Reckless in their Statements

Challenging History's Harshest Criticisms of Albert Sidney Johnston in the Civil War

Leigh S. Goggin

FONTAINE
—PRESS—

Copyright © 2025 Leigh S. Goggin
ISBN: 978-0-9924658-7-2

Published by Fontaine Press
P.O. Box 948, Fremantle
Western Australia 6959

 A catalogue record for this book is available from the National Library of Australia

Goggin, Leigh S.
Reckless in Their Statements: Challenging History's Harshest Criticisms of Albert Sidney Johnston in the Civil War / Leigh S. Goggin – First edition.
Includes bibliographical reference and index.
ISBN: 978-0-9924658-7-2
1. Johnston, Albert Sidney, 1803-1862. 2. Generals – Confederate States of America – Biography. 3. United States – History – Civil War, 1861-1865 – Biography. 4. United States – History – Civil War, 1861-1865 – Campaigns.

All rights reserved. No part of this publication may be reproduced, stored in a retrieval system or transmitted in any form or by any means, electronic, mechanical, photocopying, recording or otherwise, without the prior written permission of the publisher.

Contents

    List of Maps v
    Acknowledgements vi
    Preface 1
1. Albert Sidney Johnston – Evolution of a general 14
2. Why was the Western Department so difficult to defend? 35
3. Did Johnston implement an effective departmental strategy? 50
4. Did Johnston request enough support from the Confederate government? 73
5. Did Polk and Pillow disobey Johnston at Columbus? 85
6. Why did Johnston assume command of the Central Kentucky Army? 105
7. Was Johnston obsessed with the defense of Bowling Green? ... 118
8. Did Johnston neglect Forts Henry and Donelson? 129
9. Was Johnston aware of events in eastern Kentucky? 150
10. Did Johnston respond to the threat against Fort Henry? 167
11. Why did Johnston reject Beauregard's Covington House Strategy? 183
12. Why did Johnston delegate the defense of the Cumberland River to Floyd? 199
13. Why did Johnston reinforce Fort Donelson if it was untenable? ... 211
14. Was Johnston responsible for the blunders at Fort Donelson? ... 222
15. How serious was the threat from Buell in central Kentucky? ... 240
16. Was Johnston aware of the lack of fortifications at Nashville? ... 249

17. Did Johnston mismanage the withdrawal from Nashville?.........255
18. Did Johnston cede control of the Western Department to Beauregard?..268
19. Was Johnston's march to Corinth too slow?...........................281
20. Was Johnston too slow in ordering Van Dorn to Corinth?..........289
21. Did Johnston approve the Shiloh battle plan?......................295
22. Was Johnston or Beauregard in command of the Army of the Mississippi?...311
23. Did Johnston or Beauregard direct the battle of Shiloh?............323
24. Was Johnston foolish to personally lead a charge? 352
    Epilogue..364
    Bibliography..368
    Notes..383
    Index..428

List of Maps

The Western Department 36
Western Department Features 40
Situation, September 1861 52
Situation, November 1861 99
East Kentucky Campaigns 160
Fort Henry Campaign 181
Fort Donelson Campaign 228
Shiloh Campaign 279
Approach to Shiloh, Confederate Concept 306
Approach to Shiloh, Reality 307
Battle of Shiloh, Confederate Concept 326
Battle of Shiloh, Reality 327

Acknowledgements

I am deeply grateful to Sean Michael Chick, Don Poynton, and Ted Savas for their time and effort in reviewing this manuscript. Their insightful comments, thoughtful critiques, and general advice have greatly enhanced this work. Any remaining errors or oversights are mine alone. A special thanks to Timothy B. Smith for his kindness and generosity in providing me with primary documents from the pen of General Albert Sidney Johnston. I also extend my sincere appreciation to Hal Jesperson and Ryan Goggin for their exceptional work in creating the maps for this book. Finally, I am thankful to my parents, my wife, and my daughter for their steadfast encouragement, patience, and support during this endeavor.

Preface

Jefferson Davis, President of the Confederate States of America, was confined to bed in the Executive Mansion in early September 1861, suffering from a recurrence of malarial-related symptoms of fever, headache, and muscle pain. For the last six months, he had labored tirelessly to navigate his newly formed nation, a confederacy of eleven Southern states, through a catastrophic civil war against its former brethren, the northern, midwestern, and western states of the United States of America. The President's aides left the door of his first-floor sickroom open to facilitate the entry of fresh air and to allow Davis to hear voices in the hall down below. Upon hearing the bell and the sound of familiar footsteps, he raised himself from his sickbed and declared: "That is Sidney Johnston's step. Bring him up!"[1]

Davis and Johnston had been friends for forty years. They had first met as teenagers in 1821 while studying at Transylvania University in Lexington, Kentucky, and then formed a warm friendship while completing the arduous cadetship of the United States Military Academy at West Point, New York. Being five years younger, Davis idolized Johnston as the *beau ideal* of a soldier. In June 1826, Johnston, having been promoted from mere cadet to the adjutant of the corps of cadets, graduated from West Point ranked eighth in his class of 41 remaining cadets. Davis graduated in June 1828, but with a far less distinguished record, placed 23rd in his class of 33 remaining cadets. Despite his admiration of Johnston, the future President of the Confederacy could not replicate his friend's steadfast discipline and respect for authority. Davis was frequently cited for violations of the strict code of behavior for cadets and was even involved in the Eggnog Riot of Christmas 1826, just six months after Johnston's departure from the academy.[2]

Twenty years later, Johnston and Davis served together in the Mexican-American War, and ironically, it was the more self-possessed Johnston who led the pair into a perilous situation. In September 1846, after the victory of the United States forces at the battle of Monterrey, Davis was asked to visit Mexican General Pedro de Ampudia's headquarters to collect signed truce documents. Johnston decided to accompany him. Unfortunately, instead of his army uniform, which had been damaged in transit, Johnston was wearing a red flannel shirt, blue jeans, and a low-crowned felt hat. This outfit identified him as a Texan, who were despised by the Mexican people after years of hostility between their nation and the Republic of Texas.

The Mexican civilians and soldiers milling around the streets of Monterrey became agitated at the sight of Davis and his Texan companion. Riflemen appeared on rooftops and trained their guns on the two Americans. An old woman pointed a bony finger at Johnston and hissed "Tejano!" A crowd began to gather, and fearing the actions of an angry mob, Davis and Johnston rode up to a barricade manned by a detachment of Mexican infantry and a battery of artillery. The soldiers levelled their weapons at the two men and Johnston suggested to Davis that they raise their white handkerchiefs. This action had the desired effect, and the two riders were permitted to approach the cordon.[3] Davis requested that he and Johnston be allowed through to Ampudia's headquarters to collect the documents. A Mexican soldier was dispatched to the rear with the message but failed to return. Davis complained and two more men were sent, but each with the same result.

Ampudia's adjutant general then appeared on the scene, wishing to pass through the barricade to headquarters. Davis addressed the adjutant general, but the officer ignored him, turned to the captain of the battery, barked some orders in Spanish, and then spurred his horse to go forward. Johnston whispered to Davis, "Had we not better keep him with us?" and quickly blocked the officer's path with his own horse. Davis demanded that the adjutant general escort them to Ampudia's headquarters. Recognizing that the outbreak of any violence would result in his own death along with those of the two Americans, the officer feigned a smile and reluctantly escorted them to headquarters, where Davis received the papers. Despite inadvertently increasing the risk associated with the mission because of his attire, Davis believed that Johnston's "quick perception and decision" to take the officer hostage saved them both from an unsavoury outcome.[4]

From such examples, and a lifetime of association, Davis developed an undying faith in Johnston's abilities, remarking that "great in small things as in large ones, measuring matters with the exactness of cold calculation, yet keenly alive to every demand of honor or of courtesy, or of personal or official obligation, General Johnston was a friend to whom one could go for counsel in the most delicate affair of life, and equally rely on where personal hazards were to be taken, or values in business transactions to be balanced."[5] Now in the time of his greatest need, the President wanted his dear friend to share the heavy burden of responsibility in securing the survival of the Southern Confederacy. Davis required a trusted and experienced military commander to assume accountability for the defense of the vast western theater of operations. As a Kentuckian by birth, and a Texan by heart, Johnston was his man. In contrast to other aspiring and more egotistical Southern officers, Davis fondly recalled that after arriving at the Executive Mansion, Johnston did not ask for any specific role or command but "simply offered himself to the cause."[6]

The President awarded Johnston with the highest rank of all the Confederate field generals and dispatched him to take command of Department Number Two, also known as the Western Department, a region stretching from the Appalachian Mountains in eastern Kentucky to the plains of the Indian Territory beyond the Mississippi River. This assignment was possibly the most difficult of any faced by a general during the American Civil War. Many years later, Davis recalled that Johnston "came and by his accession I felt strengthened, knowing that a great support had thereby been added to the Confederate cause… I hoped and expected that I had others who would prove generals, but I knew I had one, and that was Sidney Johnston."[7]

Yet Johnston's contemporary reputation as a general would oscillate wildly from the time of his assumption of command to that of his death

President Jefferson Davis

on the battlefield in April 1862. At the outbreak of the Civil War, the people of the South, like Davis, regarded the general as a harbinger of miracles who would lead them to a glorious victory in the western theater of war. A Confederate officer in Texas declared that "for days I had been looking to the West as for a military Messiah in the person of Albert Sidney Johnston."[8] A journalist residing in the Confederate capital at Richmond, Virginia, recalled that Johnston, "was popularly expected… to take Cincinnati [Ohio] and march to the Northern Lakes."[9] Such sentiments were common in the South and even extended to those of the enemy. Several decades after the war, the supreme Union military commander in the Civil War and later President of the United States, Ulysses S. Grant, wrote in his memoirs that Johnston "was a man of high character and ability. His contemporaries at West Point, and officers generally who came to know him later and who remained on our side, expected him to prove the most formidable man to meet that the Confederacy would produce."[10] It was Grant that Johnston would face in his only engagement personally leading Confederate troops on the battlefield.

After the fall of Kentucky and northern Tennessee in February 1862, Southern politicians and newspapers bitterly denounced Johnston's generalship and begged for him to be replaced in command. A member of the Confederate Congress howled that Johnston's "errors of omission, commission, and delay have been greater than any general who ever preceded him, in any country."[11] Fellow Confederate general, Richard Taylor, observed that "Johnston, who had just been Alexander, Hannibal, Caesar, Napoleon, was now a miserable dastard and traitor, unfit to command a corporal's guard!"[12] Johnston's reputation had truly deteriorated from that of deliverer to pariah.

Davis ignored the obloquy and retained his friend in command of the Western Department. He informed Johnston that "we have suffered great anxiety because of recent events in Kentucky and Tennessee, and I have been not a little disturbed by the repetition of reflections upon yourself... The public, as you are aware, have no correct measure for military operations, and journals are very reckless in their statements."[13] Thanks to the unflinching support of Davis in March 1862, Johnston was thus gifted the opportunity to retrieve both his reputation and Confederate fortunes in the western theater. Johnston marshalled his forces and launched a massive surprise attack against Grant's Federal army at Shiloh Church, Tennessee, on the morning of 6th of April 1862. Unfortunately, the general was mortally wounded directing a victorious charge in the early afternoon. With Johnston's fall, the wheel of public opinion turned again, and the general was suddenly transformed into a Southern martyr of heroic proportions, whose death sealed the ultimate defeat of the Confederacy.

Novelist Thomas W. Dixon proclaimed that "great as the losses were to the North they were as nothing to the disaster which this bloody field brought the Confederacy. Albert Sidney Johnston alive was equal to an army of 100,000 men – dead; his loss was irreparable."[14] Davis was devastated and many years later wrote in his memoirs that in Johnston's "fall the great pillar of the Southern Confederacy was crushed, and beneath its fragments the best hope of the Southwest lay buried."[15] Fellow Confederate general, Randall L. Gibson, remarked that "Johnston's death was a tremendous catastrophe. There are no words adequate to express my own conception of the immensity of the loss to our country. Sometimes the hopes of millions of people depend upon one head and one arm. The West perished with Albert Sidney Johnston, and the Southern country followed."[16]

Such beliefs endured in the South over many decades following the war. Historian Richard M. McMurry related a humorous anecdote from the 8th of December 1941. He documented that a "newspaper in an unnamed Southern city is supposed to have sent a reporter out to the local Confederate soldiers' home to interview the aged veterans as to what they thought of the events at Pearl Harbor the previous day. One silver-haired old fellow reportedly drew himself erect and declared in a stentorian voice, 'It never would have happened if Albert Sidney Johnston hadn't been killed at Shiloh!'"[17]

The historiography of Johnston's generalship has assumed the same oscillating pattern of adoration and derision that marked the general's Civil War career. In 1878, his eldest son, William P. Johnston, published *The Life of General Albert Sidney Johnston: Embracing his Services in the Armies of the United States, the Republic of Texas, and the Confederate States*. As a devoted son, William was very conscious of preserving his father's legacy, remarking that "it cannot be well that such a figure should pass into utter oblivion."[18] The first full biography of the general, the book is a highly detailed and exhaustive work that required six years to complete. One reviewer of William's book noted that "the biography of his father, which he had long planned, became an almost necessity to him; first, because of the deep filial attachment for the subject of the biography; and second, to completely vindicate his father... as commander of Confederate forces."[19]

The publication of William P. Johnston's book stoked an ongoing controversy between Johnston's supporters and those of General Pierre G.T. Beauregard, his second-in-command of the Confederate forces in the Western Department. William emphasized his father's role in the leadership of the department and minimized those of Beauregard. He also accused Beauregard of ruining any chance of Confederate victory at the battle of Shiloh with a flawed battle plan and a premature withdrawal order on the first day. Beauregard and his partisans were outraged, with the general describing William's book as "shallow, confused and wrongful."[20]

Spurred on by the publication of William's book and those of other rivals, including ex-President Davis's *Rise and Fall of the Confederate Government* in 1881, Beauregard collaborated with his friend and admirer, Alfred Roman, to collate his memories and notes into a manuscript entitled the *Military Operations of General Beauregard*. Roman had served in the 18th Louisiana Regiment during the war and was a veteran of the battle of Shiloh. Published in 1884, the content of the book was Beauregard's but Roman was named as the sole author so that he could "praise Beauregard more lavishly than Beauregard could under his own name, and he could assail Beauregard's foes more bitterly than Beauregard might wish to."[21] Beauregard's manuscript predictably diminished Johnston's role and lauded himself as the true author of any Confederate successes in the Western Department.

In 1941, Stanley F. Horn, a historian from Tennessee, published *The*

Army of Tennessee, the first detailed account of the Confederate Army of Tennessee, including its previous incarnations under Johnston as the Central Kentucky Army and the Army of the Mississippi. While not focusing on the general's life specifically, Horn captured his tenure as commander of the Confederate forces in the west and offered critical assessments of Johnston's generalship, particularly regarding the Fort Donelson campaign and the subsequent loss of Southern control of the Cumberland River. Horn's writing was influenced by the reverence he held for his grandfather and other relatives who fought for the South, and he wished to honor the courage and resilience of the common soldier of the western Confederate armies. Historian Albert Castel observed that "Horn, while not neglecting the doings and misdoings of the top generals, gives ample space to the deeds of the men they led – the true heroes of the oft-defeated but ever-valiant Army of Tennessee."[22]

Accordingly, Horn took a negative view of the Confederate leadership that failed those brave men. When it came to Johnston, Horn declared that his "outstanding and incomparable military merit has become axiomatic, and to question the legend now is sheer audacity. Through a perspective of eighty years, however, it is hard to find the basis for this almost unchallenged opinion that he was the supremely qualified soldier, that his death was an irremediable catastrophe."[23] Horn clearly possessed the required level of "sheer audacity," and his history of the Army of Tennessee contains numerous critiques of Johnston's generalship.

In 1964, the World War Two veteran and historian, Charles P. Roland, produced *Albert Sidney Johnston: Soldier of Three Republics*. It was considered such a masterful biography of Johnston that no author attempted a revision for almost sixty years. Roland was born in Maury City, Tennessee, close to the scene of Johnston's near triumph and ultimate demise. He recalled that "Shiloh was hallowed ground to me in my childhood. Born and bred in West Tennessee, only an hour's drive from the famed Civil War battlefield, I visited there on countless occasions... I looked upon the spot where Albert Sidney Johnston fell at the head of the Confederate army; I pondered the effect of his death upon the outcome of the battle. His presence seemed to abide at Shiloh."[24]

As a child, Roland was fortunate to hear many first-hand accounts of Confederate soldiers' experiences during the conflict, recalling that "there were quite a number of veterans of the Civil War living in that area... They had a big barbecue every year."[25] These events spurred his interest in the battle of Shiloh and Johnston's role in the war. Roland stated that "I went to Tulane University in New Orleans to teach history. In the university library, I discovered, were Johnston's private papers." In reading through this material, Roland developed a strong admiration for the general's character, personality, and leadership, admitting that "I felt compelled to write the story of his life."[26] Roland did just that, producing a comprehensive and entertaining biography of the general. One reviewer commented that "the author leaves no doubt that Johnston is his hero, despite the fact that the hero's death came too early in the war for a definitive answer as to whether further military experience and seasoning would have confirmed him a genius of war who could have changed the course of Confederate fortunes."[27] In 2000, Roland doubled down on his sympathetic assessment, with the publication of *Jefferson Davis's Greatest General: Albert Sidney Johnston*, a short volume written for historian Grady McWhiney's *Civil War Campaigns and Commanders* series.[28]

In 1967, Thomas L. Connelly, another Tennessean historian, published *Army of the Heartland: The Army of Tennessee, 1861-1862*, which was proclaimed by many critics to be the definitive history of the principal Confederate army in the western theater of war. Like Horn's earlier work, one of Connelly's objectives in writing a history of the Army of Tennessee was to laud the fighting spirit and determination of the common Confederate soldier. However, another goal was to dismantle what he perceived to be the decades-long adoration of the Confederate commanders by historians and people alike. Connelly observed that "there has been a century of deification of some commanders which has clouded a fair estimate of their abilities. The influence of the University of the South in Southern literature and history, for example, has wrapped Leonidas Polk and Edmund Kirby Smith in protective mantles unmerited by their performance."[29] Connelly wished to rectify this situation and "avoid these dangers of hero worship and hindsight observation."[30] Thus, his book is scathing of the performance of the Confederate generals in the west.

One reviewer proclaimed that *Army of the Heartland* supplemented "Stanley Horn's earlier work with fresh interpretations. [Connelly's] is a story of frustrating Confederate leadership."[31] Castel declared "undoubtedly the outstanding feature of the work is Connelly's evaluation of the personalities and performances of the various commanders of the Army of Tennessee. These are invariably perceptive, frequently iconoclastic, and almost always critical."[32] Another reviewer exclaimed that "all top Confederates from Jefferson Davis down are roundly criticized with a polemical intensity that will shock defenders of lost causers."[33]

Johnston received the full force of Connelly's wrath. One commentator remarked that, "instances of inefficiency, if not of downright neglect, are laid at the feet of Albert Sidney Johnston."[34] Castel pronounced that Connelly "is especially harsh with Albert Sidney Johnston, who emerges as weak-willed, befuddled, and dominated by his nominal subordinate, the ambitious and conceited Beauregard."[35] Connelly took Horn's earlier work to an extreme, with possibly the most negative interpretation of Johnston's generalship in any published work. Historian Larry J. Daniel, author of *Shiloh: The Battle that Changed the Civil War* (1997) and *Conquered: Why the Army of Tennessee Failed* (2019) eagerly took up Connelly's torch and has provided withering assessments of Johnston's generalship in these two works.[36]

In 2023, Timothy B. Smith, a historian from Mississippi, but later resident of Tennessee, published *"The Iron Dice of Battle: Albert Sidney Johnston and the Civil War in the West"* – the first biography of Johnston since Roland's effort in 1964. Smith acknowledged that Roland's biography could not be materially improved and focused instead on Johnston's service during the Civil War. Smith hypothesized that Johnston's mild, even meek, personality and his seeming inability to cope with a crisis adversely impacted his generalship during the war. Although sympathetic to Johnston, with an appreciation of the general's integrity, magnanimity, kindness, and bravery, Smith disparaged his subject's military acumen, but not to the extent of Connelly and other critics.

Throughout the *Iron Dice of Battle*, Smith expressed the theory that Johnston possessed the thought processes of a methodical chess player, and when confronted with an unexpected calamity, would panic, and then make a desperate, and unsuccessful, gamble. This behavior was not conducive to military success, and according to Smith, explains Johnston's poor decisions during the Fort Donelson and Shiloh campaigns. One reviewer of the book commented that "in Smith's estimation, there is nothing in Johnston's handling of tactics, operations, and strategy to suggest high-order military genius, latent or otherwise."[37]

Johnston remains a highly polarizing figure to the present day. As commander of the Western Department from September 1861 to April 1862, he was unable to stem the relentless advance of the Union armies into the Southern heartland, and this failure has resulted in the condemnation of his generalship by Horn, Connelly, Daniel, Smith, and various authors. The positive views of William P. Johnston and Roland are now decidedly in the minority. Connelly and others have ascribed the series of reverses experienced by the Confederacy in the West largely to the decisions of Johnston during his tenure in command. However, did Connelly and others take the iconoclastic approach to Johnston too far? Smith observed that "Thomas Connelly... picked apart every single possibility of wrongdoing [by Johnston] whether factual or interpreted that way."[38]

Historian Steven E. Woodworth astutely observed, "all too often, history sorts out generals and their reputations with a logic that amounts to the assumption that if a campaign failed, the commanding general must have been incompetent, and therefore the campaign failed *because* he was incompetent."[39] Woodworth perceived that the critical assessment of a general "often takes the form of progressively more extreme vilification of a losing commander, until every mishap that befell his army is held to be the result of some egregiously, almost incomprehensively wrongheaded decision on his part."[40] Connelly's *Army of the Heartland* is replete with such interpretations, especially regarding Johnston. However, such explanations are simplistic and ignore the geographical, political, logistical, and interpersonal environment in which the general had to operate.

This book was written to question history's harshest criticisms of Johnston during his time in command of the Western Department, particularly those presented by Connelly. Are the series of defeats experienced by the Confederate army attributable primarily to the strategy and tactics employed by Johnston? Or were other factors at play? Have historians treated Johnston justly? Are the condemnations of Johnston substantiated by the evidence at hand? Have authors like Connelly misinterpreted or even distorted documented history to depict Johnston in the most unflattering light? In this book, the most disparaging assessments of Johnston's generalship will be critically analyzed, with an examination of the political and military context behind the general's decisions.

As an introduction, chapter one will offer a brief sketch of Johnston as a general, including a discussion of his military philosophies. Chapter two will detail the multitude of difficulties that were associated with the defense of the Western Department and how they influenced the military strategy adopted by the Confederate government. Chapter three will discuss how Johnston adapted to the constrained military environment that he found himself in. Each subsequent chapter will assess the validity of a condemnation of Johnston by one or more reputable historians. Did the general formulate a strategy for the defense of the Western Department? Connelly did not seem to think so. Historian Benjamin F. Cooling, author of a volume on the fall of Forts Henry and Donelson, concurred with Connelly and attributed this lack of strategy as a major cause of the loss of Confederate control of the Tennessee and Cumberland rivers. Yet there is ample evidence that Johnston devised and implemented an effective strategy in the context of his constrained political and military environment.

Did Johnston request enough support from the Confederate central government in Richmond? Again, Connelly argues in the negative, blaming the general's poor communication skills for the lack of assistance for the Confederate forces operating in the Western Department. However, historians have access to reams of correspondence between Johnston and the Richmond government from September 1861 to April 1862, and there exists sufficient evidence to determine both the clarity and level of persistence regarding Johnston's appeals for aid. Did the general's subordinates responsible for the defense of the Mississippi Valley, Major General Leonidas Polk and Brigadier General Gideon J. Pillow, ignore or disobey Johnston's orders on multiple occasions? Connelly, Woodworth, and Smith believe that this was the case and blame Johnston for timidity in dealing with these seemingly rebellious officers. However, there are other elements to consider. The Union disposition of troops and misleading information reported to Johnston's headquarters had a profound influence. Polk, a dear friend of the general, was not as stubborn and recalcitrant as depicted in *Army of the Heartland*.

Why did Johnston purportedly relegate himself to mere district rather than department command when he situated himself at Bowling Green, Kentucky, for five crucial months from October 1861 to February 1862? Connelly, Cooling, and Beauregard biographer, T. Harry Williams, castigate Johnston for such behavior. They are baffled by the general's decision to assume personal command of the Central Kentucky Army when capable subordinates such as Major General William J. Hardee and Brigadier General Simon B. Buckner were both available for the role. However, the suitability of these officers may now be questioned. Did Johnston neglect the defenses at Fort Henry on the Tennessee River and at Fort Donelson on the Cumberland River? Connelly, Smith, Daniel, and numerous historians, even the usually sympathetic Roland, have rebuked the general for his supposed carelessness. Yet an examination of Johnston's correspondence reveals a deep concern for the river forts. The failure to defend these points was attributable to multiple factors that were likely impossible to overcome.

Why did Johnston send 12,000 reinforcements to the threatened Fort Donelson? A number that was supposedly too few to ensure a victory but too many to lose to the fort's inevitable surrender. Historians have been baffled by this decision for over 150 years. Horn, Williams, and Connelly offered vituperative criticism of the general whereas Roland could only shrug and lament Johnston's supposed error. However, there exists evidence that explains the evolution of Johnston's thought processes and his strategy regarding the campaign for the fort on the Cumberland River. Did Johnston mismanage the withdrawal of the Central Kentucky Army from Bowling Green and Nashville? Perhaps insurmountable military, political, environmental and logistical factors existed to impede the ability of Johnston to implement an orderly withdrawal.

Did a disconsolate and confused Johnston cede control of the Western Department to Beauregard? This theory is a central tenet of Connelly's *Army of the Heartland*, echoing and expanding on statements made by his mentor, T. Harry Williams. While it is true that Beauregard was both vain and ambitious, this theory is flawed in that it fails to consider factors such as the general's health and the military situation at the time. Why was Johnston's superior battle plan for the offensive against Grant's Union army at Shiloh Church substituted for Beauregard's supposedly execrable alternative? This is another Johnston conundrum that has never been adequately resolved by historians. Some use the event as proof of Beauregard's usurpation of command, with Johnston meekly acquiescing to the modification. In contrast, Johnston's son claimed that Beauregard altered the plans without his father's knowledge. Others, such as Smith, believe that Johnston simply delegated the planning to Beauregard because he disliked the minutiae of paperwork. However, simple logic dictates another explanation for the outcome.

Was Johnston or Beauregard in command of the Army of the Mississippi at the battle of Shiloh? Beauregard himself propagated the notion that he, by virtue of his position at the rear of the battlefield, was responsible for the general direction of the engagement, whereas Johnston, by leading from the front, was acting like a mere brigade commander. Williams and Connelly supported Beauregard's sentiments and condemned Johnston for his alleged abrogation of army command. However, when each tactical movement of the army is considered, it becomes clear which general was more influential on the battlefield, regardless of his position. Should Johnston be castigated for personally leading a charge on the eastern section of the battlefield in the early afternoon of the 6th of April? Or was such behavior commonplace at the time? Could Johnston's life have been saved if the tourniquet in his pocket was used to stem the bleeding from the back of his right leg? What do modern surgeons think?

This book will examine each major criticism of Johnston's performance as commander of the Western Department, using the available documentary evidence, contextual information, and basic logic to interrogate the validity of the critiques from various historians. Although Johnston ultimately failed to arrest the invading Union columns into Kentucky and Tennessee, Woodworth judiciously observed that "there is far more to be learned in trying to understand how and why a general fell short – why a particular course of action seemed desirable to a highly intelligent and motivated man – than there is in multiplying denunciations of his alleged stupidity."[41]

1.
Albert Sidney Johnston – Evolution of a general

Albert Sidney Johnston had taken a calculated risk. He was standing before the Board of Examiners at the United States Military Academy in January 1825, ready to receive the mathematical problem whose resolution was required for graduation. The twenty-one-year-old cadet had thoroughly studied the entire course, except for two problems, but was unconcerned. The protocol at the academy dictated that if a cadet was unable to solve a particular problem, he had the opportunity to pass and ask for a second question. Ironically, for this was a mathematics examination, Johnston felt that the odds of both his unstudied questions being asked in sequence was highly improbable. Yet this is precisely what occurred. He floundered and the professors gravely ordered the humiliated cadet back to his seat.[1]

Immediately after class, an agitated Johnston wrote a letter to the superintendent and Board of Examiners explaining his situation. He implored them to interrogate him on any other section of the course, but his impassioned appeal was frowned upon. Fortunately, Major WilIam J. Worth, the commandant of the Corps of Cadets, interceded on Johnston's behalf, and the Board relented. The cadet was re-examined, and he managed to solve the mathematical question presented to him. Johnston's grade was reduced due to his "misadventure," but he still graduated eighth in his class.² Worth was fond of the cadet. Johnston's roommate and close friend, Leonidas Polk, mentioned in a letter home that Johnston was "popular among the officers of the staff on account of his strict attention to duty and steadiness of character."³ Worth's intercession saved the young man's military career.

At 6'1 (1.85 m) and of muscular proportions, Johnston possessed a natural soldierly bearing. In 1823, he had been rewarded with an appointment to color corporal on the staff of the Corps of Cadets. In subsequent years, he was promoted to sergeant and then sergeant major in the first company of the corps. Even after the examination incident, Johnston was appointed adjutant of the corps the following year, considered the most prestigious position by the cadets, and tasked with the responsibility of preparing all orders disseminated from the commandant's office. Worth had clearly taken a shine to the young man, but he was not the only one. A fellow cadet observed that "no one of his large class at the Academy enjoyed more than he the respect of all who knew him, and none had a larger share of the affectionate regards of his classmates."⁴

Born on the 2nd of February 1803, in Mason County, Kentucky, Johnston's interest in military matters was piqued by tales of heroism by the United States Navy in the War of 1812 and the Second Barbary War of 1815. A couple of years later, two of his close friends obtained warrants as midshipmen in the navy, and Johnston wished to abandon his studies at Transylvania University and join them. However, this notion was quickly rejected by his father. Disappointed, Johnston sojourned for a period with his stepbrother's family in Louisiana but then returned to his studies at the university. The family hoped that Johnston would follow in his father's footsteps and become a qualified medical physician.⁵

It was not to be. Inspired by the exploits of Simón Bolívar and other notables during the Spanish American Wars of Independence, Johnston abruptly changed his mind regarding a medical career and sought appointment to the United States Military Academy. This time his father conceded, and through the political influence of his stepbrother, a United States Congressman, Johnston's appointment to West Point was confirmed in 1822. Johnston adapted well to the gruelling but tedious regime of military instruction at the Academy and graduated in June 1826 with the brevet rank of second lieutenant. The top five cadets were offered positions in the elite Corps of Engineers, so Johnston was left with the choice of serving in the artillery or the infantry. He chose the infantry, believing it to be the more active and adventurous branch of service, as those in the artillery were typically stationed in coastal fortresses.

While on several months of furlough, Johnston visited his stepbrother in Washington D.C. and was introduced to such luminaries as President John Quincy Adams, Senators Daniel Webster and Henry Clay, and one of the nation's most famous military figures, General Winfield Scott. Known as "The hero of Lundy's Lane," a bloody battle in the War of 1812, Scott was commander of the Eastern Military Department. The general took a liking to Johnston and offered him a position as his aide-de-camp, a considerable honour and a rare opportunity for rapid career advancement. To the disbelief of all, Johnston declined the offer, preferring active service in the field to a life of administrative duty in a large city. Having made this career defining decision, Johnston left Washington and following orders, travelled to Madison Barracks at Sackets Harbor, New York, arriving sometime in November 1826.[6]

After a monotonous six months, spent mostly in drill and practice at the lightly manned post, Johnston was ordered to join the 6th Infantry Regiment at Jefferson Barracks near St. Louis, Missouri. In August 1827, he participated in his first expedition, organized as a response to the killing and scalping of several white settlers in the Wisconsin River area by a group of Ho-Chunk (Winnebago) led by *Red Bird* and other warriors in late June. The peaceful surrender of the culprits averted conflict with the Ho-Chunk for the time being. In 1828, possibly due to his experience as adjutant of the Corps of Cadets at West Point, Johnston was appointed as adjutant of the regiment by Brigadier General Henry Atkinson, the commanding officer at Jefferson Barracks.

The Black Hawk War

In May 1832, Johnston's regiment was ordered to participate in the Black Hawk War, a brief but significant conflict between the United States and a coalition of Native Americans led by the Sauk leader *Black Hawk*. The war began when Black Hawk and his followers crossed the Mississippi River into Illinois, attempting to reclaim their ancestral lands after being forced to cede them under disputed treaties. Taking advantage of the chaotic situation, some Ho-Chunk and Potawatomi warriors unaffiliated with Black Hawk conducted their own raids along the frontier, striking terror into the hearts of the white settlers. There were instances of marauding bands surprising and butchering isolated white families and small travelling parties. Johnston soon became accustomed to this style of warfare, commenting that "an active and cruel enemy was now busy in the work of death and destruction... Their mode of warfare is such that, while you keep a sufficient force in motion against them to contend with their main body, you must necessarily keep troops at every available point on the frontier to hold in check small parties, which it is their custom to detach to a great distance."[7]

Black Hawk and his followers were finally corralled and defeated at the battle of the Bad Axe in August 1832. Johnston served as assistant adjutant general and aide-de-camp to Atkinson during the campaign, and thus, did not command troops on the front lines. Instead, he was involved primarily in administrative tasks, and "learned the importance of careful planning for supply and logistics, especially in operations across a country void of roads and provender."[8] Johnston was close to Atkinson, possessed the general's confidence, and likely offered advice in relation to the key decisions of the campaign. He was praised by Atkinson in this role, with the general declaring that Johnston "has talents of the first order, a gallant soldier by profession and education and a gentleman of high standing and integrity."[9] A fellow officer remarked that Johnston "acquired a very high reputation for his wise and successful conduct during the Black Hawk War."[10]

Family Tragedy

After the conclusion of the Black Hawk War, Johnston resigned from the United States Army to care for his ailing wife, Henrietta, who was likely suffering from tuberculosis. They moved back to Kentucky, but she succumbed to the illness in August 1835. This tragic event was compounded by the recent losses of Johnston's father, closest stepbrother, and newborn daughter in the two preceding years. He was now unemployed and lost in sorrow. However, early the next year, Johnston was approached by an agent from the Republic of Texas, with a request for his assistance in defending the newly independent country against military invasion by the Republic of Mexico, which refused to recognise Texas's sovereignty. Johnston was stirred by the challenge and left Kentucky in the summer of 1836. Historian Timothy B. Smith claimed that Johnston's decision to move to Texas was the first manifestation of a psychological tendency to react to a crisis, in this case the catastrophic loss of close family members and unemployment, with an irrational and flawed response.

Smith asserted that "in his move to Texas, Johnston displayed numerous attributes of a desperate man gambling on the future to regain his self-worth and peer acceptance," and that Johnston was "trying hard to resecure his future. In doing so, he almost began to panic and gamble on decisions that were always not the best option." Smith concluded that "unlike the methodical chess player he always envisioned himself as being, these frantic decisions were made in haste and perhaps without proper context and contemplation."[11] However, Smith's theory is questionable. A more prosaic explanation is that Johnston was a career soldier with little experience in any other profession and Texas simply offered him the rare opportunity to utilise his training and experience to help secure a nation's freedom against a larger and more powerful aggressor. And he was not alone. Hundreds of men from the United States volunteered to fight for Texas during this time.

The Texas Army

The Texas Army was encamped near the Coleto River, and upon arrival, Johnston was assigned to the cavalry by the commander, Brigadier General Thomas J. Rusk, merely by virtue of his possession of a horse. Almost 2,000 strong, the army consisted of volunteers, described by Charles P. Roland as "true soldiers of liberty mingled with adventurers seeking only the spoils and glory of conquest."[12] Johnston's son wrote that they were "some of the best and some of the worst people in the world… without discipline, subordination, or effective organization, so that obedience was a mere matter of choice. Released from such necessary restraints, these fiery bands were easily stirred to turbulence and mutiny by the demagogues of the camp."[13] Rusk was impressed with Johnston's soldierly bearing, made some enquiries, and then appointed him as adjutant general, hoping that the experienced officer could bring some order to the unruly volunteer army.

The Texas Secretary of War soon became aware of Johnston's presence and called him to the capital in October 1836. He appointed Johnston adjutant general of the Republic with the rank of colonel and set him to work to implement administrative reforms and increase the efficiency of the Texas military. Johnston performed well in this role, but in January 1837, he was ordered to return to field duty. The new President, Sam Houston, wanted Johnston to personally lead the Texas Army. Unfortunately for Johnston, the acting commander, Brigadier General Felix Huston, perceived the appointment as a slight from the government. Huston, a Kentuckian like Johnston, claimed to have personally recruited 500 of the Texas Army's volunteer soldiers from the Mississippi Valley region and believed that this entitled him to the command of the whole army. Unable to challenge the President to a duel, he threw down the gauntlet to his new commander instead.

Johnston had "but little respect for the practice of duelling," but a refusal to fight Huston would have branded him as a coward in the eyes of the rowdy volunteers. This would have made it impossible for Johnston to command the Texas Army, as the soldiers would only follow officers of conspicuous bravery and audacity. Thus, Johnston accepted the challenge "as a public duty," correctly assessing that the "safety of the republic depended upon the efficiency of the army; and that, again, upon the good discipline and subordination of the troops, which could only be secured by their obedience to their legal commander. General Huston embodied the lawless spirit in the army, which had to be met and controlled at whatever personal peril."[14]

Johnston was shot in the right hip. The attending surgeon pronounced the wound as a mortal injury and Huston immediately expressed his profound regret, promising to serve under Johnston if he recovered. The "effect of the duel was a complete revolution in the sentiment of the army; and the excitable feelings of the troops were warmly enlisted for his recovery."[15] Johnston survived the wound, but his recovery was slow, remaining bedridden for more than a month. Huston pledged his obedience to Johnston's command, and his destructive influence on the discipline of the army dissipated.[16] Johnston had risked his life to nullify the influence of Huston and his cadre of supporters in the Texan army, who had only recently defied the authority of the government and even threatened to impose a military dictatorship.

After a period of leave to recover from his wound, Johnston resumed command of the Texas Army in December 1837. He was tasked with defending the long Texas border with Mexico with few troops and even fewer supplies. There were frequent false alarms of Mexican incursions and Johnston had to scramble to assemble some form of defense with his often unpaid and poorly equipped soldiers. In this role, Johnston became intimately familiar with the complexities of managing the volunteer soldier. Although he had won their respect in the confrontation with Huston, he now had to maintain their morale, discipline, and cohesion in trying circumstances. Johnston tried "with good results to improve the discipline of the army by drill and occupation in other military duties; and the troops were kept as much in motion as was safe and practicable."[17] The general understood that idle troops confined to camp would succumb to the temptation of whiskey and other mischief.

In the coming months, Johnston became all too aware of the disposition of the volunteer soldiers, and how it influenced the operational capability of his army. He "believed that Texas had the men for an army of invasion and could dictate a peace better within the boundaries of Mexico than beyond them; and that [his volunteer soldiers], admirable for offensive warfare, were a burden while idle. Five times as many men would have been required to guard the frontier securely as to invade."[18] President Houston did not support this view, and the Texas Army remained on the defensive. Fortunately for the Republic, hostilities between Mexico and France, combined with ongoing domestic turmoil, precluded any organized aggression from the Mexican military.

Johnston forged strong relationships with his subordinate officers, including Huston, in his time as army commander. As a product of nineteenth century Kentucky customs, schooling, and instruction, Johnston personified the stereotype of a Southern gentleman. Educated, courteous, and chivalrous, the general held a deep regard for personal honor, duty, and gallantry in all aspects of his daily life. One associate observed that the general treated his subordinates with "high-bred courtesy, which gained him the affection of all who came near him… In bringing one's duties before them, it was done in such a way as to make them feel it was suggested by their own sense of right and not his."[19] Some historians have interpreted this command style as evidence of timidity in Johnston's dealings with his subordinates, but this is misguided. He maintained a firm discipline over his officers, overruling Huston on several occasions and quietly removing a group of junior officers involved in a whiskey-fuelled rebellion from the army.[20]

The Cherokee War

Disillusioned by the policies of the Texas government and the lack of military action against Mexico, Johnston took a second leave of absence from the army and returned to Kentucky to visit his children, family, and friends. In December 1838, Johnston was appointed the Secretary of War of the Republic of Texas in the administration of Mirabeau B. Lamar. The general was enthused by the appointment and in one of his first acts, recommended the establishment of regular armed forces, consisting of four regiments of infantry, one regiment of cavalry, one regiment of artillery, and a supporting body of engineers and ordnance troops. Unfortunately, the Texas Congress only authorized the creation of one regiment to patrol and protect the frontier with Mexico, and more disappointingly for Johnston, the regiment failed to fill its ranks. The men of Texas were more concerned with their business and civilian pursuits, typically volunteering for military service only in times of national emergency.

With the Mexican frontier remaining quiescent for the time being, President Lamar turned his attention to the Native American population living in Texas. Responding to the occasional depredations on the ever-encroaching white settlers over the years, Lamar determined to remove the Cherokee and other tribes from northeastern Texas. In July 1839, Johnston and other representatives from Lamar's administration travelled to the council grounds of Chief Bowles (*Di'wali*), spokesman for the Cherokee, to commence negotiations. Lamar offered the Cherokees financial compensation for their land and crops, on the proviso that they peacefully exited the Republic of Texas. The negotiations dragged on for two days and Johnston and the other emissaries began to worry that the Cherokees were deliberately delaying the discussions to gain time to gather and ready their warriors for battle.

At noon on the 15th of July 1839, the discussions with the chiefs ended without a mutually acceptable treaty having been signed. The Texas delegation informed the Cherokee that their soldiers would be marching on their camp immediately and those willing to leave peacefully should raise a white flag. Brigadier General Kelsey H. Douglass then ordered 500 of his Texas troops forward. Both Johnston, Secretary of War, and David G. Burnet, Vice President of the Republic of Texas, accompanied Douglass and his soldiers. The Texan forces advanced to the Cherokee campsite but found it abandoned. They pursued the retreating Cherokees for ten miles (16km) until they encountered about 800 warriors drawn up in a defensive position at the top of a hill. Skirmishing broke out between the two sides before nightfall ended the fighting. Early the next morning, the Texas soldiers continued their pursuit, eventually gaining on the Cherokee band around noon.

The Cherokee warriors attacked the Texas soldiers, which had now been reinforced by additional units. The Texans repulsed the attack and then launched a counterattack of their own. Johnston rode close to the front line, and at one point, gently admonished a retreating soldier: "My young friend, you are going the wrong way. Think a moment. Rejoin your command and do your duty." The youth replied, "You are right, sir," turned about, and re-entered the fray.[21] The Texan charge broke apart the Cherokee formation, Chief Bowles was killed in action, and the remaining warriors retreated into a swamp at the bottom of the Neches River. They were soon driven from this position by the victorious Texans, and after a futile attempt to reach Mexico, the surviving Cherokee warriors and their followers were expelled into Arkansas and the Indian Territory.

Although acting in the capacity of a government official, this was Johnston's first significant experience in direct combat on the battlefield, and he demonstrated courage and coolness under fire. In Douglass's report of the battle of the Neches, the general commended both Johnston and Burnet "for active exertions on the field in both engagements" and "having behaved in such a manner as reflects great credit upon themselves."[22] Johnston was subsequently feted with praise and ceremonial dinners throughout the Republic. As with the duel against Huston for command of the Texas Army, Johnston was clearly willing to risk his life to secure the obedience of the volunteer soldier and fulfil his public duty to the people of Texas. The fact that he survived both the duel and the battle against the Cherokee mostly unscathed helped to reinforce such bravery in dangerous situations.

The Comanche War

With the removal of the Cherokee from northeastern Texas, President Lamar turned his attention to breaking the "predatory spirit" of the Comanche tribe residing in the western border of the Republic. Tasked with this difficult mission, Johnston advocated an offensive strategy that would seize the initiative from the enemy. He proposed the establishment of nine frontier posts across central Texas, supported by three military bases behind the line, each garrisoned by one regiment of infantry and one regiment of cavalry. Johnston stated that he "would not merely supinely defend these posts; rather, he would use them as bases for striking at concentrations of [Comanche] strength, wherever they might occur."[23] The Texas troops in the northeast of the Republic were immediately transferred to the western frontier and purchase orders were dispatched to foundries in the United States for the acquisition of artillery and small arms.

Johnston's son noted that his father, "while never an aggressor in his dealings with the Indians, believed in such a policy as would protect the white people and compel the [Comanche] to observe peace by severely punishing its infraction." After several months of clashes between the Texas Army and the Comanche raiding parties in the western region of the Republic, the chiefs presented themselves to negotiate a treaty of peace with the Texan government. They also promised to return all the white captives and stolen property in their possession. Johnston's son applauded his father's successful offensive strategy toward the Native Americans, concluding that "this decisive treatment led to a short but bloody struggle with the Comanches, ending in their severe chastisement and in comparative security to the harassed frontier."[24] Based on this experience, Johnston would regularly turn to an offensive strategy which would seize the initiative from his enemies.

Return to Kentucky

Johnston resigned his position as Secretary of War in March 1840, and returned to Kentucky. Smith used this decision to bolster the theory of the duality between chess player and gambler in Johnston's psychology, claiming it as "yet another gamble made when matters of life boiled up to the point that he had to make long-odds decisions just to catch up," since Johnston was abandoning a regular income.[25] Again, this theory is overplayed. There were three important reasons for Johnston's resignation. Firstly, he had grown weary of administrative duty. Johnston's son attested that his father's primary "motive for leaving public life… was a great distaste for the routine of civil office. General Johnston felt a strong impulse and entire fitness for military command." This corresponds with Johnston's earlier rejection of a staff position under General Winfield Scott in 1826. Secondly, it was apparent by early 1840 that "Johnston saw no hope of such a concentration of resources and power as would enable him to punish the insolence of Mexico. His motive for remaining in office therefore failed." Finally, Johnston had "formed an attachment for a young lady of great beauty, talents, and accomplishments, Miss Eliza Griffin" during his visits to Kentucky, and wished to secure her hand in marriage.[26]

Johnston returned to Kentucky, and after several years, married Eliza in a ceremony at Lynch's Station near Shelbyville in October 1843. Like many Southerners, Johnston now focused on agricultural pursuits and purchased the *China Grove* plantation in Brazoria County, Texas. Smith also criticized this decision, professing that Johnston "launched into another gamble that, like many beforehand, came up lacking and nearly ruined him financially."[27] Such condemnation, to support the theory of Johnston's duality between chess player and gambler, is particularly harsh. The fact is that thousands of individuals in the United States at this time aspired to land ownership and commercial success. And a large proportion failed. Weather extremes, pests and diseases, labor shortages, water scarcity, soil degradation, market volatility, and many other factors could result in financial distress. It was such a common experience that examples can be found even amongst future Civil War generals, including Braxton Bragg, Ulysses S. Grant, Theophilus H. Holmes, and Leonidas Polk.

The Mexican-American War

After several years on the plantation, Johnston was drawn back into the military sphere when the United States Congress declared war on the Mexican Republic in May 1846 following the annexation of Texas and a subsequent dispute over the border between the two nations. Brigadier General Zachary Taylor, commander of the United States army on the border, called upon the Texas legislature for volunteers to supplement his forces. The Texan Governor contacted Johnston and asked to meet him at Point Isabel, Texas, near the Rio Grande, and promised him an appointment as an officer in the Texas contingent. Johnston readily agreed, but promised his wife that he would not extend his service longer than six months without her consent, and departed his home near Galveston, Texas, for the 300-mile (483km) journey to the Rio Grande.

Johnston was unable to secure lodging on a ship, so had to make do travelling on horseback, where an increasing number of eager volunteers and adventurers joined him. When he finally arrived at Point Isabel on the 6th of June 1846, over three hundred men accompanied him. Johnston discovered to his dismay that the Governor was not permitted to make his desired appointments, and he was left without a command. Fortunately, he was then selected by the three hundred volunteers he had collected along his journey to be their colonel, organized as the 1st Texas Infantry Regiment. By this time, the Mexican forces had retreated beyond the Rio Grande after defeats at the battles of Palo Alto and Resaca de la Palma. After a month of training and instruction, the 1st Texas, now numbering 650 men, was included in Taylor's expedition into the Mexican interior.

Cognisant of logistical concerns from his experience in the Black Hawk War, Johnston wrote to a friend on the 10th of July: "General Taylor is making most strenuous efforts to prosecute the campaign with vigor, though I must say that his exertions are not sustained as they should be by the Government. There has been great deficiency of supply in the quartermaster's department."[28] In August 1846, the 1st Texas was the first regiment of the volunteer division to travel up the Rio Grande to Camargo, the site of Taylor's advance base. The summer weather was scorching, reaching 112 degrees (44°C), and the town was swarming with insects. Worse still, its water supply was polluted. Conditions in the camp became insufferable. Taylor's troops gathering in Camargo became sick, with many succumbing to their illnesses.

This experience had a profound effect on Johnston. He wrote that "few comprehend the ravages and perils of war. They are not to be found in the reports of the battlefield; [these] account for but a small portion of the waste of life... Privations without number, hard marches, under a vertical sun or in the chilly hours of the night... make up a bill of mortality, treble that of the fiercest warfare... [This] has been particularly so with our [army] in this war."[29] Johnston was always solicitous of the care of the soldiers and animals under his command. Even in childhood, his eldest sister recalled: "His dog and his horse he always treated with the kindest consideration. I have often known him to walk, and lead his horse, when it had become fatigued."[30] At Camargo, Johnston "felt gratification that, while a good deal of sickness prevailed among the volunteers, only three men of his regiment had died; and those not with the command, but in a company of unacclimated Germans, and on detached service. The health of the regiment was due to its discipline, and to regard for sanitary precautions not usually observed."[31]

The situation at Camargo only reinforced Johnston's attention to the welfare of his men and animals as an army commander in future campaigns. Clean water sources and proper disposal of waste were encouraged to reduce outbreaks of dysentery, typhoid, and other waterborne illnesses. He oversaw the layout of camps to ensure proper spacing between units and minimize overcrowding, which could lead to the rapid spread of infectious diseases. Although Johnston's resources were often limited, he supported the establishment of hospitals and the procurement of medical supplies for his troops. During the Civil War, Johnston ensured that his soldiers were vaccinated against smallpox to prevent the spread of the deadly disease. Such measures reflected Johnston's understanding of the importance of disease prevention in maintaining an effective fighting force.[32]

The Battle of Monterrey

The enlistment term of Johnston's regiment expired during its delay at Camargo, and despite his urging the volunteers to re-enlist, over half of them decided to abandon the army and return home. The remaining men were distributed to the other regiments and Johnston was again left without a command. Fortunately, Taylor possessed a high opinion of the displaced colonel, and he was soon assigned to the position of inspector general on the staff of Major General William O. Butler, commander of the entire division of volunteers. In late August 1846, Taylor's army finally marched out of pestilent Camargo and advanced upon the white cathedral city of Monterrey. Here Mexican General, Pedro de Ampudia, lay in wait in a strong defensive position, his army outnumbering that of the United States forces.

On the morning of the 21st of September, Johnston accompanied Butler and his men on the extreme right of the advance. The volunteers were first subjected to a heavy artillery bombardment, and then having reached the outskirts of Monterrey itself, were exposed to artillery and musketry fire in vicious street battles. In two hours, the volunteer division lost approximately a quarter of its men killed or wounded. Butler was injured and carried to the rear, replaced by Brigadier General Thomas L. Hamer as division commander. The United States soldiers battled the Mexican forces in the streets for the rest of the day but could not break through the city's defenses. Taylor reluctantly ordered the withdrawal of his troops from the eastern end of the city, but in doing so, ceded the initiative over to the Mexican forces, which counterattacked with a mounted column of lancers.

The volunteers panicked and the withdrawal quickly became a rout, with many soldiers discarding their weapons and fleeing into a nearby cornfield. Johnston remained calm, and riding his horse through the frightened mob, he ordered them to turn and form a line to repulse the victorious lancers. Captain Joseph Hooker, future commander of the Union Army of the Potomac during the Civil War, witnessed Johnston's rallying of the men, and later wrote: "It was through [Johnston's] agency, mainly, that our division was saved from a cruel slaughter... The coolness and magnificent presence [that he] displayed on this field... left an impression on my mind that I have never forgotten."[33] The lancers were repulsed and Johnston and his soldiers found refuge in a sheltered position taken earlier in the day.

The Mexican army, finding itself cut off from supplies and reinforcements, and suffering heavy losses, grew demoralized. General Ampudia sent out a flag of truce on the 24th of September, and after protracted discussions, surrendered the city but not his army. Taylor's army occupied Monterrey, and the United States forces remained in control of the city until June 1848. Johnston had made a conspicuous target by remaining on horseback during the battle and his mount was wounded three times. He explained to his son that "he was unwilling to risk separation from his horse, as his efficiency would be greatly impaired if left on foot."[34] Such risky behavior followed on from that of the 1837 duel and the battle of the Neches and was now essentially a hallmark of Johnston's leadership. He had no hesitation in hazarding his own life to provide an example of bravery that would rally and inspire his demoralized volunteer soldiers. Taylor was duly impressed and declared that Johnston was "the best soldier he had ever commanded."[35]

Return to Texas

Johnston did not remain with Taylor's army after the battle of Monterrey. He had the promise to his wife in mind, and in the absence of a formal offer of command following the expiration of his enlistment period, he did not even have to ask her permission to stay. Johnston was hurt not to receive such an offer, having demonstrated superb leadership in the recent battle of Monterrey and having received the compliments of Taylor, Butler, and Hamer on his conduct. It was believed political machinations within the army were to blame. In early October 1846, he departed Mexico to join his wife and infant child back at China Grove in Texas. However, Johnston remained a keen observer of the Mexican-American War and became a fierce proponent of the military philosophy of concentration of military power. In his mind, this was the best way to create opportunities to attack and destroy an isolated section of the enemy's forces.

Johnston wrote a letter to a friend criticizing the fragmentation of the invading United States army into separate detachments of troops. He recognized the vulnerability of divided troops, writing that "an acknowledged principle of war is that, when the line of operations is pierced or even interrupted, the army is in danger."[36] He asserted that "instead of concentrating its power with the paralyzing shock of the thunderbolt on some vital point, [our government] has wasted its momentum by breaking up the force into army corps, which, from the vast extent of the country they operate in, have in every instance been isolated and placed *en prise*, from which positions the indomitable courage of our gallant soldiers has alone extricated them... Our armies, whenever employed, have acquitted themselves admirably; but, being separated, their efforts have produced no results. The simplest knowledge of mechanical power would indicate the folly of dividing our forces."[37]

The Department of Texas

Despite the perceived flaws identified by Johnston in the strategy of the United States leadership in Mexico, the better disciplined troops, modern weaponry, and naval superiority of the United States military proved decisive. Johnston spent several years working on his plantation in Texas and then returned to the United States army as a paymaster. In March 1855, he was appointed colonel of the newly formed 2nd United States Cavalry regiment by his dear friend, and now Secretary of War, Jefferson Davis. The 2nd Cavalry was to patrol the western frontier region of Texas, curb the raiding parties of the Comanche, and halt their depredations on the white settlers in the area. Based on his previous success against the Comanche, Johnston's response to the mission was characteristically aggressive. He had previously written that "to give peace to the frontier and that perfect security so necessary to the happiness and prosperity of communities, the troops ought to act offensively, to carry the war to the homes of the enemy."[38]

This was Johnston's fundamental military philosophy, and it even permeated into a February 1856 letter that he sent to his eldest daughter. He teased: "You have some of the high and rare qualities of a good General. You know when to take the initiative. You anticipate my attack by making one."[39] In March 1856, Johnston received an unexpected promotion to temporary command of the entire Department of Texas, replacing Brigadier General Persifor Smith, and he ordered his forces to relentlessly pursue the Comanche raiding parties and destroy their bases of operation. He wrote to his daughter: "The Indians harass our frontiers, and [the] 2nd Cavalry and other troops thrash them wherever they catch them."[40]

Later that August, he could report a measure of success: "So far, since my administration of the affairs of this department, our frontiers have been free from Indian incursions. Our troops have driven them far into the interior, and I hope they will not soon venture in again. This is, of course, only a hope; for there is nothing in the nature of the country offering any obstacle to their movements. The country, as you know, is as open as the ocean. They can come when they like, taking the chance of chastisement. If they choose, therefore, it need only be a question of legs."[41] Yet Johnston persisted with his aggressive strategy against the Comanche and the clashes of arms continued unabated. In one issue of Johnston's General Orders, the department commander complimented his subordinates for eleven successful sorties against the Comanche warriors.

Newspaper accounts offered high praise for Johnston and his troops in the Department of Texas during his tenure in command. One stated that "Johnston's regiment has been quite successful in operating against the Indians. They have acquired considerable character as Indian fighters… [Johnston's] conduct, since he has been in command of the Texas frontier, challenges the admiration and esteem of his fellow citizens. He has shown himself an able and energetic commander." Another declared: "We believe we express the common sentiment of our frontier people, that no predecessor has given more satisfaction to them, or inspired them with more confidence in the United States Army, than this gallant officer and well-known citizen."[42] The offensive strategy Johnston employed against the Comanche, while not foolproof, was clearly the most effective option in deterring raids against the white settlers of Texas.

The Mormon War

In August 1857, Johnston was ordered to assume command of a military expedition destined for the Utah Territory. Trouble had been brewing in the Territory due to intractable differences between the United States government and the Church of Jesus Christ of Latter-day Saints, also known as the Mormons, regarding theocracy and polygamy in the region. The President of the United States, James Buchanan, decided to relieve the Mormon leader, Brigham Young, of his position as Territorial Governor of Utah, and appointed Alfred Cumming of Georgia to the role. Buchanan also dispatched a force of 2,500 soldiers to construct a military post in the territory and enforce the laws of the United States, but Young did not receive word of his replacement because of the recent annulment of the Utah mail contract. Young therefore considered the military expedition as an army of invasion and mobilized the Mormon militia in response. Tragically, the militia slaughtered over 120 innocent civilians, including women and children, travelling in an emigrant train from Arkansas to California at Mountain Meadows on the 7th of September.

In increasingly cold conditions, Johnston led his small army across the country to Fort Bridger, located 125 miles (201km) northeast of Salt Lake City, as the location offered freshwater and some shelter from the elements. A powerful blizzard struck the column on the 6th of November, which resulted in the loss of hundreds of horses, mules, and oxen from the bitterly cold conditions. On some nights, the temperature plunged to minus 16 degrees (-26°C) and froze the grease on the wagon axles. Yet Johnston managed to guide his forces through the blasting wind and sleet to Fort Bridger without the loss of a single man. One subordinate wrote that "Johnston footed along at the head of the command, setting an example of endurance that checked complaint, and turned these trials into matter for jest and good humor." Another reported that "duty is severe upon the men, but not a word of complaint have I heard. We have all endured alike, and the fact that Colonel Johnston has on the march "footed it," as did the men, suffers the same exposure, and will not permit the officer to receive more than the soldier, has endeared him to all."[43]

Upon arrival, the United States forces discovered that Fort Bridger had been burned by the retreating Mormon forces, so Johnston ordered it repaired and armed with cannon. With his army suffering from the freezing weather and isolated from any support, the Mormon leadership expected Johnston to abandon the campaign. But to their consternation, Johnston procured food, supplies, and livestock from nearby mountain men, friendly Native Americans, and the inefficient War Department logistics network. The discipline and organization of the army was preserved through regular training drills, instruction, and reviews. To ward off boredom in their isolated camp, Johnston also supported regular band concerts and the establishment of an amateur theatre, library, and photography booth. The Mormon newspaper, the *Deseret News*, begrudgingly reported that "it takes a cool brain and good judgment to maintain a contented army and healthy camp through a stormy winter in the Wasatch Mountains."[44]

With the thaw in temperatures in March 1858, Young agreed to negotiate terms and achieve a peaceful resolution to the conflict. Johnston's army was soon invited into the valley of the Great Salt Lake and the authority of the United States government was restored in the Utah Territory without bloodshed. Johnston received a promotion to brevet brigadier general for his performance in the Utah Campaign. The commander-in-chief of the United States military, Major General Winfield Scott, proclaimed that "Johnston is more than a good officer – he is a God send to the country through the army."[45]

General Albert Sidney Johnston

In May 1858, a correspondent from the *New York Times* wrote a detailed profile: "I called on General Johnston today. He is, apparently, about 55 years of age, a plain, frank, whole-hearted soldier, equal to any emergency and always prepared for it. In simple, honest directness of manner, coolness of purpose and practical common-sense, he reminds me of the lamented General Zachary Taylor. During the time I spent in his tent I had no difficulty in understanding the magnetism which attracts to him the respect and love of his command. I am told that amid the privations of Winter the men never think of complaining of their commander, even among themselves, when they see him sharing equally with themselves the inconvenience of short rations."[46]

The American Civil War

After the Utah Campaign, Johnston was appointed as the commander of the Department of the Pacific in November 1860, but his tenure was disrupted by the eruption of civil war in the United States in April 1861.

This was the result of a decades-long antagonism between the Southern and Northern states over the role of slavery in the economy and society, the balance between State and Federal rights, the course of western expansionism, and the growth of abolitionism. Johnston was a reluctant Confederate and only resigned his commission as brevet brigadier general in the army of the United States in April after he learned of the secession of Texas. He immediately informed the United States War Department that "I felt, as soon as I learned the course adopted by my State (Texas) that it was my duty to conform to her will."[47] Johnston moved his family to Los Angeles and planned to sit out the war as a neutral citizen but news of the Southern shelling of Fort Sumter in Charleston Harbor, South Carolina, and President Abraham Lincoln's subsequent mobilization of 75,000 troops to suppress the rebellion eventually made its way to California and compelled Johnston to assist in the defense of his beloved Texas.

Johnston was obliged to undertake a perilous overland journey through the desert interior of the country to evade capture by Union patrols and join his people in the defense of the Confederacy. Escorted by Captain Alonzo Ridley's company of California Southerners, Johnston rode about 800 miles [1,288 km] from Los Angeles to El Paso, Texas, across inhospitable desert and sweeping plains. With daytime temperatures sometimes reaching 120 degrees [49°C], Johnston demonstrated great stamina and resilience to keep up with the younger men and participate in the labors of camp life. One member of the company observed that "during our trip, subjected as we were to oppressive tropical heat, scanty rations for man and beast, and scarcity of water, I could not but remark on the patience and endurance of our general... [He] at all times bore himself with cheerfulness and dignity and set an example of fortitude and self-denial."[48]

Such behavior endeared Johnston to his men and had a highly positive effect on morale and discipline. He would continue to share the dangers and privations with his soldiers throughout the upcoming Civil War. At the age of 58 years in April 1861, Johnston could have been considered elderly in the nineteenth century. For comparison, other prominent Civil War generals died around that age. After the war, George H. Thomas passed away at age 53, Nathan B. Forrest at age 56, Philip H. Sheridan at age 57, George B. McClellan at age 58, Braxton Bragg at age 59, and Robert E. Lee and Ulysses S. Grant both passed away at age 63. Yet Johnston was described as "tall, square-shouldered, full-chested, and muscular. He was neither lean nor fat, but healthily full, without grossness, indicating great bodily strength."[49] Johnston's endurance, youthfulness, and impressive appearance contributed significantly to his charisma, magnetism, and leadership on the battlefield.

The Western Department

President Jefferson Davis's appointment of his dear friend to the command of the Western Department was seemingly an inspired choice. Combined with his high character, personal attributes, and extensive military experience, Johnston had succeeded in highly challenging situations, ranging from the wilderness of the Michigan Territory, the vast open plains of Texas, the horrors of street warfare in Mexico, and the freezing mountains of the Utah Territory. Johnston had developed the skills to deal with the challenges associated with the defense of a vast amount of territory with few troops, poor equipment, scanty supplies, and a determined foe. He understood the mindset of the volunteer soldier and knew how to shape such men into an effective army.

Johnston was forever looking to the concentration of his forces and offensive actions to grasp the initiative from his enemies, even when on the defensive and constrained by limited military resources. He would bring these military philosophies of aggression and concentration to the senior leadership of the Confederate States of America. When crossing the desert from California, Johnston pondered the conflict against the more populous and industrialized Northern states and responded with typical aggression. He declared: "If we are to be successful, what we have to do must be done quickly. The longer we have them to fight, the more difficult they will be to defeat."[50]

2.

Why was the Western Department so difficult to defend?

On the 10th of September 1861, the Confederate government announced that General Albert Sidney Johnston was "assigned to the command of [the Western Department], which will hereafter embrace the States of Tennessee and Arkansas, and that part of the State of Mississippi west of the New Orleans, Jackson & Great Northern and Central Railroad; also, the military operations in Kentucky, Missouri, Kansas, and the Indian country immediately west of Missouri and Arkansas."[1] It was a daunting responsibility. The Western Department encompassed an area approximately 380,000 square miles (984,200 km²) in size, comparable to that of modern Egypt.

The necessity for a territorial defense
The defense of the Western Department was possibly the most challenging assignment of the entire Civil War. Apart from its sheer extent, the department possessed topographical, political, economic, and logistical complications that made its defense extraordinarily difficult. Its fundamental strategic problem mirrored that of the entire Confederacy,

in that none of its territory could be abandoned to the Union armies. There were several important reasons for this.

Slavery

The institution of slavery was the cornerstone of the Southern economy, particularly in the agricultural sector, with enslaved people providing the labor force for the cultivation of cotton, tobacco, and other crops. The prosperity of the Confederacy was intimately tied to slavery and the seizure of land by Union troops, even momentarily, resulted in the *de facto* emancipation of the enslaved people residing in that area. The system of slavery would be dismantled and almost impossible for the Confederacy to restore. Control over plantations was essential to preserving the South's entire economic system. Loss of enslaved people to the Federal army also had a devastating impact on the Confederate war effort. Enslaved people labored on fortifications, repaired railroads, and served as cooks, bakers, blacksmiths, stable hands, hospital attendants, boatmen, laundresses, teamsters, camp servants, and grave diggers. By fulfilling these support functions, enslaved people enabled a large proportion of the Southern white men to serve as soldiers.

Conversely, enslaved people who escaped or were liberated by Union forces could voluntarily offer, or be forced to provide, their labor in support of the Northern war effort. They would also be helpful in providing invaluable intelligence and support to the Union troops operating in the South, familiar as they were with the terrain, sources of food, and other resources. There was also the genuine fear among Southerners that if Union forces penetrated deep into Confederate territory, enslaved people might feel emboldened to rebel against their masters. There had been several bloody uprisings in recent decades, and the chaos of war would only exacerbate the threat. Thus, the specter of large-scale slave uprisings was a significant concern for the Confederate government and a territorial defense was necessary to control the enslaved population.[2]

National prestige
The primary diplomatic objective of the Confederacy in the Civil War was to achieve foreign recognition as an independent nation. This would facilitate its ability to trade agricultural produce for weapons, warships, and other military supplies. It was even hoped that a powerful European nation, such as Great Britain or France would militarily intervene in the conflict on the side of the Confederacy. This aspiration for international recognition was contingent on national prestige. The Confederacy could not claim to be a sovereign nation worthy of recognition by the international community if the armies of the United States occupied its territory. President Jefferson Davis needed to project a position of strength to gain international recognition and the most effective way to do this was for the South to defend her territory and even occupy Northern land if possible.

National prestige was also crucial for sustaining domestic morale. The Confederate government needed to convince their population that they were fighting a just and winnable war. A successful territorial defense in the face of Union superiority in resources and manpower would bolster the confidence of the Southern population and help maintain their commitment to the war effort. As the largest military district in the South, encompassing populous cities such as Nashville, Memphis, Chattanooga, Clarksville, and Knoxville, and major rivers such as the Mississippi, Tennessee, and Cumberland, maintaining the territorial integrity of the Western Department was essential to safeguarding the international stature of the Confederate States of America and maintaining the spirits of the Southern citizenry.[3]

Scattered resources

The Western Department contained much of the South's agricultural and mineral resources, but these assets were widely scattered across the region and highly vulnerable to capture by enemy forces. The Confederate army was required to protect the wheatfields and cornfields in middle and eastern Tennessee, southern Kentucky, and southeastern Missouri, and the rich livestock producing areas in Kentucky, Missouri, and Tennessee. The southeast region of Missouri possessed the largest concentration of lead in the country, along with significant quantities of zinc, copper, and silver. Lead was a highly prized commodity as its high density, malleability, and low melting point made it ideal for the manufacture of minié balls, bullets, cannonballs, and other projectiles. Early in the war, 75,000 pounds of pig lead was transported by pro-secessionists from southeastern Missouri to Arkansas each month for shipment to ordnance works in Memphis. The Tennessee River basin and the Cumberland River basin were both rich in iron deposits. This *iron belt* extended across thirteen counties in Tennessee and was home to many bloomeries, rolling mills, foundries, and forges. The Confederacy desperately needed iron to plate its warships, maintain its railroad networks, and manufacture tools and equipment.[4]

The southeastern corner of Tennessee possessed the *copper basin* which provided almost 90% of the South's entire copper supply. This metal was essential for the fabrication of percussion caps, cannon shells, artillery fuses, telegraph wires, uniform buttons and insignia, ship hulls, and naval equipment. In 1860, a copper refinery, rolling mill, and wire works were constructed in southeastern Tennessee along the East Tennessee & Georgia Railroad. The mountainous regions in eastern Tennessee also contained repositories of lead and saltpetre (potassium nitrate), the latter being necessary for the manufacture of gunpowder. The Military and Financial Board of Tennessee quickly authorized the construction of several powder mills along the Cumberland River near Nashville to supply the Confederate armies with this essential resource.[5] A multitude of factories and smaller installations across the entire Western Department churned out rifles, muskets, artillery, swords, sabres, saddles, blankets, shoes, uniforms, and other accoutrements. The dispersion of so many valuable military assets across the region compelled the western Confederate generals to defend all their territory. Nothing could be sacrificed.[6]

Vulnerable rivers
The security of the Western Department was rendered pathetically vulnerable by the presence of the Mississippi, Tennessee, and Cumberland rivers. They flowed vertically, penetrating deep into the territory, providing convenient avenues for Union offensives. In contrast, the large rivers in Virginia typically flowed horizontally, limiting the Federal movement. The Army of Northern Virginia skilfully utilized these rivers to defend Richmond from a series of enemy advances from 1861 to 1863. The Confederate generals in the west would have no such advantage.[7]

The Federal government recognized the opportunity afforded by the rivers in the Western Department and commissioned the construction of a riverine ironclad fleet as early as July 1861. The first of these monsters was launched, commissioned, and ready for action by October. This rapid construction was enabled by the superior industrial capacity, resources, and availability of skilled craftsmen in the North. Unfortunately for the South, the lack of iron plating, steam plant machinery, materials, money, mechanics, shipwrights, and carpenters hampered the fabrication of a comparable ironclad fleet. This situation all but guaranteed the Union naval dominance of the Mississippi, Tennessee, and Cumberland rivers, which it could use to strike deep into the heart of the Southern nation.[8] Historian John F. Dillon concluded that the Union navy's "ability to guarantee the safe transportation of troops anywhere on the Southern coast or rivers weakened the Confederate armies in the field by requiring their commanders to disperse their forces over broad areas – many of which were never really attacked. While the Union armies gained incalculable benefits from the free and swift movements of troops, logistics, and heavy artillery, the Confederates were constantly being outflanked."[9]

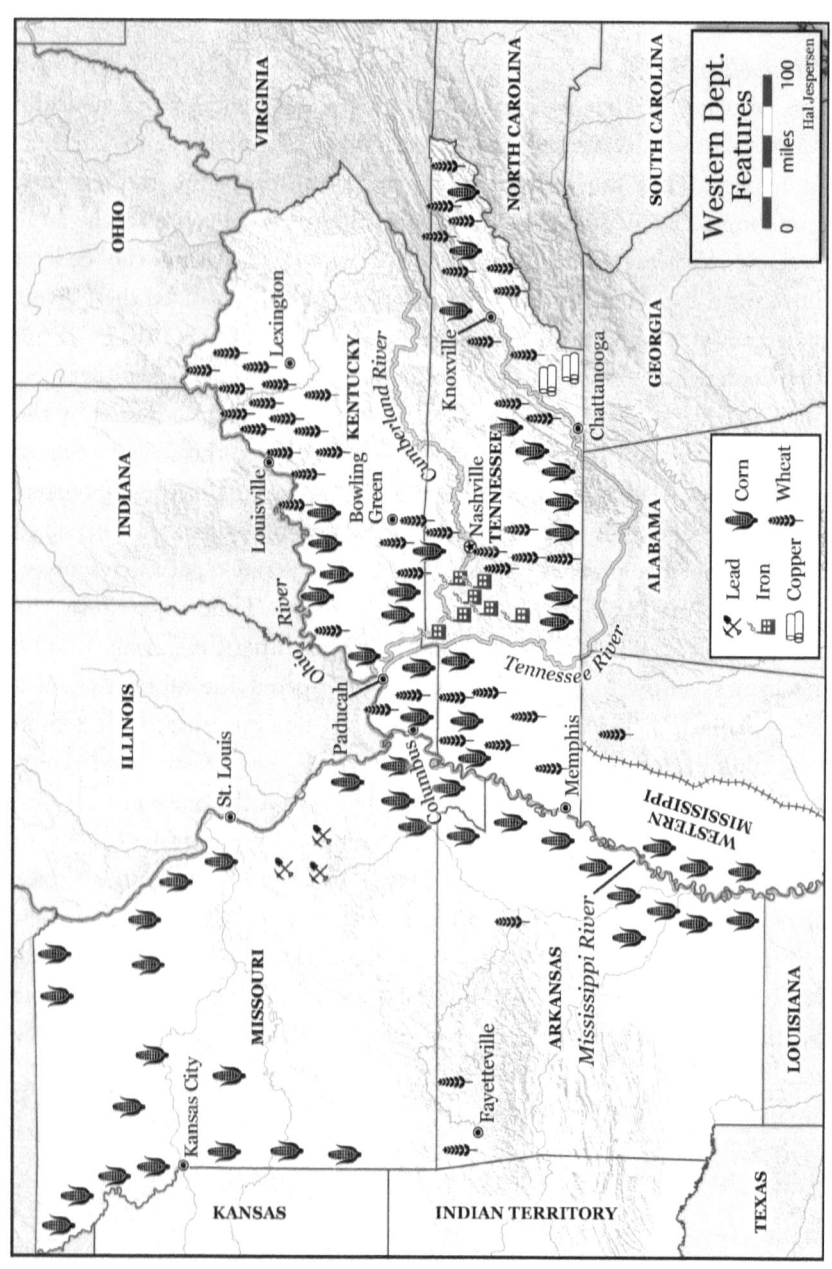

Bureaucracy
Early in the war, President Davis and the Confederate government decided to organize the defense of the country into numerous military districts. These areas were intended to be supervised by one general and be self-sustaining in terms of recruitment and supply. The appointed general was tasked with the defense of his designated war zone, responsible for both offensive and defensive planning. Yet this system had significant flaws. The departments inhibited a unified military strategy on a national level and encouraged parochialism. It was at the discretion of each department commander to choose when to cooperate with their colleagues or send their troops across departmental lines to reinforce other armies. The commanders in Virginia, the Carolinas, and the Gulf Coast were under no obligation to assist Johnston and failed to do so. In addition, Johnston was only able to draw supplies from Tennessee, Arkansas, western Mississippi, and those parts of Missouri and Kentucky under Confederate authority. Thus, the more territory he lost, the less men he could recruit and the less food he would have to supply his remaining soldiers and animals.[10]

The cordon defense and its weaknesses

Considering all these important factors, President Davis and the Confederate government committed to a rigid territorial defense of the Western Department. Troops were cordoned in key strategic locations, such as cities, ports, important railroad connections, and areas close to the rivers. The Prussian general and military theorist, Carl von Clausewitz, explained that "the term *cordon* is used to denote every defensive plan which is intended directly to cover a whole district of country by a line of posts in connection with each other."[11] The Southern government's application of the cordon defensive strategy to the Western Department was its only realistic option based on political, economic, and topographical factors, but it was fatally flawed.

Von Clausewitz explained that the cordon "is chiefly designed as an impediment to raids, and other such minor expeditions directed against single cantonments, and for this purpose it may be quite sufficient if favoured by the country… [However, the cordon has] a very small degree of defensive stamina… The object of a cordon can therefore only be to resist a weak blow, whether that the weakness proceeds from a feeble will or the smallness of the force employed."[12] Unfortunately for Johnston, the Union army and navy in the western theater were neither weak nor feeble willed, and the cordons of Confederate troops established in the Western Department would be under constant threat of being overwhelmed. They were also beset by a series of intractable problems that undermined their defensive stamina.

Lack of troops
Considering the vast area which they had to defend, Johnston had a pitifully small number of soldiers available for the task. The Union forces allocated to the campaigns in the Western Department consistently outnumbered the Confederate army by more than two to one. This discrepancy could never be rectified, as the Northern population numbered 18,500,000 compared to the Confederacy's population of only 9,000,000, of whom two-fifths, or 3,500,000, were enslaved. The border states of Missouri, Kentucky, Maryland, and Delaware possessed another 3,000,000 people, but many of these residents harbored either Unionist or anti-war sentiments.

The numerical disparity between the Union and Confederate forces in the Western Department meant that the Southern generals never had enough armed men available to garrison their cordons. The Confederate government was forced to make difficult choices about where to allocate its limited resources and troops. Accordingly, the defense of Richmond was prioritized over that of the Western Department. Richmond had been selected as the capital in May 1861 and was thus of high symbolic importance for national prestige. The city was also an industrial hub that possessed critical facilities, including the Tredegar Iron Works, which produced much of the South's heavy artillery, railroad equipment, and munitions. Such was Richmond's importance that the best equipped troops from Tennessee, Mississippi, and Arkansas all found their way to the frontlines in Virginia.[13] The Army of Northern Virginia was even able to draw food and resources directly from the Western Department.

President Davis and the State Governors also husbanded valuable troops in seaboard garrisons. The Confederacy relied heavily on ports like New Orleans, Charleston, Savannah, Wilmington, and Mobile to import weapons, supplies, and goods from Europe, particularly through blockade runners. The coastline was crucial for maintaining this lifeline, but the Union possessed a powerful maritime navy that could theoretically land troops at any point along the vast shoreline. Strong garrisons were thus required to not only protect these ports but also prevent Union amphibious operations from penetrating deep into Confederate territory where they could then disrupt internal supply lines. In early 1862, Davis emphasized the strategic importance of the Confederate seaboard, remarking that he should "much regret if any successful raid be made against the villages of our coast."[14]

Lack of weaponry
The immensely superior industrial capacity of the North ensured that the Federal soldiers were better armed and supplied than their Southern counterparts. Many of the Tennessee troops were armed with antique muskets used by their forbears in the War of 1812, and others could not find any weapons at all, drilling with sticks until the time that suitable arms could be provided. Of the flintlock muskets that still functioned, many would fail to fire in wet weather, further limiting their effectiveness. In September 1861, Colonel Lloyd Tilghman reported that "the want of arms has a most demoralizing effect" on his Tennessee brigade.[15] In October, Brigadier General Meriwether "Jeff" Thompson in Missouri grumbled, "I have been sadly disappointed in recruiting my army, as there are no arms in the country, and the people will not go without [knowing] when and where they are to receive them."[16]

In November, Colonel John W. Head, stationed in Gallatin, Kentucky, enquired of Johnston: "Three-fourths of my command are without arms. Can you spare 500 stand arms?"[17] As late as April 1862, a large proportion of Johnston's forces were still armed with outdated smoothbore and flintlock muskets, shotguns, and hunting rifles. Similarly, the western Confederate armies did not possess effective artillery batteries. The limited number of working cannons available to the Confederacy at the start of the war were typically allocated to the seaboard fortresses in preparation for Union invasions of the coastline. The South attempted to ramp up its domestic production of cannons and ammunition, but an unacceptably high proportion of output in the first months of the war was of inferior quality. A disgruntled Confederate soldier complained that "many of the guns were defective and even dangerous. One battery from the Memphis foundry lost three guns in a month by bursting."[18]

Lack of logistical support
Colonel Sydney S. Stanton, commander of the 25th Regiment Tennessee Volunteers, listed some of the many issues regarding logistical support in an imploring message to Johnston in October 1861: "My regiment, although mustered into the service more than three months ago, has not received a dime's pay, neither officers nor privates, and their clothes (only one suit each) are well-nigh worn out (inferior at first). They have but one light, small blanket each, weather getting cold, no money to clothe themselves with; have been patient, however, and as gallant a set of boys as ever entered the service. I hope you will see that they are soon to be visited with means of relief. We have no Government wagons at all and have to hire and press into the service ox and all other sorts of inferior teams, all of which retards our progress very much."[19]

Medicines were also in short supply. The concentration of so many men into poorly organized and crowded military camps facilitated the spread of disease, with measles and diarrhea causing significant mortality and morbidity within the Confederate armies. Smallpox decimated the army around Bowling Green, Kentucky, and Johnston ordered his surgeon-general to vaccinate every regiment.[20] A doctor in the 22nd Mississippi lamented that the soldiers "had come out to fight the enemies of their country in human shape, but not in the form of fever and pestilence."[21] Logistical deficiencies, particularly in warm clothing and medical supplies impaired the morale of the troops and greatly impaired their combat effectiveness.

Lack of experienced officers
The leadership of the Southern officers in the Western Department was questionable, with the senior generals a mixed bag of experience and ability. Although some possessed a West Point education and were veterans of the Seminole War, Mexican-American War, and other conflicts, there was a large cohort of inexperienced and political appointees in important positions. To build large armies of hundreds of thousands of men, both

sides had to rapidly commission officers, often promoting civilians or inexperienced militia members into leadership roles. Many officers were appointed to command due to their political influence, wealth, or personal connection to high-ranking figures in the administration. There was an alarmingly high proportion of politicians, lawyers, merchants, and planters inhabiting all ranks of the officer corps. All too frequently, they were ignorant of military strategy, the instruction of raw troops, and the application of disciplinary measures.[22]

The problems relating to the inexperience of the officers in the Western Department was compounded by the cordon defense. This system required subordinates to act autonomously and quickly to emerging threats. The lack of telegraph connections between the cordons made communications between Johnston and these men reliant on couriers, messengers, and the postal system, which could all experience significant delays and failures. Thus, Johnston could not respond to events occurring hundreds of miles away from his headquarters and was forced to rely upon the good judgment of his subordinates. This was highly dangerous when these officers were frequently lacking in education and experience.

Lack of infrastructure

The rapid transport of troops between strategic points was very challenging for Johnston. Most of the dirt roads in the region transformed into quagmires of mud during periods of heavy rain. The Southern States were primarily agricultural, and the scale of industrialization needed to construct reliable transport networks was beyond their capability. The railroad infrastructure in the Confederacy was not as developed or extensive as in the North, and many of the tracks did not connect in the major urban centers. Insufficient rolling stock crippled the South's ability to move large numbers of troops and supplies. In October 1861, Johnston's capability to rapidly move his soldiers to Bowling Green in response to a rumored Federal advance was impeded, with the general complaining that the "deficiency of rolling-stock did not permit me to make his movement more compact."[23] The rail network was also poorly coordinated. The railroad companies were typically civilian enterprises and therefore reluctant to relinquish control to a central body or fully cooperate with one another.

Then there was the placement of the tracks. The existing railroads in the South were typically in the wrong place and wrong direction to facilitate Confederate military operations. They had been constructed as short lines to connect cotton-producing areas to river or ocean ports for sale and transport. Most southern railroads extended no more than 100 miles (160 km) and often used different gauges.[24] There were no major lateral railway lines across the Western Department except for the Memphis & Charleston Railroad, but this ran so far south that it was of little assistance to the forces stationed in Kentucky or northern Tennessee. The only way of locomoting the 200 miles (322 km) from Nashville to Knoxville required a circuitous route of 400 miles (644 km) via Chattanooga to the south.[25] It took four separate railroads to transport troops from Memphis to Virginia.

The Southern States also lacked the manufacturing capability, available iron, and requisite labor force to produce new rails, rolling stock, and other essential items. Enemy actions and accidents destroyed a significant amount of the existing railroad capacity. The only new locomotives entering Confederate service would be those captured from the North.[26] The railroad companies quickly became understaffed with the transfer of their workers to the military, and many woodyards and depots lacked the manpower to operate effectively. This dearth of resources, including insufficient finances to pay for transportation costs, severely impacted the Confederacy's ability to utilize and maintain the railroads. Already inadequate in 1861, the railway network in the Western Department gradually succumbed to disrepair and inoperability throughout the war.

Likewise, the rivers flowing through the Western Department were of limited utility for transportation. At the outbreak of war, most of the riverine vessels in the west were Northern-owned and quickly secured in Union ports. The United States War Department estimated that there were 500 steamboats, 400 coal barges, and 200 freight barges in its possession in early 1861, and many of these steamboats would undergo conversions into ironclad and timberclad warships.[27] In contrast, the South had few riverine vessels and was restricted in its inability to convert them to warships.

The Union domination of the rivers had dire consequences for the cordon system of defense in the Western Department. Johnston's son noted that the Union military's "means of rapid transit were so much greater than the Confederate that they could always have opposed a superior force to any assault. The 'interior lines' are not determined by a scale of miles, but by the time required to convey troops over the intervals between commands. Facilities of transportation more than distances, therefore, decide what these interior lines are. An unlimited power of water-communication enabled [the Union forces] to cooperate fully, and practically to place what force they pleased where they pleased."[28]

Apathetic and hostile citizenry
A significant proportion of the Southern population was complacent to the war effort. Johnston's son claimed that "the victory of Manassas [in July 1861] had begotten a vainglorious confidence; and the people, fondly dreaming that no necessity existed for extraordinary effort, did not urge their youth to the field. Those at the head of affairs could not arouse them to the peril of the situation and the necessity for action. In 1861 the South was exultant and careless. Ignorant of the requirements of the hour, and undisciplined by suffering, it wasted the period of preparation and the opportunity for success. Calamity was needed to stir it to its depths, and to rouse that spirit of resistance which proved equal to the sublimest efforts."[29] Subsequent Confederate victories at Wilson's Creek, Missouri, in August, Lexington, Missouri, in September, and Ball's Bluff, Virginia, in October, only reinforced this complacency.

Some of the lack of support for Johnston's army stemmed from economic self-interest. Despite the Confederate government's desperate need for a labor force to build fortifications at key strategic points, many of the planters did not volunteer the services of their enslaved workforce, fearing that their absence would impact farming operations, or that they would escape to the Union lines. This severely impacted the construction of vital fortifications at strategic points. Johnston complained that the planters of the South "have given their sons freely enough, but it is folly to talk to them about a negro or a mule. I regret this disappointment… These people do not seem to be aware how valueless would be their negroes were we beaten."[30]

Worse still, in mountainous East Tennessee, a large proportion of the population were in active rebellion against the Southern government.

A Unionist leader in the region stated that they "could never live in a Southern Confederacy and be made hewers of wood and drawers of water for a set of aristocrats and overbearing tyrants... We have no interest in common with the Cotton States. We are a grain-growing and stock-raising people."[31] In November 1861, pro-Union guerrillas in eastern Tennessee began raiding Confederate supplies, burning bridges, destroying military installations, firing on pickets, obstructing roads, and cutting telegraph wires. The Richmond government was forced to deploy thousands of troops to the region to restore order. However, the detachment of these forces seriously weakened Johnston's cordons in Kentucky and northern Tennessee.[32]

An almost hopeless situation

The problems associated with the defense of the Western Department were insurmountable for the Confederate leadership. One of Johnston's subordinates, Colonel Randall L. Gibson, observed after the war that "there was scarcely a feature in it that did not present an advantage to the enemy, and render any disaster almost necessarily fatal, or any advance perilous except by marches of unexampled length and endurance."[33] Yet the Southern people believed that there was one general who had the experience and military skill to cope with such a daunting mission – Albert Sidney Johnston. President Davis had been inundated with petitions demanding Johnston's immediate appointment to the command of the Western Department as soon as he arrived from California.

In the meantime, Davis had entrusted the command to Major General Leonidas Polk, a mutual West Point companion and former Episcopalian Bishop of Louisiana. Polk stressed on multiple occasions that he would only serve in this capacity until Johnston was available to assume the responsibility. The bishop appreciated the complexities of the command and "was among the first, if not the very first, to nominate Johnston for appointment to the chief command in the West. No one better knew the difficulties of that position, and he nominated Johnston because he knew them. He had himself looked over the field; he had estimated its difficulties, and he saw that they were greater than at any other part of the Confederate frontier."[34]

Although appointed as the highest-ranking field commander in the Confederate army, Johnston still did not possess the authority to resolve the multiple complexities impacting the defense of the Western Department. He could not transfer idle troops in quiet areas to bolster his cordons, could not prioritize supplies for his army, and could not manufacture ironclad warships for the western rivers. Historian Steven E. Woodworth declared that Johnston "faced a situation unprecedented in his experience or in that of any other living American."[35] Similarly, Timothy B. Smith argued that "perhaps no one could emerge victorious from the situation Davis had entrusted to his friend."[36]

3.
Did Johnston implement an effective departmental strategy?

As an aggressive commander hoping to seize the initiative, General Albert Sidney Johnston must have been disappointed in the military situation he found when he arrived in Knoxville, Tennessee, on the 13th of September 1861. The Confederate forces under his command in the Western Department numbered only 46,000 men. On this eastern flank, there were about 4,000 troops under the command of former politician and newspaper editor, Brigadier General Felix K. Zollicoffer. They were poorly armed and provisioned. In the center of Johnston's defensive line were about 4,000 troops at Nashville under Brigadier General Robert C. Foster of the Provisional Army of Tennessee. This was a paltry number, considering the importance of the city and the array of factories, manufacturing installations, powder works, supply depots, warehouses, hospitals, and animal processing facilities located in the area. Almost a hundred miles (161 km) to the west of Nashville, there were about 1,000 soldiers defending Fort Donelson on the Cumberland River and Fort Henry on the Tennessee River. The largest concentration of soldiers was located on the banks of the Mississippi River. Major General Leonidas Polk had concentrated 11,000 troops at Columbus, Kentucky, and had another 2,000 at Memphis, Tennessee, 1,500 at Union

City, Tennessee, 1,000 at Fort Pillow, Tennessee, and 1,000 at Trenton, Tennessee.

Across the Mississippi River from Columbus at Belmont, Missouri, were about 1,000 cavalry under Brigadier General Meriwether J. Thompson. Near the Black River in the northeastern Arkansas, there were 4,000 troops under the command the West Point educated and experienced officer, Brigadier General William J. Hardee. To the far left of Johnston's line, in northwestern Missouri, there were Major General Sterling Price's 10,000 indifferently armed and equipped Missouri State Guard. Price was a merchant and politician, with some experience in leading militia soldiers. The Missouri State Guard had recently captured the town of Lexington in the west of the State but were about to fall back in response to a large Union offensive against the town of Springfield. Finally, at Maysville in northwestern Arkansas there were about 5,500 soldiers under brigadier generals Ben McCulloch and Nathan B. Pearce. This contingent was made up of the inadequately armed and provisioned Arkansas State Troops under Pearce and the better equipped and disciplined Confederate regular soldiers under McCulloch. The latter would assume overall command, having considerable experience and fame from fighting the Native American warriors on the frontier.

These cordons of Confederate soldiers were far too weak for any offensive operations, lacking sufficient arms, equipment, transportation, and supplies. In contrast, the Union armies in the region, under Major Generals John C. Frémont in Missouri and Robert Anderson in Kentucky, had a combined strength of almost 100,000 men. Worse still, Johnston's mission had been made immeasurably harder by the dissolution of Kentucky neutrality just a week before his appointment to Confederate command.

The fall of Kentucky

Prior to Johnston's arrival in Richmond, the northern border of the Western Department was protected from Federal invasion by the presence of Kentucky. A fellow slave state, Kentucky had looked on with horror at the eruption of civil war earlier that April and had declared itself politically neutral. Recognizing the strategic, economic, and political

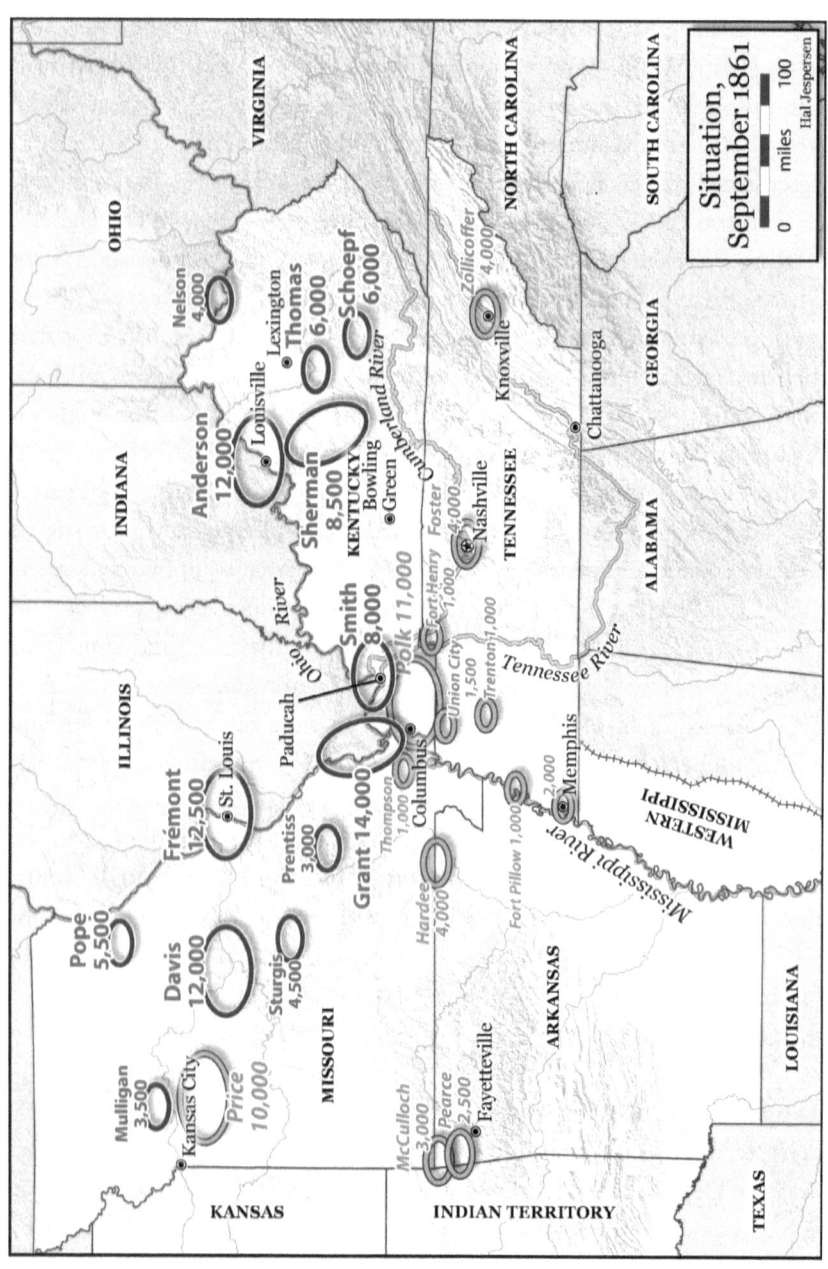

importance of Kentucky, both the United States and Confederate governments pledged to respect its neutrality and forbade their armies to enter the state. However, Kentucky's declaration of neutrality was politically naïve. Less than a month after the fall of Fort Sumter, President Abraham Lincoln decided to supply the pro-Union Kentucky Home Guard with percussion muskets. This action was to ensure that the rival Kentucky State Guard, which included many secessionists in its ranks, would not be turned against the Union cause in the state. One Northern agent recalled that the appearance of these weapons in Kentucky had a "wonderfully quieting effect in the communities into which they were introduced."[1]

Then on the 12th of June, regular Union soldiers violated the neutrality of Kentucky. The Union steamboat, *City of Alton*, chugged past the town of Columbus, transporting two companies of the 8th Illinois, under the command of Colonel Richard J. Oglesby. The Union soldiers observed a Confederate flag floating from a pole near the banks of the Mississippi River. Oglesby yelled at the townsfolk to take the flag down but was ignored. This enraged the Federal officer, and he instructed a couple of his men to swim to the shore and seize the flag. Yet the Kentucky legislature did not protest.

Eight days later, a special election for members of Congress was held in Kentucky, with both pro-Southern and pro-Northern candidates nominated on the ballots. Of the ten districts in Kentucky, nine fell to the pro-Northern candidates. The people of the Bluegrass state clearly wished to avoid the horrors of war, sandwiched as they were between the two belligerents. The *Louisville Journal* warned its readers that war is "glutted with human blood and gore" and asked them to consider the "unchained horrors and demons of hell brought to your very doors."[2] Then there was also the economic aspect of war. The same newspaper informed Kentuckians that "foraging parties will seize upon your prize cattle, your hay, housed for your farm mules next winter, and the perfect extract of corn or grape, laid by for your own use, will be confiscated to the use of war and military necessity. War confiscates everything eatable and drinkable to its capacious maw."[3]

Conversely, by remaining neutral or pro-Union, substantial war time profits could be gathered by Kentucky farmers and merchants from the increasing railroad traffic with the Northern states. The economic benefits of slavery could also be preserved. The *Louisville Journal* also warned that "the speedy, the almost immediate disappearance of slavery from our midst could be prevented by no human agency. That's a truth which every Kentuckian of common sense recognizes. The secession of Kentucky from the United States would be the secession of slavery from Kentucky."[4] This self-interest ensured that the slaveholders of the Bluegrass maintained their loyalty to the United States, and slavery was not abolished in the state until after the war, with the passage of the 13th Amendment in 1865.

President Lincoln felt emboldened by the pro-Union election results of June 1861, and ordered "10,000 stands of arms and accoutrements, six pieces of field artillery, two smooth and two rifle bore cannon, and two mountain howitzers, and ample supplies of ammunition… be carried thence through Kentucky into East Tennessee… for distribution among the men so mustered into service and men organized as Union Home Guards."[5] Again, such a provocative act was ignored by the Kentucky State Legislature. In August, Lincoln authorized the establishment of Camp Dick Robinson, a Unionist recruiting and training facility in Garrard County. The Kentucky Governor sent a letter of protest, but the President dismissed his concerns: "I believe it is true that there is a military force in camp within Kentucky, acting by authority of the United States, which force is not very large… I also believe that some arms have been furnished to this force by the United States… Taking all the means within my reach to form a judgment, I do not believe it is the popular wish of Kentucky that this force shall be removed beyond her limits; and, with this impression, I must respectfully decline to so remove it."[6]

Later that month, Colonel Oglesby ordered a squad of Union troops at Cairo, Illinois, to cross the Mississippi River into Ballard County, Kentucky, to disperse a suspicious crowd gathered on the banks of the river. Oglesby assumed that the people were Confederate troops or engineers sent to study the Union fortifications at Cairo, when they were merely civilians. The crowd fled at the arrival of the Union soldiers, except for three men, who were arrested and taken back to Cairo. The men, while secessionist in political persuasion, were innocent of any crime. They were released, but only after a detention of 44 hours.[7] This was the second time that Oglesby's Union soldiers had set foot on Kentucky soil, yet the political ramifications of these transgressions were negligible. In response to Oglesby's actions, the pro-Southern *Louisville Daily Courier* contended that "if the soldiers of Tennessee had invaded our soil, the Lincoln organs would have been rampant in their denunciations and would rest satisfied with nothing short of resorting to war to teach Tennessee to respect the inviolability of our soil."[8] Yet there were no negative political consequences for the Federal government.

The Northern generals were emboldened. On the 28th of August, Frémont issued orders to his subordinate, Brigadier General Ulysses S. Grant: "You are instructed to proceed forthwith to Cape Girardeau [Missouri] and assume command of the forces at that place... Colonel [Gustav] Waagner, chief of artillery at Cairo, left Saint Louis last night... to undertake an expedition with two gunboats, under Commander [John] Rodgers, to Belmont [Missouri], to destroy the fortifications erecting by the rebels, [and] keep possession of that place... It is intended, in connection with all these movements, to occupy Columbus, Kentucky, as soon as possible."[9]

Frémont was going to permanently violate the political neutrality of Kentucky to secure the militarily advantageous position at Columbus for the Union. The following day, Waagner and his regiment occupied the village of Belmont on the opposite bank of the Mississippi River from Columbus. Waagner's men began to construct fortifications at Belmont, which was soon detected by the Confederates. Alarmed that the Union forces were now poised to capture Columbus, Polk ordered his men to advance into Kentucky and occupy the riverbank towns of Hickman and Columbus. On the evening of the 3rd of September, Polk's enthusiastic soldiers disembarked from their transports at Hickman. The next day, they marched into Columbus, cheered on by residents waving Confederate flags. The pro-Union Kentucky legislature was outraged by the occupation and demanded that Polk remove his troops.

On the 6th of September, as the bishop moved his headquarters from Union City, Tennessee, to Columbus, Grant's Federal troops landed at the strategically critical town of Paducah, Kentucky, located at the confluence of the Ohio and Tennessee rivers. Some pro-Confederate militia under Colonel Lloyd Tilghman were in Paducah but fled at the sight of the bluecoats. Polk made no serious effort to advance his troops further northwards than Columbus and the Union forces consolidated their hold. A detachment of Federal soldiers was soon dispatched from Paducah to capture another strategically important position at Smithland, Kentucky, at the confluence of the Ohio and Cumberland rivers. In northern Kentucky, Union Major General Robert Anderson's troops occupied Louisville on the 7th of September.

While Polk and many of his soldiers were elated with their capture of Columbus, others in the South were more circumspect. A Confederate captain in the 22nd Tennessee regiment stationed at Mayfield, Tennessee, wrote to his father-in-law on the 16th of September that "the evidence of Kentucky's Union proclivities are too strong and decided to admit of a hope of [coming] over to our side except by subjugation. She is not yet ready to take the leap, and we cannot help her decide."[10] Polk's action has been frequently censured by historians, but the claim that his invasion removed Kentucky as a protective shield to the invasion of northern Tennessee is spurious because that barrier would have been broken only two days later by Frémont's planned occupation of Columbus on the 5th of September. Historian Robert I. Girardi correctly observed that "plans were in place for a Federal seizure of Columbus on September 5, but it is unlikely that, had the town been taken, the public outcry would have been as loud or the political consequences as great. Kentucky was all but locked up for the Union by the time of Polk's invasion."[11]

Johnston's Kentucky dilemma

When Kentucky declared its neutrality in the Civil War, many prominent Southerners believed that the most probable origin of a Union invasion was via the Mississippi River. Flowing 2,320 miles (3,734 km) south from Lake Itasca in northern Minnesota to the Gulf of Mexico, control of the river was an integral component of Major General Winfield Scott's *Anaconda Plan* to divide and conquer the Confederacy. As a result of this threat, the politicians, landowners, merchants, and influential citizens of western Tennessee, along with those living along the river in Mississippi, formed what Thomas L. Connelly labelled a *Mississippi River bloc*, to defend their land and commercial interests. This coalition exerted intense political pressure on Governor Isham G. Harris of Tennessee, Major

General Gideon J. Pillow of the Provisional Army of Tennessee, and the Confederate government to protect their homes and plantations along the great river from Federal invasion. They feared that any successful Northern incursions into the region could destroy their livelihoods and instigate a large-scale slave insurrection.

The *bloc* was especially powerful in Memphis, and prior to Tennessee's secession on the 8th of June, the prominent citizens of the city had drafted a resolution of unilateral secession from Tennessee itself if the state failed to join the Confederacy.[12] The persistent clamouring for the construction of Mississippi River defenses by this influential group was impossible to resist and resulted in a concentration of the limited Southern military power in the Western Department around Memphis and the Mississippi River.

Pillow was completely under the thumb of the *Mississippi River bloc*. This may have been due to his business interests in Memphis and land holdings in western Tennessee. Pillow transferred all but one of the ten artillery companies stationed in Nashville to the Mississippi River defenses.[13] He apparently had no concerns regarding the safety of central Tennessee. He announced on the 14th of June that there was "no present danger on Tennessee River – nothing of military importance to be gained by ascending Tennessee River."[14] Pillow possessed a similar attitude regarding the east of the state. When asked to strengthen the state forces in eastern Tennessee, Pillow refused, arguing that there was "not the least danger of invasion… Lincoln is too hard *pressed*."[15] This is despite one Southern official noting that "a number of Union companies are forming and drilling daily in the disaffected districts for the avowed purpose of resistance. Let the Government look closely to this movement. Unless nipped in the bud, it may become very troublesome."[16]

The neglect of central and eastern Tennessee continued after the incorporation of the Provisional Army of Tennessee into the regular Confederate military in July and the appointment of Leonidas Polk as commander of the Western Department. These important regions in Tennessee were not encompassed in his department as prescribed by President Jefferson Davis and the Confederate government, and therefore, Polk was under no obligation to assume responsibility for their defense. The unbalanced allocation of military resources in Tennessee did lead some prominent figures to express concern. In August, Governor Harris wrote to the Confederate Secretary of War complaining that we are "very much exposed upon the Kentucky border, too much so if our Kentucky friends should attempt some hostile movement."[17] Harris "urged the Government to appoint a commander for Middle Tennessee and am perfectly willing to yield to [Polk] the command and control of the Tennessee River."[18] Yet Richmond ignored the offer.

Governor Isham G. Harris

Thus, Johnston's arrival in the Western Department in September coincided with a period of intense political and military turmoil. Polk's invasion of Kentucky had completely altered the strategic situation. The sudden dissolution of Kentucky's neutrality exposed the negligence of Confederate authorities to properly fortify and defend central and eastern Tennessee, including the strategically vital city of Nashville. The sudden loss of Kentucky's barrier of neutrality, either from Polk's actual 3rd of September movement or Frémont's intended 5th of September movement, was a disaster for the Confederate defense of the Western Department.

Secretary of War Judah P. Benjamin recalled that "when we sent General A.S. Johnston to take command of the Western Department it was believed that he would proceed at once to the west of the Mississippi and conduct the campaign in Arkansas and Missouri... Before, however, General Johnston reached the Mississippi the threatened invasion of Tennessee and the advance of the Federal forces into Kentucky rendered it necessary to detain him in this latter State, equally important as Missouri to the Confederacy, and threatening more immediate danger, especially when considered in connection with the menaced attack on our lines of communication by railroad through East Tennessee."[19]

Hence, Johnston's focus was diverted from the Trans-Mississippi region to the Confederate Heartland. His first task was to decide whether to comply with the demands of the Kentucky Legislature to withdraw

Polk's forces from Columbus. Zollicoffer's small force in eastern Tennessee was also hovering dangerously on the border with Kentucky. Johnston's decision would determine the course of the Civil War in the West. It was a difficult choice, involving both political and military considerations. Simon B. Buckner, former commander of the Kentucky State Guard, wrote to Richmond on the 13th of September: "I unhesitatingly advise that the movement of General Zollicoffer be stopped at the State line. The commissioners urge the withdrawal of General Polk's force... I advise that General Johnston be ordered here at once, with discretionary authority to withdraw."[20]

Buckner and many influential figures believed that the neutrality of Kentucky could be restored if Johnston simply withdrew Polk's men from Columbus. Johnston recognized that such a belief was naïve, and he audaciously resolved to expand the invasion. He met with Zollicoffer and ordered him to march his 4,000 men northwards and seize control of the Cumberland Gap in Kentucky. Zollicoffer completed his mission without incident the next day while Johnston travelled by rail from Knoxville to Nashville. After discussions with Governor Harris, Johnston decided to capture the town of Bowling Green in central Kentucky. The occupation of Columbus and the Cumberland Gap had created a u-shaped defensive line in which both flanks were exposed. The seizure of Bowling Green corrected this strategic defect. On the 17th of September, he ordered Buckner, now a brigadier general in the Confederate regular army, to march a division of 4,000 soldiers from Nashville northwards to Bowling Green.

The Southern troops occupied the town the next day and Johnston explained his actions to President Davis: "After full conference with Governor Harris, and after learning the facts, political and military, I am satisfied that the political bearing of the question presented for my decision has been decided by the legislature of Kentucky. The legislature of Kentucky has required the prompt removal of all Confederate forces from her soil, and the governor of Kentucky has issued his proclamation to that effect. The troops *will not* be withdrawn. It is not possible to withdraw them now from Columbus in the west, and from Cumberland Ford in the east, without opening the frontiers of Tennessee and the Mississippi River to the enemy, and this is regarded as essential to our present line of defense as well as to any future operations. So far from yielding to the demand for the withdrawal of our troops, I have determined to occupy Bowling Green at once... The occupation of Bowling Green is an act of self-defense, rendered necessary by the action of the government of Kentucky and by the evidence of intended movements of the Federal forces."[21]

Johnston's refusal to withdraw Polk's troops from Columbus and his prompt seizure of both the Cumberland Gap and Bowling Green conferred two significant military advantages to the Confederacy. Firstly, the presence of three Confederate armies in the Bluegrass State provided the opportunity for Kentuckians with Southern sympathies to rise and join the Confederacy. Although a Texan by heart, Johnston was a Kentuckian by birth and shared the view of many senior officials in the Confederacy that a large proportion of his countrymen were ardent secessionists who had simply been cowed by the presence of the Union military in their state. He hoped that his occupation of Kentucky soil would encourage the people to rise and overthrow the yoke of Northern oppression. Johnston announced: "If, as it may not be unreasonable to suppose, [Kentuckians] desire to unite their fortunes with the Confederate States, to whom they are already bound by so many ties of interest, then the appearance and aid of Confederate troops will assist them to make an opportunity for the free and unbiased expression of their will upon the subject."[22]

Secondly, Kentucky possessed a significant population and rich natural resources that would be important for the Confederate war effort. The general warned that "the Government of the United States fully appreciating the vast resources to be obtained by the subjugation of Kentucky will make its greatest efforts here for this purpose," before somewhat wistfully continuing, "if we could wrest this rich fringe from his grasp the war could be carried across the border and the contest speedily decided upon our own terms."[23]

Unfortunately for Johnston, the reality of Kentucky's Unionist and anti-war sentiments soon revealed itself, and he reported that "we have received but little accession to our ranks since the Confederate forces crossed the line... [the people] appear to me passive, if not apathetic. There are thousands of ardent friends to the South in the State, but there is apparently among them no concert of action. I shall, however, still hope that the love and spirit of liberty is not yet extinct in Kentucky."[24] One Confederate officer at Bowling Green observed that "the people generally in this section of the country are... generally much opposed to our presence, and render assistance, either by information or supplies, with great reluctance."[25] Johnston concluded that "no enthusiasm, as we imagined and hoped, but hostility, was manifested in Kentucky."[26]

The anti-war sentiment of Kentuckians can be viewed in the enlistment numbers. Historian William W. Freehling estimated that 71% of the men of military age in Kentucky did not participate in the fighting during the Civil War.[27] Of those that did enlist, the majority fought in the Union armies. Only 6% of the soldiers in Johnston's Confederate army at Bowling Green were from Kentucky and the Union Army of the Ohio had fourteen times as many Kentucky infantry regiments as Johnston.[28] Without the support of this populous and resource-rich state, there would be no offensives towards the Ohio River. Johnston could only consider defensive options.

The first component of Johnston's strategy: Deception

Thomas L. Connelly maintained that Johnston "had no over-all departmental strategy."[29] However, he did acknowledge that "part of this failure was caused by the urgency of genuine problems on the Tennessee line. Before he devised a strategy, Johnston must first build an army."[30] To achieve such a difficult task, Johnston needed to implement a strategy, and despite Connelly's assertion, did so with immediate effect. The first component of this strategy was deception. Without the support of Kentucky, Johnston attempted to conceal the abject weakness of his forces and hope that a projection of power would deter the Union commanders from advancing until his army was ready for combat. The predominantly agricultural Confederate States needed time to mobilize recruits, arm, equip, and train its soldiers, construct fortifications, and develop its industrial capacity to supply artillery, munitions, locomotives, railroads, gunboats, and the assorted accoutrements of war.

Johnston would somehow have to intimidate the Union commanders in the West into quiescence for as long as possible. The general's bold advance into Kentucky purchased this precious time. He only had 4,000 soldiers available to defend Nashville and needed to occupy as much of Kentucky as he could, as quickly as possible, simply to forestall the Union offensive and buy the time necessary to construct and man fortifications at key points, such as Nashville, the Cumberland Gap, and the Tennessee and Cumberland rivers. Charles P. Roland declared that "in advancing into Kentucky, Johnston adopted what in modern warfare has been called an 'arrogant display of power.' It was a bluff; he knew that he would not be able to hold this line indefinitely, to say nothing of taking the offensive, without strong reinforcements. But he shrewdly reasoned that a bold front might deceive the enemy into believing that the Southern army was stronger than it actually was. If this could be accomplished, Johnston would be able to gain precious time for the Confederacy to build up strength in the west."[31]

Johnston's son proclaimed that "there were both moral and material advantages, for which much might be hazarded, to be secured by striking the first blow. A fertile and populous district in Kentucky would be occupied, and the semblance even of military power might keep at arm's length the troops designed for the invasion of Tennessee. General Johnston, therefore, determined, while in reality only acting on the defensive, to obtain as many as possible of the advantages of an aggressive movement."[32] In Johnston's own words, the strategy was as follows: "Believing it to be of the greatest moment to protract the campaign, as the dearth of cotton might bring strength from abroad and discourage the North, and to gain time to strengthen myself by new troops from Tennessee and other States, I magnified my forces to the enemy."[33]

He began manoeuvring his small forces in Kentucky to give an impression of strength and aggressive intent, with "frequent rapid expeditions through a wooded and sparsely-settled country, spreading rumors that had their effect at Federal headquarters."[34] One of Johnston's aides observed that "while the work [on the Bowling Green fortifications] was progressing, and while every effort was being made to get more troops, Johnston, by skillful manoeuvres, threw his men near the river which divided the two armies, and made the forces of the North believe that he was trying to decoy them across and then attack them, with a river in their rear; when, in fact, the last thing he wished was a battle, when the odds were four and five to one. His strategy succeeded. The enemy declined to cross, and Johnston continued to fortify his post and to gather together a few more regiments."[35]

On the 21st of October, Johnston issued orders to his subordinates to "impress the enemy with an expectation of an advance by us."[36] On the 9th of November, he instructed an officer to march a brigade forward and "create the impression in the country that this force is only an advance guard."[37] Johnston published false accounts of Confederate troop movements in local newspapers and sent agents north to spread misinformation and stoke the fear of the Union generals. He even developed a "plan to utilize wooden mock cannon to bolster his lines in place of actual artillery pieces."[38] This illusion of strength was applied not only to his forces in Kentucky, but all the way westward to Missouri as well. On the 18th of October, Brigadier General Meriwether J. Thompson reported to Johnston, with obvious satisfaction, that "my rapid and unexpected movements have fully convinced them that my force is very large, and I have also exercised my talents upon them with fictitious orders and reports."[39]

A soldier in the 3rd Kentucky regiment admired Johnston's tactics: "The old staunch Commander presented a bold front to the Yankees and kept his men always ready – We were marching as usual all the time to magnify our numbers I suppose, build one set of chimneys to our tents, break up camp and build a new set... Those marches what terrible long ones some of them were, and for no apparent purpose, we would march three or four days in succession and then turned back on our tracks weary and sore footed to be once more where we started from." He observed that "the people of Bowling Green thought he had over 100,000 men within [the] neighborhood. And these displays were well calculated to have that effect, for we often wondered in our ignorance why we were always reviewed at different points, changed camp so often, and when we went out on a march, always came back on the trains and vice versa."[40]

The strategy was surprisingly effective. On the 2nd of October, Colonel Joseph B. Plummer reported to Frémont from Cape Girardeau: "It is reported here by different persons who have come into town that the enemy are concentrating in large numbers upon the river opposite the town of Columbus, Kentucky, under the command of General A.S. Johnston, and intending to move for this place. It is said they expect to have, or have already, there 60,000 men... I am disposed to believe the report."[41] After seizing Paducah, Grant reported to Frémont on the 7th of October: "Information which I am disposed to look upon as reliable has reached me today that the Confederates have been reinforced at Columbus to about 45,000. In addition to this they have a large force collected at Union City and are being reinforced every day. They talk boldly of making an attack upon Paducah by the 15th of [October.]"[42] This threatened attack obviously never materialized, but on the 6th of November, Grant's successor in command at Paducah, Brigadier General Charles F. Smith, informed Washington that: "Generals A.S. Johnston and Hardee are at Bowling Green. The force there is 40,000. This I was assured of yesterday by a Northern gentleman who recently left there."[43] No doubt one of Johnston's agents.

In Louisville, Anderson was also deceived into believing that his headquarters was under imminent threat of attack. Instead of advancing on Johnston's small force at Bowling Green, Anderson allowed his subordinate, Brigadier General William T. Sherman, to pull back his Union forces in Kentucky and entrench at Muldraugh's Hill to defend the city.[44] Anderson then succumbed to the weight of his responsibilities, and resigned on the 5th of October, claiming that he "could not stand the mental torture of his command any longer, and that he must go away or it would kill him."[45] Anderson was replaced by Sherman, with the displaced commander imploring: "God grant that [Sherman] may be the means of delivering this department from the marauding bands."[46] However, Sherman would experience difficulties himself in managing the strain induced by Johnston's effective campaign of psychological warfare. In a letter to his wife, Sherman wrote: "I find myself riding a whirlwind unable to guide the storm. Rumors and reports pour in on me of the overwhelming force collected in front across Green River... To advance would be madness and to stand still folly... the idea of going down to history with a fame such as threatens me nearly makes me crazy, indeed I may be so now."[47]

Sherman then ordered his subordinate, Brigadier General George H. Thomas: "I sent a special dispatch to you last night, intimating the necessity of withdrawing your forces farther back. I am convinced from many facts that A. Sidney Johnston is making herculean efforts to strike a great blow in Kentucky; that he designs to move from Bowling Green on Lexington, Louisville, and Cincinnati. I may be in error, but he has pressed into service some 1,500 wagons at and near Bowling Green, and his force is not far short of 45,000 men, with a large proportion of artillery."[48] Thomas's withdrawal had dire consequences for President Lincoln's cherished plan to provide support to the pro-Union population living in eastern Tennessee. Such an offensive was effectively shelved for the time being.

After about a month in command, Sherman also resigned, stating that the "care, perplexities, and anxieties of the situation had unbalanced my judgment and my mind."[49] He was replaced by Brigadier General Don Carlos Buell, who arrived in Louisville on the 15th of November. Sherman's belief in Johnston's deception remained with him for life. In his memoirs, the general wrote: "I continued to strengthen the two corps forward and their routes of supply; all the time expecting that Sidney Johnston, who was a real general… would unite his force with Zollicoffer, and fall on Thomas at [Camp] Robinson, or [Brigadier General Alexander M.] McCook at Nolin. Had he done so in October 1861, he could have walked into Louisville, and the vital part of the population would have hailed him as a deliverer. Why he did not, was to me a mystery then and is now."[50]

Unfortunately, Johnston's successes against Union commanders such as Frémont, Grant, Anderson, and Sherman, were offset by an unintended consequence. A false sense of security descended upon the Southern people. Believing exaggerated newspaper accounts of Confederate strength and editorials that told of imminent offensives against Louisville, many of the people residing in the Western Department, particularly those in Nashville, fell into apathy about the war. Their confidence in Johnston and the illusory strength of the Western Department armies inhibited recruitment and the construction of fortifications around vital points. The editor of the *Richmond Examiner* later declared that "our situation in Kentucky was one of extreme weakness and entirely at the mercy of the enemy, if he had not been imposed upon by false representations of the number of our forces at Bowling Green… Our own people were as much imposed upon as were the enemy with respect to the real strength of General Johnston's forces, and while they were conjecturing the brilliant results of an advance movement, the fact was that inevitable disasters might have been known by the government to have been in store for the Southern cause in Kentucky and Tennessee, and to be awaiting only the development of a crisis."[51]

The illusion of strength that Johnston projected was successful for almost six months, or one eighth of the duration of the entire Civil War. Roland concluded that "ultimately Johnston's ruse came to naught. But it must be credited with achieving what it was meant to achieve: it purchased half a year of grace for the Confederacy in the west."[52] Johnston's son observed that his father "had made the opportunity required by the South if it meant seriously to maintain its independence. He had secured time for preparation; but it neglected the chance, and never recovered it."[53] Thus, Johnston's deceptions were borne of desperation but constituted a major component of his departmental strategy. Steven E. Woodworth observed: "If he could convince the Federal commanders that they were not strong enough to attack and if he could maintain the ruse for several months, perhaps then Richmond could spare him the troops required to set up a real defensive line. As a strategy it was a forlorn hope that should not have worked even for a week."[54]

The second component of Johnston's strategy: Expansion of the cordons

Historian Benjamin F. Cooling wrote that "feint and parry became Johnston's hallmark, but in so doing he lost sight of overall theater strategy."[55] This statement is also not supported by the evidence, since the second component of Johnston's overall department strategy was the expansion and strengthening of the cordons of troops first established by Governor Harris and Generals Pillow and Polk. The cordon defensive that Johnston inherited and then expanded in the Western Department was forced upon him by circumstances rather than choice. Roland acknowledged Johnston's lack of freedom: "In some ways, Johnston's strategic views were circumscribed by those of Davis, whose policy was that of territorial defense – voluntarily yielding no part of the Confederacy to the enemy. This dictated a cordon or line form of defense and prohibited an early concentration of Confederate forces."[56]

As an advocate for aggression, the concentration of troops, and unexpected offensives against the enemy, the cordon defensive was an anathema to Johnston. Unfortunately, this was the only option available for the Confederate army in the West. The indefensible geography coupled with scattered and vulnerable resources, and political imperatives such as the protection of slavery, obliged Johnston to adopt a rigid territorial defense with little opportunity for manoeuvre to gain tactical advantage. Johnston therefore had to curb his instinct for a bold offensive to the Ohio River and focus instead on developing a workable plan for the territorial defense of the Western Department. With the purchase of valuable time resulting from his illusions of strength, he would attempt to expand and strengthen the cordons.

After ordering Zollicoffer's and Buckner's forces into Kentucky, Johnston shuttled every available soldier in his jurisdiction to Bowling Green, including Hardee's entire army in northeastern Arkansas. He then turned to the defense of western Kentucky. Johnston ordered a detachment of about 1,200 Mississippi State militia under Brigadier General James L. Alcorn to occupy the town of Hopkinsville, Kentucky, to protect the Cumberland River and the railroad bridge spanning the river at Clarksville, Tennessee. Alcorn's men arrived on the 30th of September and established Camp Alcorn, which served as a recruitment and training center for pro-Southern citizens in the area.

Johnston also looked to the neglected region between the Mississippi and Tennessee rivers. On the same day that Hopkinsville was occupied, Johnston ordered his senior engineer to select a "suitable place in an advanced position for an intrenched camp, covering the Paducah and the Mobile Railroads, and forming also a part of the line from Columbus to Fort Henry, on the Tennessee. Looking at the map, Milburn or Mayfield would seem to fill the conditions of the problem; but it is understood that a want of water at both these places forbids the establishment of a camp at either, and that therefore the point must fall south of this line."[57] Ultimately, the camp was established just north of the Tennessee border, in the region between Hickman and Fort Henry. By the end of October, almost 3,400 soldiers under Colonel John S. Bowen were stationed at the outpost, which was soon dubbed "Camp Beauregard" in honor of the hero of Manassas. Although beset by illness, deficient equipment, and lack of training, the troops based at Camp Beauregard were successful in parrying Union raids and reconnaissance missions into western Kentucky.

Johnston also hoped to construct a primary defensive line running through Fort Henry, Fort Donelson, Hopkinsville, Clarksville, the town of Russellville in Kentucky, and Bowling Green in central Kentucky. The important city of Nashville would also be fortified from approaches via land and the Cumberland River. In October, Major Jeremy F. Gilmer was assigned to Johnston as the chief engineer of the Western Department: "After a full conference with him on the plan of defense already adopted, [Johnston] promptly sent him back to establish a second defensive line along the Cumberland from Nashville to Donelson and thence to Henry, which might prove not only a secure place of retreat in case of disaster, but an effectual barrier to the invader."[58]

However, Johnston found it difficult to build up strength in his cordons. He had no authority over the thousands of troops and artillery allocated to seaboard fortresses since the Western Department did not encompass any of the Southern coastline. The military assets devoted to seaside defenses drained the Confederacy's limited resources and deprived Johnston of much needed strength in the interior. Colonel Robert W. Woolley of Johnston's staff remembered: "I shall not be believed if I state the number of letters General Johnston wrote while at Bowling Green, urging that an indefensible coast and unimportant towns be abandoned, and that troops be sent to enable him to give battle and win a great victory. But his warning was unheeded, his requests denied... Each little town on the seacoast thought that upon its defense depended the salvation of the Southern Confederacy. Senators and Congressmen, afraid of unpopularity, demanded that the troops of their States should be kept for home protection... Except a few large towns there were no points on the seacoast of any strategic importance. The presence of garrisons at little places only invited the naval expeditions of the enemy. Had there been no troops at those points there would have been no attack."[59]

Similarly, Major General Braxton Bragg, stationed at Pensacola, Florida, wrote to Johnston: "There is a general apprehension of invasion this fall and winter, and every means in the country is being devoted to defense; some of it very injudiciously. Mobile and New Orleans are being fortified at great expense, when they should be defended in Kentucky and Missouri."⁶⁰ The allocation of troops to protect the coast was not the only major drain on Johnston's manpower and resources. The Confederate government's prioritization of Virginia also impacted the general's ability to build up strength in his cordons. Thousands of the best troops from Arkansas, Tennessee, and Mississippi were dispatched to the east to serve in the Army of Northern Virginia. Johnston was forced to call upon the State Governors for additional troops, but his calls were unable to be fulfilled.

The lack of coordinate defensive efforts

Connelly criticized Johnston's cordon defensive by declaring that "there would be no coordinate defensive effort between his district commanders."⁶¹ This is a particularly harsh statement as Johnston was obviously aware of the issue. For example, on the 23rd of September, he advised Zollicoffer that "a forward movement from your present position at this time cannot be made. Your advance into Kentucky and your route must be timed by, and in its direction combined with, the movements of General Buckner."⁶² But such coordination was almost impossible to achieve. The communication network in the Western Department was constrained by limited infrastructure. The Confederacy lacked the industrial capacity to produce the required quantities of telegraph wire, and it was unable to extend the pre-war telegraph network to any notable degree. Johnston simply did not possess the means to coordinate the actions of his subordinates across vast distances in real time. As a result, Johnston was reliant on the postal system and couriers to communicate with his officers. However, the travel time associated with these methods meant that the commanding general and his subordinates were exchanging information hours or even days out of date. Sometimes couriers were captured, killed, or delayed while undertaking their missions.⁶³

These communication issues forced Johnston to rely on his subordinates to act on their own initiative when confronted with sudden Union military movements. President Davis neatly encapsulated Johnston's predicament: "His command embraces so great an extent of territory, that its successful defense must mainly depend upon the efficiency of the division commanders."⁶⁴ But many of the officers in command of these critical strategic points lacked the experience, initiative, and ability to respond appropriately.

Another factor prohibiting coordination of his cordon garrisons was a lack of information relating to enemy movements. The Confederate intelligence network in Kentucky was stymied by both the topographical features of the land and the pro-Unionism of the resident population. The ability of Confederate scouts to accurate determine Union troop movements was marginal at best, and Johnston was therefore typically incapable of effectively coordinating the movements of his forces in response to Union actions. Johnston complained to the War Department that he found "it extremely difficult to acquire reliable intelligence of the movements of the enemy, except that which the activity of our scouts enables them to furnish, and would be glad to have $5,000 deposited in a Nashville bank to my credit for secret service."[65] Johnston established a line of reconnaissance outposts stretching from Hopkinsville in the east to Dripping Springs, Kentucky, in the west, but accurate information remained scarce.

Even if Johnston had possessed extensive telegraph networks and accurate intelligence, the problem was that the Confederacy lacked the railroad infrastructure and naval assets to rapidly transport troops between strategic points. The numerical superiority of the Union armies combined with their greater riverine mobility gave them the ability to threaten multiple Confederate cordons simultaneously and rapidly concentrate their own forces at any point. President Lincoln advised his Northern generals to menace Johnston "with superior forces at different points at the same time, so that we can safely attack one or both if he makes no change; and if he weakens one to strengthen the other, forbear to attack the strengthened one, but seize and hold the weakened one, gaining so much."[66] Johnston was aware of Lincoln's strategy to overcome the cordon defensive by launching simultaneous offensives against his line, but could do little to prevent it.

In October, Johnston informed Richmond that although he believed the enemy would make its greatest effort against Bowling Green, he was aware that "at the same time, the communications between Tennessee and Virginia, covered by Zollicoffer, and Columbus from Cairo by the river and Paducah by land… may be [subject to] a serious attack on one or the other; and for this [the Union's] command of the Ohio and all the navigable waters of Kentucky and better means of land transportation gives them great facilities of concentration."[67] Johnston acknowledged that "as my forces at neither this nor either of the other points threatened are more than sufficient to meet the force in front, I cannot weaken either until the object of the enemy is fully pronounced."[68] Until Confederate military resources in the Western Department were adequate to the task at hand, Johnston was compelled to surrender the initiative and adopt a passive stance.

Conclusion

Connelly's claim that Johnston failed to implement an overall departmental strategy is a reckless statement. It is clear from the documentary evidence that Johnston did indeed formulate a military strategy for the defense of the Western Department. Although constrained by President Davis's territorial policy and the lack of sufficient troops and resources, Johnston implemented a surprisingly successful strategy of deception and cordon expansion that kept the enemy at bay for approximately six months. His decision to invade Kentucky was bold and contributed immeasurably to the success of his subsequent illusion of strength employed against the Union commanders in the western theater of war. The possession of Kentucky territory provided the men of that state with the opportunity to join the Confederate army if they so desired, enabled Johnston's army to collect valuable agricultural produce, livestock, and other supplies, and corrected the u-shaped curve of the defensive line in the Western Department.

Johnston's deception of strength was integral to his departmental strategy, and interestingly, Connelly managed to identify and articulate this component of the general's plan. He wrote that "throughout the fall of 1861, Johnston would conduct a series of thrusts and parries designed to befuddle his central Kentucky opponent, Brigadier General William T. Sherman. The ruse utilized cavalry raids, infantry marches and counter marches, and infantry skirmishes, all designed to give the impression of a much larger force, especially in the Bowling Green area."[69] However, for whatever reason, Connelly refused to acknowledge Johnston's actions as part of a wider departmental strategy, even though the general's subordinates in other states, such as M. Jeff Thompson in Missouri, utilized the scheme and reported back to Johnston on the success on such deceptions.

Johnston worked hard to gather troops and expand the cordons in the Western Department. However, such an approach was distasteful to the aggressive general. A December 1861 letter to the Governor of Mississippi revealed Johnston's disdain for the cordon defense: "If troops are given to me, if the people can be made to feel how much suffering and calamity would be avoided by the presence now in my camp of 10,000 or 15,000 more brave men, so that I could attack the enemy, and not, from a disparity of force, be compelled to await it."[70] Johnston understood that the adoption of a territorial defensive reliant upon a series of weak cordons was a reactive strategy that yielded the initiative to the Federal generals. He also lacked the means to coordinate defensive efforts between the cordons in a timely manner. Thus, Johnston could only hope that the Confederate government would use the time purchased by his illusion of strength to furnish him with the reinforcements and resources required to wage an offensive campaign in the west.

4.

Did Johnston request enough support from the Confederate government?

When General Albert Sidney Johnston arrived in Nashville on the 14th of September 1861, the residents of the city celebrated with great fanfare. The general was gifted a new thoroughbred horse named *Fire Eater*. The people of Nashville, and the South as a whole, expected Johnston to conjure miracles in the defense of their homeland. He was more pragmatic, confiding to Governor Isham G. Harris that "the defenceless condition of this department was patent from the moment I arrived and had a hasty view of the field."[1] In a speech to an admiring crowd, the new commander of the Western Department proclaimed: "I call you soldiers, for you are all the reserved corps."[2] Johnston wanted the people of the Confederacy to know that they would need to commit fully to the war effort if they were to have any chance of success. A Nashville newspaper reported that "as a military man, he knew what was coming. The South will need all of her force. Every able-bodied man may as well make up his mind to it, and that soon."[3]

Johnston did not have much time to build his army. Historian Peter F. Walker reflected that "most armies are organized and trained in cantonments and camps far removed from the battlefield and the threat of enemy action. Though his situation was not unique, Johnston had to create his army while most of his existing force was operational and in close proximity to a superior enemy who was capable of striking almost any section of his line."[4] This was a highly challenging situation for any general. Johnston would need the unwavering support of the Confederate government to assemble an effective fighting force that was adequately armed, equipped, and supplied to defend the vast frontier of the Western Department. Yet this crucial assistance from the east never materialized. Thomas L. Connelly blamed Johnston for this situation, arguing that "Richmond's lack of understanding of Johnston's problems was due to poor communication. Johnston displayed a passive attitude toward pressing the government for things needed in his command."[5] Is Connelly's accusation fair? The documentary evidence reveals the truth of the matter.

Johnston's calls for reinforcements

Only two days after arriving in Nashville, Johnston made his first direct appeal for support to President Jefferson Davis: "I respectfully submit, considering the intended line of our defenses and the threatening attitude and increasing forces of the enemy in Missouri and Kentucky, to authorize and require of me the assurance to you that we have not over half the *armed* forces that are now likely to be required for our security against disaster."[6] Johnston called for 30,000 more volunteers from Tennessee, 10,000 from Mississippi, and 10,000 from Arkansas. However, the response was feeble as most of the willing and armed men from these states were already in service or had been transferred east. Governor Harris was compelled to release the remaining Tennessee militia in a desperate attempt to serve Johnston's request, but there were simply not enough armed men.

The general asked Richmond to evince a similar degree of solicitude for the defense of Columbus as compared to New Orleans. Johnston explained that "it is my duty to represent my own wants, and I may be pardoned if, intrusted as I am with the defense of this department, I should find the upper part of this river as important as its mouth."[7] The lack of armed troops for Columbus and other cordons prompted Johnston to ask for reinforcements from outside his own jurisdiction, such as Alabama, Louisiana, and Georgia. Yet Johnston was rebuked by the War Department for exceeding his authority. The Secretary of War, Judah P. Benjamin, lectured: "Your call for troops on Mississippi and other States will, I am afraid, produce embarrassment. When [Major General Leonidas] Polk was sent to take command of the department now under your orders, he was instructed that he might use his own discretion in the calls on Arkansas and Tennessee, but not to draw on Mississippi, Alabama, Louisiana, or Georgia without the consent of this Department."[8]

Benjamin continued his admonishment: "On other point also let me urgently fix your attention. It is understood here that you have accepted certain troops from the State of Mississippi by brigades. Now, this is against our whole policy from the beginning. If you will look at the sixth section of the act for the public defense, page 36 of the Laws of the First Session, you will see that we accept no organizations higher than a regiment. The President alone is vested with the power to form regiments into brigades and divisions."[9] Such bureaucratic red tape was frustrating and unhelpful.

In calling the various states for volunteers, Johnston specified that the men ideally should enlist for the duration of the war, but due to the pressing emergency, he would also accept twelve-month volunteers. Benjamin balked at this proposal, fearing that providing the limited weapons available to the twelve-month volunteers would deprive those who had enlisted for the duration of the war. This latter group was considered more reliable and worthy of being armed by the government. Benjamin lectured Johnston that "we are on the eve of winter. These men will be in camp four or five months, fed and paid by us, transported at great cost, provided with clothing, and then, when fairly able to do us service, we shall have to muster them out, and transport them back home at great expense."[10] Polk was also chastised for accepting twelve-month volunteers into his forces. On the 30th of December, Benjamin thundered that "we have a plenty of war men who could be sent to you, and for whom we have no arms. Pray cease accepting unarmed twelve-months' men, who are immensely expensive and utterly useless."[11]

Johnston justified his acceptance of these men: "The Government thus secured their services; otherwise, they could not have been procured, and the time between mustering in and arming was profitably employed in giving the men all practicable instructions in their duties as soldiers. This it will readily be perceived was quite as necessary to their efficiency in the field as placing arms in their hands. If the mustering-in of these volunteers had been postponed in every instance till arms were ready to be placed in their hands… we would today have been without a force to check the advance of the enemy, and our borders would have been open to the invaders. In view, therefore, of these facts and that the enemy are immediately in my front in great numbers and that we need every man it is possible to get, I reiterate a respectful but earnest hope that the order will not be enforced by the department."[12]

Unfortunately, Benjamin was determined to uphold the policy and many of the twelve-month volunteers were disbanded. The Confederate government's decision to reject these men was fatally flawed. Firstly, as Johnston described, the lack of weapons did not prohibit the drilling and disciplining of new recruits, which was an essential component of building an efficient army. Secondly, the Union army would not be idle in the winter months. Finally, Benjamin's orders to disband the twelve-month volunteers had a demoralizing effect on the troops involved and on Johnston's recruitment program. However, the whole debate over these troops must have clearly demonstrated the general's pressing need for soldiers to the Richmond bureaucrats.

Johnston's difficulty in finding armed men was further exacerbated by the Confederate government when it ordered troops from the Western Department to Virginia without even bothering to notify the general. Johnston learned that a regiment of Texas cavalry, soon to win renown as *Terry's Texas Rangers*, had been ordered to serve in Virginia. Johnston was informed that the men wished to remain in the West and was irritated that such a decision had been made without any consultation. On the 17th of September, Johnston wrote to Adjutant and Inspector General Samuel Cooper: "I can mount and use [Colonel Benjamin F.] Terry's regiment of Texas Rangers immediately if put under my orders. Please not to order any more armed companies from this department at present and order any such organized within the department to report to me here."[13]

Johnston pleaded with the Confederate government to transfer troops from less threatened points and concentrate them in Kentucky. On the

17th of October, he informed Richmond: "You know the efforts I anticipate from the enemy and the line on which the first blow is expected to fall, and the means adopted by me with the forces at my disposal to meet him. I will use all means to increase my force and spare no exertion to render it effective at every point, but I cannot assure you that this will be sufficient, and if reinforcements from less endangered or less important points can be spared, I would be glad to receive them."[14]

Johnston even attempted to draw troops from Virginia: "The enemy are crossing Green River at many points in overwhelming numbers. Their bridges are laid. I cannot meet them with more than 10,000 men between Green River and Nashville. Can [Brigadier General John B.] Floyd be sent on here?"[15] This request was met with partial success, with Benjamin apprising Johnston that "General Floyd's command will reach you by Christmas, but there are only about 2,500 men left in it. The Southern troops were sent to General [Robert E.] Lee at Charleston, where the enemy are moving with heavy force."[16] Again, the coastline took priority.

On Christmas Day, Johnston tried yet again to garner some assistance from Richmond: "Efforts have been incessantly made by me for the last four months to augment my force in the different army corps to an adequate degree of strength, but while the Governors of States have seconded my appeals, the response has been feeble, perhaps because the people did not feel or understand the great exigency that exists… I would respectfully request that the Government will earnestly and zealously aid me in my efforts to procure additional reinforcements… and that every influence should be brought to bear to convince [the Governors] and their gallant people that a decisive battle must probably be fought here for the freedom of the South, and that every man sent forward here is of importance to the Confederacy."[17]

In January 1862, Johnston offered another impassioned plea for more assistance: "I desire to ask your attention to the vast and methodized preparation of the Northern Government to carry on the war against the Confederacy with a purpose as inflexible as malignant. Their large and well-appointed army… must make every patriot contemplate its forward movement with apprehension for the safety of the country, unless, awakened to the peril which menaces it, we make a corresponding effort to meet their force and beat them back by an immediate development and application of all the military resources of the country, both of material and men, to that purpose... If necessary, let us convert our country into one vast camp of instruction for the field of every man able to bear arms, and fix our military establishment upon a permanent basis. Whenever a people will make the necessary sacrifices to maintain their liberty, they need have no fear of losing it."[18]

Johnston's pleas for weapons

The lack of troops was exacerbated by the lack of suitable weaponry. A disturbingly high proportion of the troops present for duty in the Western Department were armed with shotguns, hunting rifles, and ancient flintlock muskets. Some had no guns at all. Within days of assuming command, Johnston informed President Davis that "I have called earnestly upon the governors of Georgia and Alabama for arms, which I am assured they possess. If I fail with them, I shall appeal to your excellency for support and assistance."[19] Sadly, for Johnston, he had been misinformed, and these politicians could offer no assistance. The governor of Georgia responded that "I beg leave to state, and I do so with much regret, that it is utterly impossible for me to comply with your request. There are no arms belonging to the State at my disposal; all have been exhausted in arming the volunteers of the State now in the Confederate service in Virginia, at Pensacola, and on our own coast... Georgia has now to look to the shotguns and rifles in the hands of her people for coast defense and to guns which her gunsmiths are slowly manufacturing."[20]

Desperate for arms, Johnston learned of the rumored arrival in Georgia in September 1861 of a large shipment of rifles from Europe. He immediately contacted the President: "A steamer has arrived in Savannah with arms from Europe. Thirty thousand stand is a necessity to my command. I beg you to order them, or as many as can be got, to be instantly procured and sent with dispatch, one-half to Nashville, and the other to Trenton, on the Mobile & Ohio road."[21] Davis replied that "the steamer was a merchant vessel. We have purchased as much of the shipment as we could get – less than a sixth of your requisition. Some of the lot pledged to troops already in service. You shall have what can be sent you. Rely not on rumors."[22] Only about 1,000 rifles made their way to the Western

Department, the remainder being sent on to the armies in Virginia. Johnston wrote to Benjamin that "the inability to arm [my] troops gives the enemy a great preponderance of force with which to operate against this department, which probably has been already anticipated by you."[23]

In October, Johnston was concerned that his ordnance officer at Nashville had been "ordered to send to New Orleans and Mobile 150 barrels of cannon powder."[24] The general overruled the command since he had been informed that his army possessed but fifteen or twenty barrels. Johnston explained to Cooper: "I am aware that there is a deficiency of powder in the Confederate States, and as fully aware that, this being so, the Government must decide where the need is greatest… If Nashville is my only source of supply, no powder should be drawn thence until it is known that I can spare it."[25]

After months of pleading, Johnston sent a special envoy, Colonel St. John R. Liddell, to Richmond to meet with President Davis in January 1862. Liddell recalled that "Johnston seemed fully alive to the uncertain condition of affairs. He spoke very deliberately and clearly of everything connected with his situation in holding his present line of the Green River and of the strength and designs of the enemy under Generals [Don Carlos] Buell and [Ulysses S.] Grant. He regretted very much the inadequacy of his own force and desired me to impress the President with the necessity of sending him reinforcements and arms. Johnston thought both might be spared to him temporarily from Virginia, as no immediate movement was contemplated in that quarter since [Major General George B.] McClellan was not ready." Liddell dutifully travelled to the capital and relayed this information. The President was astonished: "My God! Why did General Johnston send you to me for arms and reinforcements, when he must know that I have neither? He has plenty of men in Tennessee, and they must have arms of some kind. Shotguns, rifles, even pikes could be used."[26]

Liddell was not deterred and conveyed Johnston's wish that troops be sent to his department from Virginia or from the idle seaboard garrisons at Charleston, Savannah, Pensacola, and New Orleans. Davis retorted "Do you think these places of so little importance that I should strip them of the troops necessary for their defense?"[27] Liddell countered that the Western Department was under immediate threat and the fall of the Mississippi River would be more calamitous than the loss of a coastal town. At a second meeting the following day, Davis softened but dismissed Liddell with the dispiriting advice: "Tell my friend, General Johnston, that I can do nothing for him; that he must rely on his own resources."[28] This statement effectively summarized the futility of Johnston's endless quest for armed soldiers in the West.

Johnston's requests for qualified officers

With the abundance of amateur generals under his command, Johnston wrote to President Davis on the 16th of September to secure the services of Major General Gustavus W. Smith: "I would be glad to have the services of G.W. Smith, if it is in the power of your excellency to assign him to my command."[29] Smith was a West Point graduate, experienced in combat, and highly regarded for his abilities. Regrettably for Johnston, an officer of such apparent quality was required in Virginia, and Smith was soon appointed commander of a division and later an entire wing of the Army of Northern Virginia. Johnston simply had to make do with the generals assigned to him by Richmond. In October, Benjamin informed the general: "I have your letter asking for the appointment of a brigadier general to command at Columbus... Your recommendation of Major A.P. Stewart has been considered with the respect due to your suggestions, but there is an officer under your command whom you must have overlooked... I refer to Colonel Lloyd Tilghman."[30] Unfortunately, Tilghman would prove a liability in the defense of Forts Henry and Donelson.

Similarly, Johnston requested the services of an experienced engineer, Captain Edward P. Alexander, but Cooper responded that "Captain Alexander cannot be spared from Manassas [Virginia]. I have tried to find you an officer but have failed. There are but few in the corps, and they are on important duties. You must have several [West Point] graduates in your command, some of whom will answer the purpose."[31] Qualified engineers were essential for the construction of fortifications, the repair and construction of roads, bridges, and railroads, the obstruction of rivers, reconnaissance missions, and the production of maps. Johnston wrote that "the necessity of engineers is pressed on my attention by the wants of every hour. Can they be furnished? If not, can I muster the engineers of Tennessee, if to be had? Please give prompt reply."[32] Again, Cooper's response was unhelpful: "Do the best you can in respect to engineers. Employ any officers you can find."[33]

Johnston's calls for logistical support

The reluctance of Kentuckians to provide food, fodder, and logistical support to the Confederate army placed great strain on Johnston's ability to maintain his forces. On several occasions, his quartermasters took much needed supplies from the Nashville depots. On the 16th of October, Benjamin reprimanded Johnston that the supplies at Nashville "were collected for the army in Virginia and have been delayed on account of the embarrassments in transportation on the railroads. The supplies in this part of the country are becoming exhausted, while in Kentucky you have a rich and fertile State, amply able to feed your army. I desire very much that you should refrain from drawing anything from the stores at Nashville, and that your commissariat be furnished by purchases in Kentucky."[34]

Johnston defended his actions, responding that "I have suspended an order of Quartermaster-General [Abraham C.] Myers to Quartermaster [John T.] Shaaff, at Nashville, to send to Richmond all stores of that depot in his hands, and I report to you my reasons by today's mail. Those reasons I beg you to hear before enforcing the order. They are weighty."[35] Johnston informed Benjamin that his procurement efforts were hindered by "the refusal of the farmers for their flour, &c., of any but gold or Kentucky paper money. While private dealers comply with their demands, we are unable to do so. We have only Confederate or Tennessee paper... There is no [usable] money in the hands of the commissary, and I should add that the quartermaster's department is also destitute. The embarrassment is peculiarly felt at this time, as without it, transportation, in which our troops are greatly deficient, cannot be obtained."[36]

Part of the problem was that the Confederate Commissary General, Lucius B. Northrop, harbored doubts that Johnston's army would be able to retain its position at Bowling Green for very long. He communicated to his chief commissary officer in Tennessee that only stores designated "for temporary use" be shipped to the army at Bowling Green.[37] Such actions by Richmond bureaucrats had a deeply injurious effect on Johnston's ability to feed, arm, supply, and move his armies. The lack of wagons and wheeled vehicles for Johnston's army was also particularly troubling. On the 27th of October, the general lamented to Cooper: "I hope soon to provide sufficient transportation to give all desirable mobility to this corps. We are quite deficient at present."[38] The dearth of transport significantly impacted the viability of the Confederate territorial defense strategy in the Western Department. Poor mobility prevented rapid internal reinforcement and weakened the effectiveness of the cordons.

A determined but futile effort

It is clear that there were almost daily petitions from Johnston to President Davis, the Secretary of War, Adjutant and Inspector General Cooper, and various government officials from September 1861 to April 1862. Special envoys such as Liddell were dispatched to Richmond to make personal entreaties for support on Johnston's behalf. Considering the voluminous correspondence and personal messengers, Connelly's criticism that the general failed to make Richmond aware of his difficulties is utterly absurd. Connelly was taking his iconoclastic approach much too far in this respect.

Liddell recorded that after personally delivering Johnston's message that the Western Department was under-resourced and vulnerable to attack, President Davis responded "I have heard similar remarks from others." Yet Liddell was left with the impression that the President "distrusted the views of others and seemed disinclined to believe the representations I made of General Johnston's critical condition. I had heard that he, General Johnston, was an especial favorite of Mr. Davis and was naturally surprised when I saw no point was stretched to afford him prompt aid." However, after further emphasizing Johnston's desperate situation, Liddell reported that the President remarked: "It is right that I should know all the facts though I might not afford the desired relief."[39]

A senior clerk in the Confederate War Department, John B. Jones, wrote on the 21st of October 1861 that "the enemy's papers represent that we have some 80,000 men in Kentucky, and this lulls us from vigilance and effort in Virginia. The Secretary of War [Leroy P. Walker] knows very well that we have not 30,000 there, and that we are not likely to have more. We supposed Kentucky would rise."[40] Several months later, on the 23rd of January 1862, Jones proclaimed: "I know, and Mr. Benjamin knows, that General Johnston has not exceeding 29,000 effective men. And the Secretary knows that General Johnston has given him timely notice of the inadequacy of his force to hold the position at Bowling Green... Well, *reinforcements are not sent.*"[41]

Another wartime correspondent declared that "the utter inadequacy of General Johnston's forces was known to the government. The authorities at Richmond appeared to hope for results without the legitimate means of acquiring them; to look for relief from vague and undefined sources; and to await, with dull expectation, what was next to happen. While the government remained in this blank disposition, events marched forward... General Johnston, thus discouraged and baffled by a government which was friendly enough to him personally, but insensible to the public exigency for which he pleaded, was left in the situation of imminent peril."[42]

Former Mississippi Congressman, Reuben O. Davis, remarked: "I had been at Bowling Green for two months, and had learned there not only to feel confidence in General Johnston's ability and devotion to the cause, but to understand something of the difficulties of his position. I knew how small his army was, and how unwilling the war department had been to allow him reinforcements."[43] Charles P. Roland concluded that Johnston "constantly warned the Richmond authorities of the imminent peril of a Federal advance against his line... [Every] communication to his superiors repeated the urgent necessity for strengthening the Confederate forces in the west."[44] More recently, Timothy B. Smith observed that Johnston "plainly told Richmond of his problems."[45] Connelly's accusation that the general did not communicate his needs is patently false.

Despite the lack of assistance from Richmond, Roland noted that Johnston "did not, however, sit idle to await reinforcement by the War Department. At the same time that he informed the Administration of his weakness, he set about vigorously to remedy it [with requests to the State Governors and fellow Confederate commanders.] All replies to these requests were disappointing."[46] Colonel Robert W. Woolley, one of Johnston's staff officers, recalled that "the army had to be built up, and the general had not only to organize the troops, but had himself to search for them."[47] After the Civil War, General Pierre G.T. Beauregard stated that Johnston "had exhausted all means of procuring more armed troops from the Confederate and State governments, and his official correspondence shows that he had done his utmost in that respect."[48] The editor of the *Confederate Veteran* magazine remarked that "in all the war the man whose life was most tried, perhaps, was that of Albert Sidney Johnston, in the organization and equipment of the western army. His pleadings with the governors of the states to call out and equip commands against the frightful conditions that confronted him were as a trial unto the death."[49]

Conclusion

Connelly's assertion that Johnston failed to make the Confederate government aware of his problems is another reckless statement. The documentary evidence of Johnston's repeated appeals is overwhelming. It was Richmond's prioritization of Virginia and the coastal defenses that deprived Johnston of any significant assistance, not the general's inability to communicate his needs. Decades after the Civil War, Davis sheepishly acknowledged this blunder by rationalizing that "so great was my confidence in [Johnston's] capacity for organization and administration, that I felt, when he was assigned to the Department of the West, that the undeveloped power of that region would be made sufficient not only for its own safety, but to contribute support, if need be, to the more seriously threatened East."[50] The failure of the Confederate government to direct the appropriate quantum of soldiery and resources to the Western Department plagued Johnston throughout his tenure of command. It is difficult to imagine that any Civil War general could have done more than Johnston in attempting to procure the necessary assistance for the defense of the Western Department. President Davis lamely excused his neglect by claiming that "the West was a field vast and distant, where the chief must act without advice or aid, and [Johnston] seemed the only man equal to it."[51]

5.

Did Polk and Pillow disobey Johnston at Columbus?

One of General Albert Sidney Johnston's first acts in command was to survey the defensive line in the Western Department. He would meet with his subordinate commanders, inspect their troops, and examine the integrity of the cordons. Johnston had already met with Brigadier General Felix K. Zollicoffer at Knoxville and Brigadier General Simon B. Buckner at Nashville, and he decided to visit Major General Leonidas Polk's fortress at Columbus next, the Gibraltar of the West. Johnston notified the government that "I am about completing the works here to meet the probable flotilla from the North, supposed to carry 200 heavy guns."[1] Johnston arrived at Columbus on the 18th of September 1861 and received a warm reception from Bishop Polk. The general's son noted that "it was a great pleasure to him to meet again, after the lapse of many years, his old comrade."[2] Polk was 55 years old, a native of North Carolina, and a West Point companion of both Johnston and President Jefferson Davis. Having served as the Bishop of the Episcopal Diocese of Louisiana for the past twenty years, Polk had immediately withdrawn his diocese from the national Episcopal Church with the outbreak of Civil War.

As a resident of the Mississippi Valley, Polk had written to Davis in May 1861 to volunteer his opinions regarding the defense of the region.

The letter was well received, and Polk was summoned to Richmond in June to attend meetings with the President and other senior officials. Surprisingly, Davis decided to entrust the defense of the Mississippi Valley to his friend until Johnston arrived from California. When asked by an acquaintance if he was discarding the gown of an Episcopal Bishop to take up the sword of a Confederate general, Polk allegedly retorted: "No, Sir, I am buckling the sword over the gown."[3]

Polk had no military experience apart from his West Point education but cut an imposing figure. Johnston's son observed that the bishop's "tall and powerful form, his resolute gray eye, broad, square, intellectual brow, aquiline features, massive jaw, and air of command, made him a striking figure, whether in the pulpit or in the saddle. His manner combined suavity, vivacity, and resolute will."[4] One acquaintance described Polk as "a grand man: a colossal nature, both physique and morale."[5] Captain Arthur J.L. Fremantle, a visiting war tourist from Britain, described Polk as "a good-looking, gentlemanlike man, with all the manners and affability of a 'grand seignior.' He is… tall, upright, and looks much more the soldier than the clergyman. He is very rich; and I am told he owns 700 negroes. He is much beloved by the soldiers on account of his great personal courage and agreeable manners."[6] Another war correspondent reported that Polk "was unrivalled for the graces of culture, native dignity, and high bearing. He was affable, self-possessed, and approachable."[7]

Major General Leonidas Polk

Johnston discussed the strategic situation in the Western Department with Polk, his second-in-command, Brigadier General Gideon J. Pillow, and the senior officers of the garrison. With the influence and support of the *Mississippi River bloc*, Polk had managed to install dozens of pieces of artillery in his new fortress. They were organized into three tiers, enabling the Confederates to fire at Union shipping with "angles varying from plunging to waterline."[8] One of the pieces of artillery was a huge 128-pounder Whitworth rifled gun, dubbed the *Lady*

Polk, after the bishop's wife. Polk proudly showed Johnston a mile-long (1.6 km) chain that he had affixed across the Mississippi River from Columbus to the opposite shore in Missouri to impede Union navigation of the river. Each link of the chain weighed about twenty pounds and five ounces (9.2 kg), so the structure had to be held aloft by barges positioned at regular intervals across the river. The chain was secured to the Columbus bluffs by a colossal anchor weighing somewhere between four and six tons, buried eleven feet (3.4 m) deep and set in place with twelve-foot oak (3.7m) logs.[9]

The two generals discussed the potential of naval mines, known as *torpedoes* or *submarine batteries*, in the Civil War era. The devices contained an air-filled compartment that enabled them to float on or just below the surface of the water. The devices were typically moored to a weight or a chain and were designed to explode on contact with a passing enemy vessel. On the 10th of October, Polk asked the Secretary of War to send an officer experienced in the construction and use of naval mines to Columbus.[10] Johnston inspected the elaborate fortifications constructed on the bluffs of the Kentucky town. The soldiers had cut down many of the taller trees to provide the artillerists with unobstructed views of the Mississippi River. These logs were then shaped into abatis for the four miles (6.4 km) of trenches protecting the site from landward assaults. Overall, Johnston was satisfied with the defensive capability of the Columbus position and Polk's handling of affairs in the Mississippi Valley District.

The troops at Columbus benefited from the presence of the departmental commander. Johnston personally inspected the garrison daily during his time at Polk's fortress. One observer noted that "while [Johnston] was not a martinet, his enforcement of discipline was admirable, and yet extremely quiet. When he reached Columbus, the discipline of the considerable forces assembled there had been visibly relaxed. Within a week after he had assumed command, a great change was apparent, and was noticed by everyone, although few could understand precisely how it was effected. I presume it was done simply by calling the attention of the higher officers to the enforcement of the army regulations. Much also was due to his habit of personal inspection. Every afternoon, in the fine October weather, he rode with some of his staff about the camps, quietly inspecting; his eye seemed to be everywhere. He had nothing whatever of the military demagogue in his composition; everyone under him was quietly but firmly kept to his proper position... The entire army, as by some instinct, soon conceived the greatest admiration of and confidence in him; he looked like a great soldier but had also a kindly face and high-bred courtesy which gained him the affection of all who came near him. He paid great attention to the health of his troops and the sanitary condition of his camps."[11]

Yet trouble was brewing. Some historians contend that the relationship between Johnston and the Columbus generals quickly deteriorated. For example, Thomas L. Connelly declared that "the ambitious Pillow and the stubborn Polk had only one interest and that was the Mississippi River defense. They would oppose and refuse cooperation with Johnston and would remain aloof at Columbus as the Tennessee line threatened to crumble around them."[12] He argued that "Polk and Pillow would maintain a disinterested attitude toward Johnston's problems in Middle and East Tennessee."[13]

The case of Lieutenant Dixon

Satisfied with the Columbus fortifications, Johnston looked to bolster the defenses in western Tennessee. On the 30th of September, his adjutant general, Lieutenant Colonel William W. Mackall, ordered Lieutenant Joseph K. Dixon, Polk's principal engineer at Columbus, to examine the terrain from the Mississippi River to Fort Henry on the Tennessee River.[14] Polk refused to release Dixon, claiming that his services were still required at Columbus. On the 7th of October, Mackall informed Polk that "General Johnston directs you to send Lieutenant Dixon to Fort Donelson, Cumberland River, instantly, with orders to mount the guns at that place for the defense of the river."[15] The bishop again protested the transfer and Mackall had to repeat the order a third time to ensure compliance.

Connelly interpreted the scenario as follows: "In October 1861 there were only three engineers in the entire [Western] Department, and [Polk] had cornered all three for work on his Mississippi River forts. Johnston ordered one of them, Lieutenant Joseph K. Dixon, to go to [Fort] Donelson and superintend the work there. Polk, in a manner that can only be described as insubordinate, first delayed the engineer's departure, and then flatly told Johnston that neither Dixon nor the other two officers could be spared. Johnston had to issue two additional orders to Polk before Dixon was sent."[16]

However, the delay in Dixon's transfer was understandable due to the lack of engineers in the Western Department and the parochialism to local areas engendered by President Jefferson Davis's division of command responsibility into defined districts. In defense of Polk, only one of the three "engineers" in the Mississippi Valley was from the engineer corps. The other two were army officers with some topographical experience. The bishop explained to Mackall that "there are but three officers assigned to duty in this department as engineers – Captain Dixon, Engineer Corps; Captain [Asa B.] Gray, infantry; and Lieutenant [J. Hudson] Snowden, infantry. The former is the only engineer officer with this command. The two latter are employed on the fortifications in the course of construction at Island Number Ten. None of these officers can well be spared, nor do I know where one can be obtained."[17]

Polk's reluctance to send the only officer from the Engineer Corps east was forgivable considering the pressing works at the recently occupied Columbus. The town had only been in Confederate hands for less than a month prior to Johnston's first request for Dixon's transfer. There were artillery batteries to embed, tiers to construct, abatis to set, and a myriad of other engineering tasks to attend to. Although Polk unsuccessfully argued his case for a few days, he did comply with Johnston's order and Dixon was at Fort Donelson by mid-October. In April 1862, Polk reported to Johnston: "Shortly after taking command of the Western Department, Lieutenant Dixon, of the Corps of Engineers, was instructed by you to make an examination of the works at Forts Henry and Donelson and to report upon them. These instructions were complied with."[18]

The transfer of troops to Clarksville

After resolving the struggle over Dixon's services, Johnston's tour of the Western Department was abruptly cut short. On the 12th of October, he received an urgent message from the commanders of the army at Bowling Green informing him that a large Union force in Kentucky was advancing southwards, and that they required his immediate presence.

Johnston hastily made his way to Bowling Green to prepare the army for action. Once in central Kentucky, Johnston observed the inherent weakness of the Confederate line in the region and turned his thoughts to building a defensive axis running from Fort Henry on the Tennessee River to Bowling Green. The problem was a lack of armed soldiers to man the line. Johnston's mind soon turned to the garrison at Columbus. Forbidden to receive reinforcements from Virginia and the coastal fortifications, the formidable defenses that Polk was constructing at Columbus seemed to obviate the need for such a large garrison to be stationed there. These soldiers could be transferred to central Tennessee or Kentucky.

On the 4th of November, Mackall notified Polk that "General Johnston directs you to send 5,000 troops, with two field batteries, to Clarksville. Let there be a fair proportion of cavalry. Put General Pillow in command. Let him use the rail or march, or do both, in his discretion, but be prompt and say nothing of his destination."[19] Polk responded that he would comply with the order but was concerned that the weakening of his garrison would leave him vulnerable to attack from the large Union forces concentrating both in Missouri and upriver at Cairo. Polk complained that "I have this evening received your dispatch ordering 5,000 troops of the force under my command to be sent forward to Clarksville. I telegraphed you in reply that measures were taken immediately to execute your orders. These measures are now being carried out... I am deeply impressed with the serious consequences that may follow from weakening the force at this place... in view of the information in our possession it [is] a matter of serious doubt whether we would be able to make a successful resistance to the large force now being concentrated in our front with so small an army as that under our command."[20]

The bishop's anxiety was completely justified. The Union commander at Cairo, Brigadier General Ulysses S. Grant, harboured a deep desire to advance on Columbus. In September, he had practically begged his superior, Major General John C. Frémont, for permission: "I telegraphed this evening that troops – artillery, cavalry, and infantry – can be spared from [Cairo] by sending those from Jackson promptly to take possession of Columbus Heights... This should be done tomorrow night."[21] This was followed by another plea less than a week later: "If it were discretionary with me, with a little addition to my present force I would take

Columbus."[22] Grant's letters to his wife during September and October were replete with lamentations concerning his rank, sphere of command, and desire to attack the enemy.

Yet Johnston would not be moved. Mackall responded to Polk: "Your force is not so great as [Johnston] would wish it to be, but, viewed from his standpoint, now that your river defenses are complete, it is fully as large, after deducting the detachment ordered, as he can spare from other parts of the field. That order, then, will be executed."[23] In desperation, Polk dispatched the persuasive and charismatic Pillow to Bowling Green to meet with Johnston in person and argue his case. As a member of the *Mississippi River bloc*, Pillow did not wish to see Columbus weakened and Memphis exposed to enemy threats. Polk's complaint was "duly considered by the general," but to no avail, and the order stood.[24] A disappointed Pillow returned to Columbus the following day.

On the morning of the 7th of November, Pillow's division commenced its march to Clarksville. However, that very morning, Grant decided to attack the Confederate camp at Belmont, opposite Columbus, on the western side of the Mississippi River. Grant's troops debarked from their river steamers and advanced on the camp. Polk immediately recalled Pillow's division and shuttled them across the river to reinforce the small garrison at Belmont. Grant's men attacked and routed the Confederate forces, thanks largely to Pillow's faulty deployment of the troops. But the retreat of the Confederates to the banks of the Mississippi River enabled the heavy guns at Columbus to fire upon the bluecoats with impunity. The incoming shells, including those from the *Lady Polk*, drove the Union forces from the camp. Grant managed to restore order and march his troops back to their transports upriver. Polk ordered more reinforcements to cross the river, and the Confederates pursued the withdrawing Federals.

Led by Pillow and other brave officers, the reinvigorated Southern soldiers surprised Grant's men with a vicious counterattack. Polk personally led additional troops across the river, and the Union expeditionary force completely disintegrated, abandoning their plunder and captured artillery. The Confederates were unable to cut off Grant's retreat and the Union soldiers rushed aboard their transports and disappeared back up the Mississippi River to safety, covered by the fire from their gunboats.

Grant's temporary capture of Belmont had cost him 607 casualties from 3,100 men engaged, whereas Polk suffered 641 casualties from about 5,000 engaged, but with never more than half of that present on the battlefield at any one time. Johnston wrote to Polk: "I was rejoiced this morning by news of your glorious victory."[24]

Some historians have declared the battle of Belmont a strategic Union victory, claiming that it focused Confederate attention on Columbus, prevented the transfer Pillow's division to Clarksville, and contributed to the neglect of Forts Henry and Donelson. Grant wrote in his memoirs that "the two objects which the battle of Belmont was fought were fully accomplished. The enemy gave up all idea of detaching troops from Columbus. His losses were very heavy for that period of the war."[26] However, Johnston's directive to transfer troops from Columbus to the east was only postponed, not cancelled, by the battle of Belmont. In a letter to the Secretary of War he wrote: "General Polk has gained a victory over the Federal troops opposite Columbus. They were routed with great loss, and I now consider his situation better than before the conflict… I therefore find still greater reason for bringing forward the troops ordered from Columbus."[27] Johnston stated that Pillow's division "has been delayed by the battle, but I hope [it] will be in time to anticipate the enemy… After deducting them and the force ordered to Clarksville, 10,000 or 11,000 effective men will be left under General Polk's command; a sufficient force for the defense of his front for the present, but much less than I would suggest for the contingencies of the future."[28]

Accordingly, on the 9th of November, Polk received a message from headquarters explaining that "the necessity for General Pillow's force at Clarksville is greater now than when ordered. The general hopes that no delay beyond that caused by the battle of the 7th instant will be made."[29] Johnston ordered several locomotives to Paris, Tennessee, to facilitate the transfer. But Polk was unable to comply. On the 11th of November, he was watching an artillery demonstration involving the *Lady Polk*. A shot had inadvertently been left in the barrel of the massive cannon following the battle of Belmont, and when fired once more to clear the barrel, the field gun exploded in a shower of shrapnel. Two officers and several soldiers were killed, and Polk was flung to the ground heavily concussed, with his uniform torn to shreds and both his eardrums damaged.

Pillow assumes command

Command devolved to Polk's second-in-command. Pillow was 55 years old, a native of Tennessee, and one of the wealthiest men in the State. He owned large swathes of land in the South, possessed hundreds of enslaved workers, and ran a profitable law practice. Pillow was charismatic, energetic, and intensely ambitious. He had run for the office of Vice President of the United States in 1852, and for a seat in the Senate in 1857, but both attempts were unsuccessful. Pillow possessed some military experience, having commanded a division in the Mexican-American War. However, he owed this appointment to his friendship with President James K. Polk rather than to any discernible talent. Pillow's commanding officer from that conflict, Major General Winfield Scott, remembered the Tennessean as "amiable and possessed of some acuteness, but the only person I have ever known who was wholly indifferent in the choice between truth and falsehood, honesty and dishonesty… ever as ready to attain an end by the one as the other, and habitually boastful of acts of cleverness at the total sacrifice of moral character."[30]

Brigadier General Gideon J. Pillow

Pillow achieved some success in the war, but his reputation was sullied by his overbearing personality and interpersonal conflicts with Scott and other officers. Renowned for his arrogance and vanity, one newspaper depicted him as a "self-inflating Pillow" in a political cartoon. Despite this personal flaw, the politically connected Pillow was appointed the senior major general in the Provisional Army of Tennessee by Governor Isham G. Harris. Pleased with the assignment, he devoted his considerable energy to recruiting, organizing, supplying, and arming the Tennessee troops. But Pillow's unrealistic belief in enduring Kentucky neutrality caused him to concentrate the State's military resources in Memphis and its surrounds.

Unfortunately for Pillow, when the Provisional Army of Tennessee was transferred into Confederate service, his militia rank of major general was downgraded to that of brigadier general in the regular army. This act enraged Pillow and led to a fractious relationship with his new superior, Leonidas Polk. An acquaintance of both men noted that Pillow's "vanity is not less conspicuous than it was in Mexico, and he is eternally carping at 'the bishop,' as he terms Polk."[31] Now in command while Polk recovered from his injuries, Pillow cancelled Johnston's order to gather locomotives for the transfer of his division to Clarksville, claiming that Columbus was threatened by another Federal offensive. Pillow argued that "we have had for several days' intelligence, from sources which we know are entitled to full confidence, that the enemy are making preparations upon a gigantic scale to assault... They are bringing all their available forces from the interior of Missouri and Illinois and will invest this place with 30,000 men."[32]

Johnston again remained firm in his resolve. Mackall informed Columbus: "Your dispatch of the 13th [of November] received. General Johnston insists that General Pillow's command move at once to Clarksville."[33] In desperation, Pillow sent a message directly to Richmond, warning the government that "from information in my possession, and from what I know of the enemy's preparations, I am fully assured that he will attack me in a few days with an overwhelming force. I beg that reinforcements may be ordered to me at the earliest moment."[34] Pillow's prayers were answered. On the 15th of November, the generals at Columbus received new orders from Mackall: "Retain General Pillow's command at Columbus. General Johnston revokes the order for his movement on Clarksville."[35]

Pillow had seemingly won the argument, defying Johnston until the departmental commander rescinded his order. Connelly argued that "to keep his men and also obtain additional troops, Pillow devised a clever scheme. On November 13, he began issuing almost daily reports of an overwhelming enemy force gathering in Kentucky to invade Columbus... Pillow's strategy was effective. Johnston believed his rumors, and... cancelled his division's transfer."[36] Connelly described Pillow as "vain, ambitious, and easily offended... These traits in Pillow's character – vanity, a quarrelsome nature, and ambition – were to be partly responsible for the trouble that [his] temporary command produced for Johnston."[37] Similarly, Steven E. Woodworth asserted that "Pillow continued to insist that Columbus was threatened by hordes of bluecoats... Finally, Johnston gave up in disgust and decided to try to find the necessary troops elsewhere."[38] But are these conclusions accurate?

A misunderstanding of strength

The reasons for the aborted transfer of Pillow's division to Clarksville were more complex. Based on personality alone, it does seem entirely plausible that Pillow connived to retain his division at Columbus. However, Connelly was too judgmental in his interpretation of events. The revocation of Johnston's transfer order had nothing to do with "clever scheming" by Pillow. Indeed, earlier that month, Johnston had successfully resisted Pillow's personal entreaties to cancel the transfer of his troops prior to the battle of Belmont.

The actual reason for Johnston's reversal involved the misunderstanding of the strength of the Columbus garrison. Johnston was under the impression that it numbered over 17,000 men based on an October return, but he soon discovered that the entire force only numbered about 11,000 men due to sickness and inaccurate counting that plagued the Confederate military organization.[39] The inexperience of commanders and their staff distorted the reporting of army strength throughout the Western Department. Disorganized and chaotic paperwork in the inchoative state and national military bureaus was a major contributor to this problem. The plenitude of militia units, independent companies, and local home guards springing into existence in 1861, coupled with various state-wide and national recruitment drives, meant that an accurate assessment of the number of effective and armed soldiers at a particular location was most difficult to obtain.

Men who were already members of the militia, home guard, reserve corps, or some other organization, were often recounted when regiments were created or transferred into the Confederate army. The naming of units also contributed to the confusion, with regiments sometimes having multiple designations. As Connelly himself noted, the 43rd Infantry Regiment of Tennessee was also referred to as the 5th East Tennessee Volunteers, and eventually, as the Mounted Infantry.[40] Commanders were also inconsistent in their use of military terminology. Polk once reported that he had four brigades of Tennessee troops, but then later referred to them as three divisions. Even when used correctly, the military terminology was not particularly informative. All regiments were supposed to have 1,000 troops, but they could have as little as 500 men. Only two of the 22 regiments organized by Governor Harris in July had over 900 soldiers in them.[41]

Accordingly, some historians have stated the strength of the garrison at Columbus as numbering anywhere from 17,000 to 21,000 men and heap scorn upon Polk and Pillow for failing to release any of these alleged hordes of soldiers to aid Johnston. For example, historian Nathaniel C. Hughes asserted that "Polk had the necessary manpower."[42] These authors have used Polk's own reports to headquarters of the number of men present for duty in his district, as documented in the *Official Records*. However, they neglect to consider important caveats related to these returns. Firstly, as discussed above, the Confederate staff often over-estimated the number of soldiers available. Secondly, a significant proportion of the army was sick and unable to take arms. Finally, Polk's figures related to his entire district, not just the fortress at Columbus. The numbers included troops stationed at various locations across his district, such as New Madrid, Island Number Ten, Union City, Fort Pillow, Camp Beauregard, and Forts Henry and Donelson. In the message revoking his order to transfer troops, Johnston asked Polk and Pillow to "send at once a return of your troops by regiments and independent companies."[43]

Johnston carefully explained the situation to Richmond: "On the 4th [of November], anticipating that the enemy would send a column in the direction of Clarksville with the view of turning the right of General Polk's line of defense, I ordered a division of that command to Clarksville. The battle of Belmont near Columbus intervening delayed the movement of the division, and finally General Polk, his generals concurring, suspended the movement, on the ground that in view of probable movements of the enemy against that position the force called for was necessary there. On the receipt of his telegram announcing that suspension of the movement of the force I reiterated my order for the immediate transfer of the division to his right at Clarksville to reinforce the force at Hopkinsville. He sends me this morning the following telegram to wit: 'We are informed beyond a doubt that there are from 20,000 to 25,000 men at Cairo and vicinity, recruits daily arriving, and that their intention is to march on this place immediately. I will nevertheless send on Pillow's division, unless otherwise ordered immediately. I will be left with about 6,000 effective men. Our defenses are unfinished.'"[44]

Johnston concluded: "I therefore revoked my order. General Polk's force is stated far below what I have estimated it, and with a knowledge of the case as he presents it, I had left but the choice of difficulties – the great probability of defeat at Columbus or the successful advance of the enemy on my left [at Bowling Green]. I have risked the latter. The first would be a great misfortune, scarcely reparable for a long time; the latter may be prevented."[45] It was a very difficult decision for the commander of the Western Department. The reduction of the Columbus garrison to only 6,000 men would have soon been discovered by Union spies and informants, leading to an assault on the fortress. Johnston could not rob Peter to pay Paul and risked a Federal advance into central Tennessee rather than along the Mississippi River.

Johnston pleaded with Governor Harris for more men to ameliorate this situation: "All my information goes to show that the danger is imminent of an invasion of the Confederate States through the northern line of Tennessee, by heavy columns of the enemy attempting to penetrate by the valley of the Mississippi; while other but little less formidable forces cover and threaten the capital by the line of the Cumberland. I therefore call upon your excellency to assist me to repel and drive back these forces by the armed forces of the State and beg you to this end to call forth every loyal soldier of the militia into whose hands arms can be placed, or to provide a volunteer force large enough to use all the arms that can be procured."[46]

Connelly naturally interpreted Pillow's repeated warnings of an imminent Union offensive against Columbus as part of his manipulation of Johnston. The alarming dispatches certainly annoyed Samuel Tate, the President of the Memphis & Charleston Railroad. He wrote to one of Johnston's staff officers: "Permit me to say to you that our people are very much exercised about General Pillow being in supreme command at Columbus. His daily sensation dispatches keep the country in alarm and commotion. If General Polk is not well enough to take command, I pray General Johnston will put some man of more prudence there. No one here has the slightest confidence in Pillow's judgment or ability, and if the important command of defending this river is to be left to him, we feel perfectly in the enemy's power. I know General Johnston has so much to do and think about, he may not feel as we do about this Columbus command… The battle of Belmont has not in the least changed public opinion about Pillow."[47]

Despite this tirade, Tate himself remained anxious about the safety of Columbus, reporting in the same letter that "my own opinion is the main attack will be made [at Columbus], and that soon. Their iron gunboats can pass any battery on shore, and we do feel uneasy here and are doing all in our power to aid our army."[48] Tate's view was shared by many, and Johnston's decision to retain the 5,000 troops at Columbus was entirely justified considering the size of the Union forces gathering in Missouri and southern Illinois.

Pillow's grand offensive

On the 22nd of November, Polk informed Johnston of the arrival of a Confederate gunboat at Columbus: "Commodore [George N.] Hollins, whose fleet I have asked for of the Secretary of the Navy, is here with one of his boats; the whole, six in number, are expected in the next two or three days."[49] Hollins's squadron was known as the *Mosquito fleet*, and consisted of civilian river steamers that had been converted into gunboats. They were intended to be used primarily as rams, with only one or two guns mounted on each ship. Hollins's fleet lacked armor and firepower and were no match for the Federal ironclads.

In Pillow's military naivety, the arrival of the *Mosquito fleet* opened a raft of possibilities. He suddenly began talk of launching an attack against the Union naval base at Cairo. Pillow's enthusiasm for an offensive was stoked by misleading reports in Northern newspapers regarding the embryonic status of the Union ironclads at Cairo. Pillow thought that if the Confederates could strike before the fleet was ready to sail then the ironclads could be destroyed in their berths and Columbus saved from a future assault. On the 2nd of December, Pillow excitedly apprised Polk, now almost fully recovered from the effects of his concussion, that "with Commodore Hollins's fleet of gunboats and our land forces acting

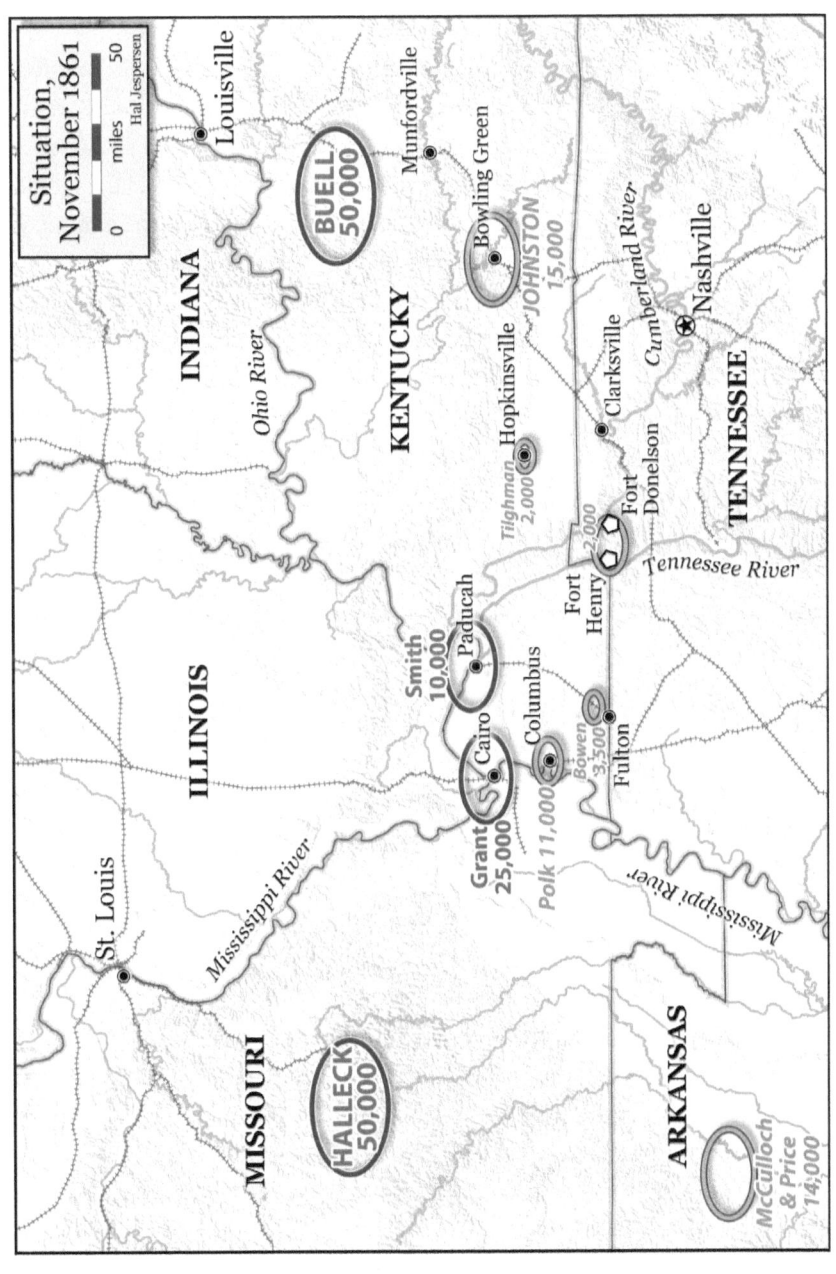

together and making simultaneous attacks by water and land we can take Bird's Point and Fort Holt and capture or destroy his unarmed gunboats, and probably Cairo."[50]

When Pillow proposed this amphibious offensive against Cairo a few days after rejecting Johnston's request for a division of troops to be transferred to Clarksville, Connelly interpreted his abrupt reversal as evidence of manipulation, claiming that "no sooner had Johnston and Harris acted than Pillow changed the tone of his reports. The enemy threat miraculously ceased, and Pillow now reported that the Columbus defenses were impregnable. In fact, Pillow suggested that conditions in West Tennessee had improved enough to allow him to undertake an offensive campaign."[51]

Connelly's assertion is incorrect. Pillow never considered the enemy threat to Columbus extinguished. His reasoning for the offensive was pre-emptive. He wrote to a subordinate that "the enemy is making preparations upon a large scale to invest [Columbus]. My opinion is that he will aim to avoid a conflict or assault on our works, but will surround my position, cut off our supplies, and aim to reduce the place by distress, at the same time harassing us with his gunboats."[52] Pillow's solution to the impending attack was to strike Cairo while the ironclads were still being fitted out. The whole episode simply illustrates Pillow's inexperience as a military commander, his overestimation of the capability of the Mosquito fleet, and his desire to be proactive in the defense of the Mississippi Valley. Polk was rightfully dubious of Pillow's scheme and consulted several of his senior subordinates, who unanimously rejected the idea.

One of Polk's generals concluded that it was "impractical with the forces at our disposal and the enemy's means of resistance… with a force of 11,000 men, and a few river boats liable to be disabled by a single shot, it is proposed that we should attack a strongly intrenched force of 34,500 men. The risks attending such an expedition are too great, and the lives of our volunteers too valuable to be recklessly sacrificed."[53] The bishop formally resumed command of the Columbus garrison on the 4th of December, and the luckless Pillow was relegated to subordinate status once again. *The New York Times* informed its readers: "That sublime ass, Pillow, was superseded by the Right Reverend Bishop Polk, who, upon the whole, proves about the best General they have got."[54]

Rather than purposeful manipulation of Johnston, Pillow's scheme for a grand offensive speaks more to his lack of military ability. Although industrious, dynamic, and an excellent organiser, Pillow was no general. In the Mexican-American War, he had earned the ridicule of much of the U.S. army when he reportedly ordered his men to entrench on the wrong side of the American fortifications at Camargo. At the recent battle of Belmont, Pillow's execrable disposition of his troops resulted in their humiliating rout from the field. He was simply out of his depth when in command at Columbus.

The transfer of troops to Bowling Green

Troubled by the advance of Brigadier General Don Carlos Buell's large Union Army of the Ohio towards the Green River, Johnston instructed Polk on the 18th of December to "send to [Bowling Green] 5,000 of your best infantry by rail direct."[55] However, Polk was wary of Grant's forces, recently reported at 35,000 men, massing in southwestern Illinois. The bishop complained to Johnston that "I have barely 12,000 men at [Columbus]. I have been working day and night to put it in a condition to enable me to hold it against the heavy force now concentrated at Cairo and threatening to attack me in the next four days."[56]

Johnston responded to Polk: "Your dispatch received. My order to you is revoked."[57] For the second time in two months, Johnston had failed to transfer troops from Columbus to the center of his defensive line. Connelly blamed Polk, describing him as "a man of little military experience who could be stubborn, aloof, insubordinate, quarrelsome, and childish. As a bishop, Polk had been trained to lead; but as a soldier, he never learned to follow. Beginning with Johnston, Polk would treat his superior officers in a manner that smacked of insubordination. Until his death in 1864, the bishop often chose to obey his commander only when it pleased him to do so."[58] Woodworth made the extreme claim that Polk "had grown accustomed to taking orders from no one below the rank of God, with whom he seemed prone to confuse himself."[59]

Connelly alleged that Polk "knew how to manipulate General Johnston, who was easily dominated by his old West Point roommate."[60] Using similar language, Timothy B. Smith remarked that "Johnston was never quite able to stand up to his old roommate."[60] The historian explained that "according to his personality as more of a methodical, gentlemanly chess player than a rough-and-tumble poker player, Johnston had shown more leniency than needed with his subordinates."[62] However, Polk's rejection of Johnston's directive to transfer 5,000 soldiers from Columbus to Bowling Green in December stems less from mulish disobedience than to a real concern regarding his strategic circumstances. Polk recognized that Johnston was hard-pressed against Buell's army on the Bowling Green front, but he was in a similar situation at Columbus. Grant's forces at Cairo were reported at 25,000 strong and there were another 10,000 Federals under Brigadier General Charles F. Smith at Paducah.

In addition, the Union forces of Major General John C. Frémont's Department of the Missouri, now under the command of Major General Henry W. Halleck, were lurking across the Mississippi River. Approximately 50,000 soldiers under the commands of Brigadier Generals Benjamin M. Prentiss, John Pope, John M. Schofield, and other officers in Missouri, could easily be brought to bear against Columbus. The military resources in the Trans-Mississippi were so abundant that in late December Halleck appointed Brigadier General Samuel R. Curtis as the commander of a new 12,000-strong Army of the Southwest to invade Arkansas. So, when Buell's threatened movement to outflank Bowling Green did not manifest, Johnston understandably revoked his order to Polk considering the terrible numerical disparity faced by the bishop. Although Columbus possessed about a quarter of Johnston's entire army and had more than 140 pieces of artillery, it was still deficient in comparison to the Union military and naval power in the region. Johnston's attempt to transfer a paltry 5,000 men from Polk's district to strengthen the Bowling Green line was pitiful in the context of the odds arrayed against him in the Western Department.

In late December, Polk received some intelligence indicating that some of Grant's forces at Cairo had been transferred to Missouri to reinforce the army under Curtis in northern Arkansas. Pillow reported to Johnston: "The forces in our front are known to have been reduced to 15,000 men. Now we could spare, until your conflict is over, 3,000 men, to be promptly returned. The forces in our front have gone against [the Confederate army in Arkansas]. This is my opinion, under the altered condition of the enemy's force."[63] The Union forces under Smith at Paducah appeared inert so Polk decided to aid Johnston by releasing the garrison at Camp Beauregard in western Kentucky: "I have resolved to send you [Colonel John S.] Bowen's command of infantry, about 5,000 strong, and have today issued orders to him to move at once... I retain his cavalry and two batteries of artillery and will replace his forces at Feliciana by four regiments sixty-days' men from Mississippi."[64] After seven weeks, Johnston's desire to shuffle a division of troops from Polk's district to the center of his defensive line was finally fulfilled. On the 30th of December, Polk informed his friend: "I have sent forward to you all of the infantry of Colonel Bowen's command, as also Colonel [Arthur E.] Reynolds's regiment... These I supposed – for it has been very difficult to get accurate returns – would make the force about 5,000. I wish I could make it 10,000."[65]

The transfer of an entire division of soldiers from Polk's district compelled the general to remove the garrison at Feliciana and entrust the protection of the region between Columbus and Fort Henry to cavalry alone: "I shall be obliged in consequence of this movement to break up Camp Beauregard and remove the Mississippi sixty-day troops from there to Union City. I shall substitute for this force a cavalry force on the Tennessee and Kentucky lines as the best and only thing left me. They will guard that line and operate freely in both Kentucky and Tennessee and will keep down the Union feeling in both States."[66] Ultimately, Polk did detach 5,000 troops from his own embattled position to assist Johnston in central Kentucky. Polk overcame both the threat of an overwhelming Northern attack and local parochialism to support his old friend in his time of need. Unfortunately, Connelly and Woodworth make no mention of Polk's sacrifice and compliance to Johnston's request, and continued to depict him as obstinate, self-righteous, and uncooperative.

Conclusion

The claims from various historians that Polk and Pillow were manipulative and wilfully disobeyed Johnston are highly embellished. The first instance of "disobedience," the transfer of Dixon, was only delayed, not disobeyed, and Polk's reasons were entirely justified. The second, the transfer of troops to Clarksville, was based on inaccurate information at Johnston's headquarters regarding the number of troops at Columbus. Once the facts were discovered, Johnston appropriately revoked his order. Pillow's calls for an offensive against Cairo were based on military naivete and the desire to protect Columbus via a pre-emptive strike rather than any manipulation of Johnston. The final incident, the transfer of troops to Bowling Green, was again only delayed and not disobeyed by Polk. The fact is that the numerical superiority of the Union armies in the Western Department meant that Columbus, Bowling Green, the Tennessee and Cumberland rivers, and various other points in the Confederate defensive line were always under threat of attack. If Johnston moved troops from one location to another, then the others would be at heightened risk of assault.

The relationship between Polk and Johnston was one of close friendship and cooperation. Johnston's son remarked that when his father assumed command of the Western Department, "it was no small consideration to feel that he had in so responsible a position [at Columbus] a friend to whose loyalty of heart and native chivalry he could trust entirely, and one who, if long unused to arms, was yet, by virtue of early training, and a bold, aggressive spirit, every inch a soldier."[67] Polk's son recounted that "one of the pleasantest moments of General Polk's life was at Columbus, where General Johnston, after inspecting his department, complimented him upon what had been done. They had been talking of the affairs of the Western Department, and General Polk, in the full confidence of that friendship which he knew General Johnston entertained for him, expressed himself concerning certain criticisms of the management of the affairs of his command. General Johnston replied to him affectionately: 'Never mind, old friend; I understand and appreciate what you have done and will see that you are supported.'"[68] Theirs was a warm and enduring friendship, and Polk would have been aghast at any accusation of disobedience or insubordination in his actions.

6.

Why did Johnston assume command of the Central Kentucky Army?

The Confederate occupation of Bowling Green on the 18th of September 1861 was of high importance for the integrity of General Albert Sidney Johnston's cordon defense. He explained that "Bowling Green was fortified... for the reasons that in my judgment... it was the most defensible point that could be selected to cover Nashville and our Southern line of defense extending from Cumberland Gap to the Mississippi River. It is naturally strong, a salient point on the railroads and turnpike roads passing through Kentucky, and the most difficult point to turn by an aggressive enemy that could have been selected."[1] Indeed, Bowling Green was highly suited for fortification, being situated on three hills that could be crowned with artillery. These guns would command a range of a mile and a half (2.4 km), making a Union offensive against the town an intimidating proposition. Possession of the town enabled the Confederates to utilize the Louisville & Mobile and Memphis & Charleston railroad connections to link the Central Kentucky Army with Major General Leonidas Polk's garrison at Columbus.[2]

Bowling Green's occupation was vital for the protection of Nashville, the capital of Tennessee with about 30,000 inhabitants. Since the commencement of the Civil War, Nashville had become an important military production center and depot of supplies for the entire Confederacy. Five railroads traversed through the city centre, enabling the transportation of materials and supplies across the South. Johnston stated that Nashville was "one of our principal depots, where large supplies of subsistence for the army East and West are accumulated, and valuable manufactories of arms, powder, clothing, &c., are established and in successful operation."[3] Agricultural products were stored in Nashville warehouses and the piggeries in the vicinity supplied thousands of pounds of pork to Confederate soldiers across the country. Nashville also possessed thirteen hospitals, which provided essential medical care for thousands of soldiers afflicted by the epidemic of camp diseases that ravaged armies throughout the Civil War.

After the capture of Bowling Green, Johnston ordered Brigadier General Simon B. Buckner and his men to commence the construction of earthworks and emplacement of artillery pieces. Colonel Robert W. Woolley asserted that "the great object was to secure Bowling Green against attack until it could be fortified and succor obtained. This was most skillfully done. The place in front soon became, in strength, the second fortress in America, and impregnable everywhere had infantry been sent to protect its wings."[4]

Satisfied with the progress of the works, Johnston departed from his headquarters at Nashville to undertake a tour of the Western Department. However, on the 12th of October, the general was urgently summoned from his inspection tour of Columbus when it was reported that 14,000 Union troops from Brigadier General Don Carlos Buell's Army of the Ohio were crossing the Green River to attack Bowling Green. The message from Major General William J. Hardee read: "The enemy is reported to be advancing from Elizabethtown. Your presence here much needed."[5] Johnston abandoned his tour and rushed from Columbus to Bowling Green, assuming personal command of the Confederate forces in central Kentucky. The enemy movement turned out to be a false alarm, but it did foreshadow the Union intentions in the region. On the 17th of October, Johnston reported to Richmond: "As at present informed, I think the best effort of the enemy will be made on this line," and decided to establish his headquarters in the town.[6]

The Central Kentucky Army

On the 28th of October, Johnston named the force of almost 15,000 soldiers gathered at Bowling Green as the Central Kentucky Army and organized it into two divisions.[7] Hardee commanded the first division, composed of three brigades under Brigadier General Thomas C. Hindman, Colonel Patrick R. Cleburne, and Colonel Robert G. Shaver. The first division commander was 46 years old, a native of Georgia, West Point graduate, and veteran of the Seminole and Mexican-American Wars. Hardee had won distinction at the battles of Medelin, Vera Cruz, and St. Augustin during the Mexican-American War, rising to the rank of brevet Lieutenant Colonel. After the war, he commanded units of Texas Rangers, served in Johnston's 2nd United States Cavalry regiment, and was the commandant of cadets at West Point. In 1855, Hardee was tasked by the Secretary of War, Jefferson Davis, to produce a drill manual, *Rifle and Light Infantry Tactics for the Exercise and Manoeuvres of Troops When Acting as Light Infantry or Riflemen*, commonly known as Hardee's Tactics.

One acquaintance described Hardee as "a tall man with solid gray eyes, a low forehead, [and a] heavy grizzled moustache."[8] Visiting English observer, Captain Arthur J.L. Fremantle, met Hardee later in the war and offered the following observation: "He is a fine, soldierlike man, broad-shouldered and tall. He looks rather like a French officer and is a Georgian by birth. He bears the reputation of being a thoroughly good soldier, and he is the author of the drill-book still in use by both armies."[9]

Johnston's son was also impressed with Hardee: "His personal appearance was striking. In form he was tall and sinewy, and his bearing was eminently military… He was good-tempered, friendly, and intelligent in conversation with men, and very charming with women. His deference and gallantry were of the old school… Hardee was an accomplished soldier. His qualities were such as command respect. He was an excellent horseman, an impressive figure on the field. Though somewhat stern and exacting as a disciplinarian, expecting full performance of duty, he was reasonable, and his judgment sound. He thoroughly knew the business of war in the camp and on the battlefield. He was a real teacher, disciplinarian, and organizer, with the troops of the West. While fond of recreation and social enjoyment, no delight could tempt him from the work of war. He was a perfectly courageous man, cool and calculating in

Major General William J. Hardee

victory or defeat. His idea was to hurt the enemy and save his own men."[10]

The second division was commanded by Buckner, a Kentuckian, and consisted of three brigades under Colonels Roger W. Hanson, William E. Baldwin, and John C. Brown. The second division commander, like Hardee, was also a West Point graduate and veteran of the Mexican-American War, featuring prominently in the battles of Churubusco, Molino del Rey, Chapultepec, Belen Gate, and the storming of Mexico City. In 1861, Kentucky Governor Beriah Magoffin appointed the 38-year-old Buckner a major general in the pro-secessionist State Guard. Buckner strived to ensure that Kentucky neutrality was respected by both sides, with the hope that, in time, Kentucky would side with the Confederacy. However, when the pro-Union State Legislature ordered the State Guard to disband, Buckner resigned his commission on the 20th of July. In the following month, Buckner received two offers from the Union high command to accept a commission as a brigadier general in the Federal army, but he declined.

Buckner was known as "Simon the Poet" due to his penchant for writing verse and other compositions. Several years prior to the Civil War, he had publicly ridiculed Brigadier General Gideon J. Pillow for his political aspirations and intrigues against their old Mexican-American War commander, Major General Winfield Scott. The egotistical Pillow had claimed credit for undertaking certain actions in the Mexican-American War, largely at Scott's expense. Buckner had a great admiration for Scott, and in October 1857, the Nashville *Republican Banner* published two "long and scathing" letters written by the Kentuckian that excoriated Pillow and his self-aggrandizing accounts of the war. Buckner's articles were "masterpieces of gibes, ridicule, irony, and sarcasm" that caused much "sidewalk and dinner party conversation." Buckner wrote under the pen name *Citizen* but notified Pillow and others that he was the author and published a third letter in February 1858. Pillow was outraged to be assailed by a man he hardly knew, and many believed the affair would result in a duel. Fortunately, the matter died down, but with lasting resentment from Pillow.[11]

Fearing arrest by the Federal authorities in Kentucky, Buckner made his way to Nashville in September 1861, followed by many of his former soldiers in the Kentucky State Guard. When Johnston ordered the Confederate forces located there to seize Bowling Green, he selected Buckner to lead the offensive. Johnston informed President Davis that "having no officer that I could place in command of the movement on Bowling Green, I have been compelled to select and appoint General Simon B. Buckner, a brigadier general, subject to your approval, which I hope it may meet."[12] Davis readily accepted Buckner's appointment. A newspaper correspondent described the Kentuckian as "in the prime of life, although his hair had turned iron gray. He was of medium stature, having a low forehead and thin cheeks, wore a moustache and meagre whiskers."[13] Johnston and Davis hoped that Buckner's presence in the Confederate army would enhance recruitment efforts in the Bluegrass state.

Brigadier General Simon B. Buckner

Along with the appointment of division commanders, Johnston's orders of the 28th of October also announced that he, despite serving as the commander of the Western Department, would also assume personal command of the Central Kentucky Army at Bowling Green. The scenario in which a departmental commander assumed personal command for a single army in his area of operations was not ideal. T. Harry Williams contended that Johnston "stayed at the far right of his line acting as a troop commander of 14,000 men, a function which he could well have relegated to one of several capable officers at Bowling Green."[14] Benjamin F. Cooling remarked that "it took only ninety days for Albert Sidney Johnston to descend from theater to district commander."[15] Timothy B. Smith concluded that "Johnston had practically made himself a district commander, which has attracted the deserved ire of historians ever since."[16]

Why did Johnston assume personal command of the Central Kentucky Army? Why did he not entrust the command to Hardee or Buckner? These two officers possessed impressive resumes, were military veterans, and appeared eminently qualified on paper. Williams deemed them "capable officers," but did this capability extend to the role of army commander?

The unsuitability of Hardee

On the 4th of December 1861, Johnston attempted to relinquish the responsibility of the command of the Central Kentucky Army to Hardee. His staff announced that "the command of the Central Army of Kentucky is devolved upon Major General Hardee... Officers in command at any points in the district will report direct to General Johnston any sudden movement of the enemy, but all other business will be submitted to the major general alone."[17] The *Times-Picayune* reported that "General Johnston, who has been actively in command of this *corps d'armee*, finding the demands of the Department on his attention so pressing as to interfere with his duties here, has turned over the active command of this division to General Hardee. General Johnston will remain [at Bowling Green], exercising a general supervision over the military department of which he is the head."[18]

The *Charleston Daily Courier* informed its readers that "an impression prevails among army officers and others who come from Kentucky to Nashville, and among well informed people here, that there will be an active campaign before long in Kentucky. It is reported that the commanding General of this department (Johnston) has assigned to General Hardee the conduct of this campaign, he holding only a supervisory or watchful position over the whole field of operations of Hardee and other Generals within the limits of his general command... He has already the favorable opinion of the people, and it appears also of General Johnston."[19] However, on the 18th of December, just two weeks after Hardee's appointment, Johnston resumed personal command of the Central Kentucky

Army. What was the cause of Hardee's promotion and almost immediate demotion? The fact was that Hardee possessed several characteristics that disqualified him for independent command of an army.

Unwillingness to assume responsibility
Despite his military credentials and combat experience, Hardee was reluctant to assume the responsibility of commanding an entire army. When stationed in northern Arkansas in July, he declared that he would "like it very much," to serve under Leonidas Polk, the military novice and bishop, and that this "would give great satisfaction" to his friends.[20] In October, Hardee urgently requested for Johnston to abandon his inspection tour of Columbus and hurry to Bowling Green in response to the rumor of a Federal advance. Instead of assessing the validity of the situation and confidently responding to the threat, Hardee and Buckner pleaded for Johnston's return. Cooling observed that Johnston's "rushing to the threatened sector of his command appeared quite correct and in character. Nobody questioned the panicky Bowling Green generals."[21] When appointed commander of the Central Kentucky Army in December, Hardee was not pleased, complaining to a female companion about his new responsibilities. He grumbled that Johnston "found the labor greater, with his other duties than he could well perform. I was well satisfied with the command I had and did not desire the additional responsibility of commanding an Army. You will think me very unambitious, and I believe it is so."[22]

Johnston's decision to resume army command was prompted by the actions of the Union Army. The bluecoats had advanced on Woodsonville, Kentucky, and commenced reconstruction of the bridges between Louisville and the Green River. Based on his behavior in October, Hardee would likely have abdicated responsibility for the army command in December to Johnston regardless. *The New York Times* commented acidly that "Hardee is so worthless that he had to be dispensed with as a commander."[23] Later in the war, General Braxton Bragg observed that Hardee was "a good drillmaster, but no more, except that he is gallant. He has no ability to organize and supply an army, and no confidence in himself when approached by an enemy."[24] Likewise, General Joseph E. Johnston is reported to have remarked to Colonel St. John R. Liddell that

"Hardee likes the show of war but dislikes its labors and responsibilities." Liddell, who knew Hardee very well, "thought there was truthfulness in this remark."[25]

In November 1863, Hardee was offered command of the Army of Tennessee after the resignation of Bragg. He responded: "I fully appreciate the compliment paid to me by the President in this expression of his confidence, but feeling my inability to serve the country successfully in this new sphere of duty, I respectfully decline the command."[26] Hardee later explained to a friend: "I do not wish to be obstinate, nor am I disinclined to bear my full share of the responsibilities of the present crisis, but I feel I can be more useful as a corps commander than [as] the commander of the army."[27] In August 1864, Southern diarist, Mary Chesnut, recorded that Davis "could not make Hardee a full general because, when he had command of an army he was always importuning the War Department for a general-in-chief to be sent there over him."[28]

This trait was evident prior to the Civil War. When Hardee was a major in the 2nd United States Cavalry regiment under Johnston in the 1850s, he pleaded that his commander's "presence is indispensable" when contemplating the possibility that the regiment would have to march to Texas without him. Johnston was presiding over a court martial case in Fort Leavenworth at the time.[29] Hardee simply lacked the confidence for leadership roles. Liddell observed that "Hardee was not self-confident – seemed to shun the weight of responsibility – and I believe was not intended by nature to be a great leader. This he had the penetration to see, and the modesty to decline, when the command was offered to him. Hardee was an able second to any leader."[30]

Social life
Hardee's ability to command an army was compromised by the prioritization of his social life. Hardee was regarded throughout the officer corps as a notorious womanizer. In January 1862, Major Jeremy F. Gilmer reported to his wife that "last evening General Hardee was here and we were teasing him about the number of lady visitors he was honored with at his house – for you must know he is the ladies' man among the officers here."[31] In 1863, Polk wrote to his wife that Hardee "is the *beau* of the army, and nothing pleases him so much as to have a bevy of ladies around

him."³² Captain Fremantle recalled that Hardee "is a widower and has the character of being a great admirer of the fair sex... He was in the habit of availing himself of the privilege of his rank and years and insisted upon kissing the wives and daughters of all the Kentucky farmers. And although he is supposed to have converted many of the ladies to the Southern cause, yet in many instances their male relatives remained either neutral or undecided."³³

In February 1862, a time of crisis for the Central Kentucky Army, Hardee appeared to spend much of his time socializing. When the army passed through Murfreesboro, nineteen year old Alice Ready noted in her diary that "General Hardee came into town with us, we have seen a great deal of him, a day has not passed without our seeing him and some member of his staff – his evenings are always spent with us, and we have found him charming... he is very unassuming and affable in his manners, perfectly at home here, calls for whatever he wants, pets Ella and me a good deal, seems to regard me as a child – [my] sister as a young lady."³⁴

Alice then reported that "Saturday morning after we had bid our brothers a sad, sad farewell, the General came, we had breakfast for him, he stayed until two o'clock... Before the General left, he took the comfort from his neck, which he had worn during the bombardment of Bowling Green and tied it around my neck, asking me to 'wear a soldier's comfort.' Bless his old heart. I love him dearly. Yesterday morning soon after breakfast, a courier came from the General with a note for me, very sweet of course. I replied to it immediately."³⁵ That Hardee could spend so much time with Alice and her sisters while the army was in a critical retrograde movement confirms the prioritization of his social life over military matters. Later in the war, an acquaintance noticed that "Hardee is eminently a devotee of society, emphatically a lady's man... The general is quite general in his attentions to the ladies generally, and it is difficult to locate him."³⁶

The unsuitability of Buckner

If not Hardee, then what about the other division commander, Buckner? He was also complicit in the failure to assume responsibility for the Central Kentucky Army in October. Colonel Liddell stated that Buckner was "affable, high-toned, and able, though not brilliant. He lacked only constancy of purpose to have made a more prominent figure in the war. I thought him inclined to be impatient with superiors and yet lacking in energy when left to himself. Hardee said to me that he was not as good an administrator of his command as General S[terling] A.M. Wood. Buckner was somewhat captious."[37]

However, the primary reason Johnston never entrusted the command of the Central Kentucky Army to Buckner was that the Kentuckian endured multiple personal misfortunes during his time at Bowling Green. The period from December 1861 to January 1862 was a terrible time for Buckner and Johnston likely did not want to entrust command to a man reeling from a series of personal calamities. In December, Buckner's young son died at Bowling Green, and to amplify the grief, the funeral procession was forbidden from passing through the lines to the family cemetery. Buell wrote to his superior: "I had a remarkable example of impudence in my neighbor Buckner last night. It was a request that his wife, two other ladies, a Confederate Army surgeon, and the corpse of his child might be allowed to pass to Louisville. I directed [Brigadier General Alexander M.] McCook to decline his request."[38] To compound the sadness, Buckner's mother passed away in January 1862 at the age of sixty due to complications from pneumonia. A widow, she had spent most of her time with Buckner and his family in Louisville since 1858 but had retired to her home at Beechland plantation in Arkansas when her son left to join the Confederate army. Buckner was very close to his mother and her unexpected death in Arkansas was a devastating blow.[39]

Buckner also suffered a sequence of devastating financial losses due to his service with the Confederate army. In September, the Federal government levied heavy taxes on his property holdings and furniture in Louisville in retaliation for his capture of Bowling Green. In November, Union troops raided his farm at Munfordville in Kentucky, making off with all his stock and much agricultural produce.[40] In December, the owners of the Nashville Railroad Company sued Buckner for $62,362 in compensation after his Confederate soldiers damaged the tracks between Elizabethtown and Bowling Green and the bridge at Munfordville. As a result of the successful court order, his Louisville home and farm were both sold for a fraction of their worth.[41]

After joining the Confederate army in September, Buckner was subjected to vituperative criticism in Kentuckian and northern newspapers. The *Courier Journal* proclaimed: "S.B. Buckner! You *were* a Kentuckian once – but *what* and *who* are you now?... Conspirator! Survey the seventy unsullied and resplendent years of this glorious and patriarchal Commonwealth, and you will see no instance of such flagrant recusancy and unnatural ingratitude as yours... You have less palliation than Attila – less boldness, magnanimity, and nobleness than Coriolanus. You are the Benedict Arnold of the day! You are the Catiline of Kentucky! Go, then, miscreant!"[42] Buckner was a proud man who believed himself to have acted honorably in the events leading up to the Civil War. He could easily have deployed the Kentucky State Guard to seize control of the legislature, telegraph offices, railroad stations, and other key infrastructure in Kentucky, but conformed to the government's direction to peacefully disband the force. Buckner believed the decision to join the Confederacy was a personal choice and the unfounded accusations of traitorous behavior were hurtful and demoralizing.

Other reasons for personal command

Thus, Hardee and Buckner were unsuitable candidates for the command of the Central Kentucky Army. Johnston must have felt that he was the only capable army commander at the important Bowling Green front. However, separate to the issues associated with Hardee and Buckner, there were three very important reasons why Johnston assumed personal command in the central Kentucky town. Firstly, by establishing his headquarters at Bowling Green rather than Nashville, Johnston acknowledged the political importance of Kentucky and signalled his commitment to defending the state and securing it as part of the Confederacy. This would assist in the recruitment of Kentuckians to the Southern army.

Secondly, the decision helped maintain his illusion of strength in the Western Department. There was a vast discrepancy in the size of the Confederate army compared to the Union forces in central Kentucky. In November, there were about 15,000 Southern soldiers defending Bowling Green and its environs. In comparison, Brigadier General William T. Sherman's last return before his resignation, submitted on the 10th of

November, reported the strength of his army at close to 50,000 troops.[43] By situating his headquarters at Bowling Green, Johnston hoped to lend credence to the perception that the Confederate forces in Kentucky were of large numbers, organized, and ready for offensive operations. If he had remained at Nashville, it may have appeared to the Union high command that the Southern army at Bowling Green was merely an outpost or understrength detachment, ripe for the picking. Knowledge of the physical location of generals had great import during the Civil War. For example, John B. Jones, the war clerk at Richmond, wrote in his diary on the 27th of November 1862 that Union Major General Ambrose E. Burnside's Army of the Potomac "*might* have [crossed the Rappahannock River in Virginia] but for a *ruse* of General [Robert E.] Lee, who appeared near Fredericksburg 24 hours in advance of the army. His presence deceived Burnside, who took it for granted that our general was at the head of his army!"[44]

Finally, the general's presence with the troops at Bowling Green had an invaluable benefit on morale and discipline. A soldier from the 3rd Kentucky regiment informed his relatives that "at our grand reviews which took place principally on Mondays, General Albert Sidney Johnston always was present, and his imposing look as he rode along our line, his eye seemed to be riveted on every man as he slowly rode by, and had a great effect – He had a severe look always, but appeared so thoroughly a soldier that it would have been strange had he looked otherwise."[45] Johnston's personal reviews had decided advantages in increasing the fighting capability of his severely outnumbered army in central Kentucky.

Connelly also alleged that Johnston "became absorbed in menial details that were really the responsibility of a post commander or staff officer," and that he "toiled over the routine matters of army management [at Bowling Green] as if he were merely a district commander."[46] These statements are incorrect. When Hardee was returned to divisional command on the 18th of December, the Special Orders specified that "the administration is devolved on the commanders of divisions."[47] Johnston was only responsible for the strategic direction of the army.

Conclusion

It was less than ideal for Johnston to assume personal command of one of the major armies in his Western Department. However, the unusual circumstances at the time mitigate the criticism of his decision. Johnston's senior officers at Bowling Green, Hardee and Buckner, were unfit for independent command, necessitating his direct leadership of the Central Kentucky Army. This also explains his later reliance on Generals Pierre G.T. Beauregard and Braxton Bragg upon their arrival in the Western Department. In addition, Johnston's personal presence at Bowling Green underscored the Confederacy's commitment to Kentucky, helped deter a Federal offensive against Nashville, and significantly bolstered the morale and discipline of the Southern soldiers. Finally, it is evident that Johnston retained his authority over the Western Department when acting as the commander of the Central Kentucky Army, with the administrative duties of the army delegated to his division commanders.

7.

Was Johnston obsessed with the defense of Bowling Green?

Thomas L. Connelly took umbrage at General Albert Sidney Johnston's personal presence at Bowling Green, and the solicitude the general harbored for its defense. Connelly made the claim that Johnston was overly concerned with Bowling Green and that "he grew certain that a Federal army would advance upon Middle Tennessee via Bowling Green and Nashville."[1] He maintained that the general "would become so intrigued in his efforts to bluff [William T.] Sherman and his successor, Don Carlos Buell, that Johnston would fail to see the danger of Federal movements in other areas."[2] Connelly then dabbled in some psychoanalysis, declaring that "Johnston's personality was... colored by a narrow outlook. He seemed able to grasp only one area of thought at a time... the defense of Bowling Green became an obsession with Johnston."[3]

Likewise, Benjamin F. Cooling argued that "Johnston deemphasized the twin river defense of the Tennessee and Cumberland. While they clearly lay within [Major General Leonidas] Polk's area of responsibility, they would remain central to Johnston's overall, cordon defense plan for the Heartland, as well as his more immediate fascination with the Bowling Green situation... His Christmas dispatches reflected an overwhelming preoccupation with the land threat to Nashville from Louisville."[4] More recently, Timothy B. Smith wrote that Johnston "fell into the trap of believing his own area, Bowling Green, was the center of enemy plans and thus became fixated on defending that locale to the detriment of others, particularly the Tennessee and Cumberland Rivers."[5]

Are these criticisms valid? Did Johnston place too much emphasis on the defense of Bowling Green? Was his concern for the town idiosyncratic or was it shared by others? Was Johnston "fixated" or even "obsessed" with the military situation at Bowling Green to the detriment of his departmental responsibilities? This chapter is devoted to examining these questions. The following chapters will address Johnston's attention to other areas in his Western Department, namely, Forts Henry and Donelson and the military operations in eastern Kentucky.

The importance of Bowling Green

Johnston was right to be concerned about the security of Bowling Green. The town was important for three main reasons. Firstly, and most significantly, it sat on the Barren River and was the only barrier in central Kentucky to a Union offensive against Nashville. As stated previously, the Tennessee capital was a vital asset for the Confederacy in terms of logistics, manufacturing, stockpiling, and medical care. Despite admonishing Johnston for his "immediate fascination" with the military situation at Bowling Green, Cooling also noted that "the warehouses [at Nashville] bulged with tons of war material. Coupled to the transportation arteries and the political significance of the city, Nashville became a beacon for Federal war planners. Johnston realized this fact."[6] Secondly, the Louisville & Nashville Railroad ran through Bowling Green, making the town a key logistical center for Confederate operations in the region. Finally, Bowling Green had been declared the Confederate capital of Kentucky, making it not only a military objective but a political one. Johnston likely believed that the Union would want to capture the town as a symbolic victory to consolidate its hold on the state.

The legitimacy of the Union threat

When historians disparage Johnston for his concern for the safety of Bowling Green, they naturally minimize the threat of Buell's Army of the Ohio. However, this view is influenced by hindsight, in that it was not operations in central Kentucky that shattered Johnston's defensive line, but the fall of Fort Henry on the Tennessee River. Yet there were numerous factors that indicated that the danger to Bowling Green was very real.

Discrepancy of forces

Bowling Green's fortifications made it a formidable prospect for the Union army to assault, but there were vulnerabilities in the Confederate defense. The major disadvantage of the position was the presence of a system of turnpikes just south of the Green River. One turnpike, the Louisville-Cave City pike, travelled through Bowling Green, but all the others bypassed the town, providing an invading enemy force with multiple routes to outflank the Southern army. Johnston had to cover all the approaches but lacked the manpower to do so. Hence his fear of a Federal offensive against the town. When the general established his departmental headquarters at Bowling Green on the 28th of October 1861, he had about 15,000 men to defend the town, far below that of the enemy. Johnston reported to the Secretary of War, Judah P. Benjamin, that Buell's Army of the Ohio "has an aggregate strength of probably more than 50,000 men to be arrayed against my force here. If the forces of the enemy are maneuvered as I think they may be, I may be compelled to retire from this place to cover Nashville."[7]

On the 8th of November, Johnston warned Benjamin that "the great superiority of the enemy's force has enabled him to place a heavy column, estimated at 20,000 men, in front of [Bowling Green], and to concentrate auxiliary forces of Kentuckians, supported by Federal troops, on my right and left, threatening flank movements. One of these movements has for its object, Nashville, Tennessee."[8] Exactly one month later, Johnston was appraised of additional Union reinforcements and an increasing disparity of strength. He informed Benjamin that "their force on this immediate line I believe ought not to be estimated over 65,000. Our returns at this place show a force of between 18,000 and 19,000, of which about 5,000 are sick (about 3,600 at Nashville), and our effective force is under 13,000 men."[9]

Such a large concentration of forces clearly signalled the enemy's intent. On Christmas eve, Johnston stated that "the enemy will energetically push towards Nashville the heavy masses of troops now assembled between Louisville and [Bowling Green]. The general position of Bowling Green is good and commanding, but the peculiar topography of the place and the length of the line of the Barren River as a line of defense, though strong, requires a large force to defend it. There is no equally defensible position as this place, nor line of defense as the Barren River, between the Barren and the Cumberland, at Nashville, so that this place cannot be abandoned without exposing Tennessee and giving vastly the vantage ground to the enemy. It is manifest that the Northern generals appreciate this, and by withdrawing their forces from Western Virginia and Eastern Kentucky they have managed to add them to the new levies from Ohio, Indiana, and Illinois, and to concentrate a force in front of me variously estimated at from 60,000 to 100,000 men which I believe will number 75,000 men. To maintain my position, I have only about 17,000 men in this neighborhood."[10]

On Christmas day, Johnston reported that "information from various sources shows that every effort has been made by Buell to concentrate all his strength for a movement upon Tennessee through Central Kentucky... A forward movement will very soon be made in this direction, but at present I can only conjecture whether they will make their attack here or turn my right, or relying upon their superiority of numbers, attempt both at the same time."[11] A couple of weeks later, Johnston declared that the Union commanders "have justly comprehended that the seat of vitality of the Confederacy, if to be reached at all, is by this route. It is now palpable that all the resources of that government will, if necessary, be employed to assure success on this line."[12]

These communications demonstrate that Johnston was deeply troubled by the massive discrepancy between the size of his Central Kentucky Army compared to that of the Union Army of the Ohio just two days march north of Bowling Green. It was a legitimate concern. Worse still, the army was in a highly vulnerable state. Confederate ordnance officer, Major George W. Rains, recalled that "this was a time of great anxiety to all concerned for had the enemy moved on General Johnston at that time, he would have had to abandon everything as he had not sufficient ammunition at that time for an extended skirmish, and there was no remedy until I could manufacture it for him."[13] The Nashville and Coffee County powder mills were the only working facilities in the region and Rains worked hard to enhance their production capacity. Accordingly, Johnston devoted much of his time and energy to projecting an illusion of strength from Bowling Green, hoping to buy time for Rains to accomplish his difficult task. If Buell had advanced during this period, Johnston could have offered but little opposition.

Buell's constraints
Soon after Buell's appointment to the command of the Army of the Ohio, Major General George B. McClellan, the Union General-in-Chief, informed him of the general strategy that he and President Abraham Lincoln had formulated: "Were the population [of Kentucky] among which you are to operate wholly or generally hostile, it is probable that Nashville should be your first and principal objective point. It so happens that a large majority of the inhabitants of Eastern Tennessee are in favor of the Union. It therefore seems proper that you should remain on the defensive on the line from Louisville to Nashville, while you throw the mass of your forces by rapid marches, by Cumberland Gap or Walker's Gap, on Knoxville, in order to occupy the railroad at that point, and thus enable the loyal citizens of Eastern Tennessee to rise, while you at the same time cut off the railway communication between Eastern Virginia and the Mississippi."[14]

This plan had been developed months ago but was thwarted by Johnston's illusion of strength. Prior to Buell's arrival in Louisville, Sherman had withdrawn the Union forces in eastern Kentucky to defend the city against Johnston's faux offensive. Consequently, the President's cherished plan to seize eastern Tennessee was in disarray, and he hoped the new general could succeed where his predecessors had failed. Yet Buell found Lincoln's plan to liberate the Unionist population in eastern Tennessee less than appealing. There was no railroad through eastern Kentucky to connect his base at Louisville with the objective of Knoxville. The countryside in the region was barren, with only numerous dirt roads winding around hilly terrain, ravines, and creeks. Buell's army would have to be supplied using a long wagon train, which would be vulnerable to Confederate attacks. If the Union army's logistical lifeline were disrupted, Buell would have to resort to the forced requisitioning of food and supplies from the people of the region, which would not only be insufficient, but would also antagonize them to the Federal cause.[15]

Another factor influencing Buell's attitude was the presence of James Guthrie, the President of the Louisville & Nashville Railroad, at the general's headquarters in Louisville. Guthrie encouraged Buell to advance his army southwards towards Bowling Green using his railway line. This would not only provide better security for the transport of the army's food and supplies, but more importantly for Guthrie, reclaim possession of his railroad from the Confederates.[16]

Apart from the logistic concerns, there were also important military considerations that Buell had to contemplate for a campaign in Kentucky. If he undertook a march through eastern Kentucky, then Johnston's Bowling Green army would be left unopposed and could theoretically advance northwards to capture Louisville. This scenario was unrealistic considering the massive numerical discrepancy between the Federal and Confederate armies in Kentucky, but still, it unnerved the leadership of the Army of the Ohio and the Unionists in the city. *The New York Times* warned that "the great defect of Louisville as a base is that it throws our army square against the works of the enemy and renders a long and hazardous flank movement necessary in order to turn them. Such a movement, apart from the intrinsic difficulties in its way, would uncover Louisville, and the rebels might, with timely intelligence of it, bring in overwhelming numbers from other quarters, make a rapid advance, cut our army off from its base before its long flank march should be completed, and... annihilate it. Thus, it will be seen that the strategic importance of [Brigadier General Simon B.] Buckner's position at Bowling Green is immense."[17]

Despite these fears, a more realistic scenario would revolve around the threat of Brigadier General Felix K. Zollicoffer's Eastern Kentucky army of about 5,000 soldiers. Although small and poorly armed, this Confederate army had fortified the Cumberland Gap and could be expected to offer fierce resistance in the highly defensible mountainous terrain. If the

Army of the Ohio became mired in a protracted battle with Zollicoffer's forces, then Johnston's army could easily move eastwards and strike the Federal rear or flank. Therefore, Buell thought it more strategically sound to march along the Louisville & Nashville Railroad in central Kentucky and attempt to capture both Bowling Green and Nashville. He reasoned that Nashville was key to the Confederate war effort in terms of manufacturing and warehousing, and that alone, made it more important in a strategic sense than the liberation of the pro-Unionists in eastern Tennessee. And once Nashville fell into Buell's possession, he could utilize the railroad from Nashville to Knoxville as another secure supply line for his army in a campaign against the Confederate forces in eastern Tennessee.

As a professional soldier, Buell did not care much for political ramifications and having decided upon the Bowling Green-Nashville route as his objective for the campaign in Kentucky, he chose to disregard both the Presidential prerogative and McClellan's instructions to advance towards eastern Tennessee. Fortunately for Johnston, Buell was reluctant to act without a simultaneous assault against one of the Confederate fortifications on the Mississippi, Tennessee, or Cumberland rivers. He wanted another Federal army to divert Johnston's attention and prevent the reinforcement of Bowling Green. However, the Union command in the Western Department was divided, with Major General Henry W. Halleck responsible for operations in the western sector. Buell and Halleck were political rivals, and much to the frustration of President Lincoln, coordination between the two men was difficult to achieve. When Halleck suggested that Buell initiate a diversionary attack to fix Johnston's army in place at Bowling Green while he advanced his own forces up the Tennessee or Cumberland rivers, Buell declared that "my position does not admit of diversion; my moves must be in earnest, and I propose to move at once."[18]

A shared concern

Johnston's apprehension regarding the safety of Bowling Green was not eccentric or unique. It was shared by many people in the South. After Polk's seizure of Columbus in September 1861, General Samuel Cooper wrote to Brigadier General Robert C. Foster of the Provisional Army of Tennessee that "Bowling Green should be occupied with sufficient force to maintain it as early as practicable."[19] A week later, John L. Helm, former governor of Kentucky warned Polk that the enemy would be "most probably thrown forward from Louisville in the direction of Bowling Green, in the center of the Green River country, in the direction of Nashville. Such a course would subjugate the people along that line, and subject those holding Southern opinions to all the atrocities which have marked the course of the Northern Army."[20] In December, Neill S. Brown, a former governor of Tennessee, warned Benjamin: "I am of opinion that [Nashville], with all its public stores, is in imminent peril. You are aware that the force of the enemy in front of Bowling Green is not less than 75,000, and perhaps 100,000. We have not half that number to oppose them."[21]

Many of the Confederate soldiers at Bowling Green anticipated imminent conflict. On the 1st of December, a private in the 3rd Tennessee wrote to his brother that "there has been great excitement among the people of Kentucky. We have been expecting a battle every day. Old Buell – the commander of Lincoln's forces above here – this was his appointed day in course to take dinner with us. The old rascal [ate] so much yesterday his stomach wouldn't lead him into danger. They are bringing in his prisoners in nearly every day. We are working on the fortification in great haste. I think the time is close at hand when we will have to fight the great battle on the Kentucky soil."[22]

The Southern newspapers regularly warned their readers of the threat of imminent conflict in the area. A sergeant in the 14th Mississippi wrote to his mother that "the newspapers are looking for a fight here soon."[23] On the 27th of December, *The Macon Telegraph* reported that "the great collision and crash in Kentucky could not be more than a few days distant; and this appears to be the idea among the Confederate army correspondents in that quarter... The Confederate force is to maintain its stand at Bowling Green and await an onslaught by the enemy."[24] In January 1862, *The Memphis Daily Appeal* cautioned that "Buell, with a large army, maneuvers his forces within the vicinity of Bowling Green, waiting for his chance to attack Johnston."[25]

The following month, *The New Orleans Crescent* declared that "the importance of Bowling Green as the headquarters of the army of [Central Kentucky], cannot well be overrated, nor have the enemy lost sight of the advantage that must accrue to him should that position be carried... Should it fall, Nashville goes with it, and an inroad is at once opened for the invasion of the Mississippi Valley."[26] The *Crescent* predicted that "the great battle of the war is evidently to be fought at Bowling Green, and its vicinity prove the field of a terrible and bloody conflict, that may be a Waterloo to one or the other of the belligerents engaged in this struggle."[27] Thus, like Johnston, thousands of Southerners were adamant that Bowling Green would be the primary target of the Union forces in the Western Department. The general was clearly not alone in his belief that the town was in danger.

Departmental responsibilities

Johnston's concern for Bowling Green did not result in the neglect of his departmental obligations. As discussed in chapter four, he spent the bulk of his time writing voluminous correspondence in the frustrating attempt to procure additional troops, arms, equipment, and artillery for all the cordons in his Western Department. President Jefferson Davis, the Secretary of War, the Adjutant and Inspector General, the State Governors, Confederate generals in other districts, and countless others received communications from Johnston requesting urgent aid. And as discussed in chapter six, the administration of the Central Kentucky Army was delegated to the division commanders, Major General William J. Hardee and Brigadier General Simon B. Buckner. The placement and construction of the fortifications around Bowling Green were overseen by Major Jeremy F. Gilmer and his engineers. The only luxury Johnston enjoyed was the review of his troops every Monday.

Finances were always a problem, and Johnston once informed the Secretary of War that "there is no money in the hands of the commissary, and I should add that the quartermaster's department is also destitute. The embarrassment is peculiarly felt at this time, as without it, transportation, in which our troops are greatly deficient, cannot be obtained."[28] Timothy B. Smith related how Johnston scrutinized the prices of beef, pork, corn, and other commodities, seeking the most advantageous terms for the armies in his department.²⁹ The general focused on optimizing the limited railroad system in the West, borrowing engines and cars from other districts to increase capacity. His departmental responsibilities also extended to the establishment of prisoner exchange protocols with Buell and the formation of tribunals to evaluate any civilians placed under military arrest.³⁰ On several occasions, Johnston was even required to deal with inventors and entrepreneurs who wanted the army to utilize their untested, and often fanciful, weaponry.

Conclusion

The criticism of Johnston's high degree of concern for the security of Bowling Green is warranted but excessive. The general's belief that Bowling Green would be the primary Union objective was based on sound military reasoning. Given the town's strategic location, its role as a transportation hub, its political significance, and the protection it afforded Nashville, he had every reason to expect that the vastly superior Union forces under Buell would soon attempt a direct overland advance toward Bowling Green. The Federal Army of the Ohio outnumbered his own Central Kentucky Army by almost four to one, and more distressingly, Johnston lacked the ammunition to fight even a small skirmish at one point. The general was not alone in his anxiety for the security of Bowling Green. Many in the South shared his conviction that the town was the primary objective of the Federal armies in the Western Department. Buell's strategic options were constrained by the lack of logistical support for his army in eastern Kentucky and his inability to campaign further west in Halleck's area of operations. Johnston's solicitude for Bowling Green was appropriate considering Buell's dilemma.

Was Johnston "obsessed" with the defense of Bowling Green? Despite the general's evident and well-documented ability to manage departmental affairs while stationed there, various historians have argued that his personal presence in the town led to strategic oversights elsewhere. The primary basis for this claim is his apparent neglect of other vital locations within the Western Department, particularly Fort Henry, Fort Donelson, and eastern Kentucky, all of which played pivotal roles in the unfolding conflict. Many historians have pointed to Johnston's failure to properly reinforce or inspect these sites as evidence that he was overly fixated on Bowling Green to the detriment of the broader defensive strategy. This critique is not without merit, as Johnston largely delegated the defense of Fort Henry to Brigadier General Lloyd Tilghman, eastern Kentucky to Brigadier Felix K. Zollicoffer, and Fort Donelson to Brigadier General John B. Floyd without direct oversight. The following chapters will examine this controversy in greater depth.

8.

Did Johnston neglect Forts Henry and Donelson?

Four months prior to General Albert Sidney Johnston's arrival in the Western Department, in May 1861, Governor Isham G. Harris instructed Brigadier General Daniel S. Donelson, of the Tennessee Provisional Army, to construct fortifications on the Tennessee and Cumberland rivers to obstruct enemy river traffic. Donelson's surveying team, civil engineer Adna Anderson and former surveyor Major William E. Foster, determined that the ideal location for the fortifications was in Kentucky, at a point in which the Tennessee and Cumberland rivers were only two miles (3 km) apart. This would allow the garrisons to support one another if one were attacked. However, Kentucky neutrality forbade such a placement. Therefore, Anderson and Foster had to find a suitable site in Confederate territory and decided that the Tennessee River fortification should be constructed on high ground at the mouth of Standing Rock Creek, about six miles (10 km) southwards. The Cumberland River fortification was sited about twelve miles (19 km) east, on high bluffs on the western side of that river. Donelson readily approved the Cumberland River location, but he was reluctant to endorse the Tennessee River site.

Donelson conducted his own survey of the region and opted to place the Tennessee River fortification on the eastern side of the river at Kirkman's Old Landing, just south of the Kentucky border. Anderson and

Foster were horrified by their leader's choice. The landing was located on a flood plain and was dominated by elevated terrain on the opposite bank of the river in neutral Kentucky. If the enemy ever seized those hills, the fort would be subject to both artillery bombardment and sniper fire. The two officers protested Donelson's selection with such vehemence that Governor Harris called in Colonel Bushrod R. Johnson of the Tennessee Corps of Engineers to resolve the disagreement. B.R. Johnson examined the area and sided with Donelson, much to the chagrin of Anderson and Foster. The fortification, named Fort Henry after Tennessee Senator Gustavus A. Henry, would be built on the low-lying terrain at the landing.[1] Thus, the foundations of Fort Henry were laid on one of the worst locations available in all of Tennessee. Why did Donelson select such a foolish site? And why did B.R. Johnson endorse it? There were a couple of reasons.

Firstly, Donelson considered the Standing Rock Creek position too remote, with no labor force available in the area to assist construction. Secondly, although Kirkman's Old Landing was located on a flood plain, it did allow for an unobstructed view of the river for about two miles (3 km). This would provide the fort's artillerists with a clear view to target approaching naval vessels.[2] Finally, it was a common belief in the South at that time that the Civil War would be over after one great battle, probably within three months or, at the most, by Christmas 1861. The possibility of rising water levels in winter may have been discounted because of the assumption that the war would be concluded by that point. The threatening hills overlooking the site on the Kentucky side of the Tennessee river may also have been ignored due to the delusion of that state's continuing neutrality. It would have seemed highly improbable for Union infantry and artillery to appear on the opposite side of the river to attack the fort, as this would involve the violation of Kentucky neutrality. Thus, myopic determinations regarding Fort Henry effectively doomed the Confederacy's defense of the Tennessee River. It was a fatal error.

In contrast, the Cumberland River fortification, named Fort Donelson after the general, was safe from flooding and protected from enemy fire from across the river. However, it was not all positive – the site possessed several features which compromised its security. One Confederate officer later remarked: "In my opinion the site itself was most unfortunate – first, because the space enclosed by the trenches formed a *cul-de-sac*, cut in the middle by an impassable backwater, thus rendering communication between the wings of our army difficult and hazardous. The whole position was surrounded by hills at the distance of from 800 to 1,500 yards [732 m to 1.4 km] higher than those occupied by us, thus giving commanding positions for the enemy's rifled field guns, from which every point in our lines could be reached."[3]

Construction of Forts Henry and Donelson progressed slowly from May to September as the Confederate government did not bother to assign a general the responsibility for the defense of central Tennessee. Major General Leonidas Polk did little to assist in the strengthening of these fortifications during his tenure as commander of the Western Department because the bastions were officially outside of his jurisdiction. In September, former Tennessee governor Neill S. Brown warned President Jefferson Davis that "Middle Tennessee is very much exposed through the Tennessee and Cumberland rivers to incursions by the enemy and will be more so when those rivers are swollen by the autumnal or winter rains."[4] Brown's warning was not heeded. Davis simply delegated the problem to his friend Johnston and hoped for the best.

Johnston confirms the sites

Johnston shared Brown's concern, and one of his first acts as departmental commander was to assign one of his subordinates the responsibility for their defense. He selected Polk and extended the bishop's jurisdiction eastwards to cover both Forts Henry and Donelson on the 21st of September. This decision may have been due to the shortage of experienced senior officers who could take immediate command of the forts. The Confederate military structure in the Western Department was still developing, and Johnston had to make do with the officers already in place. Polk was currently overseeing the defenses in western Kentucky and northern Tennessee and extending his command eastward allowed for a more unified defense under a leader who was already familiar with the region. By placing the forts in Polk's jurisdiction, Johnston sought to ensure better coordination with the defenses along the Mississippi River and those in Tennessee. Splitting the command between multiple generals may have led to disjointed decision-making.

In addition, the Tennessee and Cumberland rivers "were too low to be used by the [Union's] heavy armored flotilla; and the movements of the enemy seemed to be directed from South Carrollton [Kentucky] against Clarksville as the objective point."[5] Johnston probably felt that Polk would thus have the time to not only oversee the completion of the fortifications along the Mississippi River but also those of Forts Henry and Donelson. Unfortunately, the selection of Polk was a poor choice. The incorporation of the Tennessee and Cumberland rivers added a significant mental load to Polk's already overwhelming burden of responsibility in protecting the Mississippi Valley.

A major problem was soon identified. Captain Jesse Taylor, an artillery officer recently dispatched to Fort Henry, noticed ominous watermarks on the trees surrounding the earthwork. Taylor cautioned both Polk and Johnston that Fort Henry would be underwater with the usual rise of the river in spring. Alarmed by this report, Johnston ordered Polk to send his senior engineer, Lieutenant Joseph K. Dixon, to survey Forts Henry and Donelson and then make a recommendation regarding their relocation or continued development. Dixon arrived at Fort Henry after the delay discussed in chapter five and assessed the state of Forts Henry and Donelson. He acknowledged that their placement was not ideal, but considering the time and labor involved in establishing new defenses further north in Kentucky, recommended that Johnston progress with their construction. Major Jeremy F. Gilmer, appointed as Johnston's chief engineer later that October, concurred with Dixon's findings. The departmental commander accepted the counsel of his two senior engineers.

With an increase in the water level of the major rivers in October, the Federals sent a timberclad gunboat, the *Conestoga*, down the Tennessee River. The warship received some small arms fire from Southern infantry near Fort Henry on the 13th of October, and it fired one shot in return. Startled, Polk wrote to the Secretary of the Navy two days later, that "I am very much in need of additional boats to operate upon the Mississippi, Tennessee, and Cumberland rivers… They are indispensable to our defenses. Will you please order their purchase and armament immediately?"[6] Unfortunately for Polk, the Confederate government lacked the necessary resources and manpower to construct the vessels in time.

Johnston never personally visited the forts due to the necessity of his presence at Bowling Green. Perhaps if he had travelled to the two rivers, he may have countermanded his engineers and ordered the construction of new fortifications on better ground, but this seems unlikely due to the respect he had for Dixon and Gilmer's expert opinions.[7] Johnston's lack of visitation has resulted in much criticism. Timothy B. Smith suggested that "Johnston displayed a severe lack of concern for the twin rivers… in addition to the lack of arms, pay, and supplies, and a host of other problems, Johnston just did not recognize the weakest link in his line."[8] Thomas L. Connelly contended that Johnston was "unable to view the total command picture of his department… [he] became convinced that [Brigadier General Don Carlos] Buell's army was the main threat to the Nashville basin, even though two other Federal armies threatened in Kentucky."[9]

Larry J. Daniel stated that Brigadier General Ulysses S. "Grant and other Union generals recognized what Johnston clearly failed to see – the gaping gap between Columbus and Bowling Green."[10] The usually sympathetic Charles P. Roland also handed a rebuke to the general, commenting that "burdened with a thousand cares elsewhere, Johnston failed to give to the construction of the Tennessee forts the personal attention that coming events would prove required."[11] Are these condemnations warranted? What actions did Johnston take regarding Forts Henry and Donelson?

Johnston's initial actions

On the 16th of October, Senator Henry warned Johnston that "there is no part of the whole West so exposed as the valley of the Cumberland… [The enemy] can, unimpeded, destroy the rolling-mills on the river now manufacturing iron for the Confederate States, the railroad bridge at Clarksville, and otherwise do incalculable mischief… Dixon has not yet had time to mount his 32-pounder guns… I think the danger is not only great, but that there is no time to be lost to avert it."[12] Johnston was troubled by Henry's report and ordered Polk to "hasten the armament of the works at Fort Donelson and the obstructions below the place at which a post was intended. The operations of the enemy on the Tennessee show that the necessity of interrupting the Cumberland is urgent… You are authorized to employ [naval mines] to any extent necessary on the Mississippi, Tennessee, and Cumberland rivers... Send four companies to Fort Donelson... The necessity is urgent for them to man the works there now."[13]

Polk dispatched the 4th Mississippi regiment, three cavalry companies, and Major Alexander P. Stewart, accompanied by four artillery instructors, to Fort Henry."[14] Another regiment of Mississippians was sent to Bowling Green. Meanwhile, Johnston directed Brigadier General James L. Alcorn at Hopkinsville to "send 200 infantry of your command and a company of mounted recruits to report to Lieutenant Colonel Randal W. McGavock, at Fort Donelson, near Dover, with orders to rejoin you when McGavock receives other reinforcements, now *en route*."[15]

The Confederate engineers set to work obstructing the Tennessee and Cumberland rivers with logs and stones to prevent further Union naval incursions. On the 18th of October, Colonel Adolphus Heiman, the Confederate commander at Fort Henry reported to Polk that "Captain [H.H.] Harrison, of Nashville, is at Fort Donelson with two steamers and six barges, loaded with wood and stone, to be sunk at Ingram's Shoals, 35 miles [56 km] below Dover, for the purpose of obstructing the navigation of the river."[16] Heiman had emigrated from Prussia in 1834 and settled in Tennessee in 1837, and thus had 24 years' experience observing the seasonal fluctuations of the rivers. He informed Polk that the obstruction work "will be a fruitless operation in a river which rises from low-water mark to at least 57 feet [17 m], and which myself have often known to rise at least ten feet [3 m] in 24 hours. The general will perceive that these obstructions are no impediment to navigation in high water."[17] Nevertheless, the work proceeded due to the lack of any other options.

Johnston also considered the high ground opposite Fort Henry. Polk received a message from Johnston's Adjutant General, Colonel William W. Mackall, on the 28th of October: "General Johnston directs me to say that he wishes you to keep a vigilant eye on the Tennessee River. If possible, fortify opposite Fort Henry, to protect it from being overlooked by the enemy... No time should be lost. As soon as you are able, increase the force at Fort Henry and the point opposite."[18] Three days later, Mackall relayed Johnston's warning to Polk that his force at Columbus "is not now, nor in his calculation likely to be, more than sufficient to do the work assigned to you. Your front, and particularly your right flank, require incessant watching, and may at any moment demand all the force at your disposal. The Cumberland and Tennessee rivers afford lines of transportation by which an army may turn your right with ease and rapidity."[19]

It was too much for Polk. He was overburdened with the heavy responsibility of defending the Mississippi Valley, and begged "leave to call the attention of the general commanding to the importance of having some commander of large experience and military efficiency put in charge of the defenses of the Tennessee and Cumberland Rivers... I would suggest the propriety of having [Brigadier General Lloyd] Tilghman put in charge of those defenses... The space between [Bowling Green] and myself is now very feebly occupied."[20] Polk's son recounted that his father "had reason to know that the defense of the Mississippi would now more than sufficiently tax the capacity of any one commander, and he desired to be left free to concentrate his energies upon that work."[21] Yet the bishop recognized the importance of the twin rivers and recommended the appointment of a general to specifically oversee the construction of Forts Henry and Donelson. This act should have been undertaken by the Confederate government in July 1861.

Polk's recommended candidate, Lloyd Tilghman, was 45 years old, a native Marylander, and possessed a West Point education. However, he graduated in the lower third of his class of 1836 and resigned from the army after only three months. Prior to the Civil War, Tilghman was employed as a civil engineer and worked on various railroads in the East and South of the United States, and in Panama. He had settled in Paducah and lived in the town until evicted by the arrival of Union troops in September. Having been appointed a general officer in the Confederate army, Tilghman was perceived as a disciplinarian who could restore order to chaotic situations.

As Johnston pondered Polk's request, he received a report from Senator Henry on the 1st of November regarding the effort to obstruct the Cumberland River. The politician announced that "Dixon returned yesterday from an expedition down the river, where he had gone to blockade it by sinking old barges in the channel... Captain Harrison, an old steamboat captain, familiar with this river, concurs with Dixon that the work is effectually done. They think it will be impossible for gunboats

Brigadier General
Lloyd Tilghman

to pass Ingram's Shoals even when the water is ten feet [3 m] higher than it is now."[22] The Confederates had dumped about 1,200 tons of stone into the river and Gilmer bragged to Johnston that "in all ordinary stages of water, the obstructions render the river impassable for gunboats and for any other boats at this time."[23] Lieutenant Colonel Milton A. Haynes, the chief of the Provisional Army of Tennessee's artillery corps, was more circumspect and noted that the barrier would be effective for "any rise less than about twelve feet [3.7 m] over the present stage."[24]

As related in chapter five, Johnston directed Polk to send a division to reinforce Clarksville on the 4th of November. He informed Richmond that he would "draw 5,000 men from General Polk's command to cover the defenses of Clarksville. The Cumberland River defenses will also be thus provided for, besides enabling me to drive back the forces of the enemy concentrating at Hartford, north of the Green River, designed, I think, to operate against Clarksville and Russellville, both of which are on the Memphis & Ohio Railroad."[25] However, due to the misunderstanding regarding the true strength of Polk's Columbus garrison, the transfer did not take place until the end of the year. The river obstructions would therefore constitute the primary defense of the Cumberland River.

Unfortunately for Johnston and his engineers, the Tennessee autumn of 1861 was marked by unusually heavy rains and the water level rose dramatically. Less than a week after his first visit, Senator Henry returned to Fort Donelson and sadly notified Johnston on the 7th of November that "the enemy's gunboats have passed the place on the river where Captain Harrison sunk the barges. They constitute an ineffectual blockade."[26] This news was very demoralizing for Johnston. The placement of obstructions was one of the only available strategies to prevent incursions by the Union navy. If autumnal rains had already rendered Dixon's stone-filled barges ineffectual, then Johnston could only hope for a dry winter.

The appointment of Tilghman

On the 17th of November, Johnston complied with Polk's request for relief of the responsibility for the Tennessee and Cumberland rivers and instructed Tilghman to "repair to the Cumberland and assume command of Forts Donelson and Henry and their defenses and the defenses of the intermediate country. You will push forward the completion of the works and their armament with the utmost activity... The utmost vigilance is enjoined."[27] Tilghman was cautioned by Mackall that "the general regrets to hear that there has been heretofore gross negligence... the commander at Fort Donelson away from his post nightly and the officer in charge of the field batteries frequently absent. This cannot be tolerated. I will ask Governor [Isham G.] Harris tomorrow for four additional armed companies, which he will send to Fort Donelson. These, with the six companies now there, will make up a regiment... Your command is embraced in the division of Major General Polk, to whom you will report monthly."[28]

As Tilghman made his way to Forts Henry and Donelson, Polk continued his search for naval vessels to defend the rivers. He wrote to a friend that "I have, under the authority of the Secretary of the Navy, bought the steamer *Eastport*, and [am] now having her converted into a gunboat on the Tennessee River; the work will be done above the bridge. I am also contracting for another boat on the Cumberland, to be converted into a gunboat at Nashville."[29] Meanwhile, the lack of a labor force stifled the construction of Forts Henry and Donelson, but severely impacted Fort Heiman, the proposed fortification on the hills opposite Fort Henry, intended to protect the low-lying bastion from enemy sniper and artillery fire. Despite Johnston's order of the 28th of October to Polk to commence construction on the fort, it was only on the 21st of November that Dixon crossed the Tennessee River, surveyed the land, and sited Fort Heiman atop Stewart's Hill, Kentucky.

Fort Heiman's location was far superior to that of Fort Henry, being elevated on bluffs 150 feet (46 m) above the river and protected at the rear by seemingly impassable terrain.[30] Dixon was informed on the 21st of November that "a large force of slaves, with troops to protect them, from Alabama, would report to him for the work, which was to be pushed to completion as early as possible."[31] Tilghman arrived at the two rivers that same day and surveyed Forts Henry and Donelson. He was now the principal commander responsible for the defense of the forts.

A lack of progress

On the 23rd of November, an officer from Fort Donelson visited Johnston at Bowling Green and "laid before him the defenseless condition of the Cumberland."[32] The departmental commander was concerned at this new report and ordered Colonel John W. Head's 30th Tennessee regiment to Fort Donelson without delay. Johnston reminded Lieutenant Hugh L. Bedford, the Inspector of Artillery at the fort "that the Cumberland River cut his rear, and the occupation of Bowling Green was dependent upon the proper guarding of that stream."[33] More dispiriting news followed. The new commander of Forts Henry and Donelson, General Tilghman, already appeared dejected. On the 29th of November, he reported: "I have completed a thorough examination of Henry and Donelson and do not admire the aspect of things. I must have more heavy guns for both places at once, not less than four for each; one also of long range for each, say 64 [pounders]. Say to the general I have 1,000 unarmed men; no hope for any arms but from him… I feel for the first time discouraged but will not give up."[34]

The lack of any progress at Fort Heiman was especially disconcerting. Tilghman advised Johnston of "the absolute necessity of our occupying an eminence on the opposite side of the river… I am informed that the State of Alabama will send a full regiment to this point, with 500 negroes, for building the work… [They] will arrive in a few days (10 days)."[35] Johnston telegraphed Gilmer that same day that the construction of Fort Heiman "should not be stopped. Push them on at the same time with the obstructions at Fort Donelson."[36] The 27th Alabama and 15th Arkansas regiments arrived in early December but only managed to construct shelters for their accommodation while waiting for the enslaved workers to arrive at the two rivers.

On the 2nd of December, Tilghman wrote to Polk that "instant and powerful steps must be taken to strengthen not only the two forts in the way of work, but the armament must be increased materially in number of pieces of artillery as well as in weight of metal. I have communicated with General Johnston on the subject and learn that my wishes will be complied with on that point."[37] On the 11th of December, Lieutenant Colonel Josiah Gorgas, chief of the Ordnance Bureau, informed Johnston that two Columbiad smoothbores and one rifled smoothbore would be delivered soon. On Christmas eve, Gorgas offered a present of two more 32-pounders for the defense of the two rivers, and Johnston ordered Lieutenant Jacob Culbertson, his Chief of Artillery at Bowling Green, to repair to Fort Donelson to supervise the emplacement of the guns. Tilghman was impressed with the ability and knowledge of Culbertson and appointed him as his own Chief of Artillery.[38] On the 2nd of January, Culbertson received a massive Columbiad weighing six and a half tons from Nashville to bolster the defenses at Fort Donelson.

Unfortunately, progress on Fort Heiman stalled in December due to a lack of labor and engineering plans. Gilmer reported to Mackall that "by some unforeseen cause the negroes were not sent until after the 1st of January."[39] Several weeks later, on the 17th of January, Colonel James E. Saunders reported to Johnston that "we carried a large negro force down. They have literally done nothing, for want of the intrenchments being laid off ready to commence work as soon as the shelters were made."[40] Saunders noted that "when the engineer, Captain Hayden, was urged to his work, the answer was that General Tilghman had not passed on the plan. A courier was sent to General Tilghman on the 3rd or 4th of January, advising him that laborers were then in transit from North Alabama. The general came to Fort Henry on the 15th – and then it was, when I left, debated whether it was not too late to throw up works on the west side, as contemplated by Captain Dixon and every general who knows anything of the position of the fort. All did concur in the opinion that a failure to occupy the heights would be equivalent to abandoning Fort Henry."[41]

Johnston was shocked at the information received from Saunders and raged to his staff: "It is most extraordinary – I ordered General Polk four months ago to at once construct those works; and now, with the enemy on us, nothing of importance has been done. It is most extraordinary, most extraordinary."[42] Johnston immediately fired off a brusque telegram to Tilghman: "Occupy and intrench the heights opposite Fort Henry. Do not lose a moment. Work all night."[43] The telegram had the desired effect and Gilmer recalled that "much valuable time was thus lost, but, under [Johnston's] urgent orders when informed of the delay, General Tilghman and his engineers pressed these defenses forward so rapidly, night and day, that when I reached the fort (January 31st) they were far advanced, requiring only a few days' additional labor to put them in a state of defense."[44]

Johnston's warnings

Despite the claims of various historians, Johnston was deeply concerned about the security of Forts Henry and Donelson. On the 22nd of January, he wrote an imploring message to the Confederate government: "If force cannot be spared from other army corps the country must now be roused to make the greatest effort that they will be called upon to make during the contest. No matter what the sacrifice may be, it must be made, and without loss of time. Our people do not comprehend the magnitude of the danger that threatens. Let it be impressed upon them."[45] The general concluded that "the enemy will probably undertake no active operations in Missouri, and may be content to hold our force fast in their position on the Potomac for the remainder of the winter; but to suppose with the facilities of movement by water which the well-filled rivers of the Ohio, Cumberland, and Tennessee give for active operations, that they will suspend them in Tennessee and Kentucky during the winter months is a delusion. All the resources of the Confederacy are now needed for the defense of Tennessee."[46]

Johnston's repeated requests for additional troops and his willingness to draw 5,000 soldiers from Columbus to strengthen the center of his line show a general keenly aware of the weaknesses in his department. Major General William J. Hardee, of whom Johnston was in constant dialogue at Bowling Green, wrote to a friend on the 23rd of January that the enemy "will approach by coming up the Cumberland and Tennessee rivers. This I have always thought their safest and most practicable route... The plot is thickening, and we shall have heavy work on this line."[47] Johnston's son maintained that the forts "never ceased to be the subject of extreme solicitude to General Johnston... Extracts from his correspondence will serve to show that General Johnston not only did not lose sight of this vulnerable point but did all that he could with the means at his command... General

Johnston's letters had constantly urged upon his subordinates the prompt construction, and upon the bureaus the proper armament, of the forts."[48]

Stanley F. Horn declared that "Johnston's analysis of all the signs led him to the conclusion that [Major General Henry W.] Halleck would attempt to turn his left with an advance up the Tennessee, while Buell exerted pressure on Bowling Green. So, he used his utmost endeavors to make the river forts stronger… But it was still glaringly clear that Fort Henry and Fort Donelson were chinks in the Confederate armor. Johnston spent more than one sleepless night over them."[49]

Intractable problems at Forts Henry and Donelson

It is apparent that Johnston was anxious regarding Forts Henry and Donelson. He issued repeated instructions to his subordinates to strengthen the positions and warned Richmond multiple times regarding the enemy threat to the security of the Tennessee and Cumberland rivers. So, what factors prevented the Confederates from mounting an effective defense of the twin river fortifications? As always in the Western Department, Johnston's efforts were frustrated by intractable problems.

Lack of troops

As discussed in previous chapters, this was a fundamental weakness in the Confederate defense of the Western Department. Historian George C. Eggleston observed that "Buell, with his army of 40,000 or 50,000 men, might easily have overwhelmed Johnston's 14,000 at Bowling Green. [Brigadier General John] Pope could have so far engaged Polk at Columbus as to prevent the detachment even of a squad from that quarter for Johnston's reinforcement. Grant in the meanwhile could make his advance with 15,000 men – to be reinforced presently to 27,000 – and the gunboats, against Forts Henry and Donelson, defended as those works were by no more than 5,500 men."[50]

One example truly demonstrates the desperate situation for Johnston and his armies. On the 20th of November, Brigadier General Gideon J. Pillow stated to a delegation of Alabamians concerned about the Tennessee River defenses that "the exigencies of the service of the Confederate Government have induced it to take most of the troops raised in Tennessee and the Mississippi Valley to Virginia. [Tennessee] is not strong enough to sustain unaided the great conflict before us. Our sister State South must come to our support... If Alabama will furnish the means of constructing these works and the forces to garrison them, with arms, &c., the troops from that State will be placed in them for the purpose of defending them, thus allowing her to hold the keys of the gateway into her own territory."[51]

It was a reasonable suggestion, but Alabama simply lacked the available troops. The delegation replied: "We propose to organize a company of old men, armed, in each county in North Alabama, for forty days. Our reasons for this are that they are not only in the general better marksmen than the generation now growing up, but the very fact of gray-headed men moving to the field will give an impetus to volunteering which we need just now." After this sad proposal, the delegation plaintively asked: "We shall need transportation for men and laborers down Tennessee River, some wagons and horses, some tools for rough work, provisions, medicines, &c."[52] Ultimately this scheme provided little assistance to Fort Henry.

Of the few available armed troops available to garrison Forts Henry and Donelson, many were struck down by measles, smallpox, influenza and other diseases. Earlier that October, Tilghman had reported from Hopkinsville that the Confederate camp was "merely one large hospital, with scarce men enough on duty to care for the sick and maintain a feeble guard around them... Over one-half the entire command is on the sick list, with very grave types of different diseases."[53] It was the same situation at the river forts.

Lack of labor
Johnston's son noted that the construction of forts "required a large amount of labor. The troops worked reluctantly, and the slave-owners hired their negroes grudgingly, and were continually demanding their return. Fifteen hundred laborers were needed at Nashville, as many at Clarksville, 1,000 were called for at Fort Donelson... and the same number could have been usefully employed at Fort Henry. Instead of 5,000, not 500 could be got together at all. Much of the work was done by the soldiers, at the cost of health, drill, and discipline."[54] In October, Polk had asked planters located along the Mississippi River to volunteer their

enslaved workers for the war effort. One landowner described the request as "a most villainous call, one [Polk] has no right to make, and is the beginning of a despotism worse than any European monarchy."[55] When the bishop ordered the construction of fortifications at Island Number Ten, local planters were asked to supply 500 slaves for a period of two weeks. Only sixty were provided and they possessed but twenty shovels.

At this point in the Civil War, many Confederate soldiers refused to labor or work alongside enslaved people in the construction of fortifications, perceiving such a role to be demeaning for soldiers. This attitude would change when the troops began to appreciate the life-saving value of earthworks, but in 1861, it was not acceptable. Gilmer informed Johnston that he did "not think that the labor of troops and slaves can be combined to any advantage [unless] in imminent danger."[56] But Johnston "allowed the slave-white labor plan to stand."[57]

In December, Pillow informed the delegation from Alabama that "the work at Fort Henry is as good as we could construct in the time allowed for it and the means at our hands; but we have received but little assistance from any quarter in the construction of the works on the Mississippi, Tennessee, and Cumberland."[58] Johnston's son reported that "the fortifications had been delayed for lack of labor, and from the difficulty of employing efficiently troops unused and unwilling to build them. The call for slaves for this purpose had been responded to slowly and feebly."[59]

Johnston's labor shortage was exacerbated by his engineers. The designs for the fortifications were typically expansive, requiring long tracts of entrenchments, abatis, and other defensive structures to properly protect themselves. General Pierre G.T. Beauregard observed that "the time and labor spent upon [Bowling Green's] extensive works by [Gilmer] might have been far more judiciously applied in the strengthening of Forts Henry and Donelson – particularly the former."[60] Later in the war, General Joseph E. Johnston complained that the fortifications he had to defend were "very extensive, but slight – the usual defect of Confederate engineering."[61] This was the same situation at the two rivers. In January 1862, Tilghman protested to Polk that he had less than half of the troops required to man the fortifications at Fort Donelson.

Lack of artillery

After Polk seized Columbus, most of the cannons available in the Western Department were shipped northwards to bolster the defenses of the new citadel. He installed about 140 guns around the town. Polk's achievement was only possible because of the immense power of the *Mississippi River bloc*. There was no such comparable action group devoted to the defense of the two rivers. At their peak strength, Fort Henry possessed only seventeen guns and Fort Donelson twelve. Clarksville had but three guns mounted at Fort Defiance, an earthwork commanding the Cumberland River. Johnston's son observed that "the needs of the country for ordnance were so much greater than the ability to supply it, that Columbus alone was as yet in a state of defense."[62]

The bishop has been accused of hoarding artillery at Columbus, but the fact is that he did assist other areas. On the 15th of October he informed Johnston: "I have today ordered a battery of six guns (two howitzers, one Parrott, and three iron guns) to be shipped to [Brigadier General Felix K.] Zollicoffer at Knoxville… I have a call for two batteries from Missouri for [Major General Sterling] Price, which I shall be able to supply also in a few days… Harper's battery has gone forward to Clarksville, and is subject to your order, if not now wanted on the Cumberland River. I have ordered 24-pounders, 18-pounders, and 12-pounders, the sizes [Brigadier General Simon B.] Buckner wants, to be prepared as soon as may be, at Nashville and Memphis."[63] After the fall of Forts Henry and Donelson, Polk wrote that "all the support I could give [Tilghman] in answer to his calls was afforded. He received from Columbus a detachment of artillery officers as instructors of his troops in that arm on two several occasions, and all the infantry at my command that could be spared from the defense of Columbus."[64]

Polk recounted the difficulties associated with the armament of Forts Henry and Donelson in an April 1862 report to Johnston: "You are aware that efforts were made to obtain heavy ordnance to arm these forts, but as we had to rely on supplies from the Atlantic sea-coast, they came slowly, and it became necessary to divert a number of pieces intended for Columbus to the service of those forts." The bishop concluded that "the principal difficulty in the way of a successful defense of the rivers in question was the want of an adequate force – a force of infantry and a force of experienced artillerists. They were applied for by you and also by me, and the appeal was made earnestly to every quarter from whence relief might be hoped for. Why it was not furnished others must say. I believe the chief reason, so far as the infantry was concerned, was the want of arms. As to experienced artillerists, they were not in the country."[65]

Finally, if Polk *had* transferred a significant proportion of Columbus's 140 artillery pieces to Forts Henry and Donelson, then the Union forces at Cairo would have been emboldened to attack the Mississippi River fortress instead. It is also doubtful that additional guns would have made an appreciable difference to the Confederate defense of the Tennessee and Cumberland rivers in February 1862. Fort Henry's precarious location and vulnerability to rising floodwaters made it indefensible, and, to the surprise of many, Fort Donelson's batteries turned out to be sufficient to repel the Union ironclads when put to the test. As to the notion of establishing further fortifications south of the existing sites at Forts Henry and Donelson, the Confederacy simply lacked the political will, labor force, engineers, and experienced artillerists to do so.

Unusual weather
Lacking a riverine navy, Johnston looked to obstruct the Tennessee and Cumberland rivers with stones, logs, sunken barges, and other debris. However, there was abnormally high rainfall in Kentucky and Tennessee in early 1862. Twenty-first century meteorological analysis has determined that 1862 was characterized by a persistent La Niña weather pattern that was eventually replaced by El Niño later in the year, with the months from January to April 1862 particularly wet.[66] There may also have been cooling in the northern hemisphere because of a volcanic eruption that occurred in northeastern Africa in May 1861. The Dubbi stratovolcano exploded suddenly, "showering maritime traffic in the Red Sea with pumice and plunging coastal settlements into darkness… The volume of lava flows alone, 3.5 km^3, makes this the largest reported historical eruption in Africa. An anomalously cold Northern Hemisphere summer in 1862, recorded in tree-ring records, could be the result of Dubbi's sulfate aerosol veil."[67]

Regardless of the causes, meteorologic or volcanic or both, the cold temperatures and heavy rains recorded between January and April 1862 would not only submerge the foolishly positioned Fort Henry but render Confederate attempts to obstruct the Tennessee and Cumberland rivers utterly futile. The water level of the rivers rose significantly higher than the sunken obstructions and washed away, or ruined the gunpowder, in the naval mines scattered around the forts.

Inefficient subordinates
Steven E. Woodworth noted that although Tilghman "was concerned enough about Confederate weakness at Henry and Donelson to take the unusual step of writing directly to the president, his concern somehow failed to carry over into a sense of urgency in completing the work."[68] The general was lacklustre in his efforts to strengthen the river forts. His apathy may have been the result of illness and overwork. In a report to Richmond written in August 1862, he complained of being "nearly broken down by incessant work from the middle of June… I was not in the best condition, so late as December 15th."[69]

Another problem was Tilghman's abrasive nature. He considered one of his subordinates, Colonel George W. Stacker, commander of the 50th Tennessee, incompetent to lead the regiment and made his opinion public. Stacker subsequently resigned to avoid the awkwardness of serving under the Kentuckian. Stacker's replacement, Colonel Cyrus A. Sugg, was not fond of Tilghman either but managed to persevere in command. On the 29th of December, Private A.W. Bradley of the 30th Tennessee recounted that "the commissioned officers signed a petition to General Johnston urging him to replace Tilghman with Colonel Head. It seems the troops are dissatisfied with General Tilghman."[70]

Nothing came of this petition except increased enmity between Tilghman and Head. In early February 1862, Head "intended to resign and had gone so far as to announce the fact on dress parade," but he apparently reconciled with Tilghman and remained in command.[71] Bradley recorded that "Head acted as he did because Tilghman acted out of spite and treated the regiment more like slaves than soldiers. Head thought that there was animosity between himself and Tilghman, and by resigning, the regiment might get better treatment."[72]

In late November 1861, Tilghman, without consulting Gilmer, ordered one of the engineering teams to cease working on the obstructions in the Cumberland River. Tilghman wanted the engineers to abandon the project and focus instead on building up the landward defenses of Fort Donelson. The team leader responsible for the obstruction project instantly informed Gilmer that "General Tilghman has ordered me to suspend work. Instruct me immediately." Gilmer was infuriated and responded that "you will continue the work for obstructing the Cumberland River. It will be impossible for me to rely upon any work being done properly if each subordinate brigadier general be allowed to suspend operations ordered by me."[73]

Gilmer complained to Johnston, and Tilghman was instructed not to interfere with the engineer's work. Obstruction of the Tennessee and Cumberland rivers was one of Johnston's only defenses available, considering the absence of Southern ironclads, and he had to risk failure in the attempt. The disagreement between Tilghman and Gilmer may have contributed to the neglect of Fort Heiman, as both men focused on their respective objectives with a renewed stubborn energy. Tilghman clearly was not the best man for the job. His poor health and fractious relationships with fellow officers and subordinates delayed progress on Forts Henry, Heiman, and Donelson. Perhaps Johnston's original recommendation of Stewart for the command was the better choice, but the Confederate government enforced the appointment of officers to command in the Western Department based on seniority rather than aptitude.

Conclusion

Accusations of neglect in relation to Johnston's oversight of Forts Henry and Donelson are largely misplaced. Although at fault for assigning the overburdened Polk to command, the general soon realized his error and appointed a dedicated commander for the Tennessee and Cumberland rivers. Johnston was cognizant of the Federal threat to the river forts and attempted to strengthen their defenses. However, intractable problems quickly emerged, and these were the causative agents for the relative neglect of Forts Henry and Donelson in comparison to the works at Columbus and Bowling Green. The simple fact was that the Western Department simply lacked the armed troops, artillery, labor force, and resources to effectively defend the twin rivers. Polk possessed only 12,000 troops at Columbus to protect the Mississippi River and Johnston had less than 20,000 soldiers to defend Bowling Green and Nashville. That left but a few thousand allocated to Forts Henry and Donelson. The commander responsible for the region, Tilghman, was suffering ill health and lacked the necessary drive to accomplish critical tasks. Johnston's original choice of Alexander P. Stewart would have been the better option.

Roland pondered whether the "Western armies [ought] to have been gathered at the Tennessee and Cumberland river forts before the Federal advance began? Possibly they should have been, since this would have created a centrally located striking force capable of being moved by rail to the support of Columbus, or by water to the defense of Nashville. That this would have insured repulse of the invaders, however, does not by any means necessarily follow."[74] However, Roland quickly dismissed this notion, concluding that "Johnston concentrated the majority of his troops at the points most seriously threatened by Federal strength. The Confederate position at Columbus was exposed to a Federal army across the Mississippi and to Grant's army at Cairo. The Bowling Green position and the direct route to Nashville were threatened by Buell's force, which was larger than Johnston's entire army. To weaken either of these positions significantly was simply to open the door to the Mississippi River or to Nashville, for Johnston's adversary was capable of pinning him down with an army larger than his entire main body and of flanking him at the same time with another equally as strong."[75]

It was clearly a no-win situation for Johnston. He could not strengthen, arm, and garrison Forts Henry and Donelson without weakening the strongholds at Columbus and Bowling Green to such an extent that they themselves would become inviting targets for Federal offensives. The importance of the Mississippi River and Nashville to the maintenance of the Confederate war effort was paramount. Roland also fails to explain how Johnston and Polk could have moved the bulk of their troops with sufficient rapidity considering the deficient railroads and lack of river steamers available.

What else could Johnston have done? Polk suggested that Confederate operations in Missouri could divert Federal attention from the Mississippi, Tennessee, and Cumberland rivers. On the 3rd of January 1862, he wrote to President Davis that "so long as the Federal forces under Halleck are kept employed by Price in Missouri, they cannot cooperate with Buell against Johnston, nor be concentrated against me on my right or left flank. I hope, therefore, we shall not fail to occupy him fully with all the resources at our command. I have sent General Price several batteries; troops I have none to spare."[76] It was a forlorn hope. The thousands of Union troops in Missouri were more than sufficient to occupy Price's poorly armed and equipped militia forces.

The bishop's efforts to procure riverine ironclads also failed to have an impact. The Confederacy simply lacked the industrial capacity, materials, and skilled workers to manufacture warships on the Tennessee and Cumberland Rivers. In April 1862, Polk lamented that "one transport boat, the *Eastport*, was ordered to be purchased, and converted into a gunboat on the Tennessee River, but it was unfortunately too late to be of any service."[77] Johnston could only rely upon dubious naval mines and river obstructions. Ultimately, Richmond's policy of dispersing its available manpower in the garrisons of seaboard fortresses prohibited an effective defense of the Tennessee and Cumberland rivers. In January 1862, there were about 9,000 Confederate troops at New Orleans, 9,000 at Mobile, 7,000 at Pensacola, and a further 4,000 scattered around in eastern Florida.[78] If even half of this number had been stationed in the Western Department, Johnston would have been able to adequately garrison Forts Henry and Donelson.

9.
Was Johnston aware of events in eastern Kentucky?

One of General Albert Sidney Johnston's first acts as commander of the Western Department was to order Brigadier General Felix K. Zollicoffer to advance his 4,000 men northward from Knoxville to seize control of the Cumberland Gap in eastern Kentucky. This region was of high strategic value for several reasons. Firstly, the mineral and agricultural resources of eastern Tennessee required protection from the Federal army. Secondly, the pro-Union population invited enemy offensives into the region. Finally, the presence of Zollicoffer's small army protected the right flank of Johnston's Central Kentucky Army at Bowling Green.

Zollicoffer was 49 years old, a native of Tennessee, and descended from emigrants from Switzerland. He was a successful printer and newspaper editor, and a three-term United States Congressman representing Tennessee from 1853 to 1859. Zollicoffer had some military experience, having served as a lieutenant for one year in the Seminole War and in the Tennessee militia during times of peace. A sergeant in the 14th Mississippi regiment described him as "a tall, stern commanding-looking man, speaks cooly and deliberately. He treated us very cleverly."[1] However, Johnston's son noted that Zollicoffer "had exceptional difficulties to contend with of every possible description; and the tests to which he was subjected might well have overborne native ability of a high order [but] he could not drill a squad himself, nor was his brigade ever drilled or put in line of battle by anybody. Though he had a splendid courage, and traits that endeared him to his troops, the cast of his mind was no more military than his training. But he was a good, brave, noble, patriotic man."[2]

Brigadier General Felix K. Zollicoffer

Thomas L. Connelly's hostility to Johnston is evident from his omission of any mention of the general regarding the occupation of the Cumberland Gap in his *Army of the Heartland*. He declared that "the Confederates hoped to block a Federal invasion of the East Tennessee valley by holding Cumberland Gap. The day before Johnston took command on September 15, 1861, General Felix Zollicoffer, the East Tennessee commander, seized and fortified this position."[3] Connelly made no reference to the fact that Johnston had met with Zollicoffer in Knoxville on the 13th of September and authorized the action. Connelly apparently liked Zollicoffer, and he is one of the few Confederate generals to be praised in the *Army of the Heartland*.

When referencing Johnston's arrival in the Western Department, Connelly made the erroneous claim that Zollicoffer's forces were already deep in eastern Kentucky: "When he first arrived in September 1861, Johnston was troubled by the long curve of the Middle Tennessee line. The northeast salient was high on the Cumberland in the Mill Springs, Kentucky, area on a line 55 miles [89 km] north of Nashville. The center of the line was at Nashville, and the northwest salient was at Fort Donelson on a line 30 miles [48 km] north of Nashville."[4] In actuality, when Johnston first arrived, Zollicoffer's forces were still in Tennessee.

Johnston's supervision of eastern Kentucky
Connelly launched a scathing attack on Johnston's supervision of the Confederate military operations in eastern Kentucky, asserting that there was

a "total lack of communication between Zollicoffer and his commander. Zollicoffer had urged some coordinated action with the central force, but with no success. Johnston only made one effort to support his lieutenant during the entire fall and winter of 1861-62."[5] He concluded that "Johnston knew almost nothing of what was going on along the eastern front."[6] This accusation is unfair. Johnston's ability to direct Zollicoffer was severely compromised by the poor communication network in eastern Kentucky. Stanley F. Horn observed that "there were no direct telegraph wires, and the condition of the roads made communication by courier slow and difficult. Messages between the two generals were sometimes three or four days in transmittal."[7] Similarly, Johnston's son proclaimed that "the lack of telegraphic communication, and the wretched character of the roads, made any rapid correspondence, much more any effective cooperation, almost impossible."[8]

As comparison, newly promoted Lieutenant General Ulysses S. Grant complained to President Abraham Lincoln about the destruction of telegraph wires in his district in July 1864: "This made it take from twelve to 24 hours each way for dispatches to pass. Under such circumstances, it was difficult for me to give positive orders or directions, because I could not tell how the conditions might change during the transit of dispatches."[9] Johnston's situation in Kentucky was immeasurably worse. As department commander, he could only offer general advice to Zollicoffer via letters that took several days to arrive. Despite Connelly's diatribe, the general was *compelled* to delegate the local tactical operations to his district commanders, and trust in their judgment and competency.

Zollicoffer and Marshall

Several days after occupying the Cumberland Gap, Zollicoffer dispatched 800 men along the Wilderness Road to attack a pro-Union training camp to the northwest at Barbourville. On the 19th of September, the Confederate forces routed the Home Guard, destroyed their camp, and captured a quantity of arms and ammunition. Zollicoffer then sent additional forces to break up an encampment of Union recruits at Laurel Bridge on the 26th of September. Two days later his troops raided the Goose Creek Salt Works, capturing a vast quantity of salt and ammunition, plus several wagons and artillery pieces. Although pleased with his successful campaign to date, Zollicoffer lamented that the population in eastern Kentucky did not embrace the Confederate army. He reported to Johnston's adjutant general, Colonel William W. Mackall, that "I am without information as to the strength or movements of Camp Dick Robinson. Any information you have might be of service to me. The population here is so generally hostile I cannot push spies through."[10]

Regardless, Zollicoffer ascertained that Union Brigadier General George H. Thomas had detached a regiment of his infantry and they were now encamped at the base of Wildcat Mountain to block the Wilderness Road from future Confederate incursions. Zollicoffer determined to attack the isolated regiment with his full force of approximately 5,400 soldiers. However, he was unaware that Union Brigadier General Albin F. Schoepf had recently arrived at the camp with his entire brigade, increasing the number of Federal soldiers at Camp Wildcat to about 7,000 troops. On the 21st of October, Zollicoffer's forces attacked Schoepf's brigade, but the Union forces had the advantage of numbers and repulsed the Confederates. Zollicoffer aborted the operation and ordered a withdrawal during the night, having suffered 53 casualties in comparison to Schoepf's 43 losses. The Southern army returned to Cumberland Ford on the 26th of October. Their mission to dislodge the Union forces obstructing the Wilderness Road had failed.

On the same day as the battle of Wildcat Mountain, Union Brigadier General William "Bull" Nelson, commenced an offensive involving 6,000 troops into the Big Sandy Valley region of eastern Kentucky to disperse less than 1,000 Confederates under Colonel John S. Williams, so inadequately clothed and equipped that they were dubbed the *Ragamuffin Regiment*. The operation was successful, with the Federal forces driving the raw Southern troops from the area. In response to this offensive, President Jefferson Davis appointed Brigadier General Humphrey Marshall to command on the 1st of November. Marshall was 49 years old, a native of Kentucky, West Point graduate, and veteran of the Black Hawk War. He resigned his commission in the army to study law but retained his military ties by volunteering in the Kentucky militia. In 1846 he was elected colonel of the 1st Kentucky Cavalry and participated in the battle of Buena Vista during the Mexican-American War. After returning from

Mexico, Marshall represented Kentucky in the House of Representatives and was appointed United States Minister to the Qing Empire from 1853 to 1854.

Marshall decided to join the Confederate army in September upon the dissolution of Kentucky neutrality and the entry of Union forces into the state. Johnston's son remembered Marshall as "a very vigorous and able lawyer, a shrewd politician, and a man of wit, humor, acumen, and judgment... but he was not a man of action. Besides, his unwieldy size, weighing as he did some 300 or 350 pounds [136 to 159 kg], unfitted him for the field."[11] The President instructed Marshall to "proceed to Prestonburg, Kentucky, and assume command of the troops at that place and its vicinity for the protection and defense of that frontier [with southwestern Virginia]. You will report by letter to General A.S. Johnston at Bowling Green for such orders and instructions as he may have to communicate to you." Marshall's Army of Southwest Virginia would number about 3,000 troops after the absorption of Williams's Ragamuffin Regiment.

Brigadier General Humphrey Marshall

Although Johnston could only offer general strategic advice to his subordinates, his knowledge of events in eastern Kentucky and eastern Tennessee contradicts Connelly's assertions of complete ignorance. For example, on the 5th of November, Zollicoffer reported that 8,000 Federals were fortifying at London, and the following day, relayed alarming news of 6,000 Federals advancing towards Jamestown, about halfway between Bowling Green and Cumberland Ford. Johnston contemplated the information and responded. Mackall wrote to Zollicoffer that "your telegrams of the 5th and 6th instant just received. The movement of the enemy by Jamestown route appears to the General decided; his fortifying at London is perfectly reconcilable with this view. He will not give orders at this distance, but will only suggest that, holding the gap by your breastworks and a small force, you concentrate to meet the enemy on your left, if you have not already done so."[13] Johnston also utilized his Central Kentucky Army to assist Zollicoffer. In early November, he ordered Major General William J. Hardee to march some of the troops from his division in the direction of Jamestown. This movement spooked Brigadier General William T. Sherman into believing that a Confederate offensive against Louisville was imminent.

Sherman recalled Thomas's division from southeastern Kentucky to defend Louisville, which caused Schoepf to fear for the safety of his own flank. Schoepf ordered his troops to withdraw, but "the men straggled, abandoned their knapsacks and accoutrements, and fell exhausted from fatigue and exposure. Commissariat and ammunition wagons were abandoned, and many of the sick, subjected to the inclemency of the weather, died. In fact, the retreat partook of the character of a flight, although [Hardee] made no attempt at pursuit."[14] *The Cincinnati Commercial* reported that Schoepf's "stampede was the result of General Hardee's expedition from Bowling Green, having been reported as advancing with 100,000 men... We have no heart to comment upon such imbecility."[15] Buell soon arrived to mop up Sherman's mess, but Johnston's diversion had paid dividends. Schoepf's precipitate withdrawal cleared the path for Zollicoffer's advance to the Cumberland River. Thus, Johnston's knowledge and orders clearly had an influence on the Confederate campaign in eastern Kentucky.

The rebellion in eastern Tennessee

It was also during this time that the local Confederate authorities finally realized the depth of anti-secessionist hostility that existed in eastern Tennessee. In early November, an officer at Knoxville complained to Richmond that "General Zollicoffer has taken all the troops from here, except about 200 infantry and one company of cavalry, and most of the latter are absent on special duty. The necessity for a larger force at this point is urgent. Our commissary and quartermaster's stores are liable to be seized at any moment, as also the railroad."[16] The concerned officer argued that "it is a great mistake to suppose that the people of East Tennessee are submissive or willing to acquiesce. They have only been held quiet by the force which was at Knoxville, and now that it is gone, they are evidently preparing for a general uprising if the Lincoln Army should make any advance into Tennessee. I need at least a regiment at this place to give protection to the stores of the Government and preserve quiet. There are three companies of infantry here under the late call of the governor for 30,000, but they have no arms."[17]

Johnston was cognizant of the threat of Union partisan activity in eastern Tennessee. He reported to Richmond that "the political sentiments of the people of East Tennessee [are represented to be] extremely hostile to the Confederate Government, and that there is among them a large and well-armed force ready to act at an opportune moment."[18] The general attempted proactive measures. On the 4th of November, he notified Richmond: "I have already ordered [Colonel Sydney S.] Stanton's and [Colonel John P.] Murray's regiments and some cavalry companies from their stations in Fentress, Overton, and Jackson Counties to Jamestown, to join seven cavalry companies at that place, thence to report and await the orders of General Zollicoffer, who has been notified; also ordered [Brigadier General Leroy P.] Walker's brigade forward and any troops who might be at the rendezvous at Knoxville."[19]

However, on the 8th of November, pro-Union guerrillas destroyed five railroad bridges situated along the East Tennessee & Virginia Railroad and the East Tennessee & Georgia Railroad and cut the telegraph lines linking Chattanooga to Richmond. The next day, Johnston exhorted Governor Isham G. Harris "to use every exertion to ascertain the extent, power and organization of this insurrection if as I fear one exists, and most urgently I press your excellency to leave no means untried to put arms into the hands of your unarmed levies."[20] Johnston ordered the brigade of Brigadier General William H. Carroll from Memphis to Knoxville to assist in the suppression of the rebellion. Connelly blandly acknowledged Johnston's involvement in eastern affairs by commenting that the general "was forced to divert troops badly needed on the eastern part of his line in order to stifle the rebellion."[21]

Unfortunately for the partisans, it soon became evident that Buell's Army of the Ohio would not be marching in to relieve them any time soon. The Unionists disbanded and their leaders were arrested. On the 15th of November, Johnston informed Richmond that "General Zollicoffer is taking measures to suppress the uprising of the disaffected in

Rhea and Hamilton Counties, Tennessee... The force under Zollicoffer, as everywhere on this line, should be reinforced; but this you know without my suggestion."[22] Ultimately, the Confederacy was forced to deploy up to 8,000 soldiers to maintain order in eastern Tennessee, men that Johnston desperately needed to bolster his armies in the Western Department.

Zollicoffer crosses the Cumberland River

After dealing with the rebellion, Zollicoffer outlined his future strategy for eastern Kentucky: "Having blockaded the roads over the mountains near Jacksborough, and believing the fortifications at Cumberland Gap very strong, I do not think an army train of the enemy can pass the mountains anywhere between the Pound Gap, in Virginia, and Jacksborough, a distance of about 120 miles [193 km] ... I propose to take and strengthen a position between Monticello and Somerset, giving us facilities for commanding the Cumberland River, the coal region supplying Nashville, &c. If I can clear the banks of the Cumberland of our enemies, supplies may this winter be furnished us by boats from Nashville."[23] Zollicoffer also hoped to better mutually support Johnston's force at Bowling Green and expressed a desire to "establish and safely maintain a line of express messengers between [Brigadier General Simon B.] Buckner's outposts and my camp."[24] Johnston supported such an initiative, and Mackall informed Zollicoffer that "your dispatch of November 27 has been received and read by the general, as all heretofore received from you, with great satisfaction. Every move is entirely approved."[25]

Zollicoffer marched his troops to Mill Springs on the south bank of the Cumberland River, which commanded not only the river, but also the road network between Monticello, Somerset, and Columbia. The site also had the advantages of ample subsistence and forage, along with the presence of a gristmill and sawmill. Zollicoffer reported: "We have here an abundance of beef, pork, and corn, at low prices. The better classes of citizens sympathize with us."[26] Mill Springs was a highly defensible position, as the southern bank of the Cumberland River possessed steep bluffs whereas the northern bank was low and flat.

Ominously, on the 30th of November, Zollicoffer wrote to Johnston about his future designs: "Recent rains have much swollen the river...

[my troops] failed to seize any of the [ferry-boats]. I am now preparing to provide the means of crossing the river. The lumber and the saw-mill here will materially aid in constructing boats. The enemy's camp, 9 miles [14 km] above, on the right bank, appears to have been reinforced, but to what extent I have not been able to ascertain... Our pickets sent up on this side (opposite) today were fired on. Colonel Stanton reported to me two days ago that he had secured two ferry-boats, but it appears they have got away. He was ordered to cross the river to endeavor to cut off 800 of the enemy, then at Camp Goggin, 9 miles [14 km] above. He failed to cross for want of boats. So soon as it is possible, I will cross the river in force."[27]

As an aggressive general, Zollicoffer may have thought that if he had remained at Mill Springs on the south bank, he would be vulnerable to coordinated offensives by Federal columns employing riverine transportation to outflank his position. By crossing to the northern bank, he would be better able to observe the Union forces and gain the ability to strike isolated enemy detachments at a time of his own choosing. Yet Zollicoffer's decision was not a prudent one in a strategic sense. If attacked by a strong Federal force, his army could be trapped against the Cumberland River and forced to surrender.

Connelly claimed that Johnston had no reaction to Zollicoffer's decision to cross his army over to the northern bank of the Cumberland River. He declared that "when [Johnston] learned of the move, he did not inform Zollicoffer whether he approved or disapproved."[28] This statement is entirely incorrect. Johnston immediately responded to Zollicoffer's message: "Mill Springs would seem to answer best to all the demands of the service; and from this point you may be able to observe the river, *without crossing it*, as far as Burkesville, which is desirable."[29] Johnston's son observed that his father's "instructions [to Zollicoffer] looked to a defensive campaign by that corps, and there was nothing in its condition to warrant an aggressive movement."[30]

Likewise, Horn observed that "to stay passively on observation was not congenial to [Zollicoffer,] a man of his dynamic nature. He had been feeling his way forward into Kentucky during November until he reached Mill Springs on the south bank of the Cumberland. From this coign of vantage he could watch the movements of his adversary. Johnston thought he should go no farther and said so."[31] But it was too late. In the time it took for Johnston's response to arrive, Zollicoffer had procured enough boats to cross his army over to Beech Grove on the northern bank of the Cumberland River.

Zollicoffer's reaction to Johnston's message was apologetic: "Your two dispatches of the 4th [of December] reached me late last night… I infer from yours that I should not have crossed the river, but it is now too late. My means of recrossing is so limited, I could hardly accomplish it in face of enemy."[32] Unfortunately, most of Zollicoffer's riverine transportation had now been destroyed by the raging Cumberland River and he was loath to abandon his precious artillery, horses, and supplies in a precipitate withdrawal back to Mill Springs. Zollicoffer then compounded his error. Instead of immediately attacking the nearby Union forces under Schoepf with his entire army, thus gaining the twin advantages of comparable numbers and the element of surprise, he engaged in a series of small skirmishes with Union forces from the 2nd to the 11th of December. These minor actions alerted Schoepf to the danger of attack and resulted in the bluecoats pulling back to a strong position about three miles (4.8 km) behind the village of Somerset. Schoepf then called for urgent reinforcements.

The battle of Middle Creek

To the northeast, Marshall decided that the best way to defend the Kentucky-Virginia border was to march his army deeper into Kentucky. Without asking Johnston for approval, Marshall ordered his small army northward. By Christmas 1861, his soldiers were within sixty miles (97 km) of the Ohio River. Despite the good progress, Marshall was disappointed with both the size of his army and the attitude of the people of Kentucky. To his utmost surprise, they did not rush to swell his ranks and did little to support his campaign. Marshall wrote bitterly to Johnston in early January 1862: "I command [less than 2,000 men present and fit for duty], which I supposed when I came here would be 5,000 to commence on. This return is accurate as exhibiting the actual strength, but many of Colonel Williams's men are undrilled; some of the companies have not been in camp more than a week. I flatter myself the enemy is as green as my force… The people hereabouts are perfectly terrified or apparently

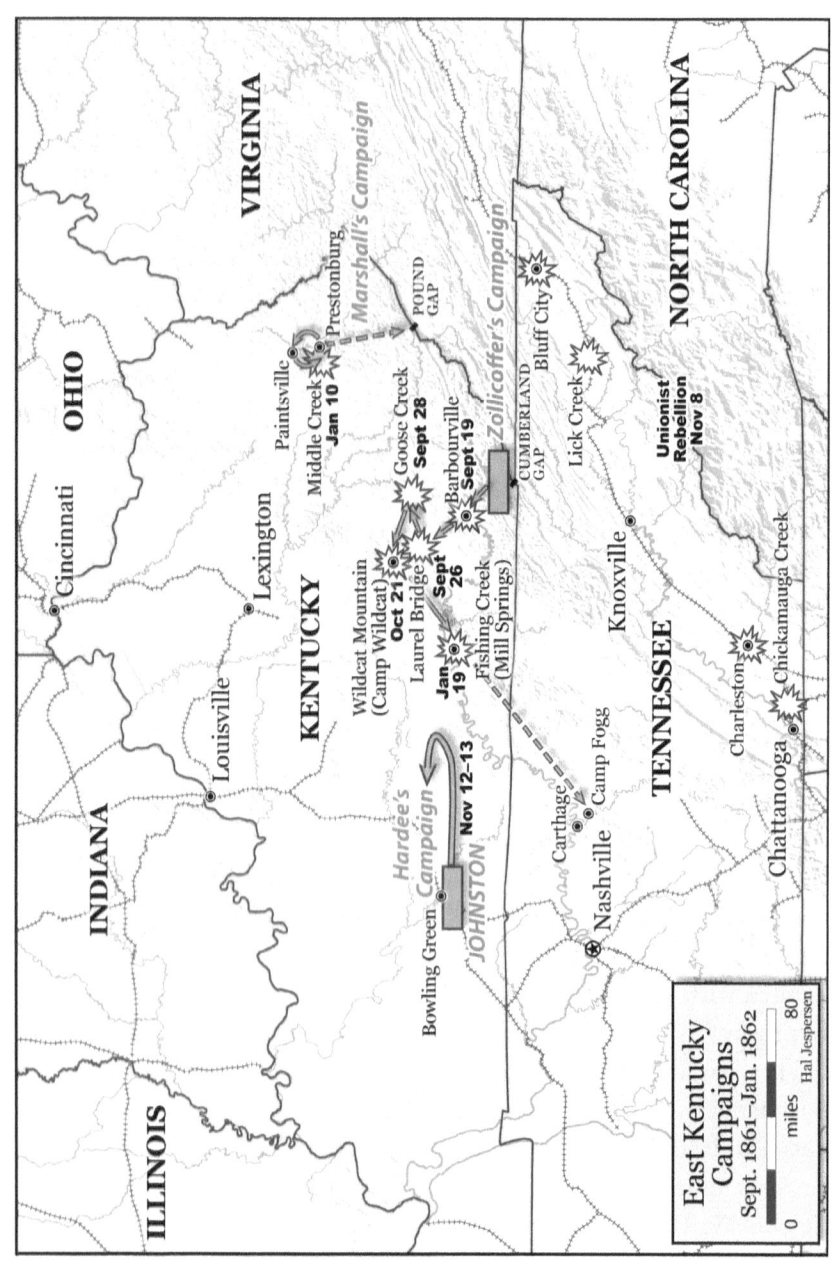

apathetic. I imagine most of them are Unionists, but so ignorant they do not understand the question at issue."[33]

At Louisville, Buell decided that Marshall had advanced far enough and dispatched a brigade under Colonel James A. Garfield to drive the Confederate forces out of northeastern Kentucky. Early on the morning on the 10th of January, Garfield's 2,200 Union soldiers skirmished with Marshall's 2,500 Southerners at Middle Creek. Neither side could gain an advantage, and the fighting sputtered out with the coming of nightfall. The inconclusive battle resulted in 27 Union and 65 Confederate casualties. Curiously, both Garfield and Marshall decided to withdraw from the battlefield during the night, thus forfeiting any claim of victory. Garfield's men were exhausted from their rapid march and Marshall's troops were close to starvation due to the lack of food and forage in the area. Marshall complained: "I am told by the commissaries that this country will be exhausted of all supplies in two or three weeks at furthest. What am I then to do?"[34] Finally, he abandoned his campaign and withdrew to the Kentucky-Virginia border.

Marshall's operation was a complete waste of time and resources. Johnston had wanted to unite Marshall's army with Zollicoffer's forces to concentrate Confederate strength in eastern Kentucky. Earlier that November, Johnston wrote to the Secretary of War that "Marshall could easily suppress the [pro-Unionist] insurrection in Carter, Johnson, and other counties, and then unite his forces with Zollicoffer."[35] This sensible request was rejected. The Confederate government had issued Marshall with specific orders to defend the southwestern border of Virginia and Johnston was given the distinct impression that he should not interfere with his erstwhile subordinate's assignment. Mackall noted that Johnston had "received no instructions from the War Department in relation to the force in East Kentucky," and thus, believed that Marshall would act according to plans that he had previously "concerted with the Department."[36] These circumstances ensured that Zollicoffer and Marshall's forces remained isolated from one another and incapable of mutual support and cooperation.

The arrival of Crittenden

Johnston received reinforcements around this time in the person of Major General George B. Crittenden, recently appointed by President Davis to command the Confederate forces in eastern Tennessee and eastern Kentucky, including those under Zollicoffer. The army under Marshall was excluded from his command due to personal animosity between the two generals. Crittenden was 49 years old, a native of Kentucky, West Point graduate, and veteran of the Mexican-American War. He had won distinction at the battles of Contreras and Churubusco. However, Crittenden's resumé was blighted by alcoholism. During his service in Mexico, Crittenden was charged with drunkenness while on duty on several occasions, and on the 18th of August 1848, his army career was terminated with a court martial. However, Crittenden's father was an influential politician and utilized his connections with government officials, including Davis, to get the conviction overturned and his son reinstated to the army. With this liability, Crittenden was a dubious asset for Johnston, but Davis used his Presidential prerogative to assign Crittenden to eastern Kentucky.

Major General George B. Crittenden

Johnston stressed the importance of Zollicoffer's safe return to Mill Springs to the new commander of the Confederate forces in eastern Kentucky. On the 16th of December, Crittenden informed Johnston that "I ordered [Zollicoffer] to recross the Cumberland and am now using all the means in my power to reinforce him."[37] But Crittenden lingered in Knoxville until Christmas day 1861, consumed with the difficult task of procuring sufficient transportation and supplies for the reinforcements he was to accompany to Mill Springs. He eventually arrived there on the 3rd of January 1862. Crittenden was troubled by the precarious situation of Zollicoffer's forces on the northern bank. Heavy rains had flooded the Cumberland River, destroying many of the boats that Zollicoffer had used to transport his army. Crittenden managed the crossing himself but was further unsettled by the feeble condition of the fortifications constructed by Zollicoffer at Beech Grove. All Crittenden could do now was to supervise the strengthening of these fortifications while waiting for the construction of additional boats to ferry the army back to Mill Springs.

Unfortunately for Crittenden, he would not be afforded the luxury of time. Union forces under Thomas had been ordered to break up the Confederate camp at Beech Grove. His division of 7,000 soldiers departed from Lebanon and struggled along the muddy and sodden roads to Logan's Crossroads, arriving on the 17th of January. Thomas halted to wait for Schoepf's 5,000 men, who were marching from Somerset to unite with him for the attack on Zollicoffer's army. The odds would be almost three to one in Thomas's favor.

The battle of Fishing Creek

The next day, Crittenden prepared his men for battle, sending a message to Johnston: "I am threatened by a superior force of the enemy in front, and finding it impossible to cross the river, I will have to make the fight on the ground I now occupy."[38] Crittenden's message was misleading. He did possess the means to transport his men back across the Cumberland. A couple of days ago, a small steamer had arrived from Nashville with supplies, and this vessel could have been utilized to shuttle the men across. The apparent impossibility was the safe transfer of the army's stores, artillery, wagons, equipment, and horses. There were simply not enough boats available for the transport of this material across the river in the time at hand. Crittenden refused to abandon these precious items to the enemy and thus made the fateful decision to fight on the northern side of the river.

Yet Crittenden did not feel confident that his 5,900 strong army could defend the 1,200 yards (1.1 km) of substandard fortifications at Beech Grove. Rather than await the Union offensive, he decided to launch a pre-emptive strike, later rationalizing that "I decided that it was best to attack the enemy, if possible, before the coming reinforcements from his rear should arrive."[39] Crittenden planned to attack while Thomas and Schoepf were still separated by the flooded Fishing Creek. The Confederate soldiers marched out of their camp just after midnight on the 19th of January towards Thomas's forces at Logan's Crossroads. Torrents of rain dissolved the dirt roads into quagmires of mud. One Northern newspaper correspondent later stated that "Zollicoffer's army had left their entrenchments in the night for the purpose of giving us a night surprise, but… were prevented by the badness of the roads, occasioned by heavy falls of rains which have been nearly incessant for the last three days."[40]

The Southern soldiers endured a cold and miserable march of over six hours just to get into position for the attack. They were exhausted and hungry, and even worse, their ancient weaponry was rendered ineffective by the drenching rain.[41] Undaunted, Zollicoffer personally led a determined Confederate attack that pushed the Federals about a mile (1.6 km) down the road. The fighting was marked by confusion, with the early morning darkness, heavy rain, wooded terrain, and gun smoke all contributing to poor visibility and lack of command and control. Zollicoffer approached some Union troops from Kentucky, mistaking them for his own men, and was shot and killed. The Confederate offensive faltered with the loss of Zollicoffer's battlefield presence, the crippling fatigue of the men, and the disconcerting failure of the flintlocks. Thomas then arrived on the battlefield with reinforcements from Logan's Crossroads and launched a powerful counterattack which shattered Crittenden's army and forced it to retreat in utter disorder back to Beech Grove. Thomas's victory at Fishing Creek cost him 262 casualties compared to Crittenden's loss of 529 men, including Zollicoffer.

Crittenden's broken army reformed at Beech Grove during the evening, closely pursued by Thomas's victorious forces. Crittenden found himself in a desperate situation: "The enemy… took positions in force on my left, center, and right. On my left they proceeded to establish a battery, which was not ready before nightfall… From the right the enemy fired upon the steamboat, which, at the crossing, was commanded by their position. Their first shots fell short; afterwards, mounting a larger gun, as it grew dark, they fired a shot or two over the boat, and awaited the morning to destroy it. The steamboat destroyed; the crossing of the river would have been impossible."[42] Crittenden had to evacuate his command or risk capture. Throughout the night of the 19th of January, the infantry, dismounted cavalry, artillery men, and sick and wounded were transported across the river, but much of critical value was left behind. The army abandoned over 1,000 horses and mules, 150 wagons, all its baggage, camp equipment, and food supplies, and eleven pieces of artillery.

Crittenden's rash decision to attack the Union forces was never sanctioned by Johnston. The general's son noted that "Crittenden's attack on Thomas was as much a surprise to General Johnston as the result could have been to the defeated commander."[43] Connelly remarked that "when the firing died down in the murky drizzle around Fishing Creek, Johnston did not know of these events. The commander of the [Western] Department, busy with details at Bowling Green, first learned that his eastern district's defenses had collapsed when he read the news in a Louisville newspaper."[44] This statement is disingenuous since the usual lag in communication between eastern Kentucky and Bowling Green was three or four days. In fact, Johnston received a telegram on the same day that he read the newspaper article. He reported to Richmond: "I have just received a telegram from [Brigadier General Thomas C.] Hindman, commanding the advance from [Bowling Green], announcing the defeat and death of General Zollicoffer at [Fishing Creek]."[45]

The loss of eastern Kentucky

Having extracted his soldiers from certain capture, Crittenden marched them about 100 miles (160 km) southwest to Camp Fogg between Chestnut Mound and Carthage, Tennessee, losing many men to desertion along the barren route. Crittenden's defeat at the battle of Fishing Creek shattered the eastern flank of the Western Department and provided Buell's army with the opportunity to outflank the Central Kentucky Army's defenses at Bowling Green. Johnston wrote to Richmond that "East Tennessee is open to invasion, or if the plan of the enemy be a combined movement upon Nashville, it is in jeopardy, unless a force can be placed to oppose a movement from Burkesville (one hundred miles [161 km] from Nashville) towards Nashville."[46] Senator Landon C. Haynes of Tennessee wrote to President Davis that "there is now no impediment whatever but bad roads and natural obstacles to prevent the enemy from entering East Tennessee and destroying the railroads and putting East Tennessee in a flame of revolution."[47] Fortunately for the Confederates,

Buell remained focused on the capture of Bowling Green via the railroad line due to the logistical concerns associated with campaigning in eastern Kentucky.

Conclusion

Connelly's omission of Johnston's initial actions in eastern Kentucky in his *Army of the Heartland* are indicative of his hostility to the general. His statement regarding the position of Zollicoffer's forces in eastern Kentucky at the time of Johnston's arrival in the Western Department is erroneous. Furthermore, Connelly's criticisms of Johnston's knowledge and influence on the campaign in eastern Kentucky are not supported by the available evidence. It has been shown that the general advised Zollicoffer on multiple occasions, implemented diversions from Bowling Green, and dispatched large numbers of troops to quell the rebellion in eastern Tennessee. Johnston's sensible desire to concentrate the forces of Zollicoffer and Marshall was rejected by Richmond. With the interminable delays in communications, he cannot be condemned for the impulsive decisions of Zollicoffer in crossing the Cumberland River and Crittenden in attacking the bluecoats at Fishing Creek. Timothy B. Smith rightly concluded that "Johnston's careful bluff of threatening an advance to mask his actual paltry numbers was now revealed for all to see. His gamble had failed because his commanders laid down their cards too soon."[48]

10.

Did Johnston respond to the threat against Fort Henry?

Sitting around a campfire in Arkansas with some of his staff, Brigadier General Ben McCulloch remarked: "Boys, we'll soon have bad news. Forts Donelson and Henry are bound to fall; [General Albert] Sidney Johnston has only 16,000 or 18,000 men at Bowling Green to meet [Brigadier General Don Carlos] Buell's 80,000, and he will be compelled to retreat to the north bank of the Tennessee, and there a great battle will be fought, and won, if the South rallies to him, if not he will fail. Manassas and [Wilson's Creek] put the South asleep but aroused the North. We have had but skirmishes compared with what is to come. Unless Johnston drives the enemy from the Tennessee, Memphis will fall. Our people have been blinded by our early success, and it will take months to rally forces that ought now to be in the field. We can recover lost opportunities by great effort, and in the end can succeed if our people are resolved to make the sacrifice."[1]

McCulloch's words may have been apocryphal, but they accurately portrayed Johnston's situation. The numerically superior Union forces in the Western Department, facilitated by riverine transportation and gunboat support, had the ability to rapidly strike any of Johnston's isolated cordons – Columbus, Fort Henry, or Fort Donelson. Overland forces could also threaten Bowling Green and eastern Kentucky with overwhelming numbers. Returning to his theory of Johnston's psychology and generalship, historian Timothy B. Smith postulated that "events began to transpire in mid-January that would not stop until disaster struck. Operations began to move swiftly, and with them came a lack of time for Johnston to methodically respond; essentially, he had to shift from being a chess-like thinker to a quick-moving poker player in response to quickened enemy movements. Unfortunately, he did not respond well."[2] Is this an accurate assessment of Johnston's actions?

The first Federal expedition against Fort Henry

On the 11th of December 1861, Johnston received a warning from Brigadier General Gideon J. Pillow at Columbus indicating that Fort Henry was under threat: "Under your instructions to give you information of the movements of the enemy I feel it my duty to say that my opinion is that the enemy are preparing to move up the Tennessee River in force. I think they will simply make a demonstration against [Columbus] to hold the force here. Will use their large water power to capture Fort Henry and pass up and take possession of Tennessee bridge and separate your command and [Major General Leonidas] Polk's."[3]

Fortunately, Johnston received an early Christmas present that would enable him to respond to the Federal threat to the Tennessee and Cumberland rivers. On the 24th of December, 2,500 reinforcements arrived at Bowling Green from southwest Virginia, under the command of Brigadier General John B. Floyd. About a week after Floyd's arrival, the 5,000 troops from the Camp Beauregard garrison also trained into Bowling Green. With the arrival of these men, Johnston now had about 23,000 soldiers in central Kentucky. After the deduction of 5,000 men from Camp Beauregard and the Columbus garrison to Bowling Green, Polk reported to Johnston that "my own force at this place, you will see, amounts to about 12,800 men ready for duty. You will see we require support. If you could give it, it would be timely and acceptable."[4] Polk's pleas were reasonable. The Confederate intelligence network continued to issue frequent false alerts regarding an imminent Union offensive against the bishop's Mississippi River fortress.

Surprisingly, the melancholic commander on the Tennessee River,

Brigadier General Lloyd Tilghman, was more optimistic with the coming of the new year. Fort Henry was a strong fortification, and despite its precarious position on a flood plain, Tilghman believed that he had effectively obstructed the passage of the river. About a mile [1.6 km] downstream from the fort lay Panther Island, a long and narrow sandbank covered in a thicket of willows, which divided the river into two channels. Tilghman had strewn the main eastern channel with naval mines and the secondary western channel was too shallow for gunboats to traverse. Tilghman informed Polk that "I reviewed and inspected the entire command at Fort Henry and am gratified at being able to report the entire command in a most admirable state of efficiency."[5]

Tilghman's sunny assessment would soon be tested. On the 14th of January, Colonel Adolphus Heiman sent an ominous warning: "A messenger reached here just now from Paducah with information from a reliable source that a division of 60,000 men, supported by eleven gunboats and thirty mortar boats, carrying not less than 160 guns, will move up Cumberland and Tennessee Rivers on next Thursday."[6] The intelligence was correct in substance but not in detail. On the 14th of January, 8,000 Union troops under Brigadier General Ulysses S. Grant moved out from Cairo to the Kentucky shore, while 5,000 more under Brigadier General Charles F. Smith departed from Paducah to reconnoitre Fort Henry.

C.F. Smith's infantry, accompanied by the timberclad gunboats, the *Lexington* and *Conestoga*, disembarked on the west side of the Tennessee River and marched to Mayfield and Murray, in the vicinity of Fort Henry. On the 17th of January, the *Lexington* lobbed four shells at the earthwork, but to no effect. Fort Henry responded with one shot, which fell short, and the gunboat withdrew. Smith concluded that "two ironclad gunboats would make short work of Fort Henry. There is no masked battery at the foot of [Panther Island], as was supposed, or, if so, it is now under water."[7]

Tilghman naturally interpreted the Union expedition as the prelude to a full-scale attack against Fort Henry and the railroad between Dover and Paris. He sent a flurry of urgent messages to both Polk and Johnston: "2,000 infantry and cavalry have landed at Eggner's Ferry and encamped six miles [9.7 km] out on road to Murray... Their object, I think, is our railroad at Paris... Will try and destroy Wood's Creek Bridge; it will impede them... Am destroying ferryboats below [Fort Donelson]. Ten-inch gun mounted at Henry at 4pm; another, 32 [pounder], will be by [midnight]. Shall return to Henry at 3am and lose no time... Smith is at Murray with, I think, 7,500 men, including 1,000 cavalry and twelve field pieces. I have possession of the hill [the site of Fort Heiman] and am fortifying hard. Can make it strong, if time is allowed... Await anxiously to know about reinforcements... I do not feel satisfied about effect of high water on earthworks at Henry."[8]

Polk quickly responded: "Have sent 1,000 cavalry to attack their column in rear and to harass them; will send also two regiments of infantry from the rear as soon as they can be put in motion."[9] Fortunately for Tilghman, the Union expedition headed back to its base at Paducah, with the Confederate cavalry detachment from Columbus cautiously following for most of the way. Grant's advance in western Kentucky also turned back. Polk was unsure of the import of the Union reconnaissance, writing to Johnston: "What the particular object of it was, has not clearly transpired. That it was intended to make a demonstration on Tennessee River seems the only thing which has been made plain."[10]

The bishop couldn't be sure that C.F. Smith's expedition was merely a diversion to distract Confederate attention from Columbus or a preparatory action for a genuine assault on Fort Henry. Johnston was also concerned about the Union expedition. On the 18th of January, his adjutant general, Colonel William W. Mackall, informed Colonel William R. Smith at Tuscumbia, Alabama: "Fort Henry, on the Tennessee River, is attacked. General Johnston directs you to move all the efficient men of your regiment by railway to the crossing of the Tennessee, and thence to Fort Henry."[11] Unfortunately, the regiment was not combat ready and failed to make it to the Tennessee River. However, two of its companies were able to reinforce the garrison at Fort Donelson later in the month.

The Russellville detachment

C.F. Smith's expedition prompted Johnston to make a daring gamble. He decided to risk the detachment of a significant proportion of the Central Kentucky Army to reinforce Russellville, Kentucky, situated between Bowling Green and Fort Henry. On the 20th of January, he directed Major

General William J. Hardee to "detach from the corps at [Bowling Green] a body of 8,000 men (due proportions of the three arms), consisting of General Floyd's brigade and so much of [Brigadier General Simon B.] Buckner's as will bring the number up to 8,000. This command will proceed to Russellville... Be instructed to protect our line from [Bowling Green] by rail to Clarksville."[12]

Thomas L. Connelly took issue with this transfer. He argued that "in January, [one of Buell's columns] moved up the Green River to South Carrollton, and Johnston considered this a threat to the weak flank west of Bowling Green. He shifted three brigades commanded by Brigadier General John Floyd... to bolster the left flank at Russellville, Kentucky. Johnston did not order this move, as some historians would later argue, because he expected a combined move up the Tennessee and Cumberland and wanted to put troops in position to reinforce Donelson. On the contrary, he expected the Donelson threat to come from the force at South Carrollton and prepared to oppose this move with troops commanded by General Charles Clark at Hopkinsville, 35 miles [56 km] northeast of the fort, and with Floyd's brigades at Russellville."[13]

Connelly's damning accusation is entirely mistaken. Johnston explained his detachment in a letter to Richmond on the 22nd of January: "The force which is going to Russellville will seize the first favorable opportunity to attack the enemy at South Carrollton, *unless* a movement in force up the Cumberland should make it necessary to go to the support of Clarksville. At Russellville, 28 miles [45 km] hence, they will be in a position to act effectively in *either* direction. Movements on my left, threatening Forts Henry, Donelson, and Clarksville, have, I do not doubt, for their ultimate object the occupation of Nashville. I have... detached 8,000 men to make Clarksville secure and drive the enemy back, with the aid of the force at Clarksville and Hopkinsville."[14] With such limited resources and insufficient numbers of armed troops, Johnston's only recourse was to distribute his forces in such a manner as to be mutually supporting. The Russellville detachment was intended to protect the garrisons at Fort Henry, Fort Donelson, and Clarksville, or assist the main army at Bowling Green, depending on the movements of the enemy. Connelly simply chose to ignore this message in his effort to malign Johnston's generalship.

Johnston's decision to detach 8,000 troops to Russellville left him with only 15,000 men at Bowling Green. This number paled in comparison to the 60,000 men of Buell's Army of the Ohio looming above him in central Kentucky. It was an audacious gamble. Johnston's son contended that "it was to General Johnston's advantage that Buell knew him only as an officer cautious and provident in military conduct, and that he could not presume him to have taken such risks as he did. It happens to be within the writer's knowledge that General Johnston regarded what he conceived to be Buell's opinion of him as one of the considerations to be weighed in determining his own course of action."[15]

The second Federal expedition against Fort Henry

On the 29th of January 1862, Major General George B. McClellan sent a telegram from Washington to his senior commanders in the western theater, Buell and Major General Henry W. Halleck, stating that "a deserter just in from the rebels says that [General Pierre G.T.] Beauregard had not left Centreville [Virginia] four days ago, but that as he was going on picket, he heard officers say that Beauregard was under order to go to Kentucky with fifteen regiments."[16] Halleck responded the next day: "Your telegraph respecting Beauregard is received. Grant and Commodore [Andrew H.] Foote will be ordered to immediately advance, and to reduce and hold Fort Henry, on the Tennessee River, and also to cut the railroad between Dover and Paris."[17] The misleading intelligence was the catalyst for the Union offensive up the Tennessee River. Johnston's son noted: "It will be borne in mind that the points of pressure, during this period, were elsewhere [Bowling Green and Columbus], and that the Federal commanders themselves came to a very sudden and unpremeditated resolution to make this their chief point of attack."[18]

Grant's forces at Cairo were delighted with the order and launched into frenzied preparation for the move up the Tennessee River. However, McClellan's information was only part accurate. The transfer of Beauregard to Johnston's Western Department was correct, but the fifteen accompanying regiments of reinforcements was entirely false. Beauregard was coming to Kentucky with a few staff only, but this misinformation was the spur that provoked Halleck into decisive action against Fort Henry. McClellan wanted Halleck to seize the fort before Beauregard's phantom regiments could reinforce the small Confederate garrison defending the Tennessee River.

On the 31st of January, the *Lexington* and *Conestoga* reconnoitred Fort Henry again and discovered the naval mines placed in the river by the Confederates. Several days later, Grant embarked his men on transports at Cairo and was escorted to Paducah by Foote's Western Flotilla, composed of four ironclad gunboats, the *Carondelet*, *Cincinnati*, *Essex*, and *St. Louis*, and three timberclad gunboats, the *Conestoga*, *Lexington*, and *Tyler*. C.F. Smith's Paducah garrison was absorbed into Grant's expeditionary force, increasing the size of the infantry component to about 17,500 men. On the 3rd of February, naval transports sent the first detachment of Grant's troops southward towards Fort Henry.

That same morning, Tilghman and Major Jeremy F. Gilmer inspected the defenses at Fort Henry. They departed for Fort Donelson at about 10am, leaving Heiman in command of the fortification. There were only 2,600 Confederate soldiers garrisoning Fort Henry, many of whom were still armed with ancient 1812 flintlock muskets from the Tennessee arsenal. Worse still, the recent heavy rains had caused the Tennessee River to rise significantly, and it was now threatening to submerge the fort itself. Only nine of the eleven pieces of artillery that faced the river remained dry and operable.

Foote's gunboats came within view of Fort Henry around 4.30am on the 4th of February, and the transports disgorged Brigadier General John A. McClernand's division on the eastern bank of the river downstream of Fort Henry. McClernand ordered his men to move inland, while the transports steamed back downriver to Paducah to collect C.F. Smith's division. Confederate scouts observed the Federal landing and fired a series of signal rockets to alert Heiman at Fort Henry. The startled officer sent out detachments of troops to guard the roads and landings near the fort. The recent downpours had made the western channel of the Tennessee River at Panther Island navigable and so Heiman ordered his men to deploy a dozen more naval mines to prevent the passage of Union gunboats through the stream.[19]

Heiman sent a courier to Fort Donelson to alert Tilghman, but the twelve-mile (19 km) journey on the narrow and muddy tracks winding through the rugged terrain between the two forts consumed about three hours on horseback. Heiman wrote that "the enemy is landing troops in large forces on this side of the river, within three miles [5 km] of the fort... They are not landing on the opposite bank [near Fort Heiman], and it will perhaps be prudent to bring some of the troops over here, but I will await your orders, or, what I would more desire, your presence. Come not without a large escort."[20]

Heiman was also disturbed by the increasing water level of the Tennessee River and noted that one of his officers had "a large force at work on the epaulements and trying to keep water out of the fort. The lower magazine had already two feet [61 cm] of water in it."[21] At about noon on the 4th of February, the Union gunboats approached Fort Henry with an ominous intent. Heiman ordered his artillerymen to open fire when the enemy vessels came within range and then sent the infantry out of the fort into the surrounding rifle pits for safety.

The Federal warships opened fire and Fort Henry responded in kind. After a thirty-minute firefight, the gunboats withdrew, with neither side inflicting much damage. Tilghman and Gilmer heard the distinct sound of artillery fire emanating from the direction of Fort Henry and wondered what was happening, but for some unexplained reason, did not bother to investigate. Heiman's courier finally arrived at Fort Donelson at about 3.30pm. Tilghman read the message and forwarded it on to Polk at Columbus. Consequently, several historians have mistakenly asserted that it was Tilghman requesting the bishop's presence at Fort Henry rather than Heiman requesting Tilghman's.[22]

Now fully alert to the danger, Tilghman ordered the two Confederate regiments stationed at Danville, the 48th and 51st Tennessee, to "repair to Fort Henry at once."[23] He transmitted a copy of Heiman's dispatch to Bowling Green, adding that Johnston "better send two regiments to Danville, subject to my orders" to replace the ones he had just summoned to Fort Henry. At 5pm on the 4th of February, Tilghman sent another message to Polk, stating: "The landing of the enemy is between rivers, perhaps from both rivers. Give me all the help you can, light battery included. Off to Henry."[25]

Questions over reinforcements

Kendall D. Gott claimed that "Tilghman sent an update of the situation to Johnston. Any reply is lost to history, but no reinforcements were sent."[26] Likewise, Connelly insisted that "Johnston was well aware of the weak condition of Fort Henry... Yet Johnston failed to aid Fort Henry. His habit of preoccupation with a single object [the defense of Bowling Green] had blinded him to his departmental responsibilities. His weakness in handling subordinates resulted in his not ordering Polk to reinforce Tilghman."[27] Connelly also claimed that "while Fort Henry was being attacked, Polk continued to hold back the badly needed reinforcements. On February 5 he finally ordered a meager force of two infantry regiments and four cavalry battalions to move towards the Tennessee River. That same day Polk announced to Johnston that he could furnish none besides these."[28] Timothy B. Smith declared: "With his attention firmly fixed on Columbus's defenses, the bishop sent no troops whatsoever."[29]

These accusations are misplaced. Polk did not "hold back" reinforcements from Fort Henry. Heiman's 4th of February dispatch was equivocally worded, only mentioning that "it will perhaps be prudent" to reinforce the fort. The nearest telegraph office was some distance from Fort Donelson, and so Polk did not receive the 3.30pm telegram from Tilghman until the next day, the 5th of February. Regardless, Polk ordered about 2,000 soldiers from Columbus to Fort Henry, certainly not a "meager" force in the context of his entire garrison of about 12,800 men.[30] Connelly also fails to explain how Polk withheld the reinforcements when he ordered them forward on the very day that he received Tilghman's first *serious* call for assistance. There was simply no time for Polk to have sent additional forces to Fort Henry. Tilghman only personally surveyed the area in the early hours of the 5th of February, and that was the day he began to earnestly request more soldiers. Polk could not teleport the reinforcements to Fort Henry.

Contrary to Gott's assertion, Johnston sent multiple reinforcements to Fort Henry. When he received Tilghman's telegram of 3.30pm on the 4th of February requesting that he send two regiments to Danville, he acted immediately, sending a newly armed regiment, Colonel William E. Baldwin's 14th Mississippi, from Nashville to Fort Donelson. Upon receiving Tilghman's urgent request for more troops at midnight on the

5th of February, Johnston dispatched heavy reinforcements, risking the safety of both Bowling Green and Nashville. Clark's brigade at Hopkinsville and Floyd's division at Russellville, a combined total of about 10,000 men, were ordered to Clarksville on the morning of the 6th of February.

Johnston's son rightly concluded that "General Tilghman's requests were not neglected... On the 5th General Johnston ordered a regiment, just armed, from Nashville to Donelson, and on the 6th Colonel [W.R.] Smith's regiment from Tuscumbia, Alabama. He also ordered Floyd, on the 6th, to proceed with his command from Russellville to Clarksville, without a moment's delay, and at the same time sent all the rolling-stock he could command to take the troops."[31] In addition, Johnston dispatched Brigadier General Gideon J. Pillow to command the small garrison at Clarksville on the Cumberland River. Pillow had resigned from the Confederate army at the end of December 1861 after months of suffering the perceived indignity of serving under Polk. He spent a few weeks at his home in Tennessee, but hearing of the defeat at Fishing Creek, presented himself to Johnston at Bowling Green, hoping to replace the disgraced Major General George B. Crittenden in command of the District of East Tennessee forces.

Johnston decided that he could utilize Pillow's services despite his checkered history with Polk and other officers. Years afterwards, Brigadier General Josiah Gorgas said that Pillow "is a man of energy and ability, and, were he content to *serve*, would, I think, be very useful; but his great ambition leads him to seek commands to which his military status is hardly equal. To a General by whom he would be controlled he would be very useful."[32] Johnston thought he could control Pillow and sent him to Clarksville, where the Tennessean could devote his considerable energy to securing that town's defenses. Arriving on the 5th of February, Pillow was disheartened by the lack of defensive works at the town. Johnston's son wrote that, "some 300 negroes were employed [at Clarksville], but the works there seem not to have been pushed vigorously. Slaves, reluctantly loaned, slothful in habits, and badly organized, could not be expected to prove very efficient laborers."[33] Regardless, Pillow set to work organizing the defenses of Clarksville while Floyd's and Buckner's troops made their way from Russellville.

Thus, Johnston had provided support for both the Tennessee and Cumberland rivers as best he could, considering the limited military resources in the Western Department. Almost a third of the Central Kentucky Army was positioned halfway between the Cumberland River and Bowling Green, and moving rapidly to the scene of action, several regiments had been ordered to reinforce Fort Henry, and the indefatigable Pillow was tasked with strengthening the defenses at Clarksville, due east of Fort Donelson, on the river's course from Nashville.

The battle of Fort Henry

Tilghman and Gilmer, escorted by Lieutenant Colonel George Gantt's 9th Tennessee Cavalry Battalion, arrived at Fort Henry just before midnight on the 4th of February. Tilghman "soon became satisfied that the enemy were really in strong force at Bailey's Ferry, with every indication of reinforcements arriving constantly."[34] Tilghman decided to transfer the two regiments of troops garrisoning Fort Heiman across the river to Fort Henry, concluding that "the extremely bad roads leading to [Fort Heiman] would prevent the movement of heavy guns by the enemy, by which I might be annoyed."[35] The evacuation of Fort Heiman was accomplished by 5am on the 5th of February, leaving only a few cavalry troops to guard the site. At 8am, Tilghman telegraphed Polk that the garrison at Fort Henry was "in good spirits, but badly armed. I will hold my position to the last, but should be reinforced amply, at once, if possible."[36] Unbeknownst to Tilghman, the Union division under C.F. Smith disembarked at about 9am. The bluecoats planned to secure a lodgement on the western bank of the Tennessee River and seize Fort Heiman. If successful, Smith hoped to blast the Confederates at Fort Henry into submission with artillery emplaced on the heights at Fort Heiman.

At 11am, Tilghman informed Johnston: "If you can reinforce strongly and quickly, we have a glorious chance to overwhelm the enemy. Move by Clarksville to Donelson and across, and to Danville, where transports will be ready. Enemy said to be entrenching below. My plans are to concentrate closely in and under Henry."[37] Polk had now received Tilghman's messages from the previous day and responded that he would send two infantry regiments and four cavalry battalions to the Tennessee River.

Tilghman was not impressed, and at midnight on the 5th of February, informed Polk: "Thank you for cavalry, but had rather have disciplined infantry. I must have two regiments, thoroughly armed and equipped, from you. Enemy strong three miles [4.8 km] below, fortifying. They were reinforced yesterday. Scouting parties engaged enemy's pickets... and our cavalry retired; lost one man. I reinforced, and enemy retired. Don't trust to Johnston's reinforcing me; we need all. I don't want raw troops who are just organized; they are in my way. Act promptly, and don't trust to anyone."[38] Tilghman then sent another midnight telegram to Johnston complaining that "I must have reinforcements and with well-drilled troops. The green men with me are wellnigh worthless. More of them would be in my way. The high water threatens us seriously."[39]

A severe storm system passed through the night of the 5th of February, bringing with it lightning, thunder, hailstones, and heavy rain. The Tennessee River continued to increase in depth and driftwood and other debris tumbled downstream, destroying the effectiveness of the naval mines. Most of the devices were washed away, and those that remained tethered were rendered useless by the high water.[40] Nevertheless, Foote's flotilla was delayed several hours by the necessity of removing the drifting naval mines. The Federal sailors fished out about a dozen of the devices and noticed that all but one had broken seals and damp gunpowder. The warships could now use the western channel of Panther Island to advance on Fort Henry, which offered more protection from Fort Henry's guns compared to the main eastern channel. The Confederate defense was severely weakened by the loss of the naval mines.

Tilghman assessed the deteriorating situation at Fort Henry and decided that the position was no longer tenable. His poorly armed 2,600 men could not contend with Grant's 17,500 strong force, and the flooded state of the river would enable the enemy gunboats to advance to a dangerous proximity. Tilghman ordered nearly all the garrison to evacuate to Fort Donelson, while remaining behind with less than a hundred men to hold off the gunboats long enough for the rest of his soldiers to make the twelve-mile (19 km) march in safety. Tilghman reasoned that "Fort Donelson might possibly be held, if properly reinforced, even though Fort Henry should fall; but the reverse of this proposition was not true.[41]

Around noon on the 6th of February, Foote opened the attack on Fort

Henry from 1,700 yards (1.6 km) with his four ironclad gunboats. The three timberclad gunboats took a position astern and inshore of the ironclads where they could lob shells into Fort Henry without risk of return fire. As the ironclads steamed forward, the guns of the Confederate fort unleashed a torrent of fire. Unfortunately for the defenders of Fort Henry, their rifled 24-pounder burst, killing three men and wounding many more. Gilmer recalled that "the effect of this explosion was very serious upon our artillerists; first, because it made them doubt the strength of these large guns to resist the shock of full charges, and, secondly, because much was expected from the long range of rifled cannon against the gunboats. Still, all stood firmly to their work, under a most terrific fire from the advancing foe, whose approach was steady and constant."[42]

The small garrison was then rattled by the destruction of one of the 32-pounder guns and its entire crew when its muzzle was hit by a Union shell. Moments later, one of the 42-pounder cannons exploded before firing its next round, killing another three artillerists, and wounding several others. Gilmer reported that soon "it was observed that the ten-inch Columbiad was silent… the priming wire had been jammed and broken in the vent… By this time the gunboats, by a steady advance, had reached positions not over 600 or 700 yards [550-640 m] from the fort. Our artillerists became very much discouraged when they saw the two heavy guns disabled, the enemy's boats apparently uninjured, and still drawing nearer and nearer."[43]

Gilmer observed that Tilghman "assisted to serve one of the pieces himself for at least fifteen minutes; but his men were exhausted, had lost all hope, and there were no others to replace them at the guns."[44] The Union fleet slowly steamed towards the fort, and the fire from both sides continued. The *Essex* received a shot in her boilers, which scalded its Commodore, 28 sailors, and 19 soldiers, and disabled the ironclad from further action. The Confederates were heartened when the stricken vessel floated downstream. However, the remaining three ironclads continued to approach the fort with their destructive fire, and about one hour and fifteen minutes after the attack began, the Confederate flag was hauled down in surrender.[45] Union casualties totalled 47 sailors whereas the Southern force suffered 35 losses, many of those inflicted by the explosions of their own artillery pieces.

Upon Tilghman's surrender, Foote's officers were able to sail through the sally port of Fort Henry on a small launch due to the high level of the Tennessee River. Tilghman bitterly recalled that "the elements even were against us, and had the enemy delayed his attack a few days, with the river rising, one-third of the entire fortifications (already affected by it) would have been washed away, while the remaining portion of the works would have been untenable by reason of the depth of water over the whole interior position."[46] Tilghman's scathing assessment was backed up by that of his Chief of Artillery: "I gave it as my opinion that Fort Henry was untenable, and ought to be forthwith abandoned, first, because it was surrounded by water, then cut off from the support of the infantry, and was on the point of being submerged; second, because our whole force, artillery, cavalry, and infantry, amounted to little over 2,000 men, a force wholly inadequate to cope with that of the enemy, even if there had been no extraordinary rise in the river... Fort Henry was of necessity compelled to surrender; if not to the gunboats, certainly to General Grant's investing army. The fault was in its location, not in its defenders."[47]

The fall of Fort Henry was a catastrophe for the Confederacy. It opened the Tennessee River to Union navigation from Paducah to northern Alabama. Following the surrender of the fort, three Union timberclad gunboats exploited the breach and steamed up the river. The vessels induced terror in the civilian populace and destroyed several transport steamers and military supplies. Most importantly, the Union navy captured the unfinished Confederate ironclad, the *Eastport*. The sudden fall of Fort Henry shocked the South. The Union navy was now free to transport bodies of infantry at any location southwest of Nashville, following the course of the Tennessee River up to the Alabama shoals. The loss of the fortification completely shattered Johnston's defense of the Western Department. St. John R. Liddell acidly commented that "the miserably spread-out policy of the Confederate Government was reaping a deplorable harvest of disasters."[48]

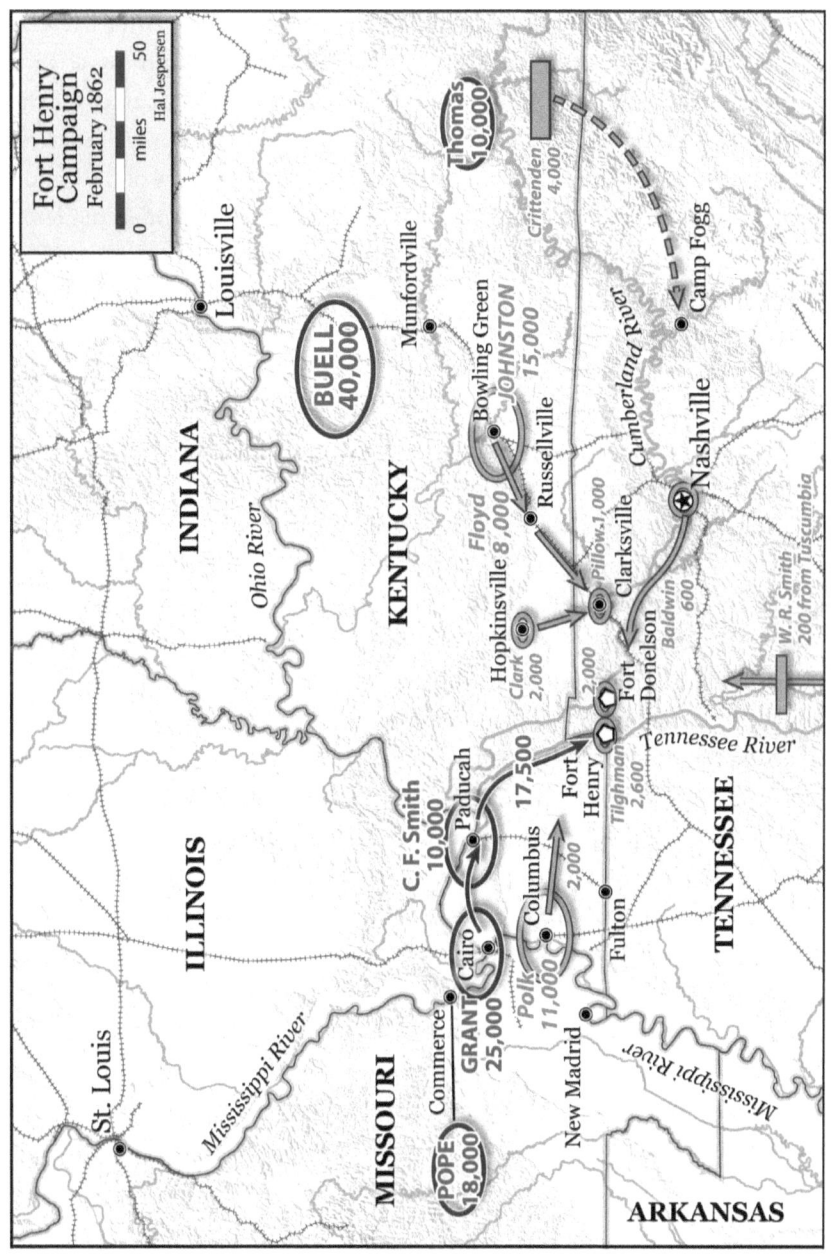

Conclusion

The denunciations from historians that Johnston did not respond quickly enough to the Federal threat to Fort Henry are mistaken. After the first raid on Fort Henry, the general made the bold decision to move a third of the Central Kentucky Army to Russellville in an attempt to cover the Tennessee and Cumberland rivers, despite the overwhelming numerical odds on the Bowling Green front. Unfortunately, the rapidity of the Union assault on Fort Henry and Tilghman's precipitate surrender rendered Johnston's actions futile. The reinforcements simply could not travel to Fort Henry in the limited time available. The Federal forces had much greater mobility than Johnston's men due to their riverine transportation. In addition, the heavy rains experienced during this period submerged parts of the Confederate fortification, opened the western channel of Panther Island to gunboat navigation, and eliminated any threat of harm from the Confederate naval mines.

The criticism of Polk's and Johnston's lack of reinforcement of Fort Henry are also misplaced. Reinforcements were clearly dispatched, but it was simply impossible for them to have arrived in time to save Fort Henry. Ultimately, Johnston's best hope for a successful defense at Fort Henry was the completion of the *Eastport*, which may have been able to hold off the enemy gunboats for enough time to allow the reinforcements to arrive and bolster Tilghman's defense against Grant's army. Unfortunately for Johnston, the Secretary of the Navy's policy of simultaneously constructing multiple large ironclads stalled progress on the *Eastport* and doomed it to capture. Without ironclad support, the fall of Fort Henry was inevitable. The one positive for Johnston from the fall of Fort Henry was that it finally stirred the Confederate government into real action. Richmond resolved to abandon its policy of husbanding troops in seaboard garrisons and decided instead to strengthen the armies in the Western Department. President Jefferson Davis, who rarely admitted his mistakes, wrote: "I acknowledge the error of my attempt to defend all the frontier, seaboard, and inland."[49]

11.

Why did Johnston reject Beauregard's Covington House Strategy?

The defeat at Fishing Creek and the fall of Fort Henry signalled the end of General Albert Sidney Johnston's strategy of illusory strength to delay Union offensives into the Western Department. Johnston now had to react to the painful fact that the Tennessee River was open to Union navigation, and thus, the heartland of the Confederacy was rendered pathetically vulnerable to invasion. The surrender of Fort Henry also exposed the two salient points of Johnston's original defensive line, Bowling Green and Columbus, to enemy flanking manoeuvres. The Confederate fortifications on the Cumberland River, Fort Donelson and Fort Defiance, were now also at risk of capture, considering the apparent power of the Union ironclad fleet.

On the Mississippi River, Major General Leonidas Polk had about 12,000 men at Columbus and another 2,000 men at New Madrid and Island Number Ten. These forces were confronted by 30,000 to 40,000 Federals under Major General Henry W. Halleck in Missouri. In the center of the Western Department, there were about 5,000 soldiers at Fort Donelson, opposed by Brigadier General Ulysses S. Grant's 17,500 victorious troops at the rapidly drowning Fort Henry. Brigadier General

Charles Clark had 2,000 men at Hopkinsville, and they were on their way to reinforce Brigadier General Gideon J. Pillow's Clarksville garrison of 1,000 men. Brigadier General Simon B. Buckner's small division of about 2,000 men was also *en route* to Clarksville from Russellville. Finally, Brigadier General John B. Floyd was in preparation to follow Buckner with the remaining 6,000 troops from Russellville.

Johnston himself had about 15,000 men at Bowling Green, facing the largest Federal force, that of Brigadier General Don Carlos Buell's Army of the Ohio, estimated at about 50,000 men. More worryingly, Johnston's eastern wing under Major General George B. Crittenden had collapsed entirely after the disaster at Fishing Creek, with his broken army retreating to Camp Fogg in Tennessee. The Union division under Brigadier General George H. Thomas in eastern Kentucky, about 10,000 strong, could now advance and threaten the right flank of Johnston's army at Bowling Green if Buell were disposed to order such a movement.

The arrival of Beauregard

After haranguing Richmond and the State Governors for more men, arms, and equipment for the past six months in an effort that had borne little fruit, Johnston was offered the services of one of the South's most famous and beloved commanders, General Pierre Gustave Toutant Beauregard, the hero of Fort Sumter and Bull Run. Ironically, it had been Beauregard's appointment and the rumors of fifteen accompanying regiments that spurred Halleck's advance against Fort Henry and the resulting destruction of Johnston's line of defense.

Beauregard arrived in Bowling Green on the 4th of February 1862. He was 43 years old, a native of Louisiana, and had placed second in the West Point class of 1838. He had served in the Mexican-American War and won distinction at the battles of Contreras, Cerro Gordo, and Chapultepec. After the war, Beauregard was employed in the United States Army Engineer Department for over a decade, repairing old forts and constructing new ones near New Orleans, Mobile, and along the Florida coast. In January 1861, Beauregard accepted an appointment as the superintendent of the Military Academy at West Point but only served for five days, as Louisiana's secession prompted the Federal government to revoke his orders.

After departing West Point, Beauregard travelled to New Orleans and offered his services to the local authorities, but President Jefferson Davis soon assigned him to take command of the Charleston Harbor defenses. Here the Louisianian won immortal fame by ordering the first shots of the Civil War, bombarding Fort Sumter into submission before it could be resupplied by a Union naval operation. Beauregard was rewarded with a prominent assignment in Virginia, commanding the largest army in the Confederacy.

On the 21st of July, Beauregard united his forces with General Joseph E. Johnston's Army of the Shenandoah to defeat the Union Army of Northeastern Virginia under Major General Irvin McDowell at the battle of Bull Run (also known as the battle of Manassas), the first major conflict of the war. Beauregard spent much of the battle on the front lines rallying the troops while J.E. Johnston directed the tactical movements of the army from the rear. After the rout of McDowell's army, the victorious Confederate forces were officially united under the command of J.E. Johnston by virtue of his seniority of rank. Although relegated to second-in-command, Beauregard retained all his popularity and celebrity among the army and the Southern people. Captain Arthur J.L. Fremantle described Beauregard as "a man of middle height... He would be very youthful in appearance were it not for the color of his hair, which is much grayer than his earlier photographs represent... He has a long straight nose, handsome brown eyes, and a dark moustache without whiskers, and his manners are extremely polite. He is a New Orleans creole, and French is his native language."[1]

General Pierre G.T. Beauregard

In the months after Bull Run, Beauregard proceeded to annoy President Davis via a series of complaints directed at the Commissary General and Secretary of War regarding the provision of adequate supplies and munitions for the Virginia army. He then enraged the President by leaking his criticisms of Davis's war strategy to the local newspapers. In

January 1862, it was suggested that Beauregard transfer to the western theater of war to assist General A.S. Johnston. The crushing Confederate defeat at Fishing Creek had finally sparked some concern in Richmond for the military situation in the Western Department. Davis hoped that Beauregard's talent for engineering would be of great benefit to Johnston and to the integrity of his cordon defenses.[2] Although reluctant, the Louisianian agreed, and Davis was no doubt relieved to be rid of the bothersome general.

The addition of Beauregard to Johnston's circle of subordinates was of mixed blessing. His arrival at Bowling Green generated much enthusiasm amongst the soldiers and citizenry of the Western Department and clearly had a positive effect on morale. Johnston anticipated that Beauregard would soon apply his engineering skills to the improvement of the fortifications at Forts Henry and Donelson, and other key areas. On the other hand, Beauregard had proven himself to be a disputatious subordinate with a penchant for criticizing the Confederate government and leaking self-aggrandizing information to the newspapers. He might continue this destructive behaviour in the Western Department and undermine Johnston's authority.[3]

Fortunately, this was not to be the case. Beauregard's friend and biographer, Alfred Roman, recounted that the general "reached Bowling Green on the evening of the 4th [of February], and there met, for the first time, General Albert Sidney Johnston, who gave him, on arrival in his department, a heartfelt greeting. The manly appearance, the simple, though dignified, bearing of this noble patriot and soldier, made a deep impression upon General Beauregard. He was drawn towards him by a spontaneous feeling of sympathy, which insured, in the future, complete harmony and effectual cooperation between them."[4] However, Beauregard had been deceived as to Johnston's strength, expecting to find 40,000 Confederate soldiers at Bowling Green and another 30,000 at Columbus, ready to assume the offensive. Instead, he was shocked to see an army of "some 14,000 effectives" at Bowling Green, with deficient arms, equipment, and transportation."[5]

In his first meeting with Johnston, the Louisianian "showed much anxiety when referring to the effects of [Brigadier General Felix K.] Zollicoffer's late disaster at [Fishing Creek]. General Buell had advanced his forces, numbering from 75,000 to 80,000 men, to within 40 miles [64 km] of Bowling Green, at Bacon Creek, on the Louisville & Nashville Railroad; General Grant was at Cairo and Paducah, with 20,000 men, pressing an expedition which was to move – General Johnston thought – either up the Tennessee River, against Fort Henry, or up the Cumberland, against Fort Donelson; and [Brigadier General John] Pope, with at least 30,000 men, in Missouri, stood confronting Major General Polk."[6] Beauregard was thoroughly disillusioned with the dire military situation in the west.

He was also very sick. Since childhood, the Louisianian had suffered from an enduring throat complaint, possibly chronic tonsillitis, and it seemed to get exacerbated during times of stress.[7] In desperation, Beauregard had consented to throat surgery prior to his departure for Bowling Green and when he arrived in Kentucky, he was acutely unwell, suffering from a bronchial infection, fever, and laryngitis. Beauregard, "realizing how useless his presence would be to General Johnston, under the existing circumstances, informed the latter that, in his opinion, he had best return at once to Virginia... General Johnston strenuously objected to his adopting such a course. He urged that General Beauregard's presence was most fortunate, and that his cooperation would be invaluable, not only in western Kentucky and western Tennessee, but in the whole Mississippi Valley."[8] Beauregard consented to remain in Bowling Green but remained bedridden for most of the next week. Unfortunately, his presence did not provide the assistance Johnston so desperately needed. He was too sick to assume command at Forts Henry or Donelson.

The Covington House Conference

On the 7th of February, soon after the surrender of Fort Henry, Johnston and Major General William J. Hardee met with the ailing Beauregard at the latter's headquarters at Covington House, Bowling Green, to discuss the military situation in the Western Department and determine a course of action. Lacking details of the fight at Fort Henry, the generals were under the impression that the Union ironclads were invincible, and that Fort Donelson could not be defended. Once the fort fell, the Cumberland River would also be opened to the Federal navy, imperilling the safety of

Johnston's army at Bowling Green.

A retreat by the Central Kentucky Army from Bowling Green to Nashville was decided as the prudent move. Beauregard recounted that "at a meeting held today at my quarters (Covington House) by Generals Johnston, Hardee, and myself... it was determined that, Fort Henry, on the Tennessee River, having fallen yesterday into the hands of the enemy, and Fort Donelson, on the Cumberland River, not being long tenable, preparations should at once be made for the removal of this army to Nashville, in rear of the Cumberland River, a strong point some miles below that city being fortified forthwith, to defend the river from the passage of gunboats and transports. The troops at present at Clarksville should cross over to the south side of that river, leaving only a sufficient force in that town to protect the manufactories and other property... From Nashville, should any further retrograde movement become necessary, it will be made to Stevenson [Alabama], and thence according to circumstances."[9]

Johnston reported to Secretary of War, Judah P. Benjamin, the next day that "no reliable particulars of the loss of Fort Henry have yet reached me. This much, however, is known, that nearly all of the force at Fort Henry retreated to Fort Donelson, and it is said that [Brigadier General Lloyd] Tilghman and about eighty officers and men surrendered the fort. Operations against Fort Donelson, on the Cumberland, are about to be commenced, and that work will soon be attacked. The slight resistance at Fort Henry indicates that the best open earthworks are not reliable to meet successfully a vigorous attack of ironclad gunboats, and, although now supported by a considerable force, I think the gunboats of the enemy will probably take Fort Donelson without the necessity of employing their land force in cooperation, as seems to have been done at Fort Henry."[10] Johnston noted that "our force at Fort Donelson, including the force from Fort Henry and three regiments of [Brigadier General John B.] Floyd's command, is about 7,000 men, not well armed or drilled, except [Colonel Adolphus] Heiman's regiment and the regiments of Floyd's command. General Floyd's command and the force from Hopkinsville is arriving at Clarksville and can (if necessary) reach Donelson in four hours by steamers, which are there."[11]

Benjamin was also informed of the risk to the Central Kentucky Army:

"Should Fort Donelson be taken, it will open the route to the enemy to Nashville, giving them the means of breaking the bridges and destroying the ferry-boats on the river as far as navigable. The occurrence of the misfortune of losing the fort will cut off the communication of the force here, under General Hardee, from the south bank of the Cumberland. To avoid the disastrous consequences of such an event I ordered General Hardee yesterday to make (as promptly as it could be done) preparations to fall back to Nashville and cross the river. The movements of the enemy on my right flank [after the battle of Fishing Creek] would have made a retrograde in that direction to confront the enemy indispensable in a short time. But the probability of having the passage of this army corps across the Cumberland intercepted by the gunboats of the enemy admits of no delay in making the movement. Generals Beauregard and Hardee are equally with myself impressed with the necessity of withdrawing our force from this line at once."[12]

The fate of Columbus

The Covington House conference also considered the security of Polk's Columbus garrison. Beauregard reported that "it was also determined that the possession of the Tennessee River by the enemy, resulting from the fall of Fort Henry, separates the army at Bowling Green from the one at Columbus, Kentucky, which must henceforth act independently of each other until they can be brought together... As the possession of the [Tennessee] river by the enemy renders the lines of communication of the army at Columbus liable to be cut off at any time from the Tennessee River as a base by an overpowering force of the enemy rapidly concentrated from various points on the Ohio, it becomes necessary, to prevent such a calamity, that the main body of that army should fall back to Humboldt [Tennessee]."[13] Beauregard announced that "at Columbus, Kentucky, will be left only a sufficient garrison for the defense of the works there, assisted by [Commodore George N.] Hollins's gunboats, for the purpose of making a desperate defense of the river at that point... Island Number Ten and Fort Pillow will likewise be defended to the last extremity, aided also by Hollins's gunboats, which will then retire to the vicinity of Memphis, where another bold stand will be made."[14]

Johnston ordered Polk to "destroy the railroad bridges from Paris to Humboldt as far as practicable" to prevent the Union forces at Fort Henry from descending on Columbus by the overland route.[15] Thomas L. Connelly misinterpreted Johnston's orders to Polk. He made the accusation that "when Grant moved on Fort Henry in early February, Johnston then expected him to turn west and strike Polk on the flank. There is no evidence that before Grant moved into the lines around Donelson, Johnston considered that he might go east instead of west to Columbus."[16] This criticism is erroneous. Firstly, on the 22nd of January, Johnston wrote to General Samuel Cooper regarding Brigadier General Charles F. Smith's reconnaissance of Fort Henry: "The badness of the roads on the route to Paris and the movement on his rear has made him relinquish his march to the railroad at Paris, which it is presumed he desired to cut before investing Forts Henry and Donelson."[17] Secondly, on the 5th of February, Johnston dispatched Pillow to Clarksville with instructions to strengthen the defenses on the Cumberland River at that point. The next day, 10,000 troops under Floyd, Buckner, and Clark were ordered to reinforce Pillow's garrison at Clarksville. No reinforcements were sent to Columbus.

Thirdly, on the 7th of February, the tenability of Fort Donelson was a central theme of the discussions between Johnston, Beauregard, and Hardee at Covington House. A day after the conference, Johnston stated to the Secretary of War that "operations against Fort Donelson, on the Cumberland, are about to be commenced and that work will *soon* be attacked."[18] No such mention was made of an imminent attack on Columbus. Finally, on the 8th of February, Johnston requested that Floyd ascertain whether the enemy would "attack Fort Donelson in conjunction with gunboats or move them against Clarksville direct."[19] Two days later, Gilmer informed Johnston that "the attack expected here is a combined one; gunboats by water and a land force in the rear."[20] These communications occurred well before Grant's army arrived at Fort Donelson on the 12th of February. Connelly simply ignored these statements to disparage Johnston's generalship.

With the endorsement of Beauregard and Hardee, the Covington House conference had thus determined Confederate strategy in the west. Bowling Green would be abandoned, and Columbus defended only by a token garrison. The defensive integrity of the Western Department was to rely on Buell's caution and the delay of Grant's forces on the Cumberland River long enough to ensure the safe withdrawal of the Central Kentucky Army from Bowling Green to Nashville. Johnston ardently desired that Beauregard assume command of the Cumberland River defenses during this difficult time, but the Louisianian's ongoing debility precluded such an option.

Beauregard was therefore assigned responsibility for the less onerous task of evacuating Columbus. Yet Johnston received a note from his second-in-command's surgeon on the 8th of February stating that "General Beauregard has been unwell all night, complains very much of his throat, and has concluded not to start in the morning. He requests that you will countermand the order for the special trains."[21] Beauregard was frustrated by his illness, writing to a friend a week later: "My health, moreover, has failed me completely lately. I was confined to my room by a wretched cold all the time I was at Bowling Green. It is the most unfortunate thing that could have happened to me, for the loss of one or two weeks now is or may be most fatal to us."[22]

Beauregard's alleged concentration plan

Over two decades after the Covington House conference, Beauregard claimed to have advocated an audacious campaign for the defense of the Cumberland River. Roman wrote that the general "thought it urgently necessary to abandon Bowling Green, except as a point of observation, and concentrate as rapidly as possible all readily available troops upon Henry and Donelson, so as to force Grant into a battle in that quarter, with decisive odds against him, and the disadvantage of isolation from immediate support… that our success must lie in following the cardinal principle of war, the swift concentration of our masses against the enemy's exposed fractions… that in war it was 'Nothing venture, nothing win.'"[23]

Stanley F. Horn also admonished Johnston for failing to concentrate at Fort Donelson: "Nashville had not been fortified; the fight to hold it must be made at Fort Donelson. He realized that Bowling Green was no longer tenable; the troops there must fall back on Nashville… Johnston was unwilling to abandon the railway and highway between Bowling Green and Nashville completely, on the score that his main object should be to gain time to remove the ammunition and provisions gathered at Bowling Green, and the immense stores of food and supplies which (against his own advice) had been piled up at Clarksville and Nashville by the Confederate Commissary and Quartermaster Departments."[24]

Horn contended that Johnston "felt that his responsibilities were too great to risk destruction of his army if he let it get penned in between Grant and Buell… Amidst all his strategic difficulties, still if the facts are considered deliberately and dispassionately, the conclusion seems inescapable that in this crisis Johnston did not display the judgment which we would be justified in expecting of his supposed genius. It was painfully obvious that, scattered as they were, his meager forces could not resist such an attack as the superior Federal power could bring against him. Equally obvious, this long-feared attack was at hand; the crisis must be faced at last."[25]

The historian condemned Johnston's conservative strategy: "Unquestionably he had very little to work with. But he acted with an excess of caution. This was no time for caution. It was a time for courage and audacity – and audacity does not seem to have been one of his outstanding qualities. He saw Buell's great threatening army lowering at him in Kentucky and knew that only his little force at Bowling Green stood between it and Nashville. Away to his left he saw his scanty garrison at Columbus, and knew it was all that blocked the way to Northern conquest of the Mississippi. He looked at that narrow neck between Forts Henry and Donelson, and knew they were the only barriers to penetration of the vitals of the South"[26]

Horn then offered an alternative: "One thing was plain: he could not possibly defend all three of these points against a sustained, well-manned attack. The indicated defensive step was to concentrate his fighting power quickly and boldly at some one point, and there attempt to deliver a crushing blow against a segment of the enemy… Fort Donelson seemed the logical place to make a stand in strength, for if it fell, Bowling Green and Columbus would almost automatically follow. But if Grant could be crushed at the fort, Buell would be forced to fall back and defend the Ohio."[27]

T. Harry Williams, concurred with Horn and asserted that "as was often the case, [Beauregard's] strategic instinct was sound. In the initial stage of the Federal move on Donelson, which started on February 12th, Grant advanced with 15,000 men. If Johnston had gone to the fort with the bulk of the troops on the right, he could have confronted Grant with a force, counting the garrison, of 30,000. He could have struck Grant before Buell arrived. With Grant defeated, Buell undoubtedly would have fallen back to defend the Ohio line."[28] Joseph H. Parks also concluded that "had Hardee's 14,000 men been added to the defense at Donelson, Grant might have been defeated."[29]

According to Roman's version of events, Johnston is said to have considered Beauregard's bold proposal, but ultimately rejected it, stating that the Confederates were "not in a condition to risk too much; that if we failed to defeat Grant, we might be crushed between his forces and those of Buell; that, even if victorious over Grant, our own forces would be more or less disorganized, and if Buell, crossing the Big Barren River, above Bowling Green, and then the Cumberland above Nashville, should place himself between us and this latter city, and force us back against the Tennessee River (then open to the Federal gunboats), without the means of crossing or of extricating ourselves therefrom, we would be destroyed or captured, Nashville would fall, and the whole Tennessee and Mississippi valleys would be left unprotected, except by the as yet ill-organized forces of General Polk, at Columbus, which were themselves threatened by greatly superior numbers assembling in southeast Missouri."[30]

Roman maintained that Beauregard refuted Johnston's argument by asserting that "Buell, being without a pontoon train [was] unable to cross the Cumberland between Nashville and Donelson, [and therefore] we could have time to escape from between the Tennessee and Cumberland rivers."[31] Roman also claimed that "General Hardee [concurred with Beauregard's plan], though not with much earnestness. General Johnston, after some discussion, adhered to the objections he had already made to this plan, and gave his own views as to the future operations of the campaign. He being Commander-in-Chief, and responsible for all that might ensue, his views necessarily prevailed."[32]

Yet there is considerable doubt that Beauregard presented such an audacious plan at the Covington House conference. The fact that Johnston informed Benjamin the day after the conference that Beauregard and Hardee were "equally with myself impressed with the necessity of withdrawing our force from this line at once," implies no such protest from Beauregard. In a letter to President Davis several weeks after the meeting, Johnston reported that "when General Beauregard came out, in February, he expressed his surprise at the smallness of my force and was impressed with the danger. I admitted what was so manifest, and laid before him my views for the future, in which he entirely concurred, and sent me a memorandum of our conference, a copy of which I send to you"[33]

Timothy B. Smith noted that a Confederate officer present at the conference "wrote contemporaneously that the Louisianian 'fully approved' the memorandum written on February 7 as well as Johnston's larger plans."[34] Charles P. Roland stressed that "no contemporary documentary evidence proves that Beauregard proposed these measures to Johnston; possibly this was another of the innumerable cases of post-bellum strategy that occupied the twilight years of so many Federal and Confederate generals."[35] However, if Beauregard *had* proposed such a strategy, would it have been possible to implement? Would Johnston have been able to crush Grant as easily as suggested by Roman, Horn, Williams, and Parks? Unfortunately, there were several fatal flaws associated with Beauregard's alleged proposal.

Pontoon bridges
At the time of the Covington House Conference, there was no way that Beauregard could have known that Buell's Army of the Ohio lacked pontoon bridges. The general had only been present in Bowling Green for three days and the inadequate Confederate intelligence service did not provide such information to Johnston or his senior officers. Thus, Beauregard would not have been able to confidently dismiss Johnston's concerns regarding Buell's army crossing the Cumberland River between Nashville and Fort Donelson as portrayed by Roman's account of the conference.

Vulnerability of Nashville
The transfer of the Central Kentucky Army from Bowling Green to the south bank of the Cumberland River would have allowed Buell's army free reign in central Kentucky and resulted in the rapid fall of Nashville, with all its essential depots, machinery, supplies, and military installations. Johnston's son declared that "this movement would have been an

abandonment to Buell of Nashville, the objective point of the Federal campaign... This desperate project, commended by General Beauregard, was exactly what the Union generals were striving, hoping, planning, to compel General Johnston to do."[36] Johnston acknowledged this fact in a letter to President Davis: "Had I wholly uncovered my front to defend Donelson, Buell would have known it and marched directly on Nashville."[37] Roland observed that Beauregard's "plan would have meant abandoning to Buell's massive army the road to Nashville in order to attempt to engage in the center a relatively small segment of the Union forces... If Johnston should fail to annihilate or capture Grant in one terrific stroke, Buell could smite the Confederate army from the rear and destroy it."[38]

Williams's confident declaration that Buell would retreat to the Ohio River in the event of Johnston concentrating his Central Kentucky Army to defeat Grant on the Tennessee or Cumberland River is also dubious. Why would Buell retreat? He had 60,000 troops and all effective opposition to his advance against Bowling Green and Nashville would have been removed. His Army of the Ohio could literally walk into both towns with no threat of danger. Buell had always wanted to capture Nashville, and the removal of Johnston's army would have encouraged him forward rather than backward in a hurried retreat. Even if Grant had been crushed, Buell could have detached 30,000 troops to the Cumberland while reserving 30,000 for the capture of Nashville.

Lack of transportation
A major flaw in Beauregard's alleged plan was that Johnston could not have moved his army to Fort Donelson with the requisite speed. To move the bulk of his soldiers, artillery, equipment, and supplies using the Memphis, Clarksville & Louisville Railroad was impossible. Colonel Robert W. Woolley reported that "there was but one road, and that almost bare of transportation. The locomotives had not been repaired for six months, and many of them lay disabled in the depots. They could not be repaired at Bowling Green, for there is not, I am informed, but one place in the South where a driving wheel can be made, and not one where a whole locomotive can be constructed."[39] This fact was made disturbingly apparent during the withdrawal of the Central Kentucky Army from Bowling Green to

Nashville in February 1862. There were few too locomotives and railcars to transport the army's soldiers after the artillery, munitions, and supplies had been loaded up. Therefore, most of the infantry had to march the 68 miles (109 km) to Nashville in freezing sleet and icy wind. There was clearly no railroad capacity for the rapid movement of 14,000 troops from Bowling Green to the Cumberland River.

Johnston couldn't rely on riverine transportation either. There were few steamers available, as Northern owners had removed their ships from Southern ports at the beginning of the war. Benjamin F. Cooling noted that "some 281 regular and transient packet boats had worked the pre-war Cumberland River, for example, but scarcely a dozen remained available for Johnston's use; probably only three or four boats existed at the end of the year. The remainder of the boats in 1861 were tied up in semiretirement at Edgefield [a suburb of Nashville] ... while most of their captains and crews had long since departed for army service."[40] In practice, only a couple of regiments could be transported from Nashville to Fort Donelson via the Cumberland River with any facility. Then there was the difficult march to Fort Henry to consider. The dirt roads that wended their way up hills and down hollows in the wilderness between Forts Donelson and Henry would have consumed another day to traverse on foot. To further complicate matters, hundreds, if not thousands, of the Bowling Green army were on the sick list and unable to endure hard marching and fighting.

Roland concluded that "if all had gone precisely according to schedule, which with the relatively untrained army and inadequate rail facilities at Johnston's disposal would seem almost beyond belief, he might have been able to close into [Fort Donelson] on the 10th [of February] ... The Confederate army would have another ten miles [16 km] to walk before reaching the outworks of Fort Henry – another half day's march. The column probably could not have covered this distance and deployed for an assault before nightfall of the 11th. Grant very easily could have withdrawn into Fort Henry and established a defensive position. Or he could have retired from the area altogether [using his transports], had he felt it absolutely necessary. He had done so at Belmont when faced with too great odds... He 'who controls the [rivers] is at liberty to take as much or as little of war as he wills.'"[41]

Fort Henry defenses
Finally, Roland asked whether Johnston could have "assaulted a position so nearly surrounded by water? In a letter of February 8 explaining his delay, Grant said: 'At present we are perfectly locked in by high water and bad roads, and prevented from acting offensively as I should like to do. The banks are higher at the water's edge than farther back, leaving a wide margin of low land to bridge over before anything can be done inland. The bad state of the roads will then prevent the transportation of baggage or artillery.' Not until the morning of February 12 was the Union column able to march on Fort Donelson, and then only after constructing a causeway across the water."[42]

Roland observed: "Although Grant initially approached Fort Donelson with only 15,000 men, he had considerably more at his disposal. A force of 2,500 men was left to garrison Fort Henry… And during the night of February 11, before Grant left for Fort Donelson, six regiments arrived on transports to reinforce him… By morning of February 12, Johnston's force of somewhere between 25,000 and 30,000 would have faced an army of approximately 22,500, entrenched in Fort Henry, surrounded by water, with flanks and rear secure on the Tennessee River, and with lines of supply and reinforcement maintained by gunboats and transports… Johnston's chances of destroying him by a *coup de main* appear to have been slight."[43]

Likewise, Johnston's son wrote that "no more fatal plan of campaign could have been proposed. Such a concentration was impracticable within the limits of the time required for success. The Confederates would have been met by a superior force under General Grant, whose position, flanked by the batteries of Fort Henry, covered by gunboats, and to be approached only over causeways not then constructed, was absolutely impregnable. It requires an utter disregard of facts seriously to consider such a project."[44] Indeed, after the battle of the 6th of February, Halleck worked frantically to strengthen Grant's position at Fort Henry. He ordered 8,000 Union reinforcements to the Tennessee River and informed his subordinate on the 8th of February that "shovels and picks will be sent to you to strengthen Fort Henry. The guns should be transferred and arranged so as to resist an attack by land… Some of the guns from Fort Holt will be sent up. Reinforcements will reach you daily. Hold on to Fort Henry at all hazards.

Impress slaves of secessionists in vicinity to work on fortifications. It is of vital importance to strengthen your position as rapidly as possible. When slaves are so impressed, they should be kept under guard and not allowed to communicate with the enemy, nor must they be allowed to escape."[45]

Conclusion

Connelly's assertion that Johnston never considered Fort Donelson as an objective of Grant's army, but rather Columbus, is a reckless statement. The documentary evidence clearly shows that Johnston was aware of the enemy threat to the Cumberland River fortification. Historians who have censured Johnston for failing to concentrate all his available forces at Fort Donelson in order to crush Grant have not recognized the major obstacles to such an operation. There were simply no transport options that could convey the 14,000 men of the Central Kentucky Army from Bowling Green to Fort Donelson in the required time. Even if such a move were possible, Bowling Green and Nashville, along with their mountains of supplies, munitions, and equipment, would have been abandoned to Buell's Federal troops in central Kentucky.

A Confederate offensive against Grant's army at Fort Henry, surrounded as it was by water and protected by gunboats, would have had a remote chance of success. Thus, Beauregard's alleged proposal to restore the integrity of the defensive line in the Western Department via a massive concentration of troops was entirely unrealistic and criticism of Johnston for not implementing it is unwarranted. Peter F. Walker surmised that the defensive plan Johnston proposed at Covington House, and endorsed by Beauregard and Hardee, was "undoubtedly sound: perhaps it was the only effective one, considering the circumstances."[46]

12.
Why did Johnston delegate the defense of the Cumberland River to Floyd?

During the Fort Henry crisis, General Albert Sidney Johnston dispatched approximately 10,000 soldiers to the town of Clarksville on the Cumberland River. This included the commands of Brigadier General John B. Floyd and Brigadier General Simon B. Buckner at Russellville, and Brigadier General Charles Clark at Hopkinsville. Johnston's senior division commander at Bowling Green, Major General William J. Hardee, instructed Floyd, the ranking commander, to "make the dispositions for the defense of Clarksville, Fort Donelson, and the Cumberland River at his own discretion."[1] Floyd was 55 years old, a native of Virginia, and an experienced politician. He had served two terms as a Member of the Virginia House of Delegates, one term as Governor of Virginia from 1849 to 1852, and one term as the Secretary of War in James Buchanan's Cabinet from 1857 to 1860. As a politician, Floyd was considered "shrewd, wary, and adroit."[2] He was Secretary of War during Johnston's time as commander of the Utah Expedition, and the two men had a congenial working relationship. Johnston even named his army's encampment near Salt Lake City in Floyd's honor.

As Secretary of War, Floyd was implicated in the "Abstracted Indian

Bonds" financial scandal and was then accused of deliberately bolstering Federal arsenals in the Southern States with weapons and heavy ordnance in the lead up to the Civil War. Ulysses S. Grant claimed in his memoirs that "Floyd, the Secretary of War, scattered the army so that much of it could be captured when hostilities should commence, and distributed the cannon and small arms from Northern arsenals throughout the South so as to be on hand when treason wanted them."[3] With the onset of the Civil War, Floyd, despite a lack of military education and experience, was commissioned as a major general in the Provisional Army of Virginia. Like the unfortunate Gideon J. Pillow in Tennessee, Floyd's rank was then reduced to brigadier general upon the Provisional Army's incorporation into Confederate service. In May 1861, Floyd assumed command of the brigade-sized Army of Kanawha and led it in the Confederate campaign to reclaim control of western Virginia.

Brigadier General John B. Floyd

Historian Charles Pinnegar observed that "when General Floyd first entered Confederate service, his potential contributions were in organization, loyalty to the cause, and a political reputation around which western Virginians might coalesce. His lack of military experience at the command level was apparent to all. To overcome this deficiency, Floyd initially employed the services of [an] inspector general and drill master."[4] Colonel Henry Heth, the inspector general, sadly remarked that "I soon discovered that my chief was as incapacitated for the work he had undertaken as I would have been to lead an Italian opera."[5] Nevertheless, Heth worked hard to drill and equip the men, even organizing night classes for the officers. Floyd's self-awareness regarding his lack of military experience and his appointment of Heth to remedy the situation was judicious indeed. As a result, the soldiers of the Army of Kanawha went into battle prepared and full of confidence. During the western Virginia campaign of 1861, Floyd won a decisive victory at the battle of Kessler's Cross Lanes on the 26th of August.

His army of 1,800 soldiers surprised and routed a Union regiment of 1,000 men, inflicting 132 casualties for the loss of only 40 of his own.

On the 10th of September, Union Brigadier General William S. Rosecrans attacked Floyd's encampment at Carnifex Ferry with a force of 5,000 men. The Confederates managed to repulse every assault, but Floyd withdrew his army during the night due to the Federal superiority in troops and artillery. Rosecrans suffered 158 casualties compared to Floyd's 32 in this engagement. When General Robert E. Lee assumed overall command of the western Virginia campaign, Floyd proved a troublesome subordinate, failing to effectively cooperate with Brigadier General, and fellow former Governor of Virginia, Henry A. Wise. After the failure of the Confederate campaign to reclaim western Virginia, Floyd's Army of the Kanawha, along with other commands in the region, were dispatched to critical areas in need. The general himself, and 2,500 of his Virginians were ordered to Bowling Green in response to Johnston's repeated appeals for additional troops in the Western Department. The remaining Confederate forces in western Virginia were allocated to the defense of Charleston in South Carolina. When Floyd arrived at Bowling Green, he ranked fourth, after Johnston, General Pierre G.T. Beauregard, and Hardee by virtue of his early date of appointment as a brigadier general.

Floyd's appointment to district command

Larry J. Daniel theorized that Johnston assigned the Cumberland River command to Floyd because he "had been a pre-war ally of Johnston. As Secretary of War, he had strongly, but unsuccessfully, argued that Albert Sidney Johnston, not Joseph E. Johnston, should be [promoted to] quartermaster general." Daniel postulated "whether or not the Fort Donelson command was a conscious reciprocation cannot now be determined."[6] Daniel's assertion has no substance. He must have confused the two Johnstons. In 1860, Major General Winfield Scott presented Secretary of War Floyd with a list of four names as possible candidates for the vacant position: Robert E. Lee, Joseph E. Johnston, Albert S. Johnston, and Charles F. Smith. Floyd preferred J.E. Johnston, and the Virginian received the appointment. Floyd chose J.E. Johnston "because he knew him better than the other nominees, because he admired his record, and because he believed that Johnston would do a good job."[7] Floyd was also the legal guardian of J.E. Johnston's niece and was the brother-in-law of his nephew.

Thomas L. Connelly criticized Johnston for entrusting "a new, untried general in the [Western Department with the] responsibility for the fate of Middle Tennessee."[8] Kendall D. Gott was baffled by Johnston's decision to appoint Floyd to command of the Cumberland River, asserting that "the tragedy is that many men of ability were available. Beauregard and Hardee were both competent generals who clearly outranked [him.]"[9] However, Floyd's appointment was not the result of nepotism, but merely the outcome of seniority of rank. Beauregard's chronic illness and Hardee's refusal to accept an independent command left Floyd as the ranking brigadier general in the Western Department. Hugh L. Bedford, the Inspector of Artillery at Fort Donelson, noted that Johnston's "generals were ready made for him; their commissions were presumptions of merit... he had no alternative but to accept the patents of ability issued to them by the War Department."[10] Johnston could not appoint men of inferior rank, as evidenced by his attempt to assign Major Alexander P. Stewart to Forts Henry and Donelson in the autumn of 1861.

At a personal level, Johnston entertained a high regard for Floyd's abilities as Secretary of War during the Utah Expedition and likely expected these to transfer to independent army command. If Johnston had any concerns regarding Floyd's military inexperience, the fact that Buckner, a West Point graduate and battlefield veteran, accompanied his command provided the necessary reassurance. Buckner should have been able to provide Floyd with sound military and engineering advice. In fact, at the time of his arrival at Bowling Green, Floyd's military credentials looked quite promising. The Virginian had recently been the commander of the Army of Kanawha, and unlike Hardee, did not shirk the responsibility of an independent army command. Johnston may have even read some newspaper articles praising Floyd's recent performance during the western Virginia campaign. After the battle of Kessler's Cross Lanes, the *Richmond Enquirer* reported that "we are also in receipt of the intelligence of a glorious victory achieved by Floyd upon the border of the Kanawha."[11] The *Sunday Delta* declared that "General Floyd led the whole command to the action, and he and his staff were all the time in the midst of the fight... The General himself, calm and composed, rode up to the column and directed the firing of some of the companies who were firing too high."[12]

Floyd also won praise for his stubborn defense at Carnifex Ferry. *The Spirit of the Age* pronounced that "Floyd's gallant little army has a greatly superior force in numbers to cope with and covered itself with glory in repelling its first attack... Floyd's defence was most gallant and his crossing of the ferry under the circumstances deliberate and well directed. His men fought with signal bravery, and their fire was admirably directed."[13] The *Weekly Raleigh Register* crowed that "General Floyd lost not a single man. This result is extraordinary. The battle lasted four hours, and the enemy's loss was heavy, while on our side there were only six men slightly wounded and not one seriously. General Floyd himself was amongst the wounded. A musket ball, at the first fire of the enemy, inflicted a flesh wound just below the elbow, but it occasioned no inconvenience to the General."[14]

President Jefferson Davis and the Confederate government also commended Floyd's actions at Carnifex Ferry. The Secretary of War wrote to Floyd that "I take great pleasure in communicating to you the congratulations of the President, as well as my own, on this brilliant affair [at Carnifex Ferry], in which the good conduct and steady valor of your whole command were so conspicuously displayed."[15] John B. Jones, senior clerk in the War Department, deemed Floyd one of the "brightest lights of the South" along with Beauregard and several other officers.[16] To further emphasize Floyd's sterling reputation at the time of his arrival at Bowling Green, Johnston later wrote to President Davis that "Floyd, Pillow, and Buckner – were high in the opinion of officers and men for skill and courage, and among the best officers of my command. They were popular with the volunteers, and all had seen much service."[17] There was no howl of outrage from Beauregard, Hardee, or the officers and soldiers of the Western Department when Floyd was assigned command of the Cumberland River.

Floyd flounders

The Covington House Conference had determined Confederate strategy for the Western Department after the sudden defeat on the Tennessee River. The fall of Fort Henry enabled Union forces to outflank both Columbus and Bowling Green, and the Confederate armies stationed at those two points were ordered to withdraw to prevent another disaster. After the capture of Brigadier General Lloyd Tilghman, the Fort Henry garrison retreated to Fort Donelson, a site that Johnston, Beauregard, and Hardee had deemed not long tenable. Pillow warned Johnston from Clarksville that "if Donelson should be overcome, we can make no successful stand here without larger force."[18] Fort Donelson's garrison now numbered almost 5,000 men due to the influx of the Fort Henry refugees. Most of Floyd's troops, including Buckner's division, were in transit from Russellville to Clarksville. Johnston advised Pillow that "if your services or Buckner's or both are most important at Donelson, go there."[19] Pillow proceeded to send the troops in Clarksville on to Fort Donelson.

On the 8th of February, Pillow sent Johnston an urgent message: "I shall stand in great need of General Buckner at Donelson and I hope you will send him down at the earliest possible moment."[20] Floyd arrived at Clarksville with his remaining troops early that same morning, and to his surprise, discovered that Pillow had already forwarded on his own two Virginia regiments and one of Buckner's regiments to Fort Donelson. It seemed that the Confederate defense of the Cumberland River would occur at Fort Donelson rather than Clarksville, due to the lack of fortifications at the latter point. Despite this independent command decision by his subordinate, Floyd did not order Pillow to recall the troops back to Clarksville. This may be because he had only just arrived in the town and was yet to familiarize himself with the situation. Pillow had also directed Clark's 2,000-strong Hopkinsville force, now under Colonel T.J. Davidson, to Fort Donelson. Pillow borrowed Clark's horse and accompanied the troops, assuming personal command of the fort early on the 9th of February.

Floyd informed Johnston that "a large proportion of the force has been sent forward to Fort Donelson, and the balance intended for that place are going there as fast as they arrive… I will take every possible means at my command to ascertain the general plan of approach of the enemy…

If the best information I can gather about these ironclad boats be true they are nearly invulnerable, and therefore they can probably go wherever sufficient fuel and depth of water can be found, unless met by opposing gunboats."[21] Alas, there would be no Confederate gunboats available to support Floyd on the Cumberland River. Johnston instructed Floyd that "although the employment of your forces after arriving at Clarksville had been left to your discretion, I deem it proper that you ascertain whether the enemy will hold his force to attack Fort Donelson in conjunction with gunboats or move them against Clarksville direct."[22] Johnston was loath to give Floyd more detailed instructions from his headquarters at Bowling Green, expecting Floyd to examine the situation and use his own initiative. He cautioned Floyd that "I cannot give you specific instructions and place under your command the entire force."[23]

Floyd considered the situation and proposed to strengthen Clarksville. He related to Johnston that "the defenses here amount to about nothing. I think they have mistaken the location of the work upon the river hill about 200 yards [183 m], whilst the one in the bottom is nearly submerged. I think the works should be strengthened here. This place is capable of being made very strong indeed. I wish it was convenient to send here at once a good engineer officer and a sufficient supply of intrenching tools."[24] Floyd's plan was highly impractical considering the lack of time and resources available to the Confederates on the Cumberland River. Unsure of himself, Floyd then begged Johnston to visit him and provide much needed advice: "I wish, if possible, you would come down here, if it were only for a single day. I think in that time you might determine the policy and lines of defense. I will, however, do the best I can and all I can with the means at hand."[25] Unfortunately, Johnston would not leave Bowling Green. Despite the errors made by Major General George B. Crittenden and Brigadier General Felix K. Zollicoffer in eastern Kentucky, the commanding general continued to adhere to President Davis's policy of reliance on the "efficiency of his subordinates."

Johnston's son justified his father's lack of specific instructions to Floyd by declaring that "Floyd was given authority to determine his movements as he might think judicious... events were moving so rapidly, and proper military action was so dependent on accurate information of the enemy, that it was necessary to leave the immediate commander untrammelled."²⁶ Similarly, Charles P. Roland explained that Johnston's delegation of command to Floyd was "faithful to his theory of command. Once he turned over an area to a subordinate, and explained the mission and general instructions, he withheld detailed orders and instead relied upon the subordinate's judgment as to how the mission could best be accomplished at that point. This 'mission concept' of command was partially the result of Johnston's inexperience in commanding a large army on a vast and exposed front. Yet it had much to recommend it. Such a policy worked splendidly with lieutenants of great skill and daring – men like 'Stonewall' Jackson or Nathan Bedford Forrest; with soldiers of less skill, it was disastrous."²⁷

Why did Johnston remain at Bowling Green?

Johnston has been condemned by numerous historians for failing to visit Floyd at Clarksville. This obloquy may be warranted but the extenuating circumstances faced by Johnston must also be considered. The Confederate forces in the Western Department faced two complex challenges in February 1862. The first mission was the defense of the Cumberland River. The Confederate soldiers concentrating at Fort Donelson confronted Grant's 15,000 troops and Flag Officer Andrew H. Foote's fleet of six gunboats. The second mission was the withdrawal of the 14,000 soldiers of the Central Kentucky Army from Bowling Green to Nashville in the face of Brigadier General Don Carlos Buell's 60,000 bluecoats from the Army of the Ohio.

Johnston decided to devote his personal attention to the latter mission, entrusting Floyd, Pillow, and Buckner with the defense of the Cumberland River. After the war, Beauregard suggested that "General Johnston should have left to General Hardee the evacuation of Bowling Green and the conduct of the retreat of its garrison upon Nashville, and should himself have repaired to Donelson, where so critical a struggle was imminent – nay, certain."²⁸ Stanley F. Horn was more adamant, declaring that "if Johnston fully appreciated the importance of the fight to be made at Fort Donelson and the tragic consequences of a defeat – and he did – it is hard to understand why he did not hasten up and assume command. Apart from the benefit of his presence at the scene of the battle, was it not the proper place for the commander of an army whose fate was at stake in pitched battle?"[29]

Horn then argued: "Could not the uncontested retreat of Hardee's division from Bowling Green have been managed by Hardee himself without Johnston's being on hand? Do history's pages record a similar picture of a commanding general marching leisurely off with a retreating column while nearby the greater portion of the army girds for a life-and-death battle under inefficient and inexperienced underlings?"[30] Likewise, Timothy B. Smith noted that "if he saw the delaying action at Fort Donelson as so critical, indeed the key to Hardee's escape, perhaps Johnston should have made it his top personal priority."[31] So why did the general choose to personally supervise the retreat of the Central Kentucky Army from Bowling Green instead of the defense of the Cumberland River? There were several important reasons.

Misleading intelligence
On the 8th of February, Johnston received some disturbing information from Buckner, who was still at Russellville: "Messenger just in from Louisville. Opinion there that [Grant's] expedition up Cumberland and Tennessee chiefly a diversion, derived from opinion of a member of Buell's staff."[32] This intelligence suggested that Grant's movement was merely a feint and that Buell's large Army of the Ohio was preparing to launch a major assault against the Bowling Green fortifications. The report also noted that Grant's army at Fort Henry numbered no more than 12,000 men. It was not an intimidating force. The Confederate troops concentrating on the Cumberland River numbered about 16,000 inclusive of the Fort Donelson garrison and would also enjoy the benefit of fortifications. The ability of Floyd, Pillow, and Buckner to conduct a successful holding operation in such circumstances seemed likely. In contrast, the evacuation of Bowling Green when outnumbered four to one appeared the more hazardous of the two assignments.

Strong leadership required
Johnston's Central Kentucky Army would have to undertake a retrograde movement in wintery conditions with Buell's army only a couple of days march away. Historian Gregory P. Liedtke stated that "few military opera-

tions are as hazardous as conducting a withdrawal in the face of an enemy. The movement of troops from one line of defense to the next exposes them to attacks at the very moment they are least prepared to counter them." Liedtke observed that "troops must have a high degree of confidence in themselves and their leaders to resist their own fears – of being left behind, trapped, caught, or killed... Leaders at all levels must be stern with their men while simultaneously exuding calm and confidence. Planning and cooperation must be worked out well beforehand to avoid confusion. Even the smallest glitch could result in panic and disaster."[33]

Not willing to risk the safety of the army to a self-doubting subordinate, Johnston felt that he must remain with the principal army in the Western Department to ensure its safe removal. Johnston's senior officer, Hardee, shunned independent command and was prone to gloom and despondency. In February 1862, Hardee wrote to his female friend: "In my judgment nothing can save us except the presence of the President, who ought to come here, assume command, and call on people to rally to his standard. We have lost Kentucky and may lose Tennessee."[34] The following month, Hardee lamented that "I have been more broken down in the last ten days than at any other time in my life... This is the darkest hour of my fortune."[35] This was clearly not the man to hold a retreating army together.

Hardee simply lacked the resilience and stoicism of Johnston. After the fall of Fort Donelson, Governor Isham G. Harris recalled: "I was with [Johnston] when the telegram announcing the surrender of the Confederate forces at Donelson was received, and had occasion to admire the philosophic heroism with which he met, not only the disaster, but the unjust censure and complaints of both army and people; the coolness and energy with which he set about the work of reorganizing the remnant of his army and the establishment of a new line of defense."[36] Hardee was not capable of such an imperturbable response which was essential to the successful withdrawal of an army in the face of an overwhelming enemy force. One author noted that "Hardee was a man of less gravity, and of a lower tone of character in every respect than Johnston."[37]

Johnston's personal leadership at Bowling Green would help maintain discipline and confidence among his troops, reassuring them that this was a strategic movement rather than a panicked flight. A retreat, especially one under pressure, can easily turn into a rout if not handled carefully. Johnston understood that if the withdrawal was not executed properly, his army could be cut off and destroyed – a disaster that could cripple Confederate operations in the Western theater. Given the stakes, he felt that his personal presence was necessary to ensure everything proceeded smoothly. The commanding general's presence with the Central Kentucky Army would also discourage desertion, a common problem when armies withdraw in the face of superior forces.

Logistical challenges
Johnston had to consider the vast quantities of supplies, artillery, ammunition, and equipment at Bowling Green that required immediate removal to Nashville and other points further south. Even if successful in their withdrawal, the troops of the Central Kentucky Army would then be required to rapidly construct the neglected fortifications around Nashville before Buell's army converged on the city. This was a significant challenge for exhausted and demoralized troops, requiring confident and firm leadership. There were also the enemy warships on the Cumberland River to consider. On the 9th of February, Johnston's chief of staff issued instructions to the local commander at Nashville: "The general is anxious that the experiment… in blocking the Cumberland should be made promptly. He orders you to procure anything in the way of tools – materials and boats he may need by requisition on Major [Vernon K.] Stevenson and put them at his disposal."[38]

Enemy reaction
It was inevitable that Union spies would discover Johnston's repositioning to the Cumberland River, and this could have served as the catalyst for a rapid Federal advance on Bowling Green, much like the effect of Beauregard's reported arrival in the Western Department on the Fort Henry offensive. Buell's Army of the Ohio may have been emboldened to immediately strike the Central Kentucky Army in its most vulnerable period.

Conclusion

Floyd's appointment to the command of the Cumberland River was not based on nepotism, as suggested by Daniel, but rather seniority. Connelly's criticism of Johnston for the appointment is baseless since the general's two ranking subordinates, Beauregard and Hardee, were both ruled out due to illness and an unwillingness to assume independent command, respectively. Floyd was simply the next ranking candidate in the Western Department, and in February 1862, his reputation as a military commander was at its zenith. However, Floyd's vacillation and request for Johnston to visit the Cumberland River and instruct him as to the correct course of action should have alarmed the departmental commander. Unfortunately, Johnston adhered to President Jefferson Davis's direction to rely on the efficiency of his subordinates and did not provide specific advice to the struggling general. Perhaps Johnston thought that the West Point educated Buckner would be sufficient for Floyd's needs? This was a reasonable conclusion at the time, but it would turn out to be a fatally flawed assumption.

Horn's claim that Johnston's decision to personally supervise the withdrawal of the Central Kentucky Army from Bowling Green was shameful is not supported in view of the circumstances. There was misleading intelligence regarding the size of Grant's army, the Central Kentucky Army required strong leadership to ensure a safe and orderly retreat, and enemy spies would have detected Johnston's movement to the Cumberland River, possibly spurring on an immediate advance against Bowling Green. If the Central Kentucky Army had been intercepted and defeated by Buell's forces, then the magnitude of that misfortune would have equalled that of the fall of Fort Donelson for the Confederacy. Historians such as Connelly and Horn would likely have blamed Johnston for dashing off to Fort Donelson and abandoning the vital Bowling Green sector to the "incompetent" Hardee.

13.

Why did Johnston reinforce Fort Donelson if it was untenable?

Arriving at Fort Donelson on the 9th of February 1862, Brigadier General Gideon J. Pillow issued a confident proclamation that was at variance with the plan formulated by General Albert Sidney Johnston, General Pierre G.T. Beauregard, and Major General William J. Hardee at Covington House. Pillow announced to the troops that he had assumed "command of the forces at this place. He relies with confidence upon the courage and fidelity of the brave officers and men under his command to maintain the post. Drive back the ruthless invader from our soil and again raise the Confederate flag over Fort Henry."[1] Not all were impressed. Lieutenant Colonel Randal W. McGavock of the 10th Tennessee wrote in his diary: "I regret very much that General Pillow has been placed in command as I have no confidence in him as an officer."[2]

Major Jeremy F. Gilmer was also at Fort Donelson, having escaped the capitulation at Fort Henry. He reported to Johnston that "the attack expected here is a combined one, gunboats by water and a land force in the rear. The greatest danger, in my opinion, is from the gunboats, which appear to be well protected from our shot... With the preparations that are now being made here I feel much confidence that we can make a successful resistance against a land attack. The attack by water will be more difficult to meet; still, I hope for success here also. I do not think it practicable to establish a boom across the Cumberland River during the freshet that now exists... We are making herculean efforts to strengthen our parapets – making narrow embrasures with sandbags, and if we can have ten days, we hope to make bomb-proofs over the guns."[3]

Johnston had not explicitly ordered Brigadier General John B. Floyd to reinforce Fort Donelson with the 8,000 troops he commanded at Russellville. The general had sent Floyd and his men, plus Brigadier General Charles Clark's Hopkinsville garrison, to Clarksville and it was up to Floyd to determine the disposition of the troops on the Cumberland River. It was Pillow who had acted unilaterally to concentrate the bulk of the soldiers at Fort Donelson, and by the 10th of February, the Tennessean had become consumed with the task of strengthening Fort Donelson's defenses. His spirits were buoyant. Pillow informed Floyd that he was "pushing the work on my river batteries day and night; also, on my field works and defensive line in the rear... I will never surrender [Fort Donelson], and with God's help I mean to maintain it."[4]

Less than a third of the three miles (4.8 km) of rifle pits surrounding the fort had been completed when Pillow first arrived, and he worked with a fury to fortify the landward defenses. The Fort Donelson garrison now numbered about 10,000 men, augmented by the reinforcements flowing in from Clarksville. Floyd did not interfere with Pillow's activities and positioned himself at Cumberland City, about halfway between Clarksville and Fort Donelson. On the 11th of February, Johnston reiterated Hardee's previous order to Floyd, stating: "I give you full authority to make all the dispositions of your troops for the defense of Fort Donelson, Clarksville, and the Cumberland you may think proper."[5]

Floyd continues to flounder

Floyd agonised over his strategy for the Cumberland River, vacillating between Clarksville, Cumberland City, and Fort Donelson as the correct base for the defense. His senior subordinates were also conflicted. Pillow was busily strengthening and reinforcing Fort Donelson while Buckner preferred to defend Cumberland City. Johnston became exasperated by Floyd's dithering between the locations and sent an admonishing telegraph: "Twice today I have telegraphed to you to command all the troops and use your judgment."⁶ Floyd was stirred into action and decided that Cumberland City should be the defensive base. He rationalized that "the position at Cumberland City is better; for there, the railroad diverges from the river, which would afford some little facility for transportation in case of necessity; and from thence the open country southward towards Nashville is easily reached."⁷ However, this proposition was dependent on the overburdened railroad network in Tennessee.

Floyd proposed to withdraw most of the Fort Donelson garrison, including his brigade of Virginians and Buckner's men, to Cumberland City. He would then sacrifice Pillow and a token garrison of a few thousand troops to Brigadier General Ulysses S. Grant's army to buy some time to fortify Cumberland City and attempt to obstruct the river. Buckner wholeheartedly supported Floyd's plan and arrived at Fort Donelson on the evening of the 11th of February to retrieve his and Floyd's troops. McGavock confided to his diary that "Buckner reached here last night from Bowling Green with a portion of his brigade. I do not know how he and Pillow will get along together, considering the dressing the former gave the latter several years ago when Pillow was trying to get into the Senate of the U.S. Pillow is a vindictive man and not likely to forget the matter."⁸ Buckner must have felt much glee at consigning Pillow to a fate like that of Brigadier General Lloyd Tilghman at Fort Henry.

Ultimately, Floyd's and Buckner's Cumberland City plan was unrealistic. A few thousand soldiers under Pillow at Fort Donelson could not hope to hold off Grant's 15,000 to 25,000 infantry for very long. Cumberland City had no existing defensive preparations and the time required to construct fortifications or attempt to obstruct the flooded river was clearly not available. Then there was the mulish Pillow. He did not want any of his troops removed from Fort Donelson. The Tennessean had already stockpiled masses of food and supplies at the wharf at Dover, a small town close to the fort. Buckner recalled that "I reached Fort Donelson on the night of February 11th, with orders from General Floyd to direct General Pillow to send back at once to Cumberland City the troops which had been designated… General Pillow declined to execute the order of which I was the bearer until he should have a personal interview with General Floyd."⁹

Pillow dashed off a telegram to Johnston: "If I can retain my present force, I can hold my position... Let me retain Buckner for the present. If now withdrawn, will invite an attack. Enemy cannot pass this place without exposing himself to flank-attack. If I am strong enough to take field, he cannot ever reach here; nor is it possible for him to subsist on anything in the country to pass over, nor can he possibly bring his subsistence with him. With Buckner's force, I can hold my position. Without it, cannot long."[10] Johnston, about a hundred miles away at Bowling Green, delegated the responsibility of the placement of Buckner and his division back to Floyd: "I do not know the wants of General Pillow, nor yours, nor the position of General Buckner. You do. You have [Pillow's] dispatch. Decide."[11] Floyd remained unsure, and Pillow departed for Cumberland City via steamer on the morning of the 12th of February to discuss the situation in person, leaving Buckner temporarily in command of Fort Donelson.

Just after 11am, the *Carondelet*, appeared in the Cumberland River and attempted to provoke the gunners at Fort Donelson into revealing the positions of their batteries. The ironclad fired ten shells from its bow guns at a long range, but the Confederates did not respond, and the warship drifted back down the river. Pillow heard the rumble of gunfire from Fort Donelson, halted his steamer, and dispatched a telegram to Floyd informing him that he was turning back. Pillow wrote that the "gunboat and transports passed up 10 o'clock last night. I have heard ten heavy discharges of artillery. I leave immediately for Donelson. Shall suspend order for Buckner to fall back at present," and then forwarded a copy of the telegram to Johnston and Governor Isham G. Harris. Buckner reported that at "about noon General Pillow returned and resumed command, it having been determined to reinforce the garrison with the remaining troops from Cumberland City and Clarksville."[13]

In the evening, Johnston telegraphed Floyd at Cumberland City: "My information from Donelson is that a battle will be fought in the morning. Leave a small force at Clarksville, and take the remainder, if possible, to Donelson tonight. Take all the ammunition that can be spared from Clarksville."[14] Floyd responded in the early hours of the 13th of February: "I *anticipated* your order which overtook me here. Shipping the balance of the troops from [Cumberland City] to Fort Donelson. I will reach there before day, leaving a small guard here."[15] Johnston had now committed all the Confederate forces on the Cumberland River, approximately 16,000 men, to the defense of Fort Donelson.

The concentration at Fort Donelson

Johnston's decision to reinforce the Fort Donelson garrison seemed at variance with the strategy for the Western Department that he formulated with Beauregard and Hardee at the Covington House conference on the 7th of February 1862. Although not explicitly stated in his message to the Secretary of War, it is assumed that the generals intended any action at Fort Donelson to consist merely of a holding action, designed to purchase time for the withdrawal of the Central Kentucky Army from Bowling Green to Nashville. If this interpretation is correct, then the reinforcement of the Fort Donelson garrison to a size larger than that of Johnston's own Central Kentucky Army or Major General Leonidas Polk's Columbus garrison appears to be an exceedingly odd action by the commanding general. Floyd arrived at Fort Donelson on the morning of the 13th of February and assumed command of this comparatively large body of Confederate troops. But for what purpose?

Historian Matthew F. Steele postulated that "Johnston, like Grant, believed [Flag Officer Andrew H.] Foote's gunboats would... be able to reduce Donelson. The query suggests itself, then, why did Johnston order Floyd to take his detachment to Fort Donelson? The answer is, Johnston did not expect Floyd to shut his army up within fieldworks, to be besieged. Fort Donelson was only a little bastioned work, less than 500 yards [457 m] in its longest dimension. It was this work that Johnston expected Foote's gunboats to knock down. The troops ordered thither were expected to oppose General Grant's army outside of the fort. General Johnston never supposed that they would place their backs to the river and build a trap of breastworks around themselves."[16]

Thomas L. Connelly suggested that Johnston disregarded the threat of the Union infantry and focused only on the ironclads of Foote's Western Flotilla. He wrote that "after the first shock of the report that Donelson was expecting an attack, he had blindly thrown troops into the area around Clarksville, thinking that the real advance would be there... Totally confused... he was still unwilling to believe the infantry force at Henry was moving to attack. There is no evidence that during this critical period he ever realized that the real danger to Donelson might be from the land side. Hence, on February 7 he ordered Pillow to take his troops to the fort, hold it as long as possible, and then retreat to Nashville, as if the Yankee land force did not exist. Blinded to a fact that he did not want to accept, Johnston saw only one side of the danger at Donelson – the river."[17]

The historian argued that Johnston "became convinced that the main threat to the fort was the Federal fleet reported to be steaming up the Cumberland, and for him defense became a question of whether the fort could hold out against the gunboats. At first, he did not think that the fleet could be stopped and issued orders for Hardee to fall back to Nashville. Johnston's strange belief that Donelson would be safe if the gunboats could be stopped perhaps explains why he ordered troops there even after he stated on February 7 that the fort was not long tenable. To him, 'untenable' meant not being able to withstand gunboats."[18] Similarly, Steven E. Woodworth concluded that Johnston "believed the Federals would take Fort Donelson with gunboats alone, without the need for land forces. If this were so, the infantry he was sending would be of no use. Perhaps he intended them to ensure that the garrison's retreat was not cut off. Perhaps he was not quite sure what they would do but thought they might be of some assistance."[19] If it were true that the general was only concerned about the enemy ironclads as posited by Connelly and Woodworth, then why would he order so many infantry reinforcements to Fort Donelson? How could these men assist in repelling Foote's flotilla? Musket balls could not penetrate the plated armor of the ironclads. Clearly, the infantry was there to engage the Union land forces under Grant. Timothy B. Smith correctly concluded that Connelly's theory "seems highly improbable and not borne out by evidence."[20]

T. Harry Williams was also perplexed by Johnston's decision: "His actions almost defy rational analysis. Having gone on record as believing Donelson to be untenable, he sent at least 12,000 reinforcements to the fort. These were not enough to stop Grant but were too many to place in a possible trap."[21] Williams concluded that "Johnston was moving temporarily in a fog of mental paralysis induced by the crisis he was facing."[22] Charles P. Roland, usually sympathetic to Johnston's actions, asked: "What defense, if any, was to be made at [Fort Donelson?] In deciding this question, Johnston made the most grievous error of military judgment of his career." Roland argued that "in spite of his previous declaration that Fort Donelson could not be held, and of his plan for a general withdrawal from the Kentucky-Tennessee line, he made the fatal decision to reinforce the doomed fort… Increasingly troubled by the prospect of sacrificing Fort Donelson without a determined stand, Johnston in effect now reversed his earlier strategy and resolved to send Pillow, Floyd, and Buckner to the defense of the fort."[23]

Smith claimed that Johnston "did not respond well, vacillating between weak leadership commensurate with his own chess-playing personality and taking major gambles in more of a poker-playing style that would risk entire wings of his army." He thought that Floyd's Cumberland City proposal or Beauregard's alleged concentration proposal were the most appropriate courses of action for the situation on the Cumberland River. Smith declared that "Johnston would have been better served to leave only the minutest force to fight [at] the fort as long as they could or to go in with all he had to make a sure thing of the defense. Johnston did neither and split the halves." However, as discussed in chapter eleven, both options were unrealistic. Yet Smith concluded that "matters were moving so fast in this high-stakes gambling game that Johnston simply did not have the needed time to think through his options or responses, as was the custom of the self-proclaimed methodical chess-player."[24]

Johnston's altered strategy

Despite the criticism from prominent historians regarding Johnston's decision to reinforce Fort Donelson, a position he had declared untenable on the 7th of February, there is substantial evidence that the general changed his mind regarding the tenability of the fort over the subsequent days.

Buckner's intelligence

The intelligence received from Buckner on the 8th of February that indicated that Grant's "expedition up the Cumberland and Tennessee [was] chiefly a diversion" also stated that "the entire land force on the two rivers was estimated at 12,000.[25] Thus, it was believed that Grant's army was relatively small, and the Confederate forces concentrating at Fort Donelson would outnumber the Federals by another third. Such favorable odds would have led Johnston to consider that rather than merely holding Fort Donelson for a time, Floyd could win a decisive victory on the Cumberland River and even attempt to reclaim Fort Henry and control of the Tennessee River.

Vulnerability of the ironclads
Several reports from the Fort Henry survivors began to trickle through to Bowling Green which suggested that the Federal ironclads were not so invincible after all. On the 10th of February, Gilmer reported that "the effect of our shot at Fort Henry was not sufficient to disable [the ironclads], or any one of them, so far as I have been able to ascertain. This was due, I think, in a great measure, to the want of skill in the men who served the guns, and not to the invulnerability of the boats themselves."[26] On the 11th of February, Floyd sent a report to Johnston describing the considerable damage suffered by the Union ironclads during the battle of Fort Henry. Johnston was elated by the new information and responded: "Your report of the effect of our shot at Henry should encourage the troops and ensure our success. If [at] long range we could do so much damage, with the necessary short range on the Cumberland [we] should *destroy* their boats."[27] The Cumberland River was far narrower than the Tennessee River, and its approach to Fort Donelson was long and straight. This feature would enable the Confederate artillerists to have an excellent view and shorter range of fire against the enemy warships.[28]

In addition, Fort Donelson had been constructed on an elevation overlooking the Cumberland River, so its guns could fire downwards on the more vulnerable decks of the ironclads. This was a major advantage. The practically submerged condition of Fort Henry during the battle of the 6th of February meant that its cannons were level with the warships, and only able to strike the heavily protected bows of the ironclads.[29] This would not be the case on the Cumberland River. Fort Donelson possessed several cannons capable of wreaking much damage on the Federal warships, primarily a ten-inch Columbiad and a rifled 32-pounder. The other guns, the eight smoothbore 32-pounders, an eight-inch howitzer, and two nine-pounders, were not capable of penetrating iron plating but could inflict damage via concussive impacts and lucky shots entering portholes and other gaps in the armor. The Confederates could feel more confident about their prospects at Fort Donelson compared to Fort Henry.

Johnston's message to Bragg
There is a message from Major General Braxton Bragg which has been repeatedly overlooked by historians when discussing the Fort Donelson campaign. On the 12th of February, Bragg wrote to a subordinate that "General A.S. Johnston, from whom I heard yesterday, feels confident of holding Fort Donelson and driving the enemy from the Tennessee soon."[30] Bragg's statement reveals that Johnston hoped not only for Fort Donelson's enduring defense, but also for a Confederate offensive to reclaim Fort Henry. On the 18th of March, Johnston explained his strategy at Fort Donelson to President Jefferson Davis: "I determined to fight for Nashville at Donelson, and gave the best part of my army to do it, retaining only 14,000 men to cover my front, and giving 16,000 to defend Donelson... I had made every disposition for the defense of the fort my means allowed, and the troops were among the best of my forces... When [Floyd's] force was detached, I was in hopes that such dispositions would have been made as would have enabled the forces to defend the fort or withdraw without sacrificing the army."[31] There was no mention of a mere holding action. Johnston had hoped for victory on the Cumberland.

Johnston's message to Floyd
On the 14th of February, during the actual battle for Fort Donelson, Johnston sent a message to Floyd stating that "if you lose the fort, bring your troops to Nashville if possible."[32] Had Johnston intended to abandon Fort Donelson all along then the "if" qualifier would not have been used. He would have said: "*when* you withdraw from the fort." Floyd's report of the battle, written on the 27th of February, also made no mention of a holding action. The Virginian stated that Johnston's "order of the 12th of this month... directed me to repair at once, with what force I could command, to the support of the garrison at Fort Donelson... Measures had been already taken by Brigadier General Pillow, then in command, to render our resistance to the attack of the enemy as effectual as possible."[33]

Nashville headquarters
Timothy B. Smith related that Johnston "travelled on February 13 to Edgefield, directly across the Cumberland River from Nashville. There he made his headquarters, outfitting it with newly bought furniture."[34] This action indicates that Johnston intended to remain in Nashville for the foreseeable future. By choosing to set up headquarters in Edgefield, Johnston was preparing Nashville to serve as his new base of operations after withdrawing from Bowling Green. He had confidence in Floyd's ability to win a victory on the Cumberland River, which would ensure the safety of Nashville from that direction. If Fort Donelson was successfully defended, it would protect Nashville's approach via the Cumberland River and allow the Confederate army to stabilize its defensive line against Buell's Army of the Ohio. Later that March, Johnston explained to Richmond that "the fall of Fort Donelson compelled me to withdraw the remaining forces under my command from the north bank of the Cumberland and to abandon the defense of Nashville, which *but for that disaster* it was my intention to protect to the utmost."[35]

Conclusion

Connelly's assertion that Johnston failed to recognize the threat from the Union land forces is a reckless statement. As discussed in the previous chapter, documentary evidence shows that that the general was keenly aware of Grant's army advancing upon Fort Donelson. The criticisms from other historians that Johnston was indecisive and sent a significant proportion of his army to Fort Donelson even though he believed it was untenable can be countered by an examination of the facts. Buckner's intelligence relating to the comparatively small size of Grant's army plus the new reports concerning the vulnerability of the ironclads were both instrumental in altering Johnston's assessment regarding the tenability of Fort Donelson. By at least the 11th of February, he had changed his mind regarding prospects for Confederate success at Fort Donelson. His communication to Bragg and resolution to remain at Nashville confirms such a transformation.

Johnston's altered strategic view opened three main possibilities for the Fort Donelson campaign. In the first, and ideal scenario, Grant's expedition would be defeated, forced to retreat, Fort Donelson secured, and Fort Henry reclaimed. Curiously enough, this was Pillow's avowed purpose all along and would restore the integrity of the Western Department. Johnston's message to Bragg confirms that this scenario was the one he was hoping to achieve. In a second scenario, Grant's expedition would be repelled, and Fort Donelson secured, providing Johnston with more time to build fortifications at Nashville using the men from the Central Kentucky Army as his labor force. The defensive plan agreed upon at Covington House was now the third, and least desirable, scenario. The Confederates would delay the Union advance at Fort Donelson long enough to ensure the successful retrograde movement of the Central Kentucky Army to Nashville. They would then abandon the fort and withdraw to the Tennessee capital themselves, possibly affording Johnston a small amount of time to fortify Nashville and obstruct the Cumberland River below the city.

It is evident that Johnston now had confidence in the viability of the first two options and was optimistic enough to discuss such an outcome with Bragg. His belief was not fanciful, since Floyd's army was comparable in size to Grant's on the 12th of February and outnumbered it for most of the 13th of February. Johnston's assessment of the effectiveness of Fort Donelson's artillery against the enemy gunboats would also be vindicated in the coming days. It is entirely reasonable to suggest that without the blunders of Floyd, Pillow, and Buckner during the battle of Fort Donelson, Johnston's forces could have defeated or repelled the Union offensive on the Cumberland River.

14.

Was Johnston responsible for the blunders at Fort Donelson?

It took almost a week for Brigadier General Ulysses S. Grant's army to move from Fort Henry to Fort Donelson due to the inclement weather and flooded terrain. Leaving a brigade under Brigadier General Lew Wallace at the submerged Fort Henry, Grant's army of about 15,000 troops marched unopposed the twelve miles (19 km) on the narrow dirt roads and arrived outside Fort Donelson on the 12th of February 1862. The Union forces partially encircled the fortress and waited for Flag Officer Andrew H. Foote's ironclads to steam up the Cumberland River. Brigadier General John B. Floyd arrived at Fort Donelson on the morning of the 13th of February, much to the annoyance of Brigadier General Gideon J. Pillow, who had been working feverishly to strengthen Fort Donelson against the impending Union attack. Floyd later reported that Pillow "had, with activity and industry, pushed forward the defensive works towards completion."[1]

Pillow accompanied Floyd on his tour of inspection, but retained an air of authority, believing himself to be the *de facto* commander at Fort Donelson. One Confederate soldier recalled that "General Floyd was present, but seemed not to be exercising command, General Pillow was giving orders and would occasionally mention one of them to General Floyd and explain it to him. Whence I inferred that General Pillow was in command."[2] In the coming days, Floyd's preference to remain at his headquarters at Dover allowed Pillow to exert tactical control over his army on the battlefield. This confused command situation was further clouded by the presence of Brigadier General Simon B. Buckner. Antagonistic to Pillow, and in a deep gloom stemming from his series of personal misfortunes, Buckner had no interest in being at Fort Donelson. As the only West Point trained officer, he should have served as Floyd's principal military advisor during the battle for the fort, but his pessimism and lack of initiative would infect the Confederate high command and contribute significantly to the disaster on the Cumberland River.

Charles P. Roland declared that "the story of the short-lived defense of Fort Donelson against Grant can hardly be matched in the annals of warfare. It is one of courage and timidity, of decisiveness and vacillation, of brilliance and stupidity – a tactical comedy of errors turned into high tragedy for Johnston and for the South."[3]

Several decades after the battle of Fort Donelson, Hugh L. Bedford, former Confederate Artillery Inspector at the post, pondered: "Is Johnston fairly chargeable with the blunders of his generals, in allowing themselves to be cooped in temporary trenches until reinforcements to the enemy could come up the Cumberland?"[4] Historian Kendall D. Gott suggested that "of the Confederate commanders involved, it is Albert Sidney Johnston who deserves the harshest criticisms."[5] What command decisions led to the catastrophe at Fort Donelson? Was Johnston responsible?

The first mistake: Lack of aggression

Most surprisingly, Pillow and Buckner failed to obstruct Grant's march from Fort Henry to Fort Donelson. The 15,000-strong Union army departed Fort Henry on the morning of the 12th of February after constructing a causeway over the floodwaters surrounding the Tennessee River bastion. The tract of land that Grant's army had to traverse between the forts was ideal for an ambush. One Confederate soldier involved in the retreat from Fort Henry wrote that "we waded creeks – plunged mudholes, ascended mountains, and crossed ravines."[6] This was highly defensible terrain, and one Federal engineer gleefully observed that "the roads had not been obstructed in any manner by the rebels."[7] Pillow was too absorbed with strengthening the Fort Donelson fortifications to consider a proactive movement. His complete lack of effort in defending the twelve miles (19 km) of wilderness between the two forts was a serious oversight. At this time, the Confederate garrison numbered almost 13,000 men, more than enough to set up ambuscades along the primitive roads.

Historian Matthew F. Steele observed that "a skilful and aggressive leader… would surely have taken advantage of the thick woods to strike the Federal columns in flank on their way across country."[8] Arndt M. Stickles declared that "no student of the battle can explain why the Confederates, who had an army at least equal to that of the Union forces on the 12th and 13th, did not risk a battle with Grant while he was advancing from the west. No gunboat was yet in sight, a force sufficiently large could have been left in charge of the river batteries, and, had the Confederates been defeated in a battle on the outside, they could still have retreated into their fortifications."[9] Benjamin F. Cooling proclaimed that "in so many ways, Henry-Donelson was a brilliantly missed opportunity for the Confederacy to smash an uncertain Union strategic thrust by an untested Yankee general."[10] Timothy B. Smith wrote that "it is remarkable that Grant's forces were able to march right up to the defenses of Fort Donelson on February 12."[11]

Floyd maintained this passivity when he assumed command on the morning of the 13th of February. With 16,000 soldiers available, he apparently did not consider the opportunity to attack the numerically inferior enemy. He blithely allowed the Union army to encircle the Fort Donelson entrenchments. Grant's biographer observed that there was "no effort to molest Grant, allowing him to continue the investment at his leisure – a blunder almost equal to that of opposing no obstacle to the march from Fort Henry."[12] Steele noted that at this time, "Lew Wallace's Union division had not yet landed. Floyd's command was then about equal in number to the Federals in line, and he had every advantage in position. If he had attacked the Union line boldly that day, he would have had an excellent chance of winning a victory."[13]

Johnston, as an aggressive commander, would have expected Floyd or Pillow to seize the opportunity to strike Grant's army on the 12th or 13th of February. He should have issued an explicit order to ensure such an action took place but failed to do. Gott observed that "in the command culture of the day, Johnston gave Floyd wide latitude as to how he would deploy his forces... But Floyd needed specific instructions on just what was expected of him. A review of Johnston's dispatches shows a presumption of a determined defense at Fort Donelson but nothing more. The novice Floyd needed far more guidance than that."[14] Steele argued that "the defense of Fort Donelson proper ought to have been left to its own little garrison. The army assembled there ought to have manoeuvred to draw Grant's army away from the fort. If it made breastworks, it ought to have placed them so as to cover its line of retreat, the Wynn's Ferry-Charlotte Road. General Pillow was responsible for the position of the Confederate fieldworks; they were built while he was in command."[15]

Perhaps Johnston felt that an explicit order was not necessary since he had already outlined such a strategy in the past. In November 1861, Johnston sent a message to Pillow while the Tennessean was in temporary command of Major General Leonidas Polk's Mississippi Valley District: "Fort Columbus being completed, your force will now be free to manoeuvre in reference to the movements of the enemy, and to act as a corps of observation to prevent the siege of the place, and should be so handled as to avoid being caught between the enemy and the river and surrounded and cut off from the magazine and reinforcements."[16] Johnston emphasized such mobility to his subordinates as the enabler to initiate offensive actions against an enemy force and as a preventative measure to avoid having their own army trapped in an encircled fortification. It was a lesson in proactive generalship that Pillow should have remembered and applied at Fort Donelson. Instead, on the 12th and 13th of February, the Tennessean timidly allowed Grant to surround Fort Donelson and trap the Confederate garrison against the Cumberland River.

The opportunity soon passed. Grant's army received significant reinforcements during the night of the 13th of February after Wallace's reserve brigade of 2,500 men at Fort Henry was ordered to Fort Donelson. It was then augmented by troops loaned from Brigadier General Don Carlos Buell's Army of the Ohio to form a third division of 10,000 men. Twelve transports deposited these reinforcements at Bear Creek Landing at about 10pm, bringing Grant's strength up to approximately 25,000 troops. Floyd received word of the Union reinforcements and informed

Johnston that "the enemy have reached the ground near the fort with eight or ten gunboats, I am uncertain which, and fifteen transports reported to have on board near 20,000 men. They are now landing. This makes their force nearly 40,000 strong."[17] This exaggeration of Grant's numbers contributed to the pessimism that enveloped Floyd and Buckner for the remainder of the campaign.

The second mistake: Pillow's aborted breakout

During the night of the 13th of February, temperatures plummeted to 10°F (-12°C) and a blizzard dumped about three inches (8 cm) of snow over Fort Donelson. At about 11am the next day, Floyd convened a council of war in his headquarters at Dover. The senior officers decided that with the arrival of heavy enemy reinforcements, they should open an escape route from Fort Donelson. Overland was the preferred option since the Union ironclads were a threat to any operations on the Cumberland River. Floyd decided to attack Brigadier General John A. McClernand's division on the Confederate left to break open a corridor before Wallace's reinforcements were fully embedded in the siege line. If successful, the Confederates would then march to the town of Charlotte, in the direction of Nashville. Just after 1pm, Pillow's brigades advanced towards McClernand's division but received an annoying fire from enemy sharpshooters. After a brief engagement, Pillow aborted the operation. He may have felt that his troops were too fatigued by the freezing weather. Or perhaps that there was not enough time left in the day to exploit any success.

Floyd remained in his headquarters during the entire action and was allegedly irate with Pillow for abandoning the offensive. One of Floyd's staff claimed that "here was, in my humble opinion, the fatal mistake at Fort Donelson."[18] The Confederates missed the opportunity to launch a major breakout attempt before Wallace's reinforcements filled the gaps in Grant's besieging line. Can Johnston be blamed for this failure? The communications between Bowling Green and the Cumberland River were sporadic. Gott noted that Floyd "sent no requests for reinforcements, nor did he update General Johnston of his plans."[19] Floyd did not bother to inform Johnston of the outcome of his conference and did not ask his superior for advice. The departmental commander was busy managing the withdrawal of the Central Kentucky Army from Bowling Green, but he should have checked in with Floyd more frequently.

Johnston's son wrote with vexation that "General Johnston's plan was general in its scope, and perfectly simple. He wished Donelson defended, if possible, but he did not wish the army to be sacrificed in the attempt... there did not seem any imminent peril to a vigilant and able commander of not being able to extricate his army from Donelson. There was nothing in the nature of a 'trap' in the situation, if the commander kept his resources well in hand, and his communications attended to... General Johnston's orders were in effect: 'Do not lose the fortress, if it can be helped; but do not lose the army anyhow.' For so much he is responsible."[20]

The third mistake: The failure to evacuate after the defeat of the ironclads

As Pillow's men skirmished with the sharpshooters on the afternoon of the 14th of February, Flag Officer Andrew H. Foote's four ironclads, the *Carondelet, Louisville, St. Louis,* and *Pittsburg*, and two timberclads, the *Conestoga* and *Tyler*, arrived and moved into position close to Fort Donelson. The ironclads opened fire as they steamed in unison towards the fort, while the timberclads followed at a safe distance, commencing a long-range bombardment. The Confederate artillerists held their fire until the ironclads were within about 400 yards (370 m) and then unleashed. Floyd sent a panicked communication to Johnston, informing him that "the fort cannot hold out twenty minutes. Our river batteries working admirably. Four gunboats advancing abreast."[21] It was now that a worried Johnston instructed Floyd: "If you lose the fort, bring your troops to Nashville if possible."[22]

Over the course of the next hour and a half, Fort Donelson's batteries pummelled the ironclads, disabling the *Louisville, St. Louis,* and *Pittsburg*. Finding himself alone, the captain of the *Carondelet* retreated from the scene of carnage. Johnston's belief that Fort Donelson's artillery could smash the ironclads was vindicated. The Confederate artillery batteries had won control of the river. It was now that Floyd could have used two river steamers at Dover to incrementally shuttle his garrison to safety across the Cumberland River while retaining a token force in the trenches.

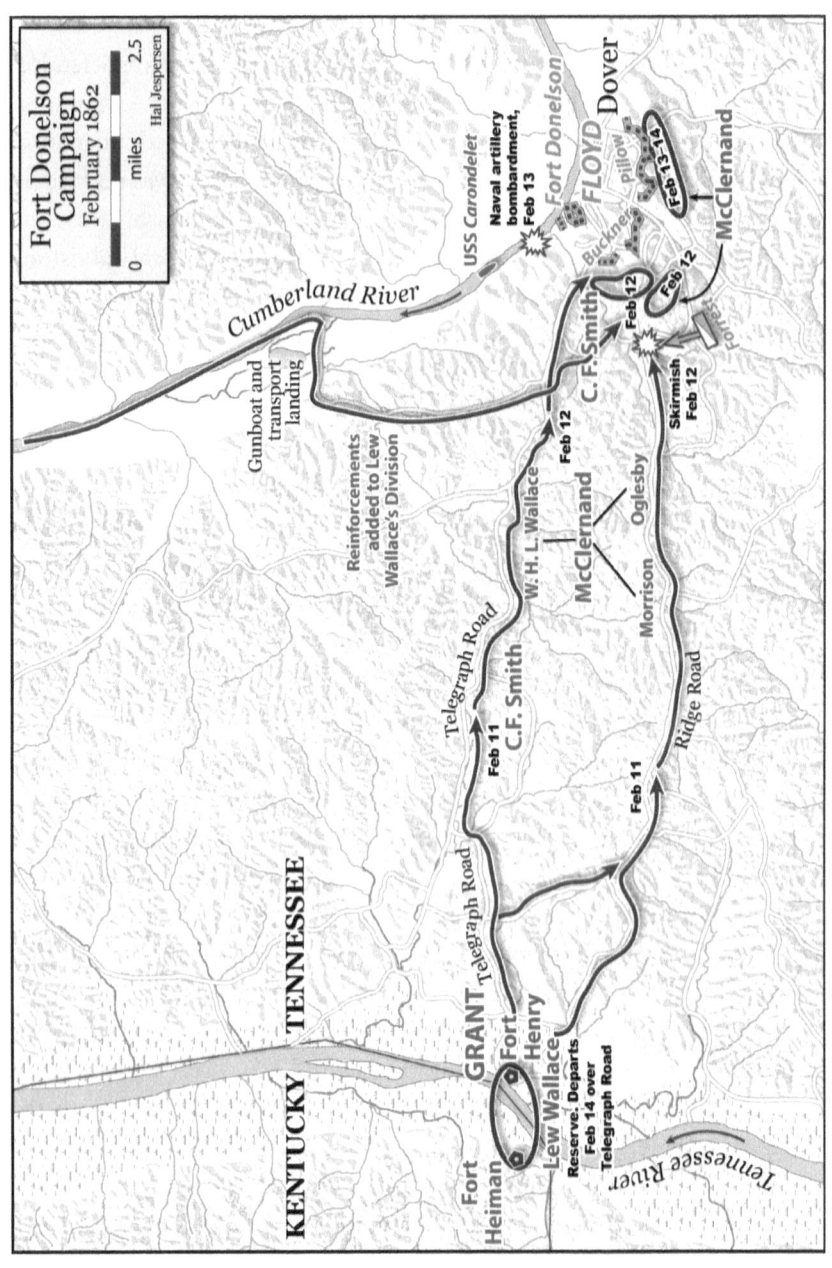

Floyd missed the opportunity. Even worse, the morning of the 15th of February would have been a perfect time for him to withdraw the garrison using the river steamers. Grant woke early before the dawn and proceeded downriver to confer with Foote. He ordered that none of his subordinates were to initiate an engagement in his absence and left no one in command of the army. The Union forces were effectively paralyzed by this foolish order. Steele commented that "with the Union gunboats away for repairs, and with two steamers in their possession, the Confederate commanders, by good management, ought to have been able to withdraw the bulk of their garrison and material to safety on the other side of the river."[23]

Unfortunately, the only thought Floyd had regarding his riverine transportation was to ship some sick and wounded soldiers upriver to Nashville. Stickles commented that "one cannot help but marvel at the thoughtlessness of the Confederate high command in not having provided for transports, barges, and all sorts of boats, which would be ready to carry their army up the river to Nashville, if the siege should appear to be ruining their chance of escape."[24] Floyd's failure to consider the Cumberland River as an escape route was highly negligent. Johnston would have expected Floyd, or at least Buckner, to have the commonsense to secure a line of retreat and consider the use of the steamboats to evacuate the garrison if the defense of Fort Donelson was becoming doubtful due to the arrival of thousands of Union reinforcements. Floyd had performed the exact action at the battle of Carnifex Ferry.

Can Johnston be blamed for Floyd's failure to utilize the Cumberland River? It would seem extremely harsh to do so. Johnston had specified such precautions in the evacuation of Columbus just a few days earlier. The Covington House memorandum of the 7th of February directed Polk to ensure that "a sufficient number of transports will be kept near that place for the removal of the garrison therefrom when no longer tenable in the opinion of the commanding officer."[25] Why didn't Floyd, or the West Point educated Buckner, take these simple precautions at Fort Donelson? Johnston later charitably wrote to Davis: "On the 14th I ordered General Floyd, by telegram, 'if he lost the fort, to get his troops back to Nashville.' It is possible this might have been done, but justice requires to look at events as they appeared at the time, and not alone by the light of subsequent information."[26]

The fourth mistake: Failure to articulate the objective of an assault

After inexplicably neglecting to consider the steamers as an evacuation method, Floyd convened another council of war on the evening of the 14th of February. Charles Pinnegar observed that Floyd "adopted the council of war as a sounding board. In this manner, Floyd could sift through the opinions of his senior officers, compare them with his own convictions, and apply the amalgam to the situation. When time and circumstances permitted, this methodology had merit for an inexperienced commander still learning his craft. Yet Floyd would have to ensure that his councils were not hijacked by a strong-willed subordinate."[27] Unfortunately, Pillow and Buckner would both serve in this role.

The Confederate leadership decided once again to attempt to break open an overland escape route through McClernand's division. Major Jeremy F. Gilmer remembered that "Generals Floyd, Pillow, and Buckner met in council soon after dark; I was present. After an interchange of views, it was decided to attack the enemy on his extreme right and right center at 5 o'clock in the morning… Pillow was to direct the movement against the right of the enemy; Brigadier General Buckner that against his right center, advancing along the Wynn's Ferry Road. A few regiments were to remain to guard the lines."[28] Yet Floyd failed to articulate his objective. Buckner and brigade commander, Brigadier General Bushrod R. Johnson, understood that the assault was a genuine break-out attempt and instructed their men to bring their knapsacks, blankets, and rations. In contrast, Pillow assumed the attack was to simply achieve a decisive victory over the Union army. Pillow asserted that "my success would roll the enemy's force in retreat over upon General Buckner, when by his attack in flank and rear we could cut up the enemy and put him completely to rout."[29]

Gilmer's interpretation aligned with that of Pillow's, and he wrote that "it was believed that the enemy might be thrown back and an opportunity secured to withdraw in safety our forces; that possibly *greater advantages* might be gained by the attack, which, if well followed up on our part, would result in disaster to the invaders… and hurl the invaders back to their transports."[30] Such confusion over the objective of the assault among the Confederate commanders could only lead to chaos. For example, Gilmer noted that "the details of preparation for carrying out the plan decided upon, such as the number of rations that should be prepared; whether blankets and knapsacks should be taken or not; what should be the order of march on retreat for the different commands; who should take the advance, and who should protect the rear, *were not arranged,* to the best of my recollection, in the council of February 14."[31] Unlike Buckner's and B.R. Johnson's troops, the soldiers of Pillow's division did not pack provisions or equipment.

At dawn the next day, Pillow's two brigades smashed into McClernand's division on the Confederate left, and over the next several hours, pushed the bluecoats back about a mile (1.6 km). Colonel Nathan B. Forrest's cavalry ranged out wide to hit the Federal's flank and rear. The astute cavalryman perceived that after hours of resistance, McClernand's division was close to shattering under the immense pressure. Unfortunately, Pillow had recently departed from the sector to investigate the failure of Buckner's troops on his right to support the offensive. Forrest approached B.R. Johnson, the senior officer on the Confederate left, for permission to lead all of Pillow's brigades in a massive charge against the crumbling ranks of McClernand's exhausted division.

Yet the hesitant B.R. Johnson did not wish to assume responsibility for the proposed attack. He came to the erroneous conclusion that the Federals "would not withdraw rapidly of their own accord after their obstinate stand unless they were trying to draw the Confederates into an ambush."[32] Instead of ordering the charge, B.R. Johnson merely agreed to advance the infantry slowly and cautiously. Forrest was disgusted and rode off to find Pillow, but the opportunity was lost. Forrest was convinced that a general charge by Pillow's infantry would have routed McClernand's entire division.[33] B.R. Johnson's disinclination to press the issue enabled the Union forces to consolidate on a new defensive line. Forrest later declared that the chance for a Confederate victory at Fort Donelson was therefore lost by a "West Pointer's reluctance to presume."[34]

Meanwhile, Buckner's supporting attack along the Wynn's Ferry Road was a feeble effort. Initially delayed by icy roads and the late arrival of one of his regiments, Buckner committed only half of his available troops to the offensive. The desultory assault was immediately stymied by the presence of a Union artillery battery ahead. Buckner explained that "in view of the heavy duty which I expected my division to undergo in covering the retreat of the army, I thought it unadvisable to attempt an assault at this time in my front until the enemy's batteries were to some extent crippled and their supports shaken by the fire of my artillery."[35] Buckner decided to deploy his soldiers in a defensive posture and bring up two batteries of his own to blast the Union artillery from its position. It was a curious decision since Buckner's artillery was composed of short-range smoothbores whereas the Union battery was made up of long-range rifled cannons. Many of Buckner's artillerists were cut down in this unequal artillery duel, while his infantry remained idle.

Pillow had become agitated at the lack of support for his offensive against McClernand and had moved over to Buckner's sector to find out what was going on. Buckner explained the situation and an exasperated Pillow ordered the Kentuckian to send his men up a hollow in the ground, using it as cover against the shells of the Union artillery. Gott contended that "Pillow's analysis of terrain was superior to that of Buckner."[36] The Kentuckian's men now managed to drive the Federals from the Forge Road and a length of the Wynn's Ferry Road, but the delay in his attack enabled Wallace's bluecoats to reinforce McClernand's exhausted division. Gott asserted that "at a decisive moment on Feb 15th, it was Buckner who hesitated to attack, allowing Pillow's attack to culminate. This hesitation prevented the Confederates from routing and possibly destroying Grant's army."[37]

The Confederate offensive sputtered to a halt around 12.30pm, but it had succeeded in driving McClernand's division back almost two miles (3.2 km) and had opened an escape route. Confusion regarding the objective of the assault now frustrated the Confederate leadership. Pillow considered the action entirely successful. An escape route was open and the Union forces on his front were defeated. He considered the bluecoats too scattered and demoralized to reinvest the fort. However, after seven hours of combat, his own division was exhausted and disorganized. The men had no rations or blankets and had used most of their ammunition in the day's fight. Wagons could not resupply his troops on the frontlines due to the difficult terrain, so ammunition had to be carried in boxes.

Pillow's division could therefore not be resupplied in time for an immediate withdrawal. The scattered and fragmented regiments would also need to be reorganized for an effective withdrawal, and this would be impossible to achieve in the limited time available before nightfall. Buckner, who was under the impression that the garrison was to utilize the breach to escape the siege immediately, and whose men had knapsacks filled with rations for three days, was aghast. He confronted Pillow and argued his case, but to no avail. Gott observed that "even at this point, it is not clear just what the final objective for the operation was. Was it to effect an escape or just to secure the means to do so when they wished?"[38]

Pillow ordered his men to collect the dead and wounded and then return to their former position in the entrenchments. He also ordered Buckner's troops to retire from the Wynn's Ferry Road. Pillow's decision to retire his own troops was justified considering the lack of ammunition, disorganization, and fatigue prevalent in his ranks. However, Pillow's order to Buckner to withdraw his men too was puzzling and entirely unwarranted. At the rear of the battlefield, Floyd was oblivious to the situation developing on his front lines, later stating that "my intention was to hold with Brigadier General Buckner's command the Wynn's Ferry Road, and thus to prevent the enemy during the night from occupying the position on our left which he occupied in the morning. I gave him orders upon the field to that effect."[39]

Charles Pinnegar asserted that "if General Floyd expected Buckner to remain astride the Wynn's Ferry Road all night subsequent to the battle, then one could argue that [Pillow's] brigades had time to return to their trenches, resupply, and march out... To fulfil this duty, [Buckner] must remain in position. Artillery support was mandatory. Not only did Pillow order his subordinate to retreat, but he also refused a request to advance the guns. So, even if we accept Pillow's interpretation that the army should resupply from the trenches before marching to Nashville, we cannot escape the conclusion that he consciously circumvented the battle plan."[40]

Floyd was shocked when he learned of Pillow's order and rushed to the frontlines to countermand it. When he encountered Pillow, the commander thundered: "General Pillow, what have we been fighting all day for? Certainly not to show our powers, but solely to secure the Wynn's Ferry Road, and now after securing it, you order it to be given up?"[41] But it was too late. Most of the troops had already been withdrawn to the entrenchments. Floyd lamented that the "movement was nearly executed before I was aware of it."[42] The removal of Buckner's men practically guaranteed that the Confederates would have to fight their way out of Fort Donelson once again on the 16th of February, unless Pillow genuinely believed that the Union forces would abandon their siege and withdraw to the Tennessee River after the day's bloody fight.

Meanwhile, Grant ordered the fresh troops of Brigadier General Charles F. Smith's division to attack the sparsely manned Southern line on the extreme right. The Union assault succeeded in capturing the outer line of entrenchments before Buckner's troops could return to defend their trenches. Despite crippling fatigue, the Confederates launched several counterattacks but failed to dislodge Smith's men. Grant also ordered Wallace to retake a portion of the ground lost that day on the Confederate left. Pillow's escape route remained open, but Grant planned to resume his offensive early the following morning.

The poorly articulated and mismanaged break-out attempt of 15th of February was a result of Floyd's passivity, Pillow's confusion, and Buckner's pessimism. The disjointed conduct of the battle, with failures by B.R. Johnson and Buckner to seize the initiative in key moments, and the lack of coordination between Floyd and Pillow in masterminding the battle plan could have been averted with someone like Johnston in command. Timothy B. Smith maintained that Johnston's "presence and direction would seemingly have ensured that everyone understood the plan during that fateful February 15 breakout attempt."[43] Unlike Floyd, Johnston preferred to lead from the front. He would have been everywhere, supervising operations on the frontlines, instructing subordinates, rallying men, and directing reinforcements to critical points. General Pierre G.T. Beauregard declared that Johnston "would have harmonized the divided counsels of the commanding officers, and undoubtedly have prevented the demoralization of their troops. It would have combined the resources of defence under his own inspiring influence."[44] Roland opined "that Johnston was remiss in not taking personal command at Fort Donelson… Had he done so, he might have been able to inflict defeat upon Grant's leaderless army on the morning of February 15."[45]

Even Grant acknowledged the challenge of facing Johnston on the battlefield as opposed to Floyd. When speaking of the battle of Shiloh many years after the war, Grant remarked: "When people wonder why we did not defeat the Southern army as rapidly and effectively as was done at other places, they forget that the Southern army was commanded by Sidney Johnston, and that to fight a general as great as Sidney Johnston was a different thing from fighting Floyd."[46] Thus, Johnston can be faulted for his absence at Fort Donelson during these decisive February days. However, as explained in chapter twelve, there were perfectly valid reasons why he chose to remain with the Central Kentucky Army at Bowling Green. The failures of Buckner and B.R. Johnson in the fighting of the 15th of February were especially damning. As the only West Point educated senior officers at Fort Donelson, they should have assumed greater responsibility for the conduct of the battle and acted more decisively.

The final mistake: A precipitate surrender

Floyd and Pillow sent Johnston enthusiastic messages describing a great victory at Fort Donelson on the 15th of February. They were pleased with the opening of the escape route and of McClernand's near rout, despite the Union gains later in the day. Forrest was also optimistic regarding the Confederate chances: "Saturday night our troops slept, flushed with victory, and confident they could drive the enemy back to the Tennessee River the next morning."[47] Johnston sent Richmond a glowing report: "We have had today at Fort Donelson one of the most sanguinary conflicts of the war. Our forces attacked the enemy with energy and won a brilliant victory."[48] One of Johnston's aides recounted that "about midnight a dispatch was received from General Pillow, announcing a 'victory complete and glorious.' We were jubilant over the result."[49]

At a council of war around midnight, Floyd discussed the situation at Fort Donelson with his subordinates. Buckner was distressed by C.F. Smith's lodgement on the right and argued that his men could not resist any further attacks. Pillow was disgusted, recalling that "Buckner gave it as his decided opinion that he could not hold his position a half hour against an assault of the enemy, and said he was satisfied the enemy would attack him at daylight the next morning."[50] The generals discussed the feasibility of a retreat through the opening in the Union line. Forrest recalled: "About 12 o'clock at night I was called in council with the generals, who had under discussion the surrender of the fort. They reported that the enemy had received 11,000 reinforcements since the fight. They supposed the enemy had returned to the positions they had occupied the day before. I returned to my quarters and sent out two men, who, going by a road up the bank of the river, returned without seeing any of the enemy, only fires, which I believed to be the old campfires, and so stated to the generals; the wind, being very high, had fanned them into a blaze."[51]

Floyd and Buckner were not convinced and discounted Forrest's opinion. They believed the fires to be the campfires of the enemy, who by now, must have now closed the escape route. Pillow refused to surrender: "The proposition was then made by [me] to again fight our way through the enemy's line and cut our way out. General Buckner said his command was so worn-out and cut to pieces and demoralized that he could not make another fight; that it would cost the command three-fourths its present numbers to cut its way out."[52] Floyd concurred. Pillow then suggested the course which they should have adopted on the morning of the 15th of February, after the defeat of the Union ironclads the previous afternoon and during Grant's absence from the battlefield. Pillow advised that Floyd should maintain a token force in the entrenchments and use the two river steamers to incrementally transport the bulk of the garrison across the Cumberland River.

Unfortunately for the Confederates, the vessels were currently occupied with the task of ferrying the wounded, sick, and prisoners to Nashville. Pillow remarked that "Floyd had sent off every steamboat we had... as matters turned out this was most unfortunate... I was not even consulted about its propriety."[53] But at least one of them would return later the next day. Pillow argued that the garrison could hold out long enough for the steamboats to return and then most of the troops could then be saved via evacuation across the river. To Pillow's fury, "General Buckner repeated that the enemy would certainly attack him in the morning and that he could not hold his position a half hour."[54] But then he changed his mind. The Kentuckian remarked that he "understood the principal object of the defense of Donelson to be to cover the movement of General A.S. Johnston's army from Bowling Green to Nashville, and that if that movement was not completed it was [his] opinion that [they] should attempt a further defense, even at the risk of the destruction of [their] entire force, as the delay even of a few hours might gain the safety of General Johnston's force."⁵⁵

"General Floyd remarked that General Johnston's army had already reached Nashville. [Buckner] then expressed the opinion that it would be wrong to subject the army to a virtual massacre when no good could result from the sacrifice, and that the general officers owed it to their men, when further resistance was unavailing, to obtain the best terms of capitulation possible for them."⁵⁶ If Buckner was willing to attempt the effort to resist further on the 16th of February to protect Johnston's withdrawal from Bowling Green, then why was he not prepared to do so to help extract most of the garrison by utilising the returning riverboats? It was mystifying logic. Captain Jack Davis of the Texas Volunteers Regiment recalled that "two boats could have taken the men and munitions of war in two hours. The enemy did not come within gunshot distance of the fort until after the surrender. Had some 5,000 men been kept in the entrenchments even on Sunday morning, we could have transferred across the river 10,000 men."⁵⁷

Regardless, Floyd was persuaded by Buckner's dismal assessment and agreed to surrender Fort Donelson and its garrison in the morning. However, neither Floyd nor Pillow wished to personally capitulate to the Union forces. Floyd feared that he would be hanged for his perceived treason as Secretary of War and Pillow vehemently opposed the decision to surrender. They abdicated command to Buckner, commandeered the available river transportation, and escaped across the Cumberland River. Floyd even managed to extract most of his Virginia troops. The indefatigable Forrest simply gathered his cavalry, and several hundred willing infantry soldiers as passengers, and trotted out of the fortification unopposed during the night. The Union troops had not closed off the escape route that his men had scouted a few hours previous. Buckner formally surrendered Fort Donelson on the morning of the 16th of February, but Grant's observance of the Confederate prisoners was so slack that B.R. Johnson and many hundreds of soldiers were amazingly able to walk through the lines to freedom. Union casualties were 2,832 of 25,000 engaged and Southern losses were 1,454 from 16,000 engaged. Yet 11,000 desperately needed graycoats passed into captivity.

If Johnston had been present at Fort Donelson, he would have done all in his power to extract the garrison by any means possible, knowing how precious armed soldiers were in the neglected Western Department. Roland declared that "Johnston could have escaped with most of the men who were lost through Floyd's indecision."[58] Likewise, T.B. Smith stated that "even though [Johnston] might have been captured himself, he most certainly would have tried to get the Donelson garrison out rather than surrender."[59] Steele also noted that "large quantities of provisions were found within the fort; and one of the boats by which Floyd and Pillow escaped had brought a large supply of ammunition for the beleaguered army. With plenty of food and ammunition there does not appear to have been any adequate excuse for surrendering at that time. Under some governments, Floyd, Pillow, and Buckner would have been tried for their lives by military court."[60]

Afterwards, Johnston informed Davis: "It appears from the information received that General Buckner (being the junior officer) took the lead in advising the surrender and General Floyd acquiesced, and they all concurred in the belief that their force could not maintain their position… Subsequent events show that the investment was not so complete as their information from their scouts led them to believe."[61] Floyd and Buckner's precipitate surrender, and failure to utilize the river transport as an escape route after the defeat of the Union ironclads, was a catastrophic error of judgment – possibly the worst of the entire Civil War. Johnston's son declared that "the answer to any criticism as to the loss of the army at Donelson is that it ought not to have been lost. That is all there is of it."[62]

Conclusion

Gott's assessment of Johnston during the Fort Donelson campaign has validity, since the general may be criticized for three oversights. He did not provide Floyd, Pillow, and Buckner with explicit orders to attack Grant's army during its march from Fort Henry to Fort Donelson. He did not issue explicit orders for them to secure a line of retreat. He did not communicate as regularly as was required with the novice Floyd. The departmental commander placed far too much trust in Buckner's professionalism, Pillow's industriousness, and Floyd's ability to command an independent force. For this much he is culpable.

The Confederates desperately needed an aggressive and competent commander on the scene who would seize the opportunity to strike the Federal army on the roads leading to Fort Donelson, issue unequivocal orders, and, if necessary, prepare for an orderly retreat. Floyd failed miserably in all these respects. Johnston's son declared that "it seems plain enough that [Floyd's duty] was to concentrate rapidly at Donelson, dispute vigorously the roads from Henry, fortify as strongly and speedily as possible, secure a transit across the Cumberland, and a line of retreat along its south bank, and then fight for Donelson as became men who held the gateway to the land – in a word, *to defend Nashville at Donelson.*"[63] The loss of three-quarters of Floyd's army and the opening of the Cumberland River to Union navigation was a calamity for Johnston. Instead of winning a decisive victory or at least safely extricating his garrison, Floyd and his generals had meekly surrendered Fort Donelson and its valiant defenders to the enemy.

The Confederate Governor of Kentucky, George W. Johnson, sent a message of consolation to Johnston after the fall of the Fort Donelson: "You had sent all to that point who could be spared from your army in the presence of Buell's army. The event showed that you had sent enough troops to that point – for we had whipped the enemy; and if the generals there commanding chose to surrender, and did so surrender, after victory and to a retreating foe, it is their fault – not yours."[64] Perhaps the most blame for the disaster at Fort Donelson belongs to the Confederate government. It is possible that even the bumbling trio of Floyd, Pillow, and Buckner could have manufactured a victory if provided with more troops. One frustrated Confederate officer remarked that "10,000 men would have converted Donelson from an overwhelming disaster to a victory – and 18,000 men were literally doing nothing under [Major General Braxton] Bragg at Pensacola and Mobile. Our President is unfortunately no military genius and could not see the relative value of position. Pensacola was nothing compared to Donelson."[65]

15.

How serious was the threat from Buell in central Kentucky?

In retrospect, it is apparent that General Albert Sidney Johnston should have assumed personal command at Fort Donelson. Brigadier Generals John B. Floyd, Gideon J. Pillow, and Simon B. Buckner made such fundamental tactical errors that any chance of victory on the Cumberland River was rendered impossible. Johnston's generalship and command style was sorely missed at Fort Donelson. He chose instead to supervise the withdrawal of the Central Kentucky Army from Bowling Green to Nashville, perceiving it to be the more perilous of the two Confederate missions in Tennessee that February of 1862. Some historians have minimized the threat posed by Brigadier General Don Carlos Buell's Army of the Ohio in central Kentucky. Charles P. Roland contended that "in electing to retire with the Bowling Green troops, Johnston exaggerated the immediate threat of Buell's advance on that line... He failed to act with the audacity and decision required by the crisis that he faced."[1] Similarly, Kendall D. Gott asserted that as of the 12th of February, "any threat from Buell was miles away and showed little sign of movement."[2] Are these assessments accurate?

Following the Covington House Conference on the 7th of February, Johnston recalled the brigades of Brigadier Generals John C. Breckinridge and Thomas C. Hindman from their advanced positions north of Bowling

Green. He employed deception once again, with Hindman instructed to "talk loudly of an advance as the only means of extricating us, that is, if you talk at all, and our invincible determination to hold on to Bowling Green at all hazards and to the last extremity."[3] One of Breckinridge's soldiers recalled that "as we marched along in platoons towards Bowling Green, I saw for the last General Albert Sidney Johnston, his gray hair and moustache was a shade grayer than when I had last seen him on parade, and a sad, care worn look about his face as he stood in silence as we passed him sitting on his horse and surrounded by his staff. As we passed him, a flush of excitement rose on my face, as I looked at his gallant head and grand appearance and felt pride in being commanded by such as him, every man in the platoon as we moved by him seemed to step more firmly."[4]

Johnston ordered the removal of the stores of artillery, ammunition, and supplies stockpiled at Bowling Green. He also instructed officials in Nashville to begin evacuation of some of the immense quantities of supplies stored in that city's depots. Colonel Robert W. Wooley of Johnston's staff proudly declared that "the first intimation the enemy had of the intended evacuation, so far as has been ascertained, was when Generals Hindman and Breckinridge, who were in advance toward his camp, were seen suddenly to retreat toward Bowling Green."[5] Unfortunately, for the soldiers of the Central Kentucky Army, there were not enough operable locomotives and rolling stock to shuttle them to Nashville. The removal of the artillery, caissons, and other precious equipment was prioritized. Some lucky soldiers managed to squeeze themselves into the cramped railcars, but most were forced to march. On the 11th of February, the troops commenced a torturous 68-mile (109 km) march to Nashville in showers of freezing rain and snow.

The Confederate soldiers destroyed bridges and felled trees to impede the enemy advance on Bowling Green. Woolley remembered that the retrograde movement was "protected by a force so small as to make doubtful the fact. Fifteen hundred sick had to be removed. Large quantities of stores and ammunition had accumulated."[6] After saving as much of the army's supplies as possible, Johnston instructed Hindman's men to burn the commissary and quartermaster stores in the town. They also burned the railroad station and platform, tore up railroad tracks, demolished telegraph lines, and obstructed the nearby railroad tunnel with heavy stones.[7] Some of the fires got out of control. In the early hours of the 13th of February, "an extensive fire occurred at Bowling Green, Ky., which resulted in the destruction of several large establishments. The soldiers worked hard and finally succeeded in extinguishing the conflagration. Generals Johnston and Hardee, in person, directed the movements of the troops."[8]

Johnston and his second-in-command, General Pierre G.T. Beauregard, departed from Bowling Green by train on the morning of the 13th of February and arrived at Edgefield later that day. Floyd's defense at Fort Donelson had protected the withdrawal of the Central Kentucky Army from an attack by the Union ironclads up the Cumberland River. Johnston expected a decisive victory there, but if Floyd was compelled to retreat, he hoped he could delay it long enough for Johnston's soldiers to construct the neglected fortifications at Nashville.

During the evening of the 13th of February, Johnston received the report from Floyd at Fort Donelson warning of 40,000 Union troops on the Cumberland River. He instructed Major General William J. Hardee to press the rearguard on to Nashville with greater urgency: "I enclose copies of dispatches from General Floyd. You will perceive the necessity of hastening your march as much as possible. It must be continued day and night until the army crosses the Cumberland."[9] Johnston was concerned with the spirits of the men: "Let it be known that the object is to secure the crossing of the Cumberland and no apprehension of the enemy in rear. You will thus preserve their morale. This order must be communicated to the rear of the column, and cavalry must be left in rear to assist the sick and bring up stragglers."[10] Similarly, Johnston sent two messages to Major General George B. Crittenden, urging him to move his District of East Tennessee forces southward to Nashville as rapidly as possible: "Every exertion [should] be made, day and night."[11] Time was running out.

Buell's advance

Historian George C. Eggleston noted that "General Johnston's position at Bowling Green was threatened by a distinctly superior army under General Buell which lay scarcely more than a two days' march to the north and east. Moreover, the position of Bowling Green was already in effect turned by [Brigadier General George H.] Thomas's advance from eastern Kentucky towards eastern Tennessee... Buell, with his army of 40,000 or 50,000 men, might easily have overwhelmed Johnston's 14,000 at Bowling Green."[12] Beauregard wrote to a friend in Richmond that "General Johnston is doing his best, but what can he do against such tremendous odds?"[13]

After the fall of Fort Henry, the Army of the Ohio began preparations to advance on Bowling Green. Buell had always urged Major General Henry W. Halleck to implement a diversion on the Cumberland River to distract the Confederates from his offensive in central Kentucky, and now it was finally in motion. On the 8th of February, Buell instructed Thomas, commander of his First Division: "Do not lose any time, but come on to Lebanon, Kentucky, as promptly as possible. I may want you immediately."[14] On the 10th of February, Buell directed Brigadier General Ormsby M. Mitchel's Third Division to march to Bowling Green via Bell's Tavern, 25 miles (41 km) northeast of the town. On the following day, Buell issued orders to his division commanders to prepare their troops for a general advance southward. The army commander informed Brigadier General Thomas J. Wood at Lebanon: "trains will be in readiness to transport your division to Bacon Creek... Encamp your division at Bacon Creek... and be always ready to move at a moment's notice."[15]

Brigadier General Alexander M. McCook's Second Division at Bacon Creek, 42 miles (68 km) northeast of Bowling Green was ordered to repair the bridges over the Green River and advance on the town. One of McCook's officers wrote "that we were marching to meet some emergency and that it was necessary to get to our destination as soon as possible."[16] On the 12th of February, the same day that Grant's army marched from Fort Henry to Fort Donelson, Buell informed Halleck that "I am advancing in some force on Bowling Green."[17]

Historian Arndt M. Stickles concluded that "another result of the fall of Fort Henry was the immediate activity exercised by General Don Carlos Buell in the vicinity of Munfordville. He moved across Green River toward Bowling Green and threatened not only the Confederate intrenchments there but Nashville as well."[18] Thus, contrary to some assertions, Buell's advance was in no way sluggish. Division commander Mitchel was determined to capture Bowling Green as rapidly as possible and he "hurried his men along, at one point impressing civilian horses and wagons to carry their knapsacks."[19] On the 13th of February, Brigadier General John B. Turchin's brigade of Mitchel's division reached the abandoned Confederate defensive line above Bowling Green. A newspaper correspondent travelling with the bluecoats reported that "the railroad appears to be a little injured. All the railroad buildings were destroyed. Some were smoking when we passed. The roads [were] obstructed by trees, which were, however, speedily removed by two companies of mechanics and engineers, who swung their axes with a will, and we were never stopped over fifteen minutes by them."[20]

Turchin's men arrived at the Barren River north of Bowling Green on the 14th of February and observed the Confederate troops in the town. Federal artillery opened fire, with the shells exploding amongst the gutted houses and buildings. The newspaper correspondent recorded that "General Turchin fired the first shell into the town, and immediately three [Confederate] regiments were seen scampering on the cars and putting off with what they had. But though within a mile [1.6 km] of Bowling Green, we were powerless to interfere, for there was Barren River, wide and unfordable, between us, and both bridges destroyed. The Texas Rangers soon began to fire all the public buildings, and we were powerless to prevent it."[21]

Hardee wrote to Johnston later that evening: "I left Bowling Green today at 3.30pm. At 12pm the enemy appeared with artillery... and opened fire on the town, and especially the depot. We were compelled to abandon the depot, which was subsequently burned. We retired at once and in perfect order."[22] Woolley observed that "the enemy pursued, and succeeded in shelling the town, while Hindman was still covering the rear. Not a man was lost."[23] Turchin's soldiers constructed an improvised bridge across the Barren River and entered Bowling Green later that evening. The Confederates had just made it out in time.

Johnston's actions

When Johnston was informed that a battle was raging at Fort Donelson on the 15th of February, he became concerned that Buell's forces might attack his own army strung out on the road between Bowling Green and Nashville. Johnston halted the Central Kentucky Army's march, placed Colonel John S. Bowen's brigade, which had been leading the withdrawal, in line of battle on each side of the road, and formed the other brigades around Bowen's men as they came up. Breckinridge's brigade marched 27 miles (43 km) that day and joined the main body of the army where it had halted. Fortunately, there was no attack. One of Breckinridge's officers recalled that during this arduous march, "the spirits of the army, however, were cheered by the accounts which General Johnston, with thoughtful care, forwarded, by means of couriers daily, of the successful resistance of Fort Donelson. The entire army bivouacked in line of battle on the night of the 15th at the junction of the Gallatin & Nashville and Bowling Green & Nashville roads, about ten miles [16 km] from Nashville. It was confidently believed that by means of boats, a large portion of the force would be sent to the relief of Fort Donelson."[24]

Colonel Edward W. Munford recalled that Johnston "had runners sent to the different commands, and troops marched as fast as practicable across the river. This movement was effected without loss of anything, and headquarters established in Nashville."[25] An officer in Breckinridge's command remembered: "At 4pm, on the 16th [of February] the head of the brigade came in sight of the bridges at Nashville, across which, in dense masses, were streaming infantry, artillery, and transportation and provision trains, but still with a regularity and order which gave promise of renewed activity and efficiency in the future. At nightfall, General Johnston, who had established his headquarters at Edgefield on the northern bank of the Cumberland, saw the last of his wearied and tired columns defile across and safely establish themselves beyond."[26]

The loss of supplies

Johnston managed to preserve his army in its perilous withdrawal but did have to abandon some supplies and equipment. The magnitude of these losses is contested. A *New York Times* correspondent travelling with Buell's army claimed that at Bowling Green "all the public buildings and several warehouses filled with pork, beef, coffee, &c., are destroyed. A pile of grain thirty feet by twenty [9 x 6 m] was burning when we arrived. Four engines and several cars were also burnt. This was their depot, and the cars had been carrying away provisions for a week. Still immense quantities were destroyed, boxes of guns, large numbers of Bowie-knives roughly fashioned of iron, and every conceivable kind of shooting apparatus, and all sorts of hardware for cooking and other uses in immense quantities. We warmed ourselves by the fires of burning corn, and heaps of pork and beef... An immense amount of provisions fell into our hands, such as sugar, molasses, over a thousand pounds of pickled beef, some few pounds of pork, a large amount of camp kettles, some few boxes of clothing, and many other articles"[27] In contrast to the account of the *New York Times*, Woolley maintained that "the provisions were nearly all secured except a large lot of spoiled pickled beef. Not a pound of ammunition, nor a gun, was lost."[28]

Conclusion

The claim that Buell's Army of the Ohio was of little threat to the Confederate forces at Bowling Green is not substantiated by the evidence at hand. The chronology of events clearly shows that the Federals moved with great rapidity and that Johnston did not have the luxury of time to orchestrate the withdrawal of the Central Kentucky Army. Turchin's troops opened fire on Hindman's men in Bowling Green itself on the 14th of February. The Union forces constructed an improvised bridge across the Barren River and entered the town later in the day. Eggleston stated that "Bowling Green was evacuated, and the Federal General Buell instantly occupied it."[29]

Not only did Johnston have to evacuate the position in the face of overwhelming numerical odds, but there were difficult obstacles to overcome. The terrible weather and scant transportation made the withdrawal an extremely challenging exercise. The 13th of February was remembered as "a night in which rain and sleet fell incessantly [and] was succeeded by a day of intense and bitter cold. Everything which could contribute to crush the spirits and weaken the nerves of men, seemed to have combined."[30] When the Central Kentucky Army departed from Bowling Green, only 500 men were in hospital, but after the long march to Nashville in frigid conditions, over 5,400 soldiers were placed on the sick list. Medical Director David W. Yandell noted "the immense number of convalescents and men merely unfit for duty or unable to undertake a march."[31]

The fact that Johnston managed to evacuate all these men is a testament to his resolve and solicitude for his army. Floyd noted that Johnston "had not slept a wink in three nights."[32] While a debatable, but likely significant, proportion of the army's supplies were lost to the advancing Federal forces, Johnston managed to preserve the integrity and morale of his army. The troops believed they were going to be transported to Fort Donelson to fight Grant's army and relished the prospect, even after such a gruelling withdrawal in freezing weather. One of Breckinridge's officers proudly claimed that Johnston "had with promptness, unrivalled military sagacity, and yet with mingled caution and celerity, dismantled his fortifications at Bowling Green, transmitted his heavy artillery and ammunition to Nashville, and extricated his entire army from the jaws of almost certain annihilation and capture."[33]

Ultimately, the evacuation of Bowling Green was a crushing disappointment to Johnston and the people of the South. The symbolic capital of Confederate Kentucky was captured, the protective barrier of Nashville removed, and the resources of the Bluegrass state lost. However, Johnston's occupation of Bowling Green for almost six months was remarkable in the context of the numerical odds between the Union and Confederate armies in Kentucky. John B. Jones, senior clerk in the War Department at Richmond, acknowledged this fact in his diary entry of the 24th of February: "General Sidney Johnston has evacuated Bowling Green with his *ten or twelve* thousand men! Where is his mighty army now? It never did exist!"[34]

With reference to Johnston's long occupation of Bowling Green, Breckinridge's assistant adjutant general, Captain George B. Hodge, noted that in September 1861, the commanding general "had found an army of hastily levied volunteers, badly equipped, miserably clad, fully one half stricken down by disease, destitute of transportation, and with barely the shadow of discipline… with these men he held at bay a force of the enemy of fully 100,000 men." Hodge argued that "the Southern States were protected from invasion. Time was obtained to drill and consolidate the volunteer force. The army was sustained in the fertile and abundant grain-producing regions of Kentucky, transportation gathered of the most efficient character, immense supplies of beef, corn, and pork collected from the surrounding country and safely garnered in depots further South for the coming summer campaign."[35] Johnston's time in central Kentucky had been highly profitable to the Confederacy.

16.

Was Johnston aware of the lack of fortifications at Nashville?

General Albert Sidney Johnston's elation at the safe withdrawal of the Central Kentucky Army from Bowling Green to Nashville was soon crushed by the news of the fall of Fort Donelson and the capture of most of its garrison on the 16th of February. His aide, Colonel Edward W. Munford remembered: "Just before daybreak, we were awakened by another messenger with 'dispatches from Donelson.' I lighted a candle, and at the general's request read to him the astounding official statement that the place 'would capitulate at daylight, and the army be surrendered by [Brigadier General Simon B.] Buckner, [Brigadier Generals John B.] Floyd and [Gideon J.] Pillow having left on steamboats for Nashville!' The general was lying on a little camp-bed in one corner; he was silent a moment, and then asked me to read the dispatch again, which I did. He then ordered the staff to be awakened, saying, 'I must save *this* army [the Central Kentucky Army].'"[1] Johnston informed General Pierre G.T. Beauregard of the catastrophe: "At 2am today Fort Donelson surrendered. We lost all."[2]

Major Jeremy F. Gilmer sympathized with his commander's predicament: "The surrender at Fort Donelson made Nashville untenable by the forces under [Johnston's] command. Situated in a wide basin, intersected by a navigable river in possession of the invader; approached from all directions by good turnpike roads and surrounded by commanding hills, involving works of not less than twenty miles [32 km] in extent, the city could not be held by a force less than 50,000. With all the reinforcements to be hoped for [Johnston's] army could not be raised to that number before the place would have been attacked by heavy forces of the enemy both by land and water."[3] With the precipitate fall of Fort Donelson, Johnston had no time to construct the necessary fortifications around Nashville. He would have to evacuate the Central Kentucky Army from the city and withdraw further southwards along the railroad line to Murfreesboro, Tennessee. To further complicate matters, Johnston would have to maintain the morale and discipline of his men while personally enduring the wrath of the people of the South for the recent disasters on the Tennessee and Cumberland rivers.

With great sadness, Johnston prepared orders for the Central Kentucky Army to abandon Nashville. He later notified Richmond that "the fall of Fort Donelson compelled me to withdraw the remaining forces under my command from the north bank of the Cumberland and to abandon the defense of Nashville, which *but for that disaster* it was my intention to protect to the utmost. Not more than 11,000 effective men were left under my command to oppose a column of [Brigadier General Don Carlos] Buell's of not less than 40,000 troops, moving by Bowling Green, while another superior force, under [Brigadier General George H.] Thomas, outflanked me to the east."[4] Johnston maintained that Brigadier General Ulysses S. Grant's forces, accompanied by "gunboats and transports, had it in their power to ascend the Cumberland, now swollen by recent flood, so as to intercept all communications with the South. The situation left me no alternative but to evacuate Nashville or sacrifice the army. By remaining, the place would have been unnecessarily subjected to destruction, as it is very indefensible, and no adequate force would have been left to keep the enemy in check in Tennessee."[5]

The Nashville fortifications

Thomas L. Connelly made a damning accusation in relation to the defensibility of Nashville, namely, that Johnston was unaware that the fortifications he had ordered had not been constructed by Gilmer and his engineers when the general decided to withdraw the army from Bowling Green. Connelly asserted that "Johnston's belief that the defenses at Nashville were being constructed [was dangerous]. There was an unjustifiable lack of communication between Johnston and Gilmer on conditions at Nashville."[6] Connelly alleged that "there is no evidence that Johnston, before he retreated to Nashville in February 1862, had any idea that the fortifications were not being built. In fact, on Christmas Day, 1861, he confidently wrote Judah Benjamin that the entrenchments 'double the efficiency of my force for the defense of this line.' When he wrote this, there was not a single yard of fortifications constructed at Nashville."[7] Similarly, historian Larry Tagg declared that "here again was evidence of Johnston's lack of attention to critical details: when his troops reached the city, they were amazed to find that there were no fortifications built around Nashville, nor any other preparation for the defense of this crucial strategic prize."[8]

However, Connelly's and Tagg's accusations can be easily refuted. Johnston's letter of the 25th of December to Benjamin in which he stated the fortifications "double the efficiency of my force," was actually referring to the defenses already constructed at Bowling Green. He referenced Nashville by stating that "I have as a further precaution ordered intrenchments *to be thrown up* under the direction of the chief engineer, Major Gilmer, at Nashville."[9] It was Johnston's entrenchments at Bowling Green, not Nashville, that he believed doubled the efficiency of his force. He knew that there were no effective fortifications at Nashville and said so much to Benjamin. It is apparent that Johnston would not have determined to "fight for Nashville at Fort Donelson" if he had believed the city was capable of any kind of defense. Connelly's criticism is based on a misinterpretation or deliberate distortion of this message. The correspondence between Johnston, Gilmer, and Governor Isham G. Harris between October and December 1861 also clearly demonstrates the departmental commander's awareness of the issue.

In October 1861, Johnston notified Governor Harris that "I have [ordered] Major J.F. Gilmer, C.S. Corps of Engineers… to Nashville, to examine the country below Nashville, in the vicinity, for the purpose of determining upon the most eligible sites for the erection of such works as will completely defend the city from all approaches of the enemy by means of the river. I ask the interposition of your aid and influence to enable him best to accomplish the object of his visit. Should it be thought necessary, after the examination, to erect the works, it can be quickly done by means of slave labor, which I presume there would be no difficulty in obtaining."[10]

Johnston dutifully notified Richmond that "I have sent Major Gilmer to make an examination at Clarksville and Nashville, with the design of constructing works of defense at both places. Many pieces of cannon will be needed for the works… I hope, as soon as we can, to get ready to make up by activity for our deficiency in number."[11] In November, Gilmer surveyed Nashville and determined that a river battery should be constructed below the city, on the south bank of the Cumberland River. This battery would help protect Nashville from Federal gunboats and the riverine deployment of enemy troops. To the north of the city, Gilmer advised the construction of breastworks across a range of hills that overlooked the roads leading into the state capital.

However, Gilmer could not procure the necessary labor. He appealed to Governor Harris on the 11th of December: "The agents heretofore employed to procure a laboring force for building fortifications for defending the approaches to this city have failed to get any more than a few negroes; a number quite insignificant when compared with the works to be undertaken. With a hope that a large force of negroes may yet be obtained by an appeal to the citizens of the vicinity and neighboring counties, I have prepared the form for the call upon them, which I submit for your indorsement. Having your indorsement, I have thought it might be advisable to have a number of copies printed and placed in the hands of some officers, say sheriffs and constables, with instructions to apply to every citizen within reach, and urge the necessity of a prompt compliance with the call."[12] The Governor heartily endorsed Gilmer's call to action and supported the engineer's campaign to enlist enslaved laborers, but encountered the same difficulties.

Despite Gilmer's and Harris's continued appeals, the Nashvillians would not release their slaves to assist in the construction of the fortifications intended for their own defense. Perhaps they did not want their slaves working in such proximity to the front lines where escape was a real possibility. Perhaps they feared the repercussions of their slaves working away from their plantations in large and potentially subversive groups. Regardless of the reason, the lack of a sufficient labor force crippled Confederate efforts to fortify the city of Nashville. On the 7th of December, Gilmer wrote in frustration to Johnston: "I have to report that the agents employed under the sanction of Governor Harris to engage the services of negroes from their masters to work on the entrenchments for defending the city of Nashville against land approach have failed to procure a force at all adequate to the magnitude of the work contemplated. In fact, the number of hands is insignificant, and the agents report that it will be impracticable to procure them at this time, as the negroes in the vicinity of this city are hired out until the end of this year and not now under the control of their masters."[13]

Gilmer concluded that "it is not probable, therefore, that any material progress can be made in the construction of the proposed defenses during the present month unless other labor can be applied. It is to be feared, too, that the call for military service has taken so large a proportion of the laboring classes from this community that it will be difficult, if at all possible, to procure white laborers at any price that will be reasonable."[14] Governor Harris also lamented to Johnston in late December that "upon your [request] I immediately appointed energetic agents to collect laborers in this and adjoining counties to construct the fortifications near Nashville, but I must say that the response to my appeal for laborers has not thus far been as flattering as I had wanted and expected."[15]

Unfortunately for Johnston, the defense of Nashville was not deemed a priority by the city officials and surrounding landowners. Colonel Munford recalled that "one day General Johnston said to me: 'I am disappointed in the state of public sentiment in the South. Our people seem to have suffered from a violent political fever, which has left them exhausted. They are not up to the revolutionary point.' I replied, 'the logic of your remark, general, is that you doubt our success?' He looked at me gravely for a moment, and said, 'If the South wishes to be free, she can be free.'"[16] The apathy of certain Southerners was especially prevalent in Nashville. Benjamin F. Cooling remarked that "allegiance to the Confederacy scarcely cloaked a preoccupation with the mounting profits from the war. They simply had no time to worry about their own defense – besides, that was Johnston's task."[17] The people felt no urgency. The illusion of strength that Johnston had cast over the Union commanders in Kentucky also enchanted the very people the general tried to protect. Munford recalled "that when [Johnston] had ordered his chief-engineer, Gilmer, to fortify Nashville, the popular sense of security was such that Gilmer was laughed at for suggesting the necessity for fortifications, was called in derision 'Johnston's dirt-digger,' and had to abandon the attempt in despair."[18]

Conclusion

Connelly's assertion that Johnston was unaware of the state of the fortifications at Nashville is another reckless statement, contradicted by the substantial documentary evidence available. Contrary to the historian's denunciations, Johnston was apprised on the lack of progress both by Gilmer and the Governor. In fact, Harris reported that "I joined Major Gilmer in an earnest and urgent appeal to the people to send in their laborers for this purpose, offering full and fair compensation. This appeal was so feebly responded to, that I advised General Johnston to impress the necessary labor; but, owing to the difficulty in obtaining the laborers, the works were not completed; indeed, some of them little more than commenced, when Fort Donelson fell."[19] Johnston ordered the impressment of 1,500 enslaved workers, but it took weeks for the army recruiters to collect only fifty men, and the entire labor force for the Nashville fortifications never totalled more than 200 men. The general was aware of the significant deficiency, but lacked the dictatorial powers required to seize the workers from the slave-owners in and around the city.

Johnston always knew that the defense of the Tennessee capital would have to be entrusted to the rapid construction of earthworks and river batteries by the soldiers of the Central Kentucky Army once they arrived from Bowling Green. This was one of the factors leading to his decision to personally command the army during the time of its withdrawal. That is also why he established his new headquarters at Edgefield. Unfortunately, he ran out of time with the precipitate fall of Fort Donelson. Looking back, it must be said that the utter failure of the Nashville elite to assist Johnston in the months prior to the Bowling Green evacuation was truly remarkable in the context of the Federal intent to capture the city and its importance to the Confederate war effort.[20]

17.
Did Johnston mismanage the withdrawal from Nashville?

The 16th of February 1862 was an emotional rollercoaster for the residents of Nashville. Colonel Edward W. Munford observed that "the people of the capital were joyous over the news of [Fort Donelson] the night before. The morning papers were full of the 'glorious victory.' In the midst of this joy came the news of the disaster. Its effects can be imagined; 'confusion worse confounded,' nay, a perfect panic prevailed, and people rushed here and there in a delirium of fear."[1] With Fort Donelson in Union hands, Nashville was completely exposed to enemy naval incursions via the Cumberland River, making a stand there untenable. Worse still, two large Federal armies under Brigadier Generals Ulysses S. Grant and Don Carlos Buell were now converging on the Tennessee capital, and any attempt to hold Nashville would have risked complete encirclement. As discussed in the previous chapter, the city had no meaningful defensive works or natural barriers that could have allowed a prolonged stand.

The people of Nashville expected hordes of bluecoats to arrive outside their city at any moment to commence the bombardment of their homes. Mobs began to roam the streets, sparking confusion and hysteria. Thousands of frightened residents frantically gathered their possessions for the trip southward. Financial institutions and commercial enterprises in the city hurriedly organized the removal of their valuables. The roads leading out of Nashville became clogged with people, animals, wagons, drays, and other conveyances. Munford remembered that "in the midst of these unhappy scenes General Albert Sidney Johnston remained calm, distributing his troops into proper positions, giving orders for the erection of batteries below the city to delay the gunboats, for the removal of public stores and property of all sorts, and receiving delegations of public functionaries and private citizens who were crowding round him for advice under the changed state of affairs."[2] Johnston advised Governor Isham G. Harris to remove the state archives to Memphis.

Captain Basil W. Duke, a Confederate cavalry officer, remembered that "during the first night after the army had reached Nashville, when the excitement and fury were at the highest pitch, and officers and privates were alike influenced by it, it seemed as if the bonds of discipline would be cast off altogether. Crowds of soldiers were mingled with the citizens, who thronged the streets all night, and yells, curses, shots, rang on all sides... Very soon all those who had escaped from Donelson began to arrive... The arrival of these disbanded soldiers, among whom it was difficult to establish and enforce order, because no immediate disposition could be made of them, increased the confusion already prevailing."[3]

In the public square, the Mayor of Nashville, Richard B. Cheatham, and other city officials gave impromptu speeches to the large crowds, advising them of Johnston's decision to surrender the city to spare its inhabitants from a devastating Union artillery bombardment. Cheatham and his colleagues implored the agitated Nashvillians to disperse and return to their homes, but the pleas went unheeded. During the night, the unruly mobs began to plunder the Central Kentucky Army's supply depots.

The appointment of Floyd

On the morning of the 17th of February, Brigadier Generals John B. Floyd and Gideon J. Pillow arrived in Nashville after their flight from Fort Donelson. Johnston received them at his headquarters "with the greatest courtesy and made the former commandant of the post at Nashville."[4] Johnston has been condemned for appointing the disgraced Floyd to this role. Stanley F. Horn claimed that "General Johnston, before moving on to Murfreesboro with the troops, assigned to General Floyd the job of restoring order in Nashville. Floyd made an ineffectual effort at carrying out this assignment."[5] Similarly, Thomas L. Connelly maintained that "John B. Floyd had been as poor at handling a post as he was at commanding a fort."[6]

However, Johnston's decision was justifiable. Firstly, knowledge of the events leading to the catastrophe at Fort Donelson were not yet fully understood. Johnston wrote to President Jefferson Davis in March 1862 that "it was impossible for me to gather the facts for a detailed report, or spare time which was required to extricate the remainder of my troops and save the large accumulation of stores and provisions, after that disheartening disaster. I transmitted the reports of Generals Floyd and Pillow without examining or analyzing the facts, and scarcely with time to read them."[7] Johnston explained that "the facts were not fully known, discontent prevailed, and criticism or condemnation was more likely to augment than cure the evil… [I deferred] to a more propitious time an investigation of the conduct of the generals; for, in the meantime, their services were required, and their influence useful. For these reasons, Generals Floyd and Pillow were assigned to duty, for I still felt confidence in their gallantry, their energy, and their devotion to the Confederacy."[8]

Secondly, Johnston required a high-ranking officer who could focus on organizing the retreat, rather than an aggressive battlefield commander, and Floyd's background made him the logical choice. The Virginian was a former United States Secretary of War under President James Buchanan and thus had intimate knowledge of military logistics, supply chains, and administration. Since Johnston wanted to remove the stockpiled provisions, munitions, equipment, and artillery as efficiently as possible before the Union forces arrived, a general with Floyd's extensive experience was a reasonable choice for handling these tasks.

Johnston detailed the 1st Missouri infantry regiment, one of the most disciplined in the Central Kentucky Army, to act as a military police force for Floyd and restore order in the capital. Duke remarked that "Floyd had no uncommon task in holding in check an infuriated mob, and in giving coherence to the routed fugitives of Donelson. His duty was, besides, to save from the wreck the most important supplies and stores."[9] Floyd later reported that "I was placed in command of the city, and immediately took steps to arrest the panic that pervaded all classes and to restore order and quiet… I immediately stopped the indiscriminate distribution of public stores by placing guards over them, and, having thus secured them from the grasp of the populace, I commenced the work of saving the stores that were in the city."[10]

After assigning Floyd as the post commander at Nashville, Johnston led the Central Kentucky Army out of the chaotic Tennessee capital on the 17th of February. He ordered Major General George B. Crittenden and the remnants of his District of East Tennessee forces to unite with his army at Murfreesboro. These two demoralized commands would need Johnston's personal presence to restore their morale, organization, and discipline for the struggles that lay ahead. Colonel Nathan B. Forrest and his cavalry arrived in Nashville on the 18th of February, after having rested for a day to recover from their exertions in the escape from Fort Donelson, and Floyd incorporated them into his Nashville police force. Over the next couple of days, Forrest's troops suppressed the rioters, with his battle-weary cavalrymen using the flats of their sabres to beat down the looters. On one occasion, Forrest even employed a fire hose to disperse a particularly large mob. The ice-cold water was a strong inducement for the plunderers to abandon their quest.

Ultimately, Floyd and Forrest were able to save and transport significant quantities of food, supplies, equipment, and munitions southward. About 250,000 pounds of bacon, 600 boxes of army clothing, thousands of pounds of flour, rifling machinery, and forty wagons of ammunition were dispatched to Murfreesboro, Chattanooga, and Atlanta, Georgia. At 10pm on the 19th of February, Floyd ordered the suspension bridge across the Cumberland River destroyed. At 3am on the 20th of February, after the railcars had left for Chattanooga, he demolished the railway bridge. At 3pm, Floyd departed Nashville and arrived at Murfreesboro on the 21st of February. Johnston summarized the results of the evacuation to Richmond on the 25th of February: "I moved the main body of my command to [Murfreesboro] on the 17th and 18th and left a brigade under General Floyd to bring on such stores and property as were at Nashville, with instructions to remain until the approach of the enemy, and then to rejoin me. This has been in a great measure effected."[11]

Critics of Johnston's decision often conflate Floyd's failure at Fort Donelson with his performance at Nashville, but the two situations were entirely different. Duke, who served under Floyd during this time, was impressed with his commander's administrative efforts. He recalled that Floyd "impressed all means of transportation available and employed them in saving ordnance-stores and other valuable property. Among other articles, he saved all the cannon, caissons, and battery wagons. He found all restraints of civil order not only relaxed but sundered. A mixed mob had possession of the city, and cupidity was triumphant."[12] Duke recalled that "nothing could have been more admirable than the fortitude, patience, and good sense, which General Floyd displayed in his arduous and unenviable task... I saw a great deal of General Floyd while he was commanding at Nashville, and I was remarkably impressed by him... He was evidently endowed with no common nerve, will, and judgment."[13] Nashville newspaper editor and publisher, Leon Trousdale, noted that "General Floyd and Colonel Forrest exhibited extraordinary energy and efficiency in getting off Government stores at that point."[14] Floyd's talents were far better suited to an administrative post than to the battlefield.

The pre-emptive movement of supplies out of Nashville

Connelly argued that "on February 8, Isham Harris suggested moving the Nashville meat stores further south, and two days later Moses Wright suggested the same for munitions. Their advice was not heeded by Johnston, and thus when Donelson fell the logistical situation became hopelessly entangled."[15] This criticism is entirely unwarranted as Johnston had already ordered such a movement, but the deficient transportation network obstructed these efforts. The general had even tried to prevent this scenario from occurring in the first place. General Pierre G.T. Beauregard recalled that prior to the Bowling Green withdrawal, Johnston "said that, at present, the main object should be to gain time to remove the supplies of ammunition and provisions collected at Bowling Green, and the still larger supplies of pork, grain, and clothing accumulated at Clarksville and Nashville, *contrary to his advice*, by the Commissary and Quartermaster Departments at Richmond."[16]

Unfortunately, the Confederate government never conceived of the need to evacuate Nashville, leaving Johnston with limited resources to manage the movement. In the capital at Richmond, war clerk John B. Jones perceptively commented that "Nashville must fall – although no one seems to anticipate such calamity."[17] Connelly's ire should have been directed at the Secretary of War and the Commissary and Quartermaster Departments at Richmond for their blithe accumulation of supplies in the Nashville depots and then their failure to provide Johnston with the necessary transportation and personnel to ensure a safe and orderly evacuation.

Lack of an evacuation plan

Larry J. Daniel declared that "even though [Johnston's] staff had five months to formulate an evacuation plan, at a time when he fully expected Buell's army to advance in overwhelming numbers, no such contingency had been devised."[18] Such a criticism may be legitimate to some degree but it must be noted that Johnston advised against the stockpiling of supplies and equipment at Nashville in the first place and then ordered the removal of such items during the Central Kentucky Army's withdrawal from Bowling Green. After the fall of Fort Donelson, Johnston's main priority was the orderly retreat of the army southwards, ensuring that it retained its fighting capability. The civilian panic at Nashville was not his responsibility and did not impact the military effectiveness of his army. Had Johnston and his men stayed in the city to control the panic, he would have risked being trapped and destroyed, an outcome far worse than temporary disorder.

In addition, it is entirely implausible that contingency plans for a withdrawal would have been endorsed and supported by the indifferent Nashville powerbrokers when they could not even be spurred to action for the purposes of their own safety from the enemy. The Nashvillians repeatedly ignored Johnston's requests for their enslaved workers to construct fortifications around the city and this indifference continued even with the general's arrival. Once at Edgefield on the 13th of February, the departmental commander ordered that a raft be constructed across the breadth of the Cumberland River to obstruct enemy gunboats, but his proposal was rejected by the influential merchants of the city, who depended on the waterway for their livelihoods. Even in such a dire military situation, the ruling class in Nashville would not compromise their economic prosperity to aid the Confederate army.

Complications

Despite the absence of an evacuation plan, Johnston successfully moved the Central Kentucky Army and its artillery out of Nashville, preventing a catastrophic Union capture of his army. The unruly scenes in the capital were largely fuelled by local civilians, fearful of an enemy bombardment and the seizure of their belongings. However, there were further impediments that impacted Johnston's ability to remove all the provisions, equipment, and munitions from the city.

Mayor Cheatham

One complication was the irresponsible actions of Mayor Cheatham, who was concerned about the safety of the city and its residents. He wanted to avert any military action taking place in Nashville itself. This lofty motivation may have influenced his behavior regarding the removal of the army's provisions. Cheatham did not want this logistical operation to serve as a catalyst for Federal military intervention in the city, and it appears that he purposefully obstructed the process. The *Richmond Times-Dispatch* reported that "Cheatham made speeches from chairs, made speeches from tables, made speeches in houses, out of houses, spoke in the streets, spoke in the suburbs, spoke loud, spoke low, button-holed men on the street corners to impress upon all this one grand fact, that he as Mayor of Nashville would never surrender the private property to the needs of the South, but would surrender the city to Buell or anybody that wouldn't interfere with the property."[19] The *Weekly Mississippian* alleged that "from the accounts which have reached us from [Nashville] it seems that Mayor Cheatham was not only anxious to surrender the place, but was extremely solicitous to conciliate [the Federals] by retaining all the Government stores for them. He endeavored to prevent the removal of Commissary stores and other articles of value to the Confederate Government."[20]

According to Forrest's biographers, on the night of the 16th of February,

Cheatham "spoke to a huge crowd of Nashville citizens and attempted to quiet their fears. By word of General Johnston, Cheatham told the people, Nashville would not be defended and would be declared an open city. The capital city, therefore, would not be destroyed. He also informed the crowd that most of the provisions warehoused in the city would not be removed by the Confederate army and would be distributed among the people. This was not to be the case, however. Whatever Johnston told the mayor about the disposition of government provisions, it was not his real plan to turn the contents of the warehouses to the people of Nashville."[21] Cheatham's speeches and actions likely instigated the plundering of the Confederate supply depots to the avaricious Nashville citizenry and the demoralized soldiers from Fort Donelson. This situation made it highly challenging for Floyd and Forrest to extricate the army's provisions southwards to Murfreesboro, as they had to fight mobs of boisterous looters encouraged by the mayor to steal as much as possible before the Union forces arrived.

Quartermaster Stevenson
Another major complication was the precipitate flight of Major Vernon K. Stevenson, the Quartermaster General of the Western Department, from Nashville. The *Knoxville Register* reported that "Mr. V.K. Stevenson, Quartermaster General, and President of the Nashville & Chattanooga Railroad, etc., instead of standing sentry at his post and protecting the immense accumulation of military stores, and controlling the railroads so as to remove them, fled. Early Monday morning [the 17th of February] he loaded several cars with his personal effects – his negroes, horses, carriages and household furniture, including his own sacred person – and hastened to [Chattanooga], where he has ever since remained."[22]

The newspaper alleged that "by his direction all the rolling stock was hurried to this end of the road, and no effort, or next to none, was made to bring any of the Government property from the doomed city. Nearly a week has elapsed, and no enemy has approached. During this time every pound of bacon and ordnance and quartermaster stores could easily have been removed to Murfreesboro, if not further. Instead of this being done, the doors of the storehouses were thrown open, and the people invited to carry off all they wished, and the torch applied to the rest! Was ever such wanton abandonment and destruction of property?"[23]

Forrest reported that "it was eight days from the time the quartermaster left the city before the arrival of the enemy, commissaries and other persons connected with these departments leaving at the same time. With proper diligence on their part, I have no doubt all the public stores might have been transported to places of safety... I saw no officer connected with the Quartermaster's or Commissary Departments except Mr. Patton, who left on Friday. I did not at any time meet or hear of Major V.K. Stevenson in the city during my stay there... From my personal knowledge I can say nothing of the manner in which Major Stevenson left the city. Common rumor and many reliable citizens informed me that Major Stevenson left by a special train Sunday evening, February 16, taking personal baggage, furniture, carriage, and carriage-horses, the train ordered by himself, as president of the railroad."[24]

Thus, Floyd and Forrest had to fill the void left by Stevenson and his staff, but it was extremely complicated without the knowledge, documentation, and physical resources of the quartermaster's department. As reported by the *Murfreesboro Post*, Stevenson's abandonment of his post and his "decision to disappear without the completion of the transportation of supplies had left the Confederate troops in a vulnerable and most impossible situation."[25] In April 1862, *The Courier-Journal* informed its readers that "a rumor has reached [Louisville] that V.K. Stevenson, Confederate Quartermaster, has been placed under arrest, upon a charge of mismanagement in his department, growing out of the evacuation of Nashville. This rumor may have grown out of the fact that an examination into the conduct of his office, as connected with that affair, has probably been ordered by the Confederate Congress."[26]

Despite the public criticisms regarding the Quartermaster General's flight and abandonment of valuable military supplies, the Confederate government never laid formal charges against Stevenson, and he continued to serve in various roles for the Confederacy. His logistical expertise, particularly with railroads, was deemed crucial, and he was allowed to resume his work without facing court-martial. Unfortunately for Johnston and the Central Kentucky Army, Stevenson's precipitate abandonment of Nashville in February 1862 severely compromised the evacuation of supplies.

Lack of transportation

Then there was the lack of railroad infrastructure and capacity. Much of the limited rolling stock was still being used to transport sick soldiers from Kentucky, and the railroad tracks themselves were in a desperate condition. The Nashville & Chattanooga Railroad had over 1,200 broken rails and the Confederacy lacked both the materials and manpower to repair them. Floyd reported that "during the interval between the morning of the 17th and the evening of the 20th of February trains were loaded and dispatched as fast as they arrived. Much more could have been saved had there been more system and regularity in the disposition of the transportation by rail. Several trains were occupied in carrying off sick and wounded soldiers."[27]

Floyd stated that "I had succeeded in collecting a large amount of stores of various kinds at the depot, but as I had no control of the transportation by rail, and hence obliged to await the action of others, much that would have been valuable to the Government was necessarily left at the depot. Among the articles saved were all the cannon, caisson, and battery wagons of which we had any knowledge."[28] Without sufficient railroad transportation, it was simply impossible for the Confederates to remove all the supplies at Nashville to safety at points further south.

Severe weather
The final major complication was the continuing extreme weather of February 1862. Floyd recalled that "the weather was exceedingly inclement during the entire time occupied… and there was an excessively heavy rain on the 19th of February."[29] Bridges and rails were washed away, roads were transformed into muddy slop, and telegraph wires were felled. Connelly and Daniel both wrote that about 70,000 pounds of bacon that had been stacked on the Cumberland River wharf was carried away by the torrential river.[30] At precisely the time of its greatest need, a large section of the road south of Nashville was swept away in floodwaters, further increasing traffic congestion and delays.

Johnston reported that "nearly all the stores would have been saved but for the heavy and unusual rains, which have washed away the bridges, swept away portions of the railroad, and rendered transportation almost impossible."[31] The horrendous weather experienced by the Confederate armies during the withdrawal from Nashville was a major impediment to Johnston's ability to move his troops, transport his supplies, and defend his fortifications. It is safe to say that even if an evacuation plan had been prepared prior to the abandonment of Nashville, it would have been rendered useless in the face of such abnormal and paralyzing weather conditions.

The fall of Nashville

The last soldiers of Forrest's command departed Nashville on the 23rd of February for Murfreesboro. Johnston quickly consolidated his disparate forces in the central Tennessee town. He notified Richmond: "By the junction of the command of Crittenden and the fugitives from Fort Donelson, which have been reorganized as far as practicable, the force now under my command will amount to about 17,000 men."[32] Buell's troops arrived at Edgefield on the same day that Forrest's men exited. Mayor Cheatham visited the Union detachment for the purpose of surrendering the city but was unsuccessful. On the 24th, Cheatham arrived in Edgefield once again, and this time Union Colonel John Kennett formally accepted the request. The bulk of Brigadier General Ormsby M. Mitchel's division arrived at Edgefield later that day, and Buell himself at nightfall, but the Union army remained on the northern bank of the Cumberland River.

On the morning of the 25th of February, Union transports steamed up the Cumberland River to the Nashville wharf and deposited Brigadier General William Nelson's division into the city. With the strains of *Dixie* filling the air and a curious crowd assembled on either side of the street, Nelson's troops marched to the capitol building and raised the Stars and Stripes over Nashville. Buell adopted a most conciliatory policy towards the residents of the city, and his army was under the strictest discipline to avoid any provocation. Cheatham and the Nashville elite must have been most relieved at this turn of events.

Conclusion

The criticism of Johnston for his appointment of Floyd as Nashville post commander does not appear warranted. Floyd's experience and skills were suited to administrative tasks, rather than battlefield actions, and historians have conflated the Virginian's failure at Fort Donelson with the chaotic, but largely successful, withdrawal of supplies and munitions from Nashville. Connelly's declaration that Johnston failed to pre-emptively remove military valuables from Nashville is erroneous, as the general had recommended such an action, but simply lacked the manpower, railroad transportation, and support of the Richmond government to do so. Daniel's condemnation of Johnston for the lack of an evacuation plan is somewhat justified, but again, this omission relates more to the factors outlined above. Even if an evacuation plan had been formulated, the extreme weather conditions and apathy of the Nashville powerbrokers would have rendered it largely ineffective.

Despite the tumultuous withdrawal of the Central Kentucky Army from Nashville, there was much that Johnston was able to achieve in those dark days of February 1862. Firstly, he was able to preserve the integrity and morale of the main army in its precipitate retreat, incorporate the disheartened soldiers from Fort Donelson into his ranks, and then unite with the remnants of Crittenden's Eastern Tennessee Army at Murfreesboro. Such an accomplishment, especially in such freezing weather, should not be discounted. Johnston correctly recognized Nashville was indefensible after the fall of Fort Donelson and avoided a suicidal stand. His retreat ultimately preserved the Central Kentucky Army for future campaigning and facilitated the massive Confederate counterstrike at the battle of Shiloh.

Secondly, Johnston salvaged as much of the supplies and equipment stored at Nashville as possible. He reported that "the quartermaster's, commissary, and ordnance stores which are not required for immediate use have been ordered to Chattanooga, and those which will be necessary on the march have been forwarded to Huntsville [Alabama] and Decatur [Alabama]. I have ordered a depot to be established at Atlanta for the manufacture of supplies for the Quartermaster's Department and also a laboratory for the manufacture of percussion caps and ordnance stores, and at Chattanooga depots for distribution of these supplies. The machinery will be immediately sent forward."[33] The ordnance shops Johnston established at Atlanta proved invaluable for the ammunition requirements of the main Confederate army in the Western Department for the remainder of the war. Benjamin F. Cooling noted that "Commissary General [Lucius

B.] Northrop told Jefferson Davis in 1879 that he had greatly admired Johnston's ability to coolly save the stores at Nashville and Shelbyville, in contrast to General Joseph E. Johnston's destruction of supplies during a similar retirement later that spring in northern Virginia."[34]

18.

Did Johnston cede control of the Western Department to Beauregard?

With the disaster at Fort Donelson and the capture of Nashville, General Albert Sidney Johnston's generalship was excoriated by Southern politicians, newspapers, soldiers, and citizens alike. President Jefferson Davis sympathized with his friend, acknowledging that "your force has been magnified and the movements of an army [measured] by the capacity for locomotion of an individual. The readiness of the people among whom you are operating to aid you in every method has been constantly asserted, the purpose of your army at Bowling Green wholly misunderstood, and the absence of an effective force at Nashville ignored. You have been held responsible for the fall of Fort Donelson and the capture of Nashville."[1]

Johnston did not publicly respond to the hateful obloquies from the people of the South. He believed that any explanation for the recent disasters would only expose the weakness of the Confederate forces in the Western Department. The general later wrote to Davis that "I observed silence, as it seemed to me the best way to serve the cause and the country... I refrained, well knowing that heavy censures would fall upon me, but convinced that it was better to endure them for the present... The test of merit in my profession with the people is success. It is a hard rule, but I think it right."[2] General Pierre G.T. Beauregard observed that "General Johnston, with that elevation of mind and uncomplaining fortitude for which he was conspicuous, bore, unflinchingly, and without explanation, the reproaches and accusations levelled against him, though he was most keenly alive to the withdrawal of public confidence from him." Johnston ignored the denunciations and focused on retrieving Confederate fortunes in the West.[3]

With such a comparatively small army now occupying central Tennessee, Johnston had yet another strategic dilemma of the greatest import. What critical region of the Western Department should he attempt to defend next? The Mississippi Valley was threatened by the forces of Major General Henry W. Halleck, particularly that of Brigadier General John Pope's army in eastern Missouri. Brigadier General Ulysses S. Grant's army at Fort Donelson could easily move westwards to threaten the Mississippi River too. If the Union seized control of the Mississippi River, they could capture two major cities, Memphis and New Orleans, and split the Confederacy in two. The Trans-Mississippi states would be isolated from the rest of the nation, and it would be difficult to transfer men, food, equipment, and supplies from one side to the other. The loss of Memphis and New Orleans would also be highly demoralizing for the Confederacy, and see large civilian populations fall under the control of the Federal authorities.

However, the fall of Bowling Green and Nashville imperilled central Tennessee to invasion by Brigadier General Don Carlos Buell's Army of the Ohio. Major Jeremy F. Gilmer worried that the Confederacy would "lose Middle and Eastern Tennessee – and most of the country producing a supply of grain and wheat."[4] The Union forces could capture Knoxville, break the railroad connection to Virginia, and then advance on Chattanooga. From this point, another city essential to the Confederate war effort, Atlanta, would be exposed. Thus, both the Mississippi Valley and central Tennessee were as important as one another to the survival of the Confederacy.

Johnston moves west

There has been much debate regarding the extent of Beauregard's influence in Johnston's decision-making during this period. Alfred Roman stated that Beauregard "sent [a message] to General Johnston, then at Murfreesboro, urging him to abandon his line of retreat, along the Stevenson & Chattanooga Railroad, which was taking him farther and farther away, and unless the enemy should anticipate, or intercept him, to turn towards Decatur, from which quarter he would then be within easy distance to cooperate with or join him."[5] Thomas L. Connelly maintained that "on February 26th, even before Johnston had left Murfreesboro, Beauregard sent two telegrams asking him to move to West Tennessee, where a Federal advance was expected. The pressure of the Louisiana general was too strong. The next day, Johnston informed Secretary of War, Judah P. Benjamin, that he was moving to unite with Beauregard in the defense of Memphis and the Mississippi River area."[6]

However, the evidence suggests that Johnston prioritized the defense of the Mississippi Valley long before Beauregard's telegrams. In November 1861, Johnston ordered his chief commissary officer to ensure that supply depots were established at Corinth and Holly Springs in northern Mississippi.[7] In January 1862, Colonel St. John R. Liddell, Johnston's special envoy to Richmond, advised President Davis that unless Johnston was reinforced, he would be "compelled to fall back before superior numbers to the Memphis & Charleston Railroad on the line of the Tennessee River."[8] On the 10th of February, Johnston ordered Major General Mansfield Lovell, the commander at New Orleans, to "send four regiments to Memphis by steamer and one to Iuka by railroad."[9]

Two days later, Johnston instructed Brigadier General Daniel Ruggles to shuttle his brigade of reinforcements from New Orleans to Corinth, only about a day's march from the Tennessee River. These troop movements indicate that the defense of the Mississippi Valley was Johnston's priority, otherwise they would have been directed to Atlanta or Chattanooga. Corinth was an obvious concentration point for the reinforcements from New Orleans as it was a nexus for several important railroad lines. Major General William J. Hardee observed that Corinth "is important [to the Confederacy as] the center of the railroad communications passing southwardly from the Ohio River, through western Tennessee, to the Gulf of

Mexico, and from the Mississippi River eastwardly to the Atlantic."[10]

After the fall of Fort Donelson, Governor Isham G. Harris travelled to Memphis to secure the state archives as recommended by Johnston during the evacuation of Nashville. While in western Tennessee, Harris met with Beauregard for an hour at the general's headquarters in Jackson. He remembered that Beauregard "requested me to urge General A.S. Johnston to concentrate, as speedily as possible, the troops under his command at Corinth."[11] Harris boarded a special train for Corinth, and on arrival, intercepted another *en route* to the bedlam that was at Nashville. The Governor recalled that "General Johnston being then in Murfreesboro, I remained in Nashville until the morning of the 22nd or 23rd of February, when I went to Murfreesboro, where I met General Johnston for the first time since the 16th. I informed him [of Beauregard's] suggestion of the importance of concentrating the two armies at or near Corinth, when General Johnston promptly answered that he was preparing, as rapidly as possible, to move the army under his command to or near Corinth, as he regarded it as important, if not absolutely necessary, that the troops commanded by [Beauregard] and himself should be concentrated in the country at or near Corinth."[12]

Harris's recollection indicates that Johnston had identified Corinth as a point of concentration prior to Beauregard's telegrams of the 26th of February. Indeed, on the 22nd of February, Johnston had already directed Hardee to dispatch Brigadier General Thomas C. Hindman's brigade to Huntsville, a point southwest of both Murfreesboro and Chattanooga, and on the route to Corinth. Timothy B. Smith concluded that "Johnston thus put in motion, as early as February 18 – just two days after Fort Donelson fell – a plan to move westward to unite with Beauregard's force."[13]

Johnston did not require Beauregard to alert him to the danger to the Mississippi Valley. There were ominous signs that the Mississippi River was under imminent threat from the Union armies in the West. Halleck eyed the Confederate fortifications at New Madrid and Island Number Ten and ordered Pope to gather his troops in Missouri and undertake an expedition to seize both strategic points. On the 21st of February, Pope concentrated an army of about 18,000 soldiers at Commerce, Missouri, and advanced towards New Madrid. Pope's infantry would be backed by a powerful navy of six ironclads and fourteen mortar rafts. If this was not concerning enough, Grant's forces were also active on the Tennessee River. Federal gunboats had made several excursions up the river since the fall of Fort Henry, and it was feared that the Union commanders would soon land their troops to destroy the bridges and railroads in the area.

More significantly, Johnston informed President Davis of a move towards the Mississippi Valley in a letter written on the 24th of February, two days before Beauregard's two telegrams of the 26th of February that were cited by Connelly. Johnston declared that "my movements have been delayed by a storm on the 22nd washing away pike and railroad bridge at [Murfreesboro]. [Brigadier General John B.] Floyd, 2,500 strong, will march for Chattanooga tomorrow to defend the central line. This army will move on 26th, by Decatur, for the valley of Mississippi; is in good condition and increasing in numbers."[14]

Stanley F. Horn remarked: "It seems clear that Johnston in retreating from Nashville had no other ultimate objective than a concentration of all his available force (including the men under Beauregard's command) south of the Tennessee River, there to turn and contest the Federal advance... He could hardly have overlooked the advantages of Corinth as a logical place to concentrate – a railroad junction, and close enough to the big bend of the Tennessee River to be a convenient base against any hostile irruption from the river banks for many miles."[15] Horn noted that Corinth's "suitability doubtless appealed to Beauregard also, but Johnston had recognized from the very first that the line of the Cumberland would be hard to defend and that he might have to fall behind the Tennessee to make a final stand. To prepare himself for the contingency he had had all this country mapped by his engineers, and there is ample evidence that he had considered its possibilities long before Beauregard called them to his notice."[16]

On the 25th of February, a day before the Beauregard telegrams cited by Connelly, Johnston informed Richmond: "Considering the peculiar topography of this State and the great power which the enemy's means of transportation affords them upon the Tennessee and Cumberland, it will be seen that the force under my command cannot successfully cover the whole line against the advance of the enemy. I am compelled to elect whether he shall be permitted to occupy Middle Tennessee, or turn Columbus, take

Memphis, and open the valley of the Mississippi."[17] Johnston concluded that "to me the defense of the valley appears of *paramount importance*, and, consequently, I will move this corps of the army, of which I have assumed the immediate command, towards the left bank of the Tennessee, crossing the river near Decatur, in order to enable me to cooperate or unite with General Beauregard for the defense of Memphis and the Mississippi."[18] Thus, the Kentucky Army would march west to the Mississippi Valley.

Johnston's decision was a huge gamble. He informed President Davis that he hoped to "join this corps to the forces of Beauregard (I confess a hazardous experiment)."[19] Major General Braxton Bragg later recalled that Johnston "acting against the advice of some of his best and ablest commanders, wisely determined to concentrate in the valley of the Mississippi."[20] Hardee, Gilmer, and even Johnston's own adjutant general, Colonel William W. Mackall, were opposed to the movement, believing the risk involved was too great. But Johnston remained firm and the fact that Beauregard also desired the concentration of Confederate forces in the Mississippi Valley likely helped steel his resolve. He held the Louisianian's opinion in higher esteem than that of the others, and Hardee's doubts over the plan was further confirmation of his unsuitability for independent command.

As for Tennessee, Johnston asked the Richmond government to appoint a district commander for eastern Tennessee, declaring that "it would be almost impossible for me under present circumstances to superintend the operations at Knoxville and Chattanooga."[21] He noted that "the department has sent eight regiments to Knoxville for the defense of East Tennessee, and the protection of that region will be confided to them and such additional forces as may be hereafter sent from the adjacent States."[22] In early March 1862, Major General Edmund Kirby Smith was appointed commander of the Department of East Tennessee.

The movement of the Kentucky Army southwards and Johnston's removal of important machinery, supplies, and equipment from Bowling Green and Nashville down to Chattanooga and Atlanta had an unintended consequence. Johnston's son observed that "the movement from Nashville, southeast by way of Murfreesboro, to a certain extent beguiled the Federal generals into the belief that General Johnston intended to retreat on Chattanooga and masked the concentration of his troops to the west. A direct retrograde would have betrayed his purpose. Had they understood his design, with larger forces, shorter lines, and better routes, they might have anticipated him at Corinth or even intercepted him at Decatur."[23] Fortunately, Grant was deceived by the activity and wrote to Halleck suggesting that "the rebels have fallen back to Chattanooga."[24] This misconception of Johnston's true intent mitigated the risk involved to the Southern army in its hazardous march to the Mississippi Valley.

Johnston's decision to move his Kentucky Army westwards rather than to the defense of central Tennessee was validated when Halleck was promoted to command of all Union forces in the Western Department. Halleck immediately instructed his former rival, a reluctant Buell, to unite his Army of the Ohio with Grant's Army of the Tennessee at the town of Savannah, Tennessee, situated on the Tennessee River. Halleck was determined to capture Corinth and its hub of railroad connections.

Beauregard's influence

Connelly devoted much energy to portray Beauregard as a wildly ambitious man who gradually assumed informal command of the Western Department from a passive and confused Johnston. He claimed that "not only was Johnston allowing Beauregard both to draw him out of Tennessee and to select the rendezvous area, but also he began to allow Beauregard to manage departmental affairs."[25] After Beauregard was assigned responsibility for Columbus at the Covington House Conference, Connelly hyperbolized the situation: "Command of the Army began to slip gradually from Johnston's hands to Beauregard's, until eventually the latter obtained virtual control... The Creole wanted more than the command of the left wing. For while he might have felt he was partly in exile, Beauregard also envisioned himself as the savior of the entire [Western] Department. He evidently believed he would be the real leader behind the scenes... Johnston seemed in a daze as he gradually handed more power to Beauregard."[26]

Connelly's assertion that Beauregard gradually assumed *de facto* command of the Western Department is not supported by the evidence. When Beauregard first arrived in Bowling Green in February 1862 and realized the weakness of the Confederate armies in the Western Department, he "immediately offered to General Johnston to waive his rank and, acting as his Chief-Engineer and Inspector-General, visit the various works and defences throughout the department, and make such suggestions for their improvement as his experience might dictate. But General Johnston was unwilling to accept so great a sacrifice, and insisted that General Beauregard should go to Columbus, there to ascertain, personally, the exact state of affairs, being convinced that, upon doing so, he would no longer hesitate to assume command."[27]

Far from desiring to seize command, this statement from Roman suggests that Beauregard actively avoided it. Johnston had to coax Beauregard into assuming responsibility of the Mississippi Valley District. The Louisianian accepted his proposal but was clearly not delighted with its prospects. He wrote to a friend from Nashville: "I am taking the helm when the ship is already in the breakers and with but few sailors to man it. How it is to be extricated from its present perilous condition Providence alone can determine, and unless with its aid I can accomplish but little."[28]

After Beauregard departed Nashville, he arrived at Corinth in time to learn of the fall of Fort Donelson. He asked Johnston for specific orders and received the following reply on the 17th of February: "Your dispatch of 16th received. You must do as your judgment dictates. No orders for your troops have issued from here."[29] Two days later, Johnston wrote to Beauregard that he "must now act as seems best to [him]. The separation of our armies is for the present complete."[30] The general's delegation of authority was not abandonment of departmental command – it was a practical measure demanded by the crisis at hand. Such a command situation was forced by circumstances. The Union had penetrated the Confederate cordon defense by capturing Forts Henry and Donelson and could utilize both the Tennessee and Cumberland rivers to invade the Southern heartland. Johnston did not have the ability to supervise and direct Beauregard from afar. It was the same arrangement as that of Brigadier General Felix K. Zollicoffer in eastern Kentucky and Brigadier General John B. Floyd on the Cumberland – Johnston's "mission concept" style of command.

Connelly then suggested that Beauregard issued a series of authoritative orders to Johnston after his assumption of independent command in western Tennessee. On the contrary, the messages reflected an anxious state of mind regarding the security of his forces. For example, on the 26th of February, Beauregard appealed to Johnston: "Appearance of an early attack on New Madrid, in force. Position of absolute necessity to us. Cannot you send a brigade at once, by rail, to assist defense as fast as possible?"[31] The brevity of words in Beauregard's messages does not imply authority. They were concise simply because they transmitted by telegraph rather than courier. Timothy B. Smith observed that "some historians have made an overblown case... some saying [Beauregard] even went so far as to give the senior general orders. These arguments... contain little to no supporting evidence."[32]

Connelly's theory also fails to appreciate the impact of Beauregard's debilitating and prolonged illness. Johnston desired that the Louisianian assume command of the Columbus garrison, but he never made it to the fortress and instead established his headquarters at Jackson in southwestern Tennessee. Beauregard then delegated the evacuation of the Mississippi River fortress, declaring that "my health is too feeble to authorize me to assume command, but I shall advise with [Major General Leonidas] Polk."[33] On the 19th of February, Governor Harris and Polk were compelled to travel to Jackson to discuss Confederate strategy in western Tennessee with the stricken general, for he was physically incapable of travel. Johnston telegraphed Beauregard on the 20th of February: "If not well enough to assume command, I hope that you, now having had time to study the field, will advise General Polk of your judgment as to the proper disposition of his army, in accordance with the views you entertained in our memoranda, unless you have changed your views. I cannot order him, not knowing but that you have assumed command, and our orders conflict."[34]

Beauregard informed Richmond on the 21st of February that "I regret profoundly to have to acquaint the War Department that my ill health has made it improper for me as yet to assume the command assigned me."[35] Beauregard became despondent, complaining that "I am in despair about my health – nervous affection of throat. Bragg ought to be sent here at once. I will, when well enough, serve under him rather than not have him here."[36] For a man apparently scheming to supersede Johnston in command of the Western Department, it seems strange that Beauregard would ask the government to replace himself with the lower-ranked Bragg and then offer to serve under that general. Beauregard also delegated the difficult evacuation of Columbus to Polk. Fortunately, the bishop extricated the entire garrison in only five days, and transferred vast quantities of food, supplies, and ordnance further southwards.[37]

When Bragg finally arrived at Corinth, he received a plaintive message from Beauregard, which was also forwarded to Johnston: "My health not permitting me yet to be with you... I hope, however, to be well enough to join you when the fighting shall have commenced, not, however, to interfere with your arrangement, but merely to assist you, if I can, and prevent misunderstandings, complications etc. My physician tells me that I must stop talking altogether and avoid any undue excitement. How in the world can that be done, at this critical moment? They might as well tell a drowning man that he must not catch at a straw."[38] Bragg visited Beauregard at his Jackson headquarters about a week later but felt that the Louisianian's state of health was so poor that he could not leave his incapacitated commander and return to his own men at Corinth. Bragg wrote to his wife that "every [dispatch] from Polk stresses him back a week. But for my arrival here to aid him, I do not believe he would now be living."[39] This does not sound like a man envisioning himself as "the savior of the entire Department" or "the real leader behind the scenes," as Connelly liked to imagine it.

The concentration at Corinth

Connelly also lavished praise on Beauregard for the unprecedented concentration of Confederate forces at Corinth. The historian claimed that "in a series of dramatic statements, he excited the attention of the Mississippi Valley people as well as the authorities in Richmond. For the first time, Richmond hastened to answer pleas from the West...Beauregard was simply more adept at stirring public opinion than Johnston had been."[40] Yet Connelly ignored the chronology of events in his effort to diminish Johnston. It was the catastrophe at Fort Henry, not Beauregard's appeals, that finally stirred Richmond into action. On the 8th of February, two days after the fall of Fort Henry, approximately 5,000 Southern troops from Lovell's garrison at New Orleans were ordered to Corinth. A further 10,000 soldiers from the coastal garrisons at Mobile and Pensacola were placed under the command of Bragg and similarly dispatched to the threatened area.

Immediately after the fall of Fort Henry, the Secretary of War, Judah P. Benjamin, informed Bragg that "the condition of affairs in Kentucky and Tennessee demands from us the most vigorous effort for defense, and General A.S. Johnston is so heavily outnumbered, that it is scarcely possible for him to maintain his whole line without large additional reinforcements. We have ordered to his aid four regiments from Virginia and 5,000 men from New Orleans, and by thus subtracting something from other points, where the pressure is not so great, we hope to enable him to defend his lines until the new levies ordered from all the States shall be in condition to take the field."[41]

Benjamin explained to Bragg that "the heavy blow which has been inflicted on us by the recent operations in Kentucky and Tennessee renders necessary a change in our whole plan of campaign… We had had in contemplation the necessity of abandoning the seaboard in order to defend the Tennessee line, which is vital to our safety… The decision is made, and the President desires that you proceed as promptly as possible to withdraw your forces from Pensacola and Mobile and hasten to the defense of the Tennessee line. We suppose it will be necessary to abandon Columbus and fall back to Island Number Ten, or possibly to Memphis… Without additional supplies of arms, we cannot hold our entire exposed coast and frontier, and we must withdraw from the defense of the whole Gulf coast except New Orleans. I shall order all troops from Eastern Florida also to Tennessee."[42]

Benjamin then informed Johnston that "the condition of your department in consequence of the largely superior forces of the enemy has filled us with solicitude, and we have used every possible exertion to organize some means for your relief… We have called on all the States for a levy of men for the war and think that in very few weeks we shall be able to give you heavy reinforcements, although we may not be able to arm them with good weapons."[43] Fortunately, Beauregard had managed to procure the services of 2,000 Louisiana militia and had organized for them to be transported to Corinth by rail. In a somewhat theatrical stunt, Beauregard called for the citizens of the Mississippi Valley to donate their plantation bells to the army, so the items could be melted down to cast cannons.

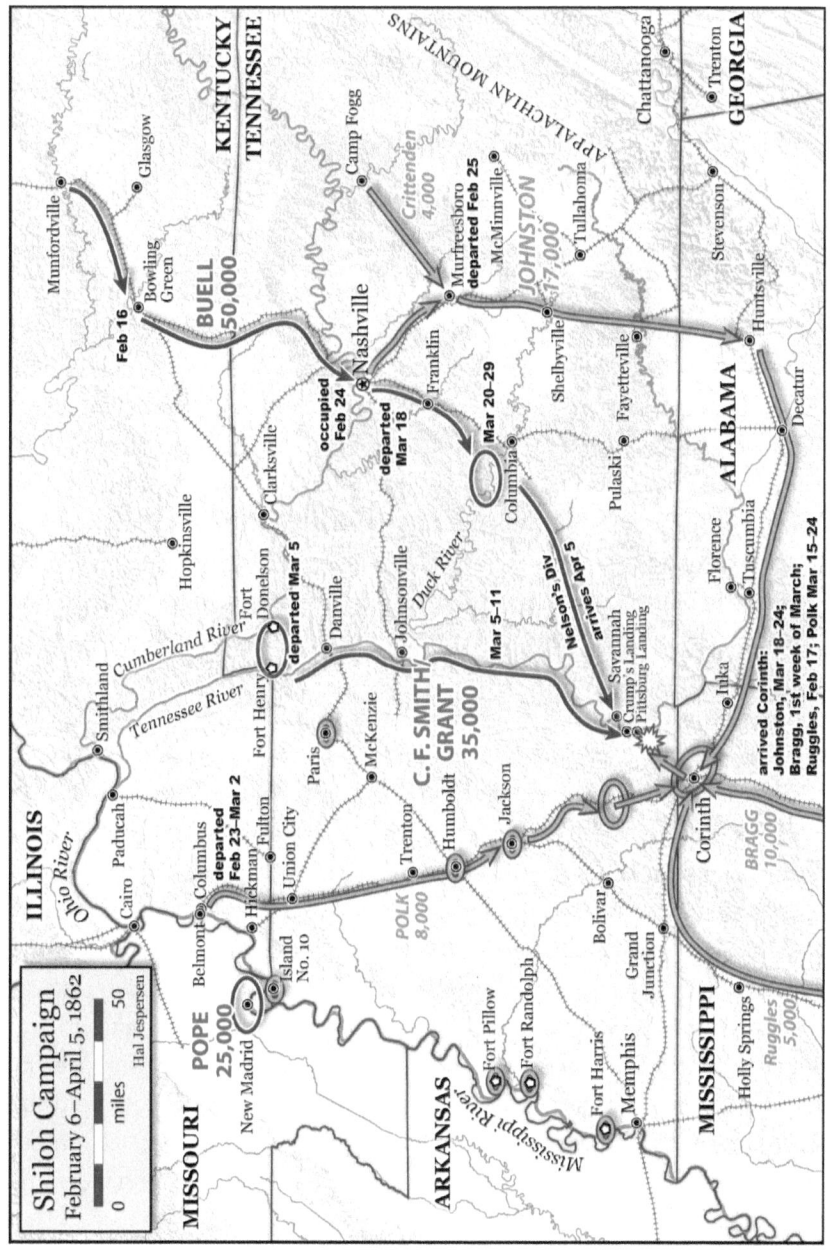

Beauregard's appeal did create a media sensation, and dozens of bells were donated. Despite the display of patriotism, the positive impact of this action on the Confederate artillery corps was negligible. Bragg considered Beauregard's petition melodramatic and informed his wife that the Confederate army lacked trained cannoneers rather than cannons, and that "there was more than enough casting metal available in New Orleans."[44]

Conclusion

Connelly's claims that Beauregard compelled Johnston to move the Kentucky Army to the Mississippi Valley rather than Middle Tennessee, that he assumed *de facto* control of the Western Department, and that he selected Corinth as the point of concentration for the Confederate forces in the West are reckless statements. It is apparent from the documentary evidence that Johnston made the decision to move westwards, against the opinion of his senior subordinates, and prior to the receipt of Beauregard's telegrams. In addition, the Louisianian's chronic illness and reluctance to assume personal command of the Confederate forces at both Columbus and Corinth lends much doubt to Connelly's theory. The latitude in command that Johnston afforded Beauregard in western Tennessee was consistent with his previous delegations of authority to subordinates separated by vast distances, such as Polk, Zollicoffer and Floyd.

Regarding the concentration at Corinth, it was the disaster at Fort Henry that galvanized the Confederate government and resulted in a change of policy. Beauregard's arrival in western Tennessee and his calls for additional support had no significant influence on this decision. While it is true that Beauregard obtained the services of some militia from Louisiana and organized the Southern troops arriving in western Tennessee, it was the catastrophe on the Tennessee River that compelled Richmond to act. Smith correctly stated that "although Johnston had been begging for arms and men for months now, only after the major blow at Fort Henry did the Confederate government understand the pending crisis and act. Richmond had provided a trickle of guns and troops in the months previous, but nothing large enough to turn the tide of war."[45]

19.

Was Johnston's march to Corinth too slow?

General Albert Sidney Johnston's Kentucky Army numbered about 17,000 troops with the absorption of the remnants of Major General George B. Crittenden's District of East Tennessee forces and the refugees from Fort Donelson. Like the people of the South, many of Johnston's officers and soldiers were demoralized by the defeats at Fishing Creek, Fort Henry, and Fort Donelson, and by the precipitate evacuations of Bowling Green and Nashville. Major Jeremy F. Gilmer remarked that Johnston "wears a very anxious face. Still, he expresses confidence that better fortune awaits us."[1] Having dispatched Brigadier General Thomas C. Hindman's brigade southwest from Murfreesboro to Huntsville on the 22nd of February 1862, Johnston prepared to lead the remainder of his troops out of the town the next day. The distance from Murfreesboro to Corinth was approximately 165 miles (266 km) and "Johnston intended the column to make fifteen miles [24 km] a day."[2] However, the Kentucky Army consumed about a month in completing the journey, resulting in an average distance of less than six miles (9.7 km) per day.

General Pierre G.T. Beauregard first referred to "General Johnston's *slow* and quiet retreat, first to Murfreesboro, thence to Fayetteville [Tennessee], Huntsville, and Decatur," in the late nineteenth century.[3]

Historian Matthew F. Steele picked up on this comment and declared: "If General Johnston fully appreciated the importance of reuniting the wings of his army 'sufficiently in rear,' and as quickly as possible, he certainly did not show his appreciation by prompt action... He reached Murfreesboro in his retreat from Nashville about the 20th of February, but he did not start from there for Corinth until the 28th of February."[4] Thomas L. Connelly argued that Johnston "dawdled on the march to Corinth, with his flank constantly exposed to attack from the river. It was a month from the time Johnston announced his decision to move until he joined Beauregard. Bad weather and the need to collect supplies were partly responsible – but Johnston also moved too slowly."[5] Larry J. Daniel concurred with Connelly's assessment, claiming that Johnston "stayed much too long at Decatur, seemingly more focused on saving pork supplies than on the concentration of troops."[6]

Despite these critical statements from Steele, Connelly, and Daniel, the fact is that there were several major factors influencing the rapidity of the Kentucky Army's march from Murfreesboro to Corinth that were completely out of Johnston's control. These factors rendered the general's stated objective of fifteen miles (24 km) per day an unattainable goal.

The first problem: Miserable weather

Steele's condemnation of Johnston for "tarrying for more than a week at Murfreesboro" is easily refuted.[7] The wet and wintery weather that had plagued the army for several weeks intensified with a massive downpour on the 22nd of February that washed away the pike and railway bridges at Murfreesboro. It took almost a week for the Confederate engineers to repair the structures, and as a result, Johnston's army could not leave the town until the 28th of February. More charitably, Steele acknowledged that "after leaving Murfreesboro, Johnston's army made the march to Corinth, by way of Decatur, as rapidly as practicable under the circumstances. The roads were terribly bad, and the streams all swollen."[8]

Once the bridges had been repaired, the Kentucky Army began its march. As Steele noted, the miserable weather severely impacted the journey. The dirt roads leading from Murfreesboro to Fayetteville were transformed into muddy bogs that greatly impeded the passage of soldiers, horses, and wheeled vehicles. Johnston's son wrote that the "incessant rains, varying from a drizzle to a torrent, flooded the roads, washed away bridges, and made encampment almost intolerable and marching nearly impossible."[9] Gilmer informed his wife that "we live and move in mud and water, and the roads have come to such a pass that we can't move much longer."[10] One soldier reported that "the state of the weather – heavy rains having set in before the command had quitted the vicinity of Nashville – foreboded evil, in retarding if not arresting the progress of the army, by swollen streams and impassable mud."[11] Another declared that "rain continued to fall almost without intermission… The passage of such numbers of horses and wagons, rendered the route literally a river of liquid mud… For miles at times the wagons would be submerged in ooze and mire up to the hubs of their wheels."[12]

On the evening of the 14th of March, a storm collapsed nearly all the tents of a Kentucky brigade in Crittenden's division and provoked a terrified herd of cattle to stampede through their campsite.[13] Crittenden reported the following morning that "owing to the condition of the roads and the water, I am unable to move my command today."[14] Likewise, Hindman informed the commanding general that "the creek at [Courtland, Alabama] is impassable… one battery of my artillery is in Courtland, and cannot be crossed except on cars. It will probably be ten days or two weeks before the water will admit of artillery moving on the dirt road to Corinth."[15] Such reports were all too common. The abnormally wet weather of February 1862, having facilitated the Union offensives against Forts Henry and Donelson, now cruelly impacted Johnston's own army's ability to move.

The second reason: Demoralization of the army

After a string of defeats and retreats, the Kentucky Army suffered from shattered morale and almost complete disorganization. Johnston had to rebuild the spirits of his troops and assemble the fragmented commands into cohesive units. He implemented a strict discipline on the troops and shared in the privations of the march. Johnston's renowned ability to inspire and cheer the men was as strong as ever, and the quality and organization of the army improved with every mile travelled. Charles P.

Roland declared that Johnston "worked tirelessly while on the march to restore the spirit of his men, and fashion them into an effective striking force. The Civil War was to witness no more remarkable transformation than he achieved in this effort."[16] Johnston reported to President Jefferson Davis on the 7th of March that "the general condition of the troops is good and effective, though their health is impaired by the usual camp disasters and a winter campaign. The fall of Donelson disheartened some of the Tennessee troops and caused many desertions from some of the new regiments, so that great care was required to inspire confidence. I now consider the tone of the troops restored, and that they are in good order."[17]

On the 11th of March, Johnston notified Beauregard from Decatur that "the force here is in good condition and fine spirits. They are anxious to meet the enemy."[18] Historian Thomas K. Hall observed that "Johnston was determined to restore the confidence of his men. His efforts paid off. He imposed strict march discipline and moved the defeated soldiers with surprising deliberation. So, while critics have panned Johnston for this move, he deserves praise for bringing the soldiers to Corinth with relative ease."[19] One of the soldiers remarked that "demoralization, almost unavoidably consequent upon the state of the public mind and the nature of a retreat, threatened to destroy the efficiency of troops who could not have been spared in case of an attack… but everything went on with a regularity and a degree of order… and [Johnston] reached Corinth with no little loss of men or munition."[20] The fact that the troops in Johnston's army could fight so doggedly less than a month later at the battle of Shiloh is a testament to the commanding general's ability to restore the morale, discipline, and confidence of a volunteer army that had nearly been ruined by military disaster, wretched weather, and epidemics of disease.

The third problem: Supplies

The necessity to transfer the army's food and supplies was a significant encumbrance. Johnston explained to President Davis that "the stores accumulated at Murfreesboro, the pork and provisions at Shelbyville and other points, and their necessary protection and removal, with the bad roads and inclement weather, have made the march slow and laborious, and delayed my movements."[21] Historian O. Edward Cunningham wrote that "General A.S. Johnston's army was burdened with large quantities of ammunition, provisions, and artillery. Hampered by a shortage of trained staff officers, the Kentuckian was able to move toward the junction but slowly."[22] The difficulty in transporting these supplies was exacerbated by the muddy roads and the deficient railroad network in western Tennessee.

Then there was also the impact of pro-Union and rebellious citizenry that inhabited certain pockets in Tennessee and Alabama. On the 9th of March, it was reported that "the citizens of Shelbyville, Bedford County, Tenn., burned a large quantity of Confederate stores, to prevent their falling into the hands of the rebel troops under A. Sidney Johnston, who were in full retreat from Murfreesboro."[23] These incidents further complicated the Kentucky Army's ability to safeguard and transfer its supplies and provender to Corinth with greater celerity.

The final problem: Degraded railroad capacity

The deplorable state of the Confederate railroads meant that Johnston's capacity to transport both the soldiers and the army's supplies was highly restricted. The general was compelled to prioritize the shipment of convalescents, food, supplies, and equipment by rail and march the healthy soldiers on foot. This resulted in significant delays due to the waterlogged dirt roads that had to be utilized instead of the railroad. After the war, Gilmer explained the effect of the constrained railroad system on the pace of Johnston's march: "It was simply impossible [to ship the men by rail] without sacrificing the supplies and munitions on which the subsistence and armament of the command depended. The entire transportation capacity of the railroads was taxed to the utmost, and even then, immense quantities of meat and other commissary supplies were left at [points along the line of march]."[24] Bragg complained that "our whole railroad system is utterly deranged and confused. Wood and water stations are abandoned."[25]

Once at Decatur, Johnston requested that Beauregard send locomotives and 400 railcars from the Memphis & Charleston Railroad to the town to facilitate his movement to Corinth. Unfortunately, most of these units had already been allocated to Bragg's transfer from the Gulf Coast. Similarly, the locomotives and 200 railcars of the Mobile & Ohio Railroad were engaged with the transport of half of Major General Leonidas Polk's troops from Humboldt to Corinth. Demonstrating great resourcefulness, Beauregard somehow managed to scrape together 160 railroad cars from the Mississippi Central Railroad for Johnston's use, but then there was yet another delay.[26]

Johnston explained the issue to Beauregard: "I had the [railroad bridge at Decatur] planked for crossing artillery and trains, but on account of the great difference in the length of axles it cannot be used for that purpose. We are now bringing them over on platform cars, which is a slow process."[27] Timothy B. Smith noted that "Johnston at first ordered planking between the rails only so both trains and troops could use the span. But the engineers soon found that the wagons and artillery wheels were too wide, so the planking had to go on the rails too. Rather than stop rail traffic, they simply decided to load everything on cars for transport across, which created a bottleneck and took even more time."[28]

Thus, there were several intractable factors that delayed Johnston's movement from Murfreesboro to Corinth. Comments from historians that he "dawdled" are unnecessarily harsh. The state of the weather and the roads, the need to restore the efficiency of the army, and the seriously deficient railroad transportation available in the Western Department were the true cause of the delays. The fact that Johnston's army still managed to traverse six miles a day (9.7 km) on average is quite remarkable. The Civil War witnessed far slower marches. Brigadier General George H. Thomas' division consumed sixteen days to march the 65 miles (105 km) from Columbia to Logan's Crossroads in Kentucky in January 1862. Between April and May 1862, Major General Henry W. Halleck's army took an entire month to cover the twenty miles (32 km) from Pittsburg Landing to Corinth. In June 1862, Major General Don Carlos Buell's army consumed almost two months to move the 230 miles (373 km) from Corinth to Chattanooga.

Vulnerable to attack

Connelly's criticism that Johnston's flank was constantly exposed to attack during the march to Corinth is also unwarranted considering the precautions that Johnston employed to mitigate the risk. His army lacked pontoon boats and the only railroad bridges that crossed the Tennessee River were located at Florence [Alabama] and Decatur. The march to Florence was faster, but Union gunboats could interfere with the crossing of the river. Johnston decided to play it safe and march directly south to Decatur, where the water was too shallow for the warships to cross.

After departing Murfreesboro, Johnston ordered Major General William J. Hardee, commanding the Kentucky Army's rearguard, to destroy every bridge over which the enemy might follow. Johnston also effectively utilized his cavalry for reconnaissance and screening operations. The movement of his army was "covered by a cloud of cavalry, [Colonel Benjamin H.] Helm's 1st Kentucky, [Colonel John] Scott's Louisiana, [Colonel William] Wirt Adams's Mississippi, and by [Colonel Nathan B.] Forrest's and [Captain John H.] Morgan's commands, who were bold and energetic in harassing the enemy."[29] Morgan's troopers scouted the area around Nashville and interfered with the activities of Buell's Army of the Ohio, currently occupying the Tennessee capital. Federal outposts were attacked, a steamer was set alight on the Cumberland River, a locomotive and several railroad cars were burnt, and over a hundred prisoners were taken.[30] Morgan's raid unsettled Buell and distracted him from any pursuit of Johnston's army.

The vulnerability of Kentucky Army was further diminished when Johnston directed the army's mail and much of the stores and ordnance rescued from Nashville to Chattanooga. The dispatch of 2,500 men under Brigadier General John B. Floyd to the town also encouraged the perception that Johnston's entire army was heading in that direction. On the 25th of February, Grant notified Halleck that Johnston was moving eastwards to Chattanooga.[31] Three days later, Buell wrote to Major General George B. McClellan that "it is stated to me quite confidentially that Columbus is being evacuated and the enemy concentrating in the direction of Chattanooga."[32] Buell even began to imagine that Johnston's army would return to fight for Nashville, informing McClellan that "Johnston is at Shelbyville, some 25 miles [40 km] south of Murfreesboro. The talk in his camp is that at Fayetteville, 20 miles [32 km] farther south, they were to meet Beauregard, with 25,000 from Virginia and South Carolina, and then return against Nashville."[33] These misapprehensions guaranteed the safe passage of the Confederate army to Corinth.

Conclusion

The criticism from various historians that Johnston dawdled in relocating the Kentucky Army from Murfreesboro to Corinth is unsupported by the evidence. Johnston worked diligently to facilitate the movement of the army, reporting to President Davis that "I am in a most hazardous movement of a large force, even the most minute detail requiring my attention for its accomplishment."[34] Unfortunately, his efforts were impeded by the terrible weather, the need to revive the spirits and discipline of the army, the need to transport supplies, and the limited railroad capacity. Governor Isham G. Harris remarked: "I was with him most of the time of his retreat from Nashville to Corinth, and not infrequently I was astonished at the coolness, vigilance, and ability with which he struggled to overcome the numerous obstacles and difficulties with which he was obliged to contend."[35]

Colonel William Preston recalled that Johnston's "two chief staff officers, Colonels [William W.] Mackall and Gilmer, deemed it impossible. Johnston persevered. He collected Crittenden and the relics of his command, with stragglers and fugitives from Donelson, and moved through Shelbyville and Fayetteville on Decatur. Halting at these points, he saved his provisions and stores, removed his depots and machine-shops, obtained new arms, and finally, at the close of March, joined Beauregard at Corinth."[36] One Kentucky soldier proclaimed that "history records no example of a retreat conducted with such success under such adverse circumstances."[37] Historian John R. Lundberg asserted that "Johnston's execution of the retreat from Nashville and junction with Beauregard at Corinth was nothing short of brilliant."[38]

20.

Was Johnston too slow in ordering Van Dorn to Corinth?

I n December 1861, the Confederate government finally recognized that the Western Department was too vast for General Albert Sidney Johnston to supervise alone. It decided to appoint a dedicated commander for the states west of the Mississippi River – Arkansas, Missouri, and the Indian Territory. Secretary of War, Judah P. Benjamin, approached Major General Braxton Bragg, commander of the Army of Pensacola in Florida, with the offer of this command. On paper, Bragg was a fine choice. He was 44 years old, a native of North Carolina, West Point educated, possessed decades of military experience, and a renowned disciplinarian. Unfortunately for the Secretary of War, Bragg declined, complaining that "the field to which you invite me is a most important one, but, under present aspects, not enticing... Without a base of operations, in a country poorly supplied at best, and now exhausted by being overrun by both armies in mid-winter, with an unclad, badly-fed, and badly-supplied mass of men, without instruction, arms, equipments, or officers, it is certainly a most unpromising field of operations."[1]

Disappointed, Benjamin approached the next candidate in mind, Brigadier General Henry Heth of Virginia, who also declined. Finally, the Secretary of War found a willing nominee in Major General Van Dorn. This officer was 41 years old, a native of Mississippi, West Point

Major General Braxton Bragg

graduate, and veteran of the Mexican-American War. Van Dorn had seen action at the battle of Monterrey, the siege of Vera Cruz, and the battles of Cerro Gordo, Contreras, Churubusco, and the Belén Gate. After the war, he performed garrison duty at various points across the country and fought in the Seminole War in Florida from 1849 to 1850. Van Dorn was promoted to Captain in Johnston's United States 2nd Cavalry regiment in 1855 and spent the next six years fighting the Seminole and Comanche in the Indian Territory, Texas, and Kansas.

Bold and impulsive, Van Dorn had relished the challenge of fighting the Comanche on the frontier. A fellow Confederate officer recalled that "Van Dorn, with his light, graceful figure, florid face, light waving hair, and bright blue eyes seemed made for love and war."[2] With his blonde curls, love of music, and immaculate uniform, Van Dorn was considered somewhat of a dandy by the Confederate soldiers in the west, but his womanizing earned him the sobriquet of "the terror of ugly husbands" from a Mobile newspaper.[3] Upon Van Dorn's appointment, Benjamin informed Johnston that "our views will be fully disclosed to Major General Earl Van Dorn, just assigned to the command of the Trans-Mississippi District, of your department, with orders to report to you in person on his way to the West."[4] Soon enough, Van Dorn developed, either in concert with Richmond or from his own imagination, a grandiose strategic offensive to defeat Union Brigadier General Samuel R. Curtis's Army of the Southwest in northern Arkansas, invade Missouri, capture Saint Louis, and then drive eastward into Illinois.

In February 1862, Van Dorn wrote to his wife of his intended campaign while at Knoxville, *en route* to Bowling Green: "I am now 'in for it,' as the saying is, to make a reputation and serve my country conspicuously or fail. I must not, shall not, do the latter. I must have Saint Louis – then Huzzah!"[5] After meeting with Johnston at his headquarters in the central Kentucky town, Van Dorn continued to Arkansas with the

Major General Earl Van Dorn

same plan in mind. Johnston apparently endorsed Van Dorn's offensive plans in the Trans-Mississippi as a diversion to relieve the pressure on his embattled line in Kentucky and Tennessee. After arriving at Pocahontas, Van Dorn informed his new subordinate, Major General Sterling Price, that the campaign against Saint Louis "seems to me the movement best calculated to win us Missouri and relieve General Johnston, who is heavily threatened in Kentucky."[6]

General Pierre G.T. Beauregard was thinking along similar lines to Van Dorn. On the 21st of February, he wrote to the new Trans-Mississippi commander that "the fate of Missouri necessarily depends on the successful defence of Columbus, and of Island Number Ten; hence, we must, if possible, combine our operations not only to defend those positions, but also to take the offensive, as soon as practicable, to recover some of our lost ground. I have just called on the governors of Tennessee, Louisiana, and Mississippi, for 5,000 men from each State."[7] Beauregard stated that he had "15,000 disposable for the field; if you could certainly join me, via New Madrid or Columbus, with 10,000 more, we could thus take the field with 40,000 men, take Cairo, Paducah, the mouth of the Tennessee and Cumberland Rivers, and, most probably, be able to take also Saint Louis, by the river. What say you to this brilliant programme which I know is fully practicable, if we can get the forces?"[8]

Yet Beauregard's scheme was not practicable at all. The governors could not provide the requested troops, and there was insufficient transportation, equipment, and supplies available for such a large-scale operation. The plan also ignored the presence of Union gunboats that could be employed to defend Cairo, Paducah, and other strategic locations on the Mississippi, Tennessee, and Cumberland rivers. In any case, Van Dorn did not receive Beauregard's message for several days, and he had already committed his army to the campaign to defeat Curtis and then march his victorious army to Saint Louis.

The battle of Pea Ridge

On the 24th of February, Van Dorn notified Johnston that he was ready to strike Curtis's forces in northern Arkansas. The Federal army had almost 12,000 troops and a powerful complement of artillery. However, in a rare instance, the Confederates outnumbered the Federals, with Van Dorn's Army of the West totalling about 14,000 men from the combined commands of Price, Brigadier General Ben McCulloch, and Brigadier General Albert Pike. However, many of the soldiers were indifferently armed and lacked discipline. Pike's troops included two regiments of Cherokee mounted infantry. Van Dorn informed Johnston that "Price and McCulloch are concentrated at Cross Hollow, twelve miles [19 km] from enemy's advance, on Sugar Creek, near Missouri line… I leave this evening to go to the army, and will give battle; of course, if it does not take place before I arrive. I have no doubt of the result. If I succeed, I shall push on."[9] Van Dorn had a good chance of victory, and if successful, Major General Henry W. Halleck would be compelled to divert troops from Major General Ulysses S. Grant's army in western Tennessee to reinforce Curtis in the Trans-Mississippi.

Although an audacious general, Van Dorn was no logistician, and he neglected the preparations essential to an offensive operation. Most of his supplies were left behind due to the rapidity of his march. By the time his army advanced on Curtis, the troops were sorely fatigued and hungry. At the ensuing battle of Pea Ridge, Arkansas, from the 7th to the 8th of March, Van Dorn's attack was repelled by Curtis and then his army broken apart by a powerful Union counterattack. Northern losses were 1,384 compared to Confederate casualties of about 2,000 men. McCulloch was killed in action, and his replacement, Brigadier General James M. McIntosh, was slain almost immediately afterward. Colonel William Y. Slack was mortally wounded, and Colonel Louis Hébert was captured. Halleck apprised Grant on the 10th of March that "the hard-fought battle and signal victory by General Curtis in the Southwest relieves the reserves intended for his support. They will be sent to you immediately."[10] Unfortunately for Johnston and his embattled forces in Tennessee, Van Dorn's efforts had not borne fruit, and the Union concentration of strength on the Tennessee River continued unabated.

The Army of the West was wrecked from its heavy defeat at Pea

Ridge and the retreat southward to the town of Van Buren, Arkansas, in miserably cold weather reduced it to a mere rabble. Over the 14th and 15th of March, most of the troops trudged into camp near the town and were welcomed by the wagons of food and supplies that had accumulated during their absence when campaigning in northern Arkansas. Stragglers continued to trickle in to camp over the coming days. The irrepressible Van Dorn reported to Johnston on the 18th of March that "I have the pleasure to inform you that the entire army I marched against the enemy some days since is now in camp a few miles from [Van Buren], and that I shall march in a few days for Pocahontas, to make a junction with whatever force that may be assembled at that place. It is my intention then to fall upon the force of the enemy in the vicinity of New Madrid or Cape Girardeau and attempt to relieve General Beauregard, and, if practicable, I shall march on Saint Louis, and thus withdraw the forces now threatening this part of the State of Arkansas... I attempted first to beat the enemy at [Pea Ridge], but a series of accidents, entirely unforeseen and not under my control and a badly disciplined army, defeated my intentions."[11]

The next day, Beauregard conveyed to Van Dorn that it was "too late for movement on New Madrid, which is in possession of enemy, but if at any time you can join your forces with mine it will be best to do so."[12] After arriving in Corinth on the night of the 22nd of March, Johnston ordered the Trans-Mississippi commander to "move your command to Memphis by the route in your judgment the best and most expeditious, and on arriving report to these headquarters."[13] Johnston decided to abandon Arkansas to the enemy for the time being and concentrate Van Dorn's army at Corinth for the confrontation with Halleck's armies.

Was the order too late?
Charles P. Roland criticised Johnston for making a "strategic miscalculation in seizing the opportunity offered by Halleck's move [to the Tennessee River] when he failed to bring together all available troops for the stroke. In Arkansas were 20,000 men under General Earl Van Dorn who could have been added to the army at Corinth."[14] Roland argued that "Johnston was remiss in failing to order Van Dorn east of the Mississippi immedi-

ately, once the Battle of Pea Ridge was lost."[15] Roland's reproach is not justified. The Confederate Army of the West had been utterly shattered by its defeat at Pea Ridge, with its senior commanders decimated. The losses of McCulloch, McIntosh, Slack, and Hébert were devastating in terms of their impact on morale, discipline, and organization.

As Van Dorn's demoralized Southern soldiers retreated through the town of Fayetteville, Arkansas, it was evident that the integrity of the army was almost gone. One observer recorded that "the army was a confused mob, not a regiment, not a company in rank, save two regiments of cavalry, which, as a rearguard, passed through near sundown; the rest were a rabble-rout, not four or five abreast, but the whole road about fifty feet [15 m] wide perfectly filled with men, every one seemingly animated by the same desire to get away. They were thoroughly dispirited. And thus, for hours, the human tide swept by, a broken, drifting, disorganized mass, not an officer, that I could see, to give an order; and had there been, he could not have reduced that formless mass to discipline or order."[16] It took a week for Van Dorn's ruined army to tramp from Pea Ridge to the safety of Van Buren in cold and inclement weather. Historians William L. Shea and Earl J. Hess wrote that "the entire army was sunk in lethargy brought on by exhaustion, malnourishment, depression, and a virtual epidemic of colds, pneumonia, and diarrhea."[17] One Confederate veteran asserted that Van Dorn's "retreat was more disastrous than a dozen battles."[18]

Conclusion

Roland's reproach of Johnston for not ordering Van Dorn's Army of the West to Corinth immediately after the battle of Pea Ridge is unfair. Considering the frightful state of Van Dorn's army after its devastating defeat and calamitous retreat to Van Buren it is quite impossible that the Mississippian could have moved his forces to Corinth earlier than he did, even if ordered to do so immediately after the battle as Roland suggested. The troops were simply in no condition to march and would require weeks to recover their health, organization, and morale. Meanwhile, events on the Tennessee River moved so rapidly, and the availability of transportation across the Mississippi River was so deficient, that Van Dorn's forces did not arrive in Corinth until after the battle of Shiloh.

21.

Did Johnston approve the Shiloh battle plan?

On the 1st of March 1862, the Union timberclad warships, the *Tyler* and *Lexington*, raided the small hamlet of Pittsburg Landing on the Tennessee River, about 19 miles (30 km) northeast of Corinth. It was the prelude to a major Union offensive up the river. Still in transit across northern Alabama, General Albert Sidney Johnston received a troubling communication from General Pierre G.T. Beauregard the following day: "I think you ought to hurry up your troops to Corinth by railroad, as soon as practicable, for here or thereabouts will soon be fought the great battle of this controversy."[1]

Beauregard's warning was timely. Major General Henry W. Halleck soon issued orders for Major General Ulysses S. Grant's senior division commander, Brigadier General Charles F. Smith, to embark on an expedition upriver from Fort Henry to Savannah, Tennessee. Smith was allocated 25,000 men and most of Grant's artillery. His objective was to "destroy the railroad-bridge over Bear Creek, near Eastport, Mississippi, and also the connections at Corinth, Jackson, and Humboldt."[2] Meanwhile, Johnston informed Richmond on the 11th of March that "my command is now crossing the Tennessee line, the advance marching toward Tuscumbia. The enemy are reported yesterday in twelve transports, about 12,000 strong, at Savannah, with thirty or forty more transports expected. It is supposed

[Major General Don Carlos] Buell will concentrate the main force there to cooperate with Grant."[3]

The next day, the first division of C.F. Smith's expedition landed at Savannah on the eastern side of the Tennessee River. On the 13th of March, Brigadier General Lew Wallace's division disembarked at Crump's Landing, roughly parallel to Savannah on the western side of the river.[4] Brigadier General William T. Sherman's division then disembarked at Tyler's Landing on the mouth of Yellow Creek, a tributary of the Tennessee River, on the evening of the 14th of March, and the bluecoats marched inland with the intention to cut the Memphis & Charleston Railroad. Fortunately for the Confederates, the miserable weather that had been plaguing Johnston's march from Murfreesboro also impacted Sherman's expedition and he was forced to return to Pittsburg Landing.

Grant arrived in Savannah on the 17th of March to assume command of the Union Army of the Tennessee from C.F. Smith. He was encouraged by Sherman's enthusiasm regarding the defensive potential and spaciousness of the terrain at Pittsburg Landing and ordered the bulk of his forces to move to that location.[5] It was a very risky decision. The Union forces were protected by the Tennessee River at Savannah and moving across the river to the western side made them vulnerable to a Confederate attack. However, Halleck, recently promoted to overall command in the western theater, now ordered Buell's 70,000-strong Army of the Ohio to leave Nashville and unite with Grant's forces at Savannah.

Buell detached 18,000 soldiers to garrison the Tennessee capital and dispatched another 15,000 men under Brigadier General Ormsby M. Mitchel southwards to Fayetteville to cut the Memphis & Charleston Railroad. Buell's remaining 37,000 troops would march southwest to link up with Grant at Savannah. Hoping to delay the unification of Grant's and Buell's armies at Savannah, Johnston ordered Captain John H. Morgan's cavalry to destroy the bridge over the Duck River. When Buell's first division arrived at Columbia, Tennessee, they were greeted by the sight of the ruined structure. The bridge had been 180 feet (55 m) long, and due to the torrential state of the river, the Union engineers struggled to rebuild it. Buell ordered the construction of a temporary pontoon bridge, but progress was slow, and his army's union with Grant was delayed by nearly two weeks.[6]

The lead elements of Johnston's Kentucky Army arrived in Corinth on the 18th of March, and the general himself set foot in the town on the night of the 22nd of March. Major General Leonidas Polk had arrived a day earlier, bringing one division of his Columbus garrison to Corinth and another to Bethel Station, 24 miles (39 km) north of Corinth, to guard against an advance of Wallace's division at Crump's Landing. The final division of Polk's garrison was transferred to the fortifications at Island Number Ten. Johnston was pleased to have his old friend in his company once more. However, Johnston's relief at seeing Major General Braxton Bragg's forces from Pensacola and Mobile was palpable. These 10,000 highly trained troops would make all the difference. Bragg wrote to his wife that "Johnston almost embraced me when I met him, saying that 'your prompt and decisive move [to Corinth] has saved me and saved the country.'"[7] Beauregard, still sick, made the effort to travel to Corinth to meet his commander-in-chief, arriving on the 23rd of March. The rearguard of the Kentucky Army dribbled in daily, with the last troops arriving on the 27th of March.

Johnston had now successfully concentrated a sizeable Confederate army at Corinth before the unification of the equally formidable Union armies under Grant and Buell. Now was the time to strike. Johnston received a letter from General Robert E. Lee on the 26th of March: "I need not urge you when your army is united, to deal a blow at the enemy in your front, if possible, before his rear gets up from Nashville."[8] Charles P. Roland wrote that "Johnston saw clearly the necessity of uniting Confederate forces for a counterattack against this fraction of the enemy that now lay isolated and exposed at Pittsburg Landing."[9] Some years after the war, Grant lamented that "if Buell had reached us in time, we would have attacked Sidney Johnston; but, of course, Johnston knew Buell was coming, and was too good a general to allow the junction to take place without an attack."[10]

The opposing armies

It was not a simple assignment. Grant had debarked four divisions of infantry from his transports on the Tennessee River, and they were now scattered around a small log chapel, known as Shiloh Church, about 2.3

miles (3.7 km) from Pittsburg Landing. His army numbered about 35,000 men, with Wallace's additional 5,000 troops still encamped two miles (3.2 km) downriver at Crump's Landing. More Union reinforcements arrived after the success of Brigadier General Samuel R. Curtis's army in Arkansas, and on the 26th of March, a sixth division was created and placed under the command of Brigadier General Benjamin M. Prentiss, bringing the number of Union soldiers encamped in the area up to about 40,000. To the east, Buell's engineers finally rebuilt the bridge across the Duck River to a sufficient degree to allow the passage of the army. There was some concern in Buell's army for the safety of Grant's forces isolated on the western side of the Tennessee River at Pittsburg Landing. Brigadier General William Nelson exclaimed: "By God, we must cross the river at once, or Grant will be whipped."[11] Time was running out for Johnston to launch his offensive against Grant's army, but the Confederate forces assembling at Corinth were themselves too raw and disorganized.

Bragg described the Southern army at Corinth as "a heterogeneous mass, in which there was more enthusiasm than discipline, more capacity than knowledge, and more valor than instruction. Rifles, rifled and smoothbore muskets – some of them originally percussion, others hastily altered from flint-locks by Yankee contractors, many still with the old flint and steel – and shot-guns of all sizes and patterns, held place in the same regiments. The task of organizing such a command in four weeks, and supplying it, especially with ammunition suitable for action, was simply appalling."[12]

On the 29th of March, Johnston announced that the disparate Confederate forces aggregating at Corinth would be formally known as the Army of the Mississippi, a term previously used by Polk in reference to his Columbus garrison and Beauregard in reference to his troops in western Tennessee. The army was organized into three corps under Bragg, Polk, and Major General William J. Hardee, with a reserve force under Major General George B. Crittenden. Several decades after the war, Beauregard claimed the credit for creating such a structure but acknowledged that he discussed the matter with Johnston prior to the implementation. In fact, the three corps and one reserve corps army structure mirrored that of Johnston's Kentucky Army in its march from Murfreesboro to Corinth. Johnston had organized his army into three divisions under Hardee, Crittenden, and Brigadier General Gideon J. Pillow, and created a reserve force under Brigadier General John C. Breckinridge. The Army of the Mississippi had the same structure with corps rather than division designations.

The newly formed army was soon rocked by a series of command changes. The indefatigable Pillow was finally relieved of command of his division pending an investigation into his dubious conduct at the battle of Fort Donelson. Then Reserve Corps commander, Crittenden, and his senior subordinate, Brigadier General William H. Carroll, were arrested for intoxication while on duty. The stresses and disappointment of the last few months had broken Crittenden's spirit and Breckinridge replaced him as commander of the Reserve Corps. Breckinridge was 41 years old, a Kentuckian, experienced lawyer, and career politician. He served as a member of the House of Representatives representing Kentucky from 1851 to 1855 and was the fourteenth Vice President of the United States from 1857 to 1861. He was beloved by his troops, especially those from Kentucky.[13]

Brigadier General John C. Breckinridge

Johnston, Breckinridge, and his senior commanders worked tirelessly to improve the cohesion, discipline, and morale of the Army of the Mississippi. Beauregard played a key role in the organization of the troops and his mere presence boosted the spirits of the Confederate soldiers. After the war, Bragg noted that the organization of the army was undertaken by Johnston "with a cool, quiet self-control, by calling to his aid the best knowledge and talent at his command, which not only inspired confidence, but soon yielded the natural fruits of system, order, and discipline."[14] In just two weeks after his arrival at Corinth, John R. Lundberg described Johnston's army as a "reasonably well-organized, disciplined, and supplied force capable of giving battle."[15]

It was none too soon. On the 1st of April, Sherman led an expedition from Pittsburg Landing to Eastport. Johnston issued a warning for his troops to "be placed in readiness for a field movement and to meet the enemy within 24 hours."[16] Fortunately, Sherman's troops soon turned back. The following day, the commander of Polk's division at Bethel Station reported a sudden westward movement of Wallace's division at Crump's Landing to Polk and Beauregard. The latter interpreted the Union activity as an indication that Grant's army was commencing an offensive against the Mobile & Ohio Railroad. Before retiring to bed, Beauregard advised Johnston that "now is the moment to advance and strike the enemy at Pittsburg Landing."[17]

To further emphasize the import of this message, Johnston also received intelligence from Colonel Nathan B. Forrest that Buell's army was now approaching the Tennessee River. Not wishing to awaken the sickly Beauregard, Johnston conferred with the Louisianian's Adjutant General, Colonel Thomas Jordan, and they proceeded to Bragg's headquarters. The three officers sat in Bragg's bedroom late on the night of the 2nd of April and discussed the situation. Johnston resolved to order an immediate attack.

The four corps commanders were instructed to prepare three days rations and have their men ready under arms by 6am on the 3rd of April, in preparation for a strike against Grant's army at Pittsburg Landing. After dissemination of the orders, signed receipts were received from Hardee and Polk at 1:40am on the 3rd of April, while Breckinridge, whose corps was at Burnsville, Mississippi, was notified via telegraph. Beauregard was not informed until daylight, as Johnston wished to give his ailing second-in-command some more rest in preparation for the stressful events ahead.

Johnston sent a hurried note to President Jefferson Davis, informing him of the decision to attack Grant's army: "General Buell is in motion, 30,000 strong, rapidly from Columbia by Clifton to Savannah; Mitchel behind him with 10,000. Confederate forces, 40,000, ordered forward to offer battle near Pittsburg. Division from Bethel, main body from Corinth, reserve from Burnsville converge tomorrow near Monterey. On Pittsburg, Beauregard second in command; Polk, left; Hardee, center; Bragg, right wing; Breckinridge, reserve. Hope engagement before Buell can form junction."[18]

The order of battle

At daylight on the 3rd of April, an aide dispatched by Jordan roused the sleeping Beauregard and informed him of Johnston's decision to attack the Union forces at Pittsburg Landing. Beauregard quickly jotted down his thoughts regarding the organization of the advance and battle plan on the backs of various envelopes and telegrams. Johnston visited Beauregard's headquarters soon after to discuss these arrangements. After Johnston left, Beauregard passed his notes to Jordan to formalize into the marching orders of the army. The adjutant general utilized both Beauregard's notes and Napoleon Bonaparte's orders for the French army at the battle of Waterloo to draft Special Order Number Eight, which outlined the order of march and battle plan for the Army of the Mississippi.

However, prior to the completion of the Special Order, Jordan was called into another meeting with Johnston, Beauregard, and Bragg at the Louisianian's headquarters to review the road network north of Corinth. There was only one map of the roads, which Beauregard and Jordan had both studied, but the adjutant general had left it in his own quarters. Instead of retrieving the document, Beauregard simply drew a rough sketch of the roads leading out of Corinth onto a tabletop in the room. Hardee and Polk arrived soon afterwards, and all the officers studied the diagram. Beauregard explained that since Jordan had not finished drafting the Special Order, and that time was of the essence, he would verbally describe the order of march to them, and that their respective corps should be ready to depart at noon.[19] After Beauregard had finished, it took Jordan a few hours to prepare the orders, and they were disseminated sometime in the afternoon.

There were two main roads from Corinth to Pittsburg Landing, and Hardee was instructed to march his 3rd Corps on the northernmost path, the Ridge Road, while Bragg marched his 2nd Corps on the direct road to Pittsburg Landing, through the small village of Monterey. Polk's 1st Corps and Breckinridge's Reserve Corps would follow on each respective route. Stanley F. Horn observed that "Beauregard's plan was designed to bring the army into action in somewhat unusual fashion – the first two corps (Hardee's and Bragg's) arrayed in single parallel lines, one behind the other, with Polk supporting the left and Breckinridge the right. The more orthodox style of attack was for each corps to face the enemy on a designated part of the front."[20]

Many historians consider Johnston's 3rd of April telegram to President Davis as evidence that he had devised an alternative battle plan involving a linear formation of corps side-by-side, and that this superior arrangement was subsequently replaced by the cumbersome stacked corps arrangement concocted by Beauregard and Jordan. After the war, Bragg asserted that "the general plan (Johnston's) was admirable, the elaboration simply execrable."[21] When ex-President Davis was invited to unveil a monument to Johnston at Metairie Cemetery in New Orleans in 1887, he spoke wistfully of his friend's original battle plan. He even referred to a second telegram that he allegedly received from Johnston prior to the battle of Shiloh in which the general once again described a linear arrangement with the corps of Polk, Hardee, and Bragg side-by-side with Breckinridge in reserve.

However, Johnston's purported second telegram to Davis has never been found, and it is likely never to have existed. Davis was simply using the monument dedication to publicly censure Beauregard for altering the battle plan. Davis declared that Johnston "made but one mistake. He had planned that battle and sent me a telegram which has been lost. In that telegram he described how it was to be fought. It was fought and won, and it is the only battle in the world's history which was fought just as intended. The mistake he made was in letting someone else take charge of the order of march. That one mistake delayed the arrival of troops one day, and it enabled Buell to approach Grant."[22] Beauregard was outraged and emphatically denied that Johnston had a different plan in mind for the battle.

It is also claimed that Johnston was completely unaware that his own supposed battle plan had been discarded. The general's son claimed that "unfortunately [Beauregard] changed what seems evidently General Johnston's original purpose… into an array in three parallel lines of battle, which produced extreme confusion when the second and third lines advanced to support the first and intermingled with it."[23] Roland stated that "in his message of April 3rd to Davis, Johnston indicated a superior attack formation… No satisfactory explanation can be given for the disparity between these two plans."[24] Joseph H. Parks believed that Beauregard changed the battle plan without Johnston's knowledge or approval, arguing "whether Johnston agreed to the change or Beauregard disregarded Johnston and went his own way is not a matter of record, but the latter seems more likely."[25]

Steven E. Woodworth opined that "the resulting arrangement was drastically different from what Johnston had envisioned... by the time Johnston discovered what Beauregard had done, it was too late to rearrange the troops."[26] Most recently, Timothy B. Smith stated that "Johnston, who despised minutia and paperwork, whether as the Texas secretary of war or as army commander, had unwisely left it to Beauregard to draft the full orders for the advance... It was very different than what Johnston had intended, and historians have wrangled for decades over the reasoning for the disparity."[27] Yet there is considerable evidence that Johnston abandoned his linear battle plan on the 3rd of April after discussions with Beauregard at his headquarters. The fact is that the stacked column of corps battle plan was deemed more advantageous than a linear arrangement by Johnston, Beauregard, Bragg, and Jordan for three important reasons.

The first reason: Rapidity of movement necessary for surprise

The limited road network and heavily wooded terrain from Corinth to Pittsburg Landing would naturally constrain the army's movement. Jordan explained that "as for marching in the manner indicated in General Johnston's dispatch to Mr. Davis, of April 3rd, by three separate columns, an examination of the maps extant of the period will suffice to show that such an order of movement was out of the question, as also that the plan of Beauregard was the one of all others most likely to assure the least confusion with the greatest possible celerity, whether with raw or seasoned troops."[28] The stacked column of corps arrangement enabled each corps to use one of the two primary roads from Corinth to Pittsburg Landing. Once in the proximity of Pittsburg Landing, the four corps of the army would attack the Federals in the order of their deployment. A forward movement with the three corps arranged in a linear orientation, followed by the reserve, was just not feasible due to the thick vegetation, streams, swamps, and rugged terrain in the area.

The stacked order of battle was also vital to maintain the element of surprise. It allowed the corps to deploy in the order that they marched along the main Corinth Road. It would not waste precious daylight hours by requiring the corps to arrange themselves in a linear fashion across the heavily wooded landscape. The time consumed in such a redeployment to a wider formation would have afforded the Union forces with more opportunities to discover the Confederate vanguard and alert all the Union division commanders of the impending Southern attack.

In a post-war interview, Beauregard explained that his previous experience "had shown him the great difficulty and hazard of attempting to move simultaneously, by many orders from [the commanding general], the several main divisions of a new army to execute with precision a definite plan of battle." Thus, for the battle of Shiloh, "the entire first line would then move, together, upon a single order from [the commanding general], and the second and third lines would follow, respectively, each in turn. As the whole essence of the plan of attack was in a surprise, it was indispensable that it should be commenced and followed up [properly]; that is that the lines should move with [cohesion] and rapidity through as few orders and [occasions] for mistake or accident as possible. Under a different arrangement the lines of attack would have been, in all likelihood, too [fragmentary] and disjointed for a surprise, besides being exposed to division and separation through a lack of [celerity] in the movement (as happened several times the next day) owing to mistaken orders or the broken and wooded character of the country. The adhesion and [integrity] of the lines were also better [maintained] through the mutual support from right to left along the entire front."[29]

The second reason: Poor maps

The Confederate leadership misinterpreted the spatial dimensions of the battlefield due to poor maps. Alfred Roman blamed this situation on Richmond's repeated negligence of the Western Department: "The lack of competent engineers was also a source of great annoyance, as without them it became next to impossible to make necessary reconnaissance's, and map off the country lying between the two opposing armies. The sketches prepared by staff officers, untrained and inexperienced in such matters, were very imperfect."[30] Beauregard had previously delegated the command of the Confederate forces concentrating at Corinth to Bragg due to his ongoing illness, and that general was reputed to have a poor spatial awareness. One officer claimed that Bragg could not understand a map and that "it was a spectacle to see him wrestle with one, with one finger painfully holding down his own position."[31]

Unfortunately, the only maps of the area in Beauregard's possession were rudimentary sketches, made without compass or scale. They indicated that Corinth was twice as far from Pittsburg Landing in the lateral direction (i.e., east to west) than it was in the vertical direction (i.e., north to south). Unbeknownst to the Confederates, Corinth was twice as far from Pittsburg Landing in the vertical direction than it was in the lateral direction. Timothy B. Smith stated that due to this error, Johnston "believed Pittsburg Landing lay far south of its actual location, thus putting it within easier striking distance of the Confederate attack."[32] The maps also signalled that the presence of Owl and Lick Creeks would prohibit a wide attack formation, and therefore, the Army of Mississippi would have to be wedged through a relatively narrow opening to attack the Union camps.[33] A stacked column of corps was thus considered the only formation that would avoid the disrupting impact of the presence of these creeks. A linear formation would simply get blocked at each end of the line at the creeks and would have to somehow funnel itself through the space.

The final reason: Deception

Johnston employed his illusion of strength strategy once again in the planning for the battle of Shiloh. The stacked formation of corps would obscure the actual number of soldiers present in the Confederate army. Roman explained that the formation was "designated not only for the purpose of deceiving the enemy as to the number of our troops, which we wished to exaggerate, but also to inspire our own men with greater confidence."[34] Similar to Johnston's deceptions with the manoeuvring of the Central Kentucky Army in the heartland from September 1861 to February 1862, this ruse was eminently successful, for when Grant requested urgent reinforcements from Buell's army after the Confederate attack on the morning of 6th of April, he claimed that Johnston's forces were over 100,000 strong. This illusion endured for many years after the

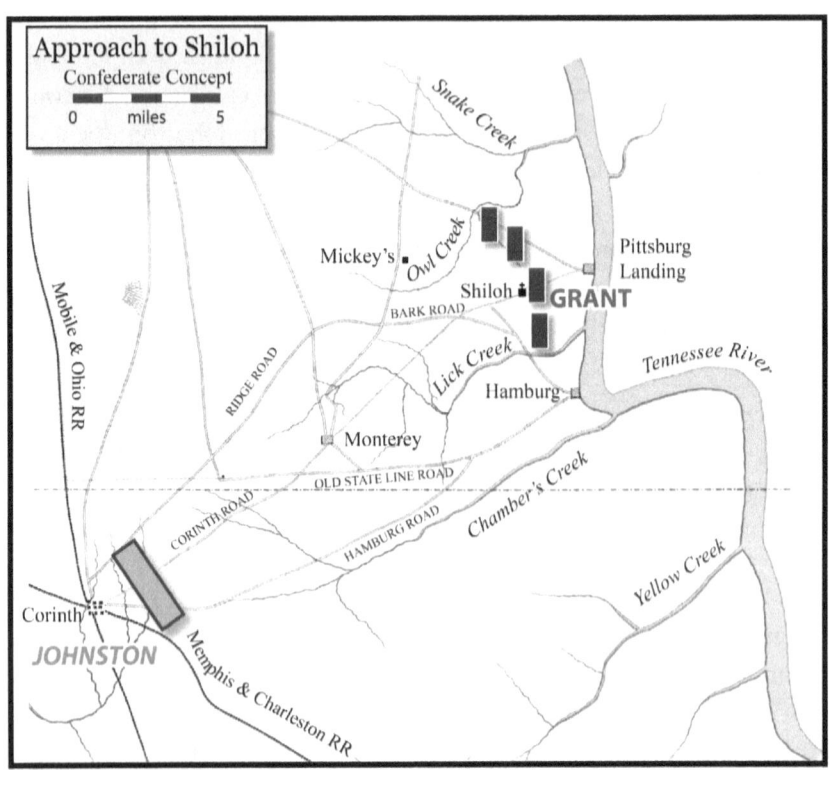

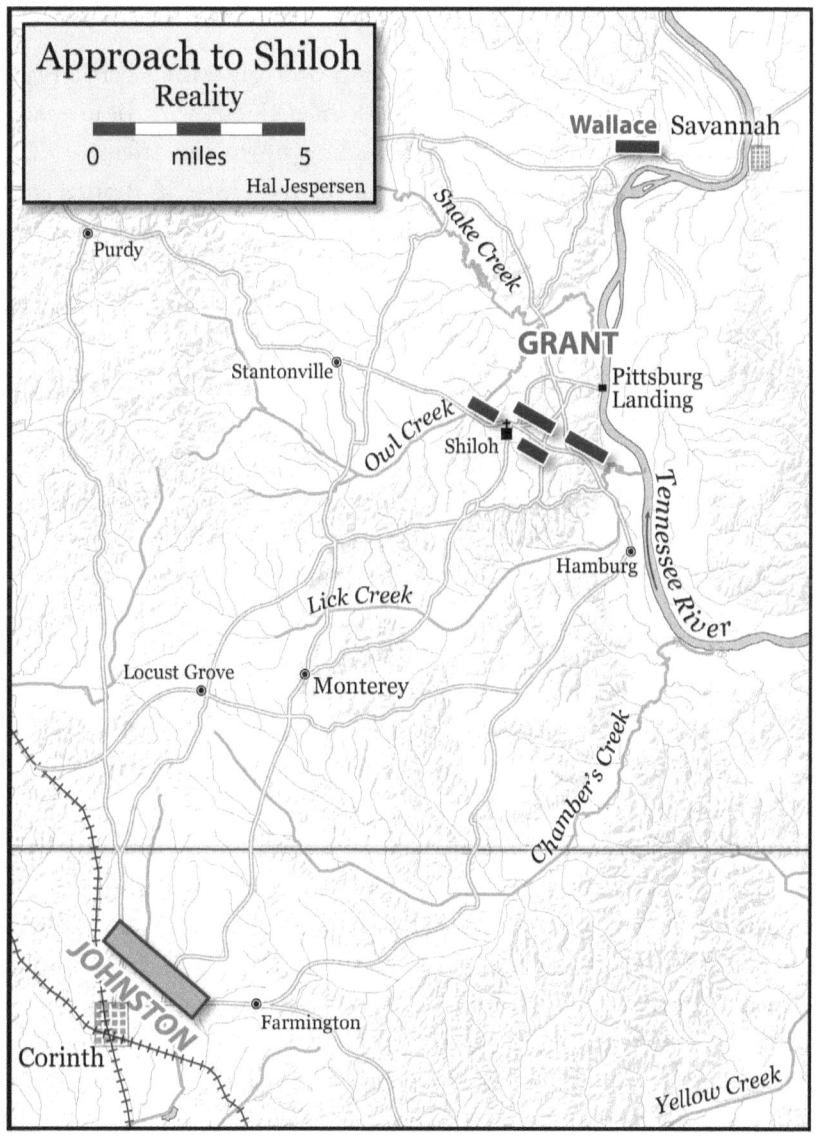

war. Even into the 1890s, some Union veterans remained convinced that Johnston had upwards of 70,000 men.

Johnston's endorsement

The notion that Johnston and Beauregard had contrasting battle plans is highly dubious. Johnston was in constant dialogue with Beauregard, Bragg, and Jordan in the 48 hours leading up to the offensive. The commanding general was present during the conference in Beauregard's quarters on the 3rd of April, in which his second-in-command sketched the details of the road network on a tabletop. Johnston was also in the room when Beauregard verbally instructed Bragg, Hardee, and Polk as to the convoluted sequence of marches. Johnston's son recalled that his father "did not undervalue the importance of details. No man regarded more closely all the details subsidiary to a great result than he."[35] Colonel Edward W. Munford wrote that "General Johnston was most active in his attention to all the details of reorganization and preparations for the battle."[36] Jordan recounted that "General Johnston weighed all that was said with much deliberation, and not until every detail had been very thoroughly discussed, did he decide to make the movement, as [Beauregard] proposed it."[37]

Colonel St. John R. Liddell once noted that Johnston "listened to, and yet was not confused by, the various opinions of his subordinates."[38] Beauregard himself stated that "I prepared the order of march and of battle, which were submitted by me to Generals Johnston and Bragg, in the presence of Colonel Jordan, chief of staff of the whole army, and they were accepted *without one word of alteration*. They were then put in proper form by Colonel Jordan and furnished to the corps commanders."[39] Beauregard emphatically declared that "Johnston had agreed to the formation."[40] Indeed, Thomas K. Hall noted that "Beauregard would have had a difficult time trying to justify ignoring his superior's plan, especially since there were other officers in the room witnessing the discussion."[41]

Hence, Johnston was obviously aware of the stacked column of corps battle plan, considered it the most advantageous arrangement to the situation at hand, and authorized its implementation. On the morning of the 4th of April, Johnston reviewed the published order of battle and did not modify it. When departing his headquarters in Corinth that same morning, Munford remembered that the general paused "on the doorstep, lost in thought, and how, looking up, he muttered, half aloud, 'Yes, I believe I have overlooked nothing.'"[42]

The plan's impact on the battle

The stacked corps formation adopted by Johnston and Beauregard has been relentlessly criticized over the years. Like Johnston's son and many historians, Hall opined that "Beauregard formed the attack with the four corps lined up behind each other. The result was units becoming intermingled with one another resulting in a complete breakdown of any semblance of command and control. Commanders, from regiment all the way to division, wound up commanding whatever troops happened to be closest to them."[43] However, Buell took a different view, remarking that "when the three Confederate lines were brought together successively at the front, there was, of course, a great apparent mingling of organizations; but it was not in their case attended with the confusion that might be supposed, because each division area was thereby supplied with a triple complement of brigade and division officers, and the whole front was under the close supervision of four remarkably efficient corps commanders."[44]

The terrain around Pittsburg Landing was so heavily wooded and criss-crossed with streams and other impediments that *any* army formation would have disintegrated rapidly into intermingled groups of disorganized men shooting at one another. The battle of Shiloh was one of the first major engagements of the war, and the inexperience of all involved, coupled with the difficult terrain, guaranteed chaos. In the overall scheme of things, the impact of the stacked corps formation versus a linear arrangement on army disorganization and command confusion seems much overstated by authors in the past.

Roman accurately surmised that the fact that "the commands got very much broken and mixed up during the battle was not surprising and was due less to the order of battle than to the rawness of the troops, including officers, the broken and wooded nature of the field, and the severity of the contest. General Beauregard is of the opinion that any other order of battle would have resulted similarly, under like circumstances. The Federals were also in the same mixed-up condition, according to their own reports, when the battle had lasted only a few hours."[45]

Finally, historian David A. Powell noted that at the battle of Chancellorsville in May 1863, Lieutenant General Thomas J. "Stonewall" Jackson's deployment of troops was characterized by a "long line of battle, more than a mile wide and three divisions deep, all in heavily wooded terrain not unlike Shiloh. Unsurprisingly, a great deal of confusion arose as Jackson's three lines became intermingled… But Jackson's attack is considered one of the tactical masterpieces of the war, while Johnston's was, in Wiley Sword's words, fatally flawed. And yet both assaults used the same standard formation."[46] As Johnston's famous words attest, success really does seem to be the test of merit for generals in the Civil War.

Conclusion

Many historians have grappled with the discrepancy between the order of battle described by Johnston in his 3rd of April telegram to President Davis and that employed by the Army of the Mississippi at the battle of Shiloh. They claim that the formation was altered without Johnston's knowledge, that he discovered the change too late to do anything about it, or that he was simply not interested in the tedious details. However, the evidence suggests that Johnston abandoned his linear arrangement of corps in favor of a stacked column of corps when confronted by the realities of the rugged terrain and limited road network in the Corinth-Pittsburg Landing-Tennessee River area. The stacked column of corps arrangement was deemed preferable by the senior Confederate leadership due to the rapidity of deployment it promised, their need to surprise the Federals, the constraints of the spatial dimensions as indicated by the inaccurate maps, and the impression of larger numbers that it would provide. Johnston was present during the various discussions between Jordan and the corps commanders and obviously agreed with and confirmed the order of battle. He also had the time to correct the plan if he considered it mistaken. The complaint that the stacked columns of corps led to intermingling of units and confusion is a legitimate one, but the terrain at Shiloh was so difficult that any formation would have suffered similar consequences.

22.

Was Johnston or Beauregard in command of the Army of the Mississippi?

About a month prior to the battle of Shiloh, General Pierre G.T. Beauregard issued a memorandum from his headquarters in Jackson, Tennessee, on the 5th of March 1862. It read: "Soldiers, I assume this day the command of the Army of the Mississippi, for the defense of our homes and liberties, and to resist the subjugation, spoilation, and dishonor of our people."[1] At this time, General Albert Sidney Johnston was occupied directing the perilous movement of the Kentucky Army from Murfreesboro to Corinth. It is likely that he never read or had any knowledge of Beauregard's proclamation.

Historian Thomas K. Hall made much out of this incident, writing that "as the troops began gathering at Corinth the confusion between Beauregard and Johnston as to who exactly was in charge began to take shape… On March 5, while still trying to close on Corinth, Beauregard issued a memorandum assuming command of the Army of the Mississippi… he had to have confused some of them as to who was really in charge"[2] However, Beauregard was referring to the amalgamation at Corinth of the troops under his supervision, namely, Major General Leonidas Polk's troops from Columbus, with those of Major General Braxton Bragg's from

Pensacola and Mobile, and those of Brigadier General Daniel Ruggles from New Orleans. It was these three separate forces that Beauregard was uniting under the name of the Army of the Mississippi. In fact, Polk had previously used the same term for his Columbus garrison.

It is obvious that the troops of Johnston's Kentucky Army were excluded from Beauregard's declaration. Earlier that February, Johnston had warned the Louisianian that "the separation of our armies is for the present complete," and that he must act independently.[3] The two generals led distinct armies separated by a hundred miles or more and Beauregard's proclamation was confined to the troops under his immediate supervision. It was expected that once Johnston's army arrived in Corinth, the departmental commander would assume control of the entire Southern force.

Johnston's proposition

Yet Johnston was full of surprises. Once at Corinth, he offered Beauregard the tactical command of all the Confederate forces now gathered in the northern Mississippi town. Colonel Edward W. Munford, was aghast at his commander's gesture and remonstrated that "this battle may regain [Tennessee and Kentucky], and re-establish your jeoparded fame; yet you, on such an occasion, would invite another to win the glory of redeeming what you had lost." Johnston smiled and said: "I think it but right to make the offer."[4] He assured Munford that "I will be present at the battle and will see that nothing goes wrong."[5]

A startled Beauregard quickly declined Johnston's proposal. The Louisianian recalled that "when General Johnston first met me at Corinth, he proposed, after our staff officers had retired, to turn over the command of the united forces to me, but I positively declined, on his account and that of the *cause*, telling him that I had come to assist, but not to supersede him, and offering to give him all the assistance in my power. He then concluded to remain in command. It was one of the most affecting scenes of my life."[6] Johnston responded warmly that "we two together will do our best to secure success."[7]

Johnston's offer to delegate command of the Southern army to Beauregard has been interpreted as an abdication of responsibility. T. Harry Williams contended that "under a storm of criticism for the disasters in the West, he may have realized that he had erred in not exercising central command and was now trying belatedly to assume his proper function. Or he may still have wished to avoid large responsibility by placing the greater part of his forces under Beauregard's direct command."[8] Similarly, historian O. Edward Cunningham wrote that "Albert Sidney Johnston's generous offer has caused much speculation, but the probable reason for it was that the Kentuckian felt that the army and the people no longer trusted his judgment."[9] The interpretations of Williams and Cunningham certainly appear reasonable, but there have been several explanations for Johnston's surprising proposition to Beauregard.

A boost to morale
Johnston was aware of the vituperative criticism directed his way due to the falls of Fort Henry, Fort Donelson, Bowling Green, and Nashville, whereas Beauregard was still considered the hero of Fort Sumter and Manassas. Perhaps Johnston thought the morale of the troops would be strengthened if they knew that it would be Beauregard leading them onto the battlefield. Hall stated that "a high-profile name like Beauregard would, indeed raise confidence in the ranks. Johnston was motivated more by his concern for the soldiers rather than Beauregard's ego."[10] This interpretation may have some element of truth, but Johnston was a charismatic general in his own right with much experience in managing the volunteer soldier.

Johnston had restored the spirits and organization of the Kentucky Army after the devastating blows of Fishing Creek, Forts Henry and Donelson, the withdrawal from Bowling Green, and the fall of Nashville. Johnston would have been confident that he could do the same with the combined forces at Corinth, and his efforts over the two weeks prior to the battle of Shiloh demonstrate his success in raising the morale of the Confederate soldiers. Although cognizant of the public censure of his generalship, it does not seem likely that the general would cede command on this basis alone.

Colonel St. John R. Liddell recorded: "General Johnston told me that he utterly disregarded the public clamor against him for evacuating Kentucky and Nashville. When the facts became fully known, his course would be fully approved and justified. Beauregard had approved the step, or the necessity for such. Johnston said his mind was not in the least disturbed by foolish newspaper publications, which often misled public opinion and might change at any moment. When the true history of the war was finally written, his course would be fully vindicated... his manner was calm, very plain, and earnest."[11] Similarly, Jefferson Davis declared that Johnston was "of calm judgment, concentrated will and iron nerve" and "was as little likely as any man I have ever known to be influenced by popular clamor."[12]

A power play
Some have suggested that Johnston's proposal was a Machiavellian power-play designed to reassert his command over the Confederate army. They argue that if Beauregard declined the responsibility, then the Louisianian's influence over military operations in the Western Department would diminish and Johnston could reassume complete control. This interpretation stems from Thomas L. Connelly's theory that Beauregard had gradually become the dominant leadership figure in the West. However, Connelly's theory is not supported by any evidence, and it is highly unlikely that Johnston perceived Beauregard as a threat to his authority.

Johnston would not have indulged in such deception either. Liddell noted that "no one inspired more respect for integrity of character... General Johnston had good sense, and he made no professions of superiority, which certainly was something to his credit in these times of military pretension and arrogance of official station."[13]

A beau geste
Finally, the proposal may have been a *beau geste*, a magnanimous gesture but ultimately meaningless in substance, a mark of respect. Beauregard himself had offered to serve under his junior, Bragg, but a few weeks prior. In accordance with the tacit understanding of a *beau geste*, Bragg also politely declined the overture. Johnston's son remarked that his father "felt constrained to make this offer, because he had brought with him the smaller fraction of the united forces, and he was on a field that he had set apart for Beauregard's control. That officer had been for some time on the ground, and he was unwilling that a subordinate should suffer by his arrival. He would make any sacrifice himself rather than take one laurel from the brow of a fellow-soldier."[14]

He concluded that it was Johnston's "wish to give General Beauregard the command of the troops in the field, which would have secured to that officer whatever of glory might be won at Shiloh; but it was in no wise his intention to abdicate the supreme command, or the superintendence of affairs in the management of the department or the movements of the army. His offer to Beauregard was certainly an act of rare magnanimity."[15] One student of the battle of Shiloh, Anne B. Hyde, declared that Johnston offered the command to Beauregard "in a moment of chivalric generosity." She wrote that "Beauregard declined the offer, though he apparently considered it as an evidence of self-distrust on the part of General Johnston, but no one who studies that great character can construe it other than an act of unselfishness."[16]

Beauregard's own recollection of the event support the notion of a *beau geste*. He wrote that he refused the departmental commander's offer "in a spirit of disinterestedness and generosity which equalled that of General Johnston."[17] The Louisianian also added that he "could not think of commanding on a field where Sidney Johnston was present."[18] Likewise, Munford's recollection that Johnston intended to remain with the army regardless of Beauregard's decision to ensure that nothing went wrong, suggests that the offer was not a serious one, and that there was no abdication of responsibility.

The General Orders of the 29th of March stated that Johnston "assumes the command and immediate direction of the armies of Kentucky and of the Mississippi, now united, and which, in military operations, will be known as the 'Army of the Mississippi.' General G.T. Beauregard will be second in command to the Commander of the Forces."[19] Johnston decided to retain the Army of the Mississippi appellation as this made more sense than the "Kentucky Army." That state had been abandoned to the enemy. Hence, there was no confusion for the troops as to which general was in command. Johnston's decision to preserve the name "Army of the Mississippi" for the aggregated force may have led to Hall's misunderstanding. Johnston was the commanding general in both name and action. Bragg remarked that "Beauregard, who, having recently come out from the army in Virginia, and being in feeble health, was assigned no special command, but was designated in orders as 'second in command,' and as such aided the commander-in-chief with his counsel and advice."[20]

Johnston upholds the offensive

The Army of the Mississippi commenced its march from Corinth to Shiloh Church on the afternoon of the 3rd of April. The massive surprise attack had been scheduled for dawn on the 5th, but this objective quickly became unrealistic. Inexperienced officers had difficulty managing the expeditious movement of so many troops, animals, and wagons along the two primary roads from Corinth to Pittsburg Landing. Beauregard observed that "the slowness of the march… was mainly attributable to the rawness of the troops and the inexperience of the officers, including some of superior rank."[21] The advance was plagued by confusion and delays.

The roads themselves impeded rapid movement. They were narrow, dirt tracks that wended their way through a countryside composed of thick woodlands, farmer's fields, orchards, gullies, and marshes. The roads were entirely unsuitable for the transit of an army numbering 40,000 men and encumbered with supply wagons, artillery batteries, horses, and animals. Bragg found conditions on the Monterey Road so poor as to divert the march of his 2nd Corps to the Ridge Road, which then delayed the passage of Polk's 1st Corps. Then the curse of bad weather, which had tormented Johnston's forces in the Western Department and significantly contributed to the defeats at Fishing Creek, Fort Henry, and Fort Donelson, continued to thwart the aspirations of the Southern army. Heavy rain on the morning of the 4th of April turned the dirt roads into torrents of mud and hampered the ability of the wheeled vehicles to maintain pace with the rest of the army.

Lieutenant George W. Baylor, one of Johnston's aides, wrote that "the only reason why [Major General Ulysses S.] Grant's army was not destroyed or captured was that the rain of Friday night [the 4th of April] prevented our getting our army into line of battle and making the attack at daylight Saturday morning [the 5th of April]."[22] This sentiment was echoed by J.B. Ulmer, one of Johnston's cavalry escorts during the battle. Ulmer stated that except for the delay "on account of the narrow muddy roads, and the miring ordnance and artillery teams… the battle would have opened on Saturday. What might have been the result had the plans of the general been carried out can now only be left to conjecture. Certain it is, [Major General Don Carlos] Buell would not have been in reach, for on that day his army was 25 miles [40 km] away, and the history of the second day would not so have been written."[23]

It was a very trying time for Johnston. In addition to the inclement weather and poor roads, there were other frustrating incidents. When Major General William J. Hardee's 3rd Corps finally deployed for battle on the morning of the 5th of April, it was discovered that the left wing of Bragg's corps in the second line of battle was missing. The culprit, Ruggles's division, was at the rear of the army, resting in a field. Earlier that morning, Ruggles had found Polk's corps blocking the road, and so he decided to bypass the bishop's men by tramping his division into the wilderness by the side of the path. Ruggles then heard some skirmishing between Hardee's corps and an enemy patrol and feared that the battle had begun. He halted his men in a nearby field and sent scouts forward to determine the best route forward. Bragg and his aides had no idea where Ruggles had disappeared to, and after an hour of futile searching, reported their bafflement to Johnston.

The army commander became irate, declaring: "This is perfectly puerile! This is not war! Let us have our horses," and he mounted *Fire Eater* to personally hunt for Ruggles's division.[24] Johnston untangled the snarl of wagons obstructing the road and eventually found Ruggles and his men in the field. The errant division was directed to its proper place, and Bragg's second line of battle was complete. Yet the whole process consumed another four hours.[25] The delays caused by weather, muddy roads, and inexperienced subordinates compelled Johnston to delay the attack until the morning of the 6th of April. Some historians criticize the Confederate high command for such a tardy advance, but Charles P. Roland took a charitable view of the situation and concluded that "taking into account the want of training of officers and men and the nature of roads and weather, perhaps it was remarkable that the Southern force moved and deployed as expeditiously as it did."[26]

The delay in the Army of the Mississippi's march and deployment troubled Beauregard. He was convinced that the Federals were now aware of the impending attack. To exacerbate the issue of the postponement, there had been several heavy skirmishes between Hardee's corps and Union pickets during the Confederate advance. Beauregard observed that "during the advance of the 4th of April, a reconnaissance in force was injudiciously made by a part of the cavalry of the 2nd Corps, with such audacity – capturing an officer and thirteen men of the enemy – that it ought to have warned the Federal commander of our meditated attack."[27] Several more clashes occurred throughout the next day, the 5th of April, which further disturbed Beauregard. However, the Union soldiers taken prisoner during the clashes were interrogated and confessed that Grant and the senior leadership of the Federal Army of the Tennessee remained oblivious to the impending attack.[28] But could their statements be trusted? Perhaps the prisoners were goading the Confederates to attack their now fully prepared and fortified army at Shiloh Church.

The Army of the Mississippi had also been noisy during the march. Many of the soldiers had been firing their weapons to test functionality after the heavy rains. Some shot at pheasants, rabbits, and other game that appeared amongst the underbrush. The soldiers also cheered every time Johnston, Beauregard, or some other high ranking officer rode past them. The commanding general was compelled to ride along the line to discourage the firing. Major Dudley M. Hayden, volunteer aide to Johnston, remembered: "When they began to cheer his approach, he checked them, because it would call the attention of the enemy to their position."[29]

At around 5pm on the 5th of April, Beauregard, Hardee, and Bragg met at the rear of the first line of battle. Beauregard was in a sullen mood and launched into a scathing review of the army's performance, complaining that "the maladroit manner in which our troops have been handled on the march and the blunder of the noisy, offensive reconnaissance... satisfy me that the purpose for which we had left Corinth had been essentially frustrated and should be abandoned as no longer feasible."[30] Bragg blamed Polk for the delay, being contemptuous of the bishop's military credentials and the discipline of his 1st Corps troops. When Polk appeared on the scene, Beauregard berated him: "I am very much disappointed at the delay which has occurred in getting the troops into position." Bristling at the criticism, Polk explained that "so am I, sir; but so far as I am concerned my orders are to form on another line, and that line must first be established before I can form upon it."[32]

Several decades after the battle, Colonel Thomas Jordan defended Polk from such accusations, stating that "Polk's corps... seems to have been moved with as little delay as might be expected, and not to have been at all responsible for the delay of Bragg's troops, as I heard General

Bragg sharply complain to General Beauregard in the afternoon of the 5th of April – a report made with such circumstantiality at the time as to induce the latter to speak to General Polk of the belatement and of its grave consequences."[33] Johnston overheard the animated discussion and rode up to the group of corps commanders. Brigadier General John C. Breckinridge arrived moments later, but feeling ill, lay on a blanket spread out on the damp ground.[34]

Beauregard remained distressed and repeated the concerns he had previously discussed with Bragg. He asserted that Grant's Army of the Tennessee would now be "intrenched to the eyes, and ready for our attack."[35] Beauregard pointed out the weakness of their own army. The men were exhausted from their three-day march, and many had already consumed all their rations. Beauregard implored Johnston to abandon the attack and withdraw the army back to Corinth. The departmental commander was not convinced and asked Bragg for his opinion. The irascible general sided with Beauregard and urged a judicious retreat. Hardee remained silent. Johnston then turned to his old comrade, Polk, and asked the same question. The bishop declared that "my troops are in as good condition as they have ever been. They are eager for battle. To retire now would operate injuriously upon them. I think we ought to attack."[36] Breckinridge raised himself into a sitting position and added his endorsement to Polk's position. Johnston reflected for a moment. He admitted that Beauregard's statements carried much weight but still hoped that the attack would surprise and rout the enemy. Johnston announced: "Gentlemen, we shall attack at daylight tomorrow."[37]

As Johnston walked away from the group, he commented to one of his staff officers that "I would fight them if they were a million. They can present no greater front between these two creeks than we can, and the more men they crowd in there, the worse we can make it for them. Polk is a true soldier and a friend."[38] Munford recalled that after the conference, Johnston "said with a glowing countenance, 'I have ordered a battle for tomorrow at daylight, and I intend to hammer 'em!'"[39] The army's Medical Director, Dr. David W. Yandell, remembered the general declaring that "tomorrow at twelve o'clock we will water our horses in the Tennessee River."[40]

Yet Johnston was troubled about the depressed spirits of Beauregard and discussed the matter with several confidants. Colonel Jacob Thompson, of Beauregard's staff, wrote that "General Johnston took my arm, and remarked, 'I perceive that General Beauregard is averse to bringing on the attack on the enemy in the morning, on the ground that we have lost an opportunity by delay.' I replied that I knew that such was the feeling of General Beauregard, and he seemed wonderfully depressed in spirits... 'But,' says General Johnston, 'don't you think it is better to fight, and run the chances of defeat rather than retreat? Our troops are in high spirits, eager for the trial of arms, and confident of victory; and the effect of an order to retreat will not only disappoint them but depress their spirits, and I fear it would have the same effect as a defeat.'"[41] The general confided to Dr. Yandell that "Beauregard is sick... I don't think much of the opinions of a sick man in matters that require action."[42] Yandell concurred, stating that Beauregard was still suffering from the effects of his severe throat ailment and that he was not yet capable of commanding men on the field of battle. Johnston pressed ahead with the attack.

Fortunately for the Confederates, the Union high command remained oblivious despite the skirmishing between the forces over the past few days. On the 5th of April, Brigadier General William T. Sherman informed Grant that "all is quiet along my lines now... The enemy has cavalry in our front, and I think there are two regiments of infantry and one battery of artillery about two miles out. I will send you ten prisoners of war... I have no doubt that nothing will occur today more than some picket firing. The enemy is saucy, but got the worst of it yesterday, and will not press our pickets far. I will not be drawn out far unless with certainty of advantage, and I do not apprehend anything like an attack on our position." That same day Grant informed Major General Henry W. Halleck that "I have scarcely the faintest idea of an attack (general one) being made upon us."[45]

When Brigadier General William Nelson's division from Buell's army arrived at Savannah, Grant told one of its brigade commanders that "there will be no fight at Pittsburg Landing; we will have to go to Corinth, where the Rebels are fortified. If they come to attack us, we can whip them, as I have more than twice as many troops as I had at Fort Donelson."[46] Nelson was not convinced, remarking that "Sidney Johnston is not a man to be underestimated. I think Grant is wrong. We should be over there now."[47] Yet Nelson's division would remain at Savannah on the eastern side of the Tennessee River while Grant's army resided on the western side at Pittsburg Landing. As a result of the nonchalant attitude possessed by Grant and Sherman, most of their troops were unprepared for the audacious Confederate offensive scheduled for the morning of Sunday the 6th of April.

At dawn on the 6th of April, Johnston and his staff rode forward through woodlands about a mile (1.6 km) southwest of Fraley's cotton field near Shiloh Church. The general established his headquarters near an intersection of the Corinth-Pittsburg and Bark Roads. Beauregard and the corps commanders gathered around his campfire to discuss the planned attack. One observer noted that "they ate thin crackers and sipped coffee – some talking, General Johnston, mainly a listener."[48] Beauregard repeated his arguments of the previous day and insisted that the army retreat, but Johnston remained firm in his decision. At 5:14am, the sound of gunfire echoed through the early morning mist. Johnston cut off any further protests from Beauregard by stating that "the battle has opened gentlemen. It is too late to change our dispositions."[49]

A Union patrol had stumbled into the skirmishers of Hardee's 3rd Corps in Fraley Field, opening the battle of Shiloh. Johnston and his officers prepared for action. At about 6:40am, the commanding general mounted *Fire Eater* and rode off toward the front line, trailed by some of his staff. Johnston announced that "tonight we will water our horses in the Tennessee River."[50] After his discussions with Yandell the previous night, Johnston decided to place Beauregard at the rear of the battlefield, where he could assume the less burdensome role of directing reinforcements and munitions to the front line. The Louisianian's pulse was measured at over a hundred and his laryngitis made it difficult for him to speak.[51] Beauregard later maintained that "I only went to the battle at the urgent request of General Johnston, for I was so unwell at the time."[52]

Conclusion

The contention that the soldiers and officers of the Army of the Mississippi were confused as to whether Johnston or Beauregard was in command is misplaced. Although Johnston used the same designation for the army that Polk and Beauregard had previously employed for their own forces at Columbus and in western Tennessee, respectively, the General Orders issued on the 29th of March clearly stated the command structure. Johnston's proposition to relinquish battlefield command of the Army of the Mississippi to Beauregard can be considered a *beau geste*, very similar to that offered by the Louisianian to Bragg only a few weeks prior. Johnston's decision to uphold the surprise attack despite vehement opposition from Beauregard, his second-in-command, and Bragg, the commander of his largest corps, demonstrates his authority over the Army of the Mississippi.

The 6th of April was likely to be the only opportunity to attack Grant's forces prior to the arrival of Buell's army, and a withdrawal now would only demoralize the Confederate soldiers. Johnston's determination to strike forward and relegate a sick Beauregard to a support role at the rear of the army was indicative of his complete grasp of command. Despite siding with Beauregard at the time, Bragg later realized that Johnston's decision to progress the attack on the morning of the 6th was ultimately the correct choice: "Contrary to the views of such as urged an abandonment of the attack, the enemy was found utterly unprepared, many being surprised and captured in their tents, and others, though on the outside, in costumes better fitted to the bedchamber than to the battlefield."[53] Although close, Buell's forces would not be able to arrive until the evening, providing the Confederates with almost a full day in which to drive Grant's army into the swamps of Owl Creek.

23.

Did Johnston or Beauregard direct the battle of Shiloh?

There has been much debate as to whether General Albert Sidney Johnston or General Pierre G.T. Beauregard directed the Army of the Mississippi during the battle of Shiloh. The two generals assumed contrasting roles. T. Harry Williams described the arrangement: "While the commanding general pressed the attack at the front, Beauregard was to command the troops in the rear sector, particularly the two 'reserve' corps, [Major General Leonidas] Polk in rear of [Major General Braxton] Bragg and [Brigadier General John C.] Breckinridge in rear of [Major General William J.] Hardee. At the right moment he was to commit them to battle and to send forward any other troops to points where they were needed."[1] After the war, Beauregard wrote that Johnston gave him "the general direction" of the battle.[2] Several historians have agreed with this statement, contending that Beauregard, by remaining at the rear, was afforded an overall strategic view of the situation and therefore acted as the true commander of the Confederate forces.

Williams claimed that "by going from unit to unit at the edge of the battle, exhorting the men to charge and offering to lead them, Johnston was performing more like a corps or division general than a commander."[3] Likewise, Thomas L. Connelly opined that "although Johnston commanded the Army, during the early hours of the battle he behaved more like a brigade or regimental commander than an army chieftain."[4] Larry J. Daniel derisively wrote that "Johnston needlessly flitted about while Beauregard established what amounted to command headquarters."[5] Most recently, Timothy B. Smith declared that "Beauregard was more in command of the army overall than Johnston."[6] Are these statements an accurate description of the situation? Which general's actions during the engagement were consistent with the battle plan formulated at Corinth in the preceding days?

The battle plan

The Confederate battle plan was compromised from the very beginning due to the inaccurate maps drafted by the scouts. Historian Stacy D. Allen examined the Shiloh battlefield "in a way no other historian had done before. By reviewing contemporary maps, plotting the troop movements on modern maps, and examining the troop positions," he deduced "that the Confederate command authority, most notably Johnston, misread the Union deployment at Pittsburg Landing in the context of the geography of the site. Johnston believed the Union camps lay in a line from north to south, facing west, but in actuality, the front line of camps ran east and west, facing south."[7] After conducting his topographical analysis, Allen stated that "the maps indicated that the Confederate front faced east, toward the river, and further illustrated that the Union army, with its right on Owl Creek and its left on Lick Creek, faced west. In reality, the plateau and the Federal deployment was arranged much differently... the Federal front faced south (not west), with the right on Owl Creek and the left on the Tennessee River, not Lick Creek as the Confederates appear to have believed."[8]

Johnston's memorandum to his corps commanders contained the assumption "that the enemy is in position about a mile [1.6 km] in advance of Shiloh Church, with its right resting on Owl Creek, and its left on Lick Creek."[9] A western facing orientation of the enemy seemed perfectly reasonable to the Confederate high command, as the flanks of the Union army would be protected by the creeks, and the rear secured by the Tennessee River, which was the source of its reinforcements and supplies. Federal gunboats lurking in the river would also be available to protect the ground forces by lobbing shells over their troops into the advancing graycoats. Steven E. Woodworth noted that Johnston's "prebattle comment that the Federals could 'present no greater front between these two creeks than we can,' suggests that he believed the Union line more or less spanned the space between the creeks and thus ran due north and south, facing west."[10] Indeed, Sherman's orders specified that "each brigade must encamp looking west, so that when the regiments are on their regimental parades the brigades will be in line of battle."[11] However, this instruction was ignored and the Union brigades were encamped in a haphazard manner, some facing southwards and others south-westerly. Several decades after the battle, Colonel Thomas Jordan was still under the impression that the enemy faced westwards, commenting "that our adversary's position at Pittsburg Landing, with his back against a deep, broad river, in a *cul-de-sac* formed by the two creeks (Owl and Lick), would make his defeat decisively disastrous."[12]

Johnston's battle plan required the Army of the Mississippi to smash into the "southern flank" of Major General Ulysses S. Grant's Army of the Tennessee, which was assumed to be facing west, roll it up, and drive the startled bluecoats northward into the confluence of Owl and Snake Creeks. Here the Federals would be trapped and compelled to scatter or surrender. Johnston's memorandum announced that "in the approaching battle every effort should be made to turn the left flank of the enemy so as to cut off his line of retreat to the Tennessee River and throw him back on Owl Creek, where he will be obliged to surrender. Every precaution must also be taken on our part to prevent unnecessary exposure of our men to the enemy's gunboats."[13] It was a bold plan, but unfortunately for Johnston, the inadequate reconnaissance and lack of Confederate understanding of the topography and disposition of the Federal forces sabotaged its chances of success.

Instead of an orderly, linear formation, Grant's five divisions were spread out in a large, disjointed semicircle, with gaps of up to one mile (1.6 km) between some units. Brigadier General Benjamin M. Prentiss's 6th Division was in the middle of the formation on the Eastern Corinth Road. Most of Major General William T. Sherman's 5th Division was posted to the west and behind Prentiss, on the western edge of the battlefield, between Owl Creek and Shiloh Church. Brigadier General Stephen

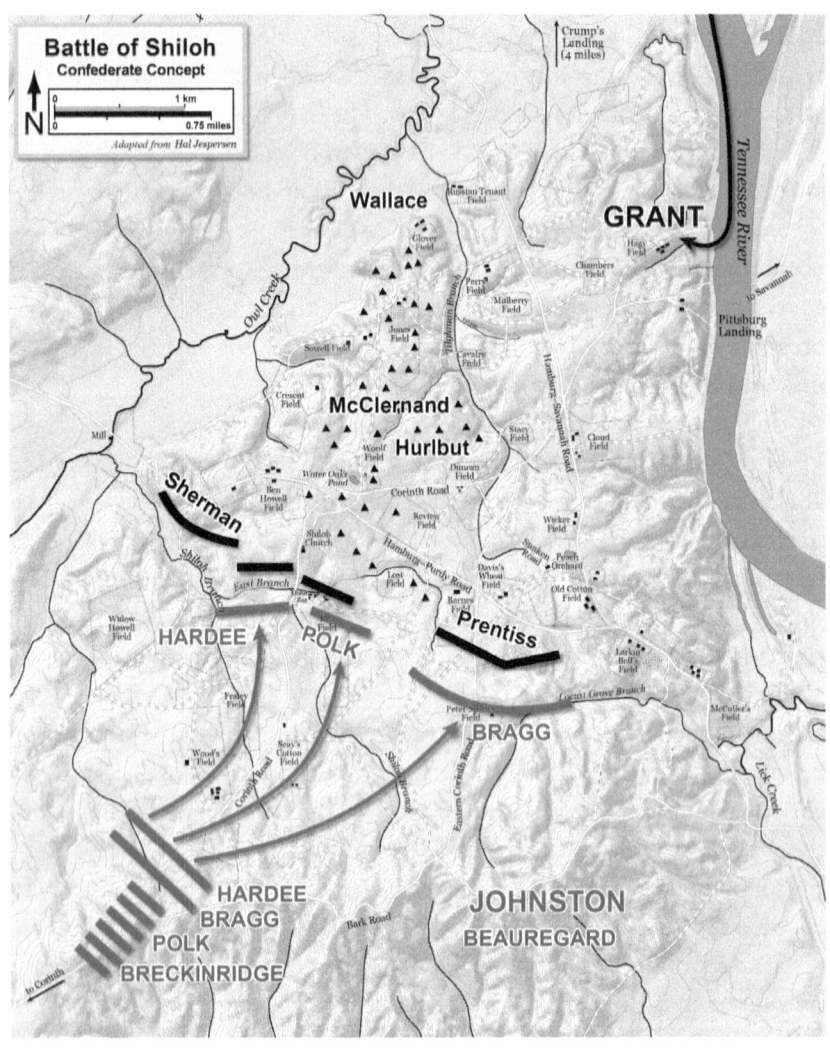

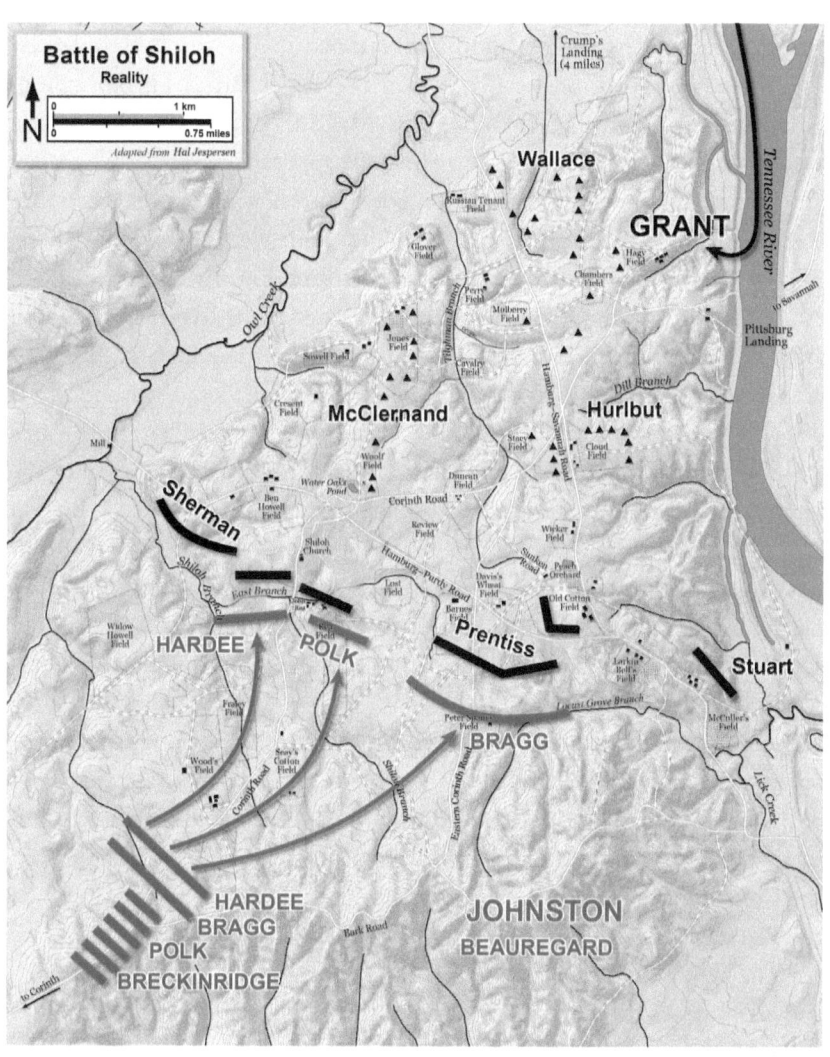

A. Hurlbut's 4th Division was located to the east and behind Prentiss, about three-quarters of a mile (1.2 km) from Pittsburg Landing. Then there were the two divisions in reserve. Major General John A. McClernand's 1st Division was situated about 200 yards (183 m) to the east and rear of Sherman. Brigadier General William H.L. Wallace's 3rd Division was situated closest to the landing, encamped in a position bounded by the Tennessee River, Snake Creek, and the River Road. Finally, one of Sherman's brigades, under Colonel David R. Stuart, was settled on the eastern edge of the battlefield, guarding the approaches over Lick Creek.[14]

Johnston's son wrote that the Confederates "knew that in the recesses of that forest, between those creeks, 50,000 invaders were posted; but where, or how, and with what preparation, no man could tell."[15] Despite having established an outpost at Pittsburg Landing prior to the arrival of the Union army, Brigadier General Daniel Ruggles had not adequately scouted the area in which the battle was to be fought. The Confederates also found it difficult to collect accurate intelligence from the local citizens in the area and therefore lacked crucial information regarding the topography of the region, including the Tennessee River and its tributaries. When Johnston arrived at Corinth on the 22nd of March, he ordered that "a corps of at least twenty reliable citizens who are familiar with this section of country, particularly that portion of it lying between the Memphis & Charleston and Mobile & Ohio Railroads and the Tennessee River [be created to] serve as guides."[16]

The contemporary maps available to Johnston and Beauregard also failed to identify Dill Branch and the various ravines on the eastern sector of the battlefield. These would seriously impede any Confederate advance in that direction. Beauregard stated that "it must be remembered that the Confederates had no accurate knowledge of the ground occupied by the Federals, and they had no proper staff officers to make the necessary reconnaissance, if practicable."[17] Ultimately, the presence of Dill Branch and the surrounding rough terrain on the east of the battlefield would make the anti-clockwise rotation of the Confederate attack against the Union army extremely difficult to achieve.

The direction of the battle

The battle of Shiloh commenced when an early morning patrol sent by Colonel Everett Peabody, the commander of the first brigade of Prentiss's division, encountered skirmishers from Hardee's 3rd Corps in Fraley Field at about 4.55am on the 6th of April. The sound of the resulting firefight echoed through the woods, alerting Johnston and his staff to the commencement of hostilities. The Confederate attack had achieved surprise at a strategic level, but not at a tactical level due to Peabody's vigilance.[18] Hardee's men were in the middle of breakfast when the skirmishing with Peabody's patrol broke out, and it took the Georgian about an hour to ready his troops, get them in line, and advance. At about 6am, Hardee's corps moved forward, but its progress was impeded by rough terrain, ravines, and impenetrable thickets, which compelled the regiments to separate, and veer left or right around the various obstacles. The corps of Bragg, Polk, and Breckinridge dutifully shuffled forward behind Hardee's soldiers.[19]

The battle of Shiloh would be a soldier's fight. As Hardee had just experienced, the dense vegetation and rough terrain of the battlefield broke up formations, created confusion, and made coordinated manoeuvres difficult. This led to a more personal and immediate type of warfare. The troops on both sides were often engaged in brutal, close-quarters combat. Success on the battlefield depended on the quick-thinking, bravery, and initiative of individual soldiers and small units rather than the larger, coordinated strategies of higher command. Nevertheless, Johnston and Beauregard had critical roles to play, and both generals influenced the movements of the Army of the Mississippi on the 6th of April. However, the Louisianian's statement that he had the "general direction" of the battle, which garnered the support of numerous sympathetic historians, is open to debate. An examination of the significant large-scale movements of the Confederate army during the battle of Shiloh clearly indicate that Johnston was the causative agent for many of them.

Johnston secures the flank

As Johnston rode *Fire Eater* to the front lines trailed by staff officers, he cheered on the troops and instructed them to, "shoot low boys; it takes two to carry one off the field."[20] It was here that he made his first significant tactical decision of the day. Encountering Colonel George E. Maney's 1st Tennessee regiment of Polk's corps, Johnston ordered five companies to proceed to Greer's Ford near the Tennessee River. These troops would protect the eastern flank of the Confederate army as it advanced forward.

A soldier in the regiment recalled Johnston's speech: "My countrymen, I have selected you for the post of honor today. As our army forces the enemy down the river, which I confidently expect, our rear becomes exposed from a possible attack from the river at or near Hamburg. Should [Major General Don Carlos] Buell, whose army is moving rapidly to General Grant's assistance, cross the Tennessee at Hamburg, under cover of the gunboats, and attack our rear from that point without successful resistance, he would place our army in jeopardy, and probably wrest from us the great victory which we hope confidently to win today. I have heard good accounts of your campaigns in the mountains of Virginia, and on that account have selected you for this post of honor. Colonel [Nathan B.] Forrest, of whom you have doubtless heard, and his regiment will be with you. I have made this frank statement to you, my countrymen, in order to impress upon you the importance of holding your position at all hazards. No matter in whatever numbers the enemy come, hold your position until I can get to you.""[21]

Maney's troops were likely disappointed in receiving such an assignment far from the glory of the battlefield, but it was a real possibility that Buell's Army of the Ohio could land at Hamburg on the Tennessee River and then strike the Southern army's right flank during its assault on Grant's army at Pittsburg Landing, or, just as worse, get between the Confederates and their base at Corinth. In fact, Grant had informed Major General Henry W. Halleck on the 5th of April that "General [William] Nelson's division has arrived. The other two of General Buell's column will arrive tomorrow and next day. It is my present intention to send them to Hamburg, some four miles [6.4 km] above Pittsburg, when they all get here."[22]

Johnston's speech mollified and inspired the men. Out of earshot, he directed Maney to assume command of all the troops at the ford and "watch and resist any demonstration of the enemy against the extreme right flank or the rear of the army from the direction of Hamburg."[23] Johnston explained that his orders were discretionary and permitted

Maney to bring the troops guarding Greer's Ford to join the main battle if no Union threat towards Hamburg manifested. Maney and Forrest concluded that no threat existed by about 11am and moved northward to join the battle. Although Buell's men never materialized at Hamburg, Johnston's orders were prudent in securing the safety of his army.

Johnston drives the attack

As the first rank of Brigadier General Sterling A.M. Wood's brigade of Hardee's corps advanced into Fraley's Field, the commander of Peabody's patrol feared that his men were about to be outflanked and ordered a withdrawal at about 6.30am. However, Prentiss had sent a relief force of five companies to reinforce the patrol, and the two Union forces met in Seay Field just east of the Corinth-Pittsburg Road. The Federal commander of the relief force assumed command and established a new defensive line. Brigadier General Thomas C. Hindman's brigade joined Wood's men and advanced to drive the Union troops from the field. To the west, Hardee's third brigade, under Brigadier General Patrick R. Cleburne, also advanced forwards. One of Johnston's aides remembered: "General Johnston then passed to the left at a point in front of the camps, near two cabins, subsequently used as a hospital. A field of a hundred acres fringed with forest extended to the northeast. Through this General Cleburne's brigade moved in beautiful order, and with loud and inspiring cheers in the direction of the advanced camp. Heavy firing was heard as they neared it."[24]

Cleburne's troops had slammed into one of Sherman's brigades near Rea Field. The Southerners encountered challenging terrain, peppered by inundated creeks, dense undergrowth, and swamp land, which broke up the brigade's formation and weakened its attack. Sherman rode to the front of his division at about 7am to investigate the rattle of musketry and was shocked to see thousands of Confederate soldiers approaching. He exclaimed, "My God, we are attacked!" and Cleburne's men unleashed a volley in his direction.[25] Sherman was hit in the hand and an aide riding at his side was killed instantly. The stunned general turned his horse and rushed off to find reinforcements. Fortunately for the bluecoats, Sherman's division was in a strong defensive position behind the flooded Shiloh Branch, and it was buttressed by powerful artillery.

Johnston moved eastwards to Seay Field and personally observed the action against Peabody's reinforced patrol from the woods bordering the clearing. The Arkansas troops from Hindman's brigade drove Peabody's men out of Seay Field, but the Federals reformed with the remainder of their parent brigade on a low wooded ridge just south of their campsite near a branch of Shiloh Creek. Hindman's soldiers pursued, but, with the shock of first contact with Peabody's full brigade, several Arkansas regiments disintegrated and fled to the rear. A soldier in Johnston's escort company observed that "instantly [the general] quickened to a gallop, with the staff and escort following, and right into the melee we plunged."[26] Johnston exclaimed: "Men of Arkansas! They say you boast of your prowess with the bowie knife. Today you wield a nobler weapon – the bayonet. Employ it well!"[27]

One of Johnston's aides remembered that "Hindman's brigade was suffering under a heavy fire. Some of the men were breaking ranks, and there were many dead and wounded. General Johnston in person rallied the stragglers."[28] As the general approached Colonel John S. Marmaduke, commander of the 3rd Arkansas, and a fellow veteran of the Utah Expedition, he placed his hand on the young man's shoulder: "My son, we must win this day – conquer or perish."[29] Marmaduke later claimed that he felt braced "tenfold" after this interaction with the army commander. Johnston was able to quickly reassemble the fragmented and dispirited troops by virtue of his position on the front lines. This safeguarded the momentum of the Confederate offensive. Stanley F. Horn remarked that "displaying rare valor and hardihood but dubious discretion, General Johnston was active along the right front, urging the men on and leading them himself when there was any sign of faltering."[30]

Johnston extends the line
While Peabody's brigade battled Wood's and Hindman's troops, Prentiss ordered his second brigade, under Colonel Madison Miller, to advance into Spain Field, a little to the east of Peabody, and prepare his men for imminent conflict. Two batteries of Prentiss's artillery were deployed in the northwest corner of the field. Johnston followed Hindman's troops as they struggled to drive Peabody's soldiers from the ridge. Johnston and the Confederate commanders believed that the divisions of Sherman and

Prentiss constituted the entire width of the Union left flank, and that the remainder of the Federal army was arrayed to the north, facing west.

However, Sherman's and Prentiss's divisions formed the west and center of the Union line, with McClernand's division lurking behind. The divisions of Hurlbut and Wallace, plus Stuart's isolated brigade, hovered undetected between the Confederate army and the Tennessee River. Johnston soon realized that the divergence of Lick and Owl creeks was much greater than that indicated by the map. In response, he ordered Brigadier General Adley H. Gladden's brigade of Bragg's corps, currently on the second line of the army, to move forward and extend the right of Hardee on the first line. Due to the incorrect map, the Confederate generals did not know that Lick Creek curved abruptly to the northeast, and therefore, the gap on the right would only expand further as the troops moved forward.[31]

At the rear of the Confederate army, Beauregard responded to the movement of Bragg's troops. Roman wrote that "Generals Polk and Breckinridge were now hastened forward, and, reporting to General Beauregard, at half-past seven, were by him deployed in column of brigades, General Breckinridge on the right, General Polk on the left. They received from General Beauregard brief general instructions to keep at a proper distance in rear of General Bragg's line and apart from each other, until called on for assistance, when they should move promptly with concentrated forces wherever needed, and, if in doubt from the hidden and broken character of the country, to move upon the sound of the heaviest firing."[32]

In this movement of the Army of the Mississippi, Johnston played the active role and Beauregard the passive role. The commanding general personally observed the divergence of Lick and Owl creeks from his position at the head of the army and ordered Bragg's soldiers forward to extend Hardee's line. Johnston possessed the tactical insight from his direct observation of the terrain. Beauregard responded to the realignment of the army's corps by bringing forward the troops under Polk and Breckinridge and instructing them to move towards the sound of most intense combat.

Johnston reacts to a threat from the left

As Gladden's brigade moved forward to strike Miller's troops in Spain Field, Johnston rode over to the west of his line to observe Cleburne's offensive against Sherman's division positioned in Rea Field and the area west of the Corinth Road.[33]

Concerned by the lack of progress in this sector, the general galloped back across the Confederate line to direct the assaults against Prentiss's division, still erroneously believed to constitute the entire left flank of the Union army. With the collapse of Prentiss, the division under Sherman could be threatened from two sides. Prentiss's infantry numbered about 5,400 men and were supported by two batteries of artillery. At about 8am, Gladden's troops rushed forward to assault Miller's brigade in Spain Field, but were bloodily repulsed under a hail of musketry, artillery shot, and shell. Gladden was mortally wounded and his brigade disintegrated. Johnston rode into the wavering mass of soldiers, exhorting them to reform. Meanwhile, Hindman's struggle against Peabody's brigade on the low wooded ridge was assisted by the advance of Wood's brigade on his left, which outflanked the Federals. The right flank of Peabody's brigade began to give way under the intense pressure.[34]

To the west, Cleburne's assault on Sherman's division was faltering badly. The impenetrable, marshy ground around the flooded Shiloh Branch wreaked havoc on Cleburne's formation. His brigade only managed to attack in uncoordinated fragments. The Union infantry, supported by the concentrated firepower of multiple Union artillery batteries, easily repulsed Cleburne's offensive and inflicted heavy losses. The 6th Mississippi regiment suffered 300 casualties out of its 425 soldiers engaged, one of the worst attrition rates for any regiment reported during the entire Civil War.[35]

In response to Cleburne's failure, Beauregard ordered up three more Confederate brigades, Brigadier General Patton Anderson's and Colonel Preston Pond's from Bragg's corps and Colonel Robert M. Russell's from Polk's corps, and sixteen cannon to dislodge Sherman's division from its strong position. Beauregard's order has been cited as evidence that the Louisianian ignored the battle plan and deprived Johnston of much need strength for the planned flanking manoeuvre on the right. However, at this point in the battle, Johnston and Beauregard were under the impression that Sherman's and Prentiss's divisions constituted the "southern" edge of the Union army, which was facing west. Beauregard's decision to send an additional three brigades to support Cleburne was justified, as Sherman's resistance would need to be broken for Johnston's turning manoeuvre on the right to succeed. Unfortunately for the Confederate generals, the Federal army was facing southwest, and Prentiss's division was the centre.

While directing the fight against Prentiss's division, Johnston received some inaccurate information from a scout that additional Union troops had also appeared on Cleburne's left and threatened to outflank him. The Union troops belonged to Colonel John A. McDowell's brigade of Sherman's division, and they were simply manoeuvring to a better defensive position, with no aggressive intent. Johnston, of course, could not know this, and he responded decisively, deciding to send Breckinridge's entire Reserve Corps to this sector.[36] One of Beauregard's staff officers recalled that "the battle was then raging furiously. General Johnston was sitting on his horse where the bullets were flying like hailstones. I galloped up to him amid the fire, and found him cool, collected, self-possessed, but still animated and in fine spirits."[37] Johnston remarked, "say to General Beauregard, we are sweeping the field before us, and in less than half an hour we shall be in possession of their camps, and I think we shall press them to [Owl Creek]. Say, also, I have just learned from a scout, or messenger, that the enemy is moving up in force on our left, and that General Breckinridge had better move to our left to meet him."[38]

As this was unverified information from a scout, Johnston qualified his instructions, "Do not say to General Beauregard that this is an order, but he must act on what additional information he may receive. The reports to him are more to be relied on than to me."[39] Johnston acknowledged that he did not have a comprehensive view of the entire battlefield and entrusted Beauregard with the responsibility of guiding reinforcements to the most important areas. The Louisianian did not oppose or countermand Johnston's directive. Roman wrote that "three brigades of General Breckinridge were accordingly set in motion as an additional reinforcement for that quarter."[40]

Johnston's concentration of forces
Turning his thoughts back to the offensive against Miller in Spain Field, the point at which he would launch the anti-clockwise turning movement of the army, Johnston ordered the brigades of Brigadier General James R. Chalmers and Colonel John K. Jackson of Bragg's corps to fill the

expanding gap between Owl and Lick Creeks. Timothy B. Smith noted that "Johnston realized that his right far outflanked the enemy left in this area. In fact, the sounds of battle could be heard far to the west, all the way to and past Shiloh Church. But absolutely nothing was heard to the east. Johnston thus decided he had located the enemy flank, and according to his plan, he began to turn it."[41] Chalmers's men on the far right advanced, "by a gradual left wheel" in accordance with Johnston's battle plan.[42] The commanding general also directed Colonel James H. Clanton's Alabama Cavalry regiment to reconnoitre and guard the army's right flank.

Having dispatched Breckinridge's corps, the army's final reserve, to the left, Johnston needed to find some more weight on the right for the turning movement. He rode westwards to the Corinth Road and encountered his friend Polk. They conferred for several moments and then Johnston ordered the bishop to send one of his brigades to strengthen the right. This was the last time that Johnston and Polk would ever meet. Polk selected Brigadier General Alexander P. Stewart's brigade, and Johnston personally led it to the desired position. Stewart remembered that "we continued to advance, until General A.S. Johnston came up and directed me to move my brigade to the right, to support of General Bragg… No one who saw him on the field of battle on that fateful morning of April 6th could fail to be struck by his bearing. His whole mien was singularly noble and soldierly, characterized by a calm dignity that was inspired by a consciousness of power and confidence."[43]

Regarding Johnston's previous order to move Breckinridge's troops to the eastern sector of the battlefield, historian David A. Powell stated that "Johnston directed Breckinridge's Reserve Corps to move toward the Confederate left opposite Sherman; Beauregard had fortuitously overridden this advice since it turned out the troops were unneeded there."[44] However, this was not the case. Roman recorded that "a courier came in from General Johnston, with information that the enemy was not strong on the left and had fallen back."[45] Thus, Beauregard did not override Johnston's order, he merely responded to new intelligence received from the commanding general. Roman recounted that "General Beauregard thereupon ordered General Breckinridge to send but one brigade to the left, and lead his remaining two brigades to the right of Gladden, so as to share in the forward movement of the first line, and extend his own right as far as possible towards Lick Creek."[46] Accordingly, Brigadier General John S. Bowen's brigade and Colonel Walter S. Statham's brigade were redirected to the right while the third, under Colonel Robert P. Trabue, continued onwards to fight Sherman. This conformed to Johnston's original battle plan.

Leaving Stewart's brigade, Johnston rode back to the Spain Field and Eastern Corinth Road area to direct the assault against Prentiss's stubborn division. The commanding general had now amassed almost 10,000 Confederates from Wood's, Hindman's, Gladden's and Chalmer's brigades with which to crush Prentiss.[47] Johnston ordered a bayonet charge and the screaming graycoats flung themselves at the enemy lines. Hit on two sides, Prentiss's division reeled backwards to its original campsites. Peabody, having already been wounded four times, was hit once more and fell dead. His brigade disintegrated and retreated in wild disorder. Miller's men were unable to resist the onslaught and joined the rout.

Many of the Union soldiers did not stop running until they reached the safety of Pittsburg Landing. Two pieces of artillery were abandoned. The Confederates pursued the fleeing Federals and soon discovered a cornucopia of abandoned food, equipment, supplies, and trinkets in Prentiss's campsites. The hungry Southerners halted to eat, rummage through the tents, exchange their weapons for superior models, and gather valuables. Johnston was disturbed by the number of soldiers engaged in the looting and galloped over to reform his troops. He witnessed a Confederate officer emerge from an enemy tent triumphantly grasping several valuable items and lost his temper, shouting, "None of that, sir; we are not here for plunder!" Seeing the officer's crestfallen expression, and feeling that he had been too harsh, Johnston reached down and picked up a tin cup from a table, pronouncing, "let this be my share of the spoils today."[48] Such a response endeared Johnston to his men. A group of Union prisoners, many of whom were German immigrants and barely able to speak English, threw themselves at *Fire Eater's* hooves, begging for mercy. Johnston was stunned and exclaimed, "Why men, you don't suppose we kill prisoners, do you? Go to the rear and you will be safe there."[49]

Grant arrived at Pittsburg Landing from his headquarters at Savannah and was shocked at the sight of thousands of demoralized and panicked

Union soldiers crowding around the landing. He sent an urgent appeal to Buell, stating that "the attack on my forces has been very spirited from early this morning. The appearance of fresh troops on the field now would have a powerful effect both by inspiring our men and disheartening the enemy. If you can get upon the field, leaving all your baggage on the east bank of the river, it will be a move to our advantage and possibly save the day to us. The rebel force is estimated at over 100,000 men."[50] At Savannah, Nelson's division from Buell's army was ordered to advance to Pittsburg Landing as quickly as possible, but it was difficult to find a knowledgeable guide and they would not debark at the landing until later that evening. Brigadier General Lew Wallace's division downriver at Crump's Landing was also directed to march to the battlefield, but the orders were confusing, and Wallace took the wrong road. His troops would also not arrive until later that evening. Grant's army would have to survive the afternoon unaided from both Buell and Wallace.

It was Johnston's concentration of Confederate forces on the right that enabled the success against Prentiss's division. He was the general that organized the brigades and personally directed them against the Federal position. It was also Johnston's order that prompted Beauregard to cancel the movement of Breckinridge's entire corps to the left of the army and redirect two of the brigades back to the right to confront Prentiss in accordance with the original battle plan.

Johnston's grand turning movement
After capturing Prentiss's camp, Johnston heard intense fighting to the left, where Cleburne's brigade and three other brigades were battling Sherman's division in the valley of Shiloh Branch. McClernand had brought forward his division to the east of Sherman, about three quarters of a mile (1.2 km) to the northwest of Prentiss's campsite. Johnston was informed of this movement, and as there appeared to be no enemy confronting Chalmers's brigade to the right of the Confederate line, he assumed that he had successfully outflanked the Union army. Stacy D. Allen observed that "in the first four hours of combat, the Confederate right, under Johnston's personal supervision, manoeuvred one and three-quarter miles [2.8 km] east and one mile [1.6 km] north... [this angle of approach] conformed to the Confederates' inferior maps. In overrunning

Prentiss's camp, the Confederates turned what Johnston probably believed was the Union left, but actually he had hit the Union center."[51] Johnston had Wood's, Hindman's, Gladden's, and Chalmers's brigades available at Prentiss's captured campsite, and these troops were soon joined by two of Bragg's brigades under Jackson and Gibson. In addition, two brigades from Polk's corps, Stewart's and Colonel William H. Stephen's, also arrived in the vicinity.

Johnston now had a total of eight brigades available between the Corinth Road and the Eastern Corinth Road for the swing to the northwest, the decisive action designed to turn the Union army and push it into Owl Creek.[52] One of Hardee's officers recalled that "after reforming my line I was ordered to make an oblique change of front to the left, with the view of making an attack upon an encampment to the left and rear of the camp just captured."[53] Allen explained that "Johnston shifted the better part of the force in Prentiss's camp to his left, which moved northwest to participate in the attack on McClernand's camp, hoping to force the Federal army back on Owl Creek."[54] Johnston intended for over half of the entire Confederate army to participate in this enormous turning movement.

Eight brigades would drive the bulk of Grant's army into the swamps while Sherman's reinforced division would be defeated, or at least fixed in place, by the five brigades already fighting in that sector. Johnston's son stated that "General Johnston was carrying forward the movement by which his entire right wing was swung around on the center, Hindman's brigade, as a pivot, so that every command of the Federals was taken successively, in front and flank, and a crumbling process ensued by which the whole line went to pieces."[55] Timothy B. Smith deemed that Johnston's turning movement as "one of the major command decisions at Shiloh – one that would have a profound effect on the rest of the battle."[56]

Johnston reacts to a threat from the right

Just as Johnston was about to launch his massive anti-clockwise rotation of the army, he received alarming intelligence from Bragg's chief engineer, Captain Samuel H. Lockett, who had conducted a pre-dawn reconnaissance of the eastern sector of the battlefield. Lockett discovered Stuart's brigade encamped near Lick Creek but could not determine the strength of the Union force. He therefore misinterpreted Stuart's presence as part of Union preparations for a movement to outflank the Confederate army and attack from the rear. The scout also made the erroneous assumption that Stuart's brigade of 2,100 men was another Federal division of up to 10,000 soldiers.

After receiving Lockett's unsettling report, Johnston pondered the situation for a while. The unwelcome discovery of Stuart's force compelled Johnston to divert some of his turning force to deal with the new threat. He ordered the brigades of Chalmers and Jackson to disengage from their positions on the front line and march to Lick Creek.[57] Historian Alexander Mendoza wrote that Johnston, "probably did not intend the 4,500 men he thus dispatched to cut off Grant's army from the river. He seems to have believed, thanks to inaccurate maps, that he had substantially accomplished that already by taking Prentiss's camps. Chalmers and Jackson would have the task of securing the Confederate flank against this errant Union 'division.'"[58]

Johnston and Hardee then rode to the north of Prentiss's campsite to reconnoitre the area and made another most unwelcome discovery – a second line of Union infantry. Hurlbut's division had come up and established a position in Sarah Bell's old cotton field to the east of the Hamburg-Savannah Road. Hurlbut had deployed three batteries of artillery, and they soon spotted the two high ranking Confederate generals and fired upon them. Johnston and Hardee beat a hasty retreat. With the removal of Chalmers's and Jackson's brigades from this sector, Johnston needed additional firepower to deal with Hurlbut. Fortunately, one of Beauregard's aides arrived at Prentiss's captured camp seeking instructions from Johnston. The aide remembered: "General Beauregard directed me to seek General Johnston, who was in the front, learn from him the condition of things there, and know of him what order he had to give as to the disposition of the reserves commanded by General Breckinridge."[59]

Johnston ordered Bowen's and Statham's brigades to deploy to the Confederate right flank in accordance with his battle plan. One of Johnston's cavalry escorts later remembered "that a young officer came up at full speed and said something to the general, who listened intently, then suddenly throwing out his right arm and bringing it in with a curve said: 'Tell General Breckinridge to sweep them.'"[60] Hardee felt confident that Johnston was "in person directing the battle" on the right and moved off to the left to support Cleburne.[61] Meanwhile, Chalmers and Jackson received their orders to move to the extreme right of the battlefield to contain the phantom Union division, which was really the isolated brigade of Stuart, at about 9.30am. They extracted their men from the front line and waited about half an hour for a guide to appear. At 10am, they commenced their circuitous march to the southeast, crossing some of the most difficult terrain of the battlefield.

Lockett returned from his reconnaissance at about 11am and reported in person to Johnston. He remembered: "I came to General A.S. Johnston and his staff standing on the brow of a hill watching the conflict in their front. I rode up to General Johnston, saluted him, and said I wished to make a report of the state of affairs on our extreme right. He said he had received the report and a sketch from Captain Lockett, of the engineers. I told him I was Captain Lockett. He replied, 'Well, sir, tell me as briefly and quickly as possible what you have to say.'"[62] Lockett continued: "When my report was finished, he said, 'That is what I gathered from your note and sketch, and I have already ordered General Breckinridge to send forces to fill up the space on our right. Ride back, sir, toward the right, and you will probably meet General Breckinridge; lead him to the position you indicate."[63]

However, historian William C. Davis noted that "Breckinridge, like his fellow corps commanders, had little or no knowledge of the terrain of the field, no maps, and may well have been lost or blindly groping his way toward the river when Johnston's officer found him."[64] The delay involved in dispatching Chalmers and Jackson to the far right and waiting for Breckinridge's two brigades to fill the gap had profound consequences. Stuart's brigade was of little threat to the Confederate offensive, remaining inert while awaiting orders to either hold their ground or retreat. When Chalmers and Jackson veered off to the right to deal with Stuart, the pressure on the Union center abated. It took precious hours for Breckinridge's brigades to arrive and fill the void in the central sector of the battlefield.

This delay gifted the Federals time in which to reform, consolidate their fragmented regiments, and receive reinforcements. W.H.L. Wallace's division and Prentiss's remnants reformed in some thick oak woods behind an old wagon trail to the west of Hurlbut's division. Here the Union troops were protected by dense vegetation, and the Confederate approach to the farm lane was covered by thick brambles. Many years later, this position would earn the sobriquet of the "Hornet's Nest." It was a formidable position and the way it dissected the battlefield provided a natural line of defense to Grant's army.[65] Thus, Johnston's decision to divert the brigades of Chalmers and Jackson to contain the threat posed by Stuart's phantom division had a momentous impact on the battle. Although a prudent move based on Lockett's misinformation, the reallocation of the Confederate forces to the right resulted in a critical delay that may have saved the Union army from defeat.

Johnston's attenuated turning movement
Johnston's eight brigade turning movement to the left against McClernand's division was reduced to five brigades due to the removal of Chalmers's and Jackson's brigades, and the exhaustion of Gladden's brigade, which was left behind to defend Prentiss's old campsite. Johnston's son wrote that "all the Confederate troops were then in the front line, except two of Breckinridge's brigades, Bowen's and Statham's, which were moving to the Confederate right, and soon occupied the interval to the left of Chalmers and Jackson. Hardee, with Cleburne and Pond, was pressing Sherman slowly but steadily back."[66] The weight of the five brigades sent against McClernand's position was too much for the Union defenders and they were forced back to the Hamburg-Purdy Road, exposing Sherman's left flank. After about three hours of determined resistance, Sherman's division finally crumbled, and about 10am, the Northerners abandoned their campsites to fall back to the northeast toward the Hamburg-Purdy and Corinth-Pittsburg Landing crossroads.

As with the capture of Prentiss's campsite, the Confederate soldiers on the left halted their advance to ransack Sherman's encampment. This delay enabled Sherman and McClernand to reform their battered divisions north of the Hamburg-Purdy Road. Between 10.30am and 11am, the five brigades under Hardee consolidated with the brigades sent in by Johnston. The Confederate forces reformed and launched an offensive against Sherman and McClernand's new position. Two thirds of the entire Confederate army was involved in this action, and the Union line buckled and broke under the pressure.[67]

By 11.30am, Sherman's and McClernand's men had been pushed back

1,300 yards (1.2 km) to Jones field. However, during the offensive on McClernand's position, Hindman's brigade, situated on the far right of the Confederate assault force, was surprised to receive a heavy enfilade fire on its right flank, which compelled his troops to find shelter in some woods to the west. Hindman's men had inadvertently discovered W.H.L. Wallace's and Prentiss's men in the Hornet's Nest. Gladden's brigade arrived to join the fray but was also repulsed. Ultimately, Johnston's battle plan was deranged by the unexpected disposition of the Union army and the topography of the battlefield. His anti-clockwise striking force coalesced with the brigades on the western edge of the battlefield and the defeated Federals under McClernand and Sherman fell back to the northeast towards Pittsburg Landing rather than the northwest towards Owl Creek. Smith noted that "the Confederate push had inadvertently sent the Union right rearward, toward, not away from, Pittsburg Landing."[68] Neither Johnston nor Beauregard ever intended such an outcome.

Johnston's third attempt at a turning movement
Leaving Prentiss's captured campsite, Johnston rode to the east of his line to supervise the attack on Hurlbut's division in the Sarah Bell cotton field. The army commander issued orders to Colonel Joseph Wheeler's 19th Alabama regiment, a Texas regiment, and some other units to press the attack. One of Jackson's soldiers remembered Johnston declaring: "My noble boys we have achieved a grand victory, a very great victory!"[69] Johnston crossed Locust Grove Branch and ascended to some high ground to observe Jackson's and Chalmers's men advance against Stuart's brigade on the extreme right. A member of Johnston's staff recalled that "we sat on our horses, side by side, watching [Chalmers's brigade] as it swept over the ridge; and, as the colors dipped out of sight, the general said to me, 'That checkmates them.' I told him I was glad to hear him announce 'checkmate,' but that 'he must excuse so poor a player for saying he could not see it.' He laughed, and said 'Yes, sir, that mates them.'"[70]

Chalmers's and Jackson's brigades reached the north bank of Locust Grove Branch on the far right of the Confederate line just before 11am and engaged in a firefight with Stuart's advanced skirmishers. Stuart's brigade effectively utilized the rugged terrain to stall the Confederate attack. Mendoza wrote that "the carnage near the Hamburg-Savannah

Road devastated Stuart's force, but the brigade's refusal to yield their ground readily to Chalmers and Jackson had bought precious time for the Federals on the right and center."[71] Jackson's men eventually captured Stuart's campsite but then stumbled into the path of Brigadier General John A. McArthur's brigade, positioned to the east of Hurlbut's position in Sarah Bell's field. Jackson attacked but failed to dislodge McArthur's men, and Chalmers experienced similar difficulty in his attempt to break Stuart's new position on a ridge overlooking a steep ravine.

At 11am, Beauregard ordered Stephens's brigade of Polk's corps to assault the Hornet's Nest, but his advance was caught in a crossfire between the troops hiding in that dense thicket and those of McClernand's division to the northwest, and the Confederates were repulsed with great loss. After the successful effort to overwhelm Sherman's and McClernand's divisions, elements of Johnston's turning strike force were directed east to break the Federal resistance at the Hornet's Nest.[72] The assault from this disorganized mass of Southern troops was also beaten back, and so Bragg brought up Gibson's brigade to lend some more weight to the Confederate offensive. Gibson's men fared no better, and after several attempts, the graycoats fell back bloodied and out of ammunition. The diversion of the best part of six brigades to assail the Hornet's Nest, and the fatigue, disorganization, and lack of ammunition of the Confederate troops on the left of the line, resulted in a loss of momentum in this sector of the battlefield.

The brigades of Hardee's and Polk's corps halted to rest, resupply, and loot the Union camps, and this created an opportunity for the Union to regain the initiative. Sherman and McClernand had both received fresh troops from Pittsburg Landing, and at 12pm, they launched a fierce counterattack from Jones Field that pushed the Southerners back about half a mile (800 m). The Union soldiers reclaimed their campsites from that morning and Beauregard responded by dispatching Trabue's brigade of Breckinridge's corps to staunch the Union offensive.[73]

On the other side of the battlefield, Breckinridge and the two brigades of his reserve corps, under Bowen and Statham, arrived on the right of the Confederate line at 12pm to assist Jackson and Chalmers. Johnston rode to some high ground south of the Hamburg-Purdy Road in which to oversee the movements of his right wing. Johnston had gathered five brigades, those of Stephens, Statham, Bowen, Jackson, and Chalmers, to dislodge Hurlbut's division from the Bell's cotton field and Peach Orchard area. Johnston personally guided Breckinridge's two brigades into action, leading the men over a series of gullies and ravines. As Bowen's brigade approached the Federal line, Johnston shouted to the men: "Only a few more charges and the day is ours!" and then fell back to a small hollow at the rear of the brigade.[74] Hurlbut's division, supplemented by McArthur's brigade, formed an eastward extension of Prentiss's and W.H.L. Wallace's Hornet's Nest defensive line. Hurlbut's men were arrayed behind an old fence, smothered in tangled vines and thick vegetation. The attacking Confederates had to cross an open expanse of ground with little cover, a particularly daunting aspect since McArthur's brigade on the eastern side of Hurlbut's line was bolstered by powerful artillery.

Bowen's Arkansas troops rushed forward but were beaten back by the deadly canister shot from the Union cannons.[75] Governor Isham G. Harris of Tennessee, acting as a volunteer aide to Johnston, remembered the general becoming inpatient at the stalled progress and declaring: "They are offering stubborn resistance here. I shall have to put the bayonet to them."[76] Harris and other staff officers relayed Johnston's order for Bowen's and Statham's brigades to charge Hurlbut's position in the Peach Orchard to Breckinridge. There would be no more reinforcements or transfers of troops – the entire Confederate army was now engaged in the battle.[77] Johnston had gathered Breckinridge's two brigades to bolster his attack on Hurlbut's division. This was the army commander's third attempt to drive the Union Army of the Tennessee into the swamplands around Owl and Snake creeks.

Beauregard must be credited for dispatching Trabue's brigade to the left in response to the counterattack by Sherman and McClernand, but his instructions for rallied troops to simply go where the firing was heaviest meant that the Hornet's Nest became the focal point of two thirds of the Confederate army. Thomas K. Hall declared that "the two senior commanders were working towards different goals: Johnston wanted the main effort on the Confederate right; Beauregard spread the troops out all over the field with no particular main effort."[78]

Johnston breaks Hurlbut's division
As Johnston waited for Bowen's and Statham's brigades to charge Hurlbut's position, Breckinridge galloped up in great distress and exclaimed: "General, I have a regiment of Tennesseans that refuses to fight. I have been doing my utmost to rally them and get them in." This assertion stung Governor Harris's state pride, and he interrupted: "General Breckinridge, show me that regiment!" Breckinridge apologetically pointed to the command, and Johnston said: "Let the Governor go to them."[79] Harris galloped over to the demoralized regiment and managed to cajole the Tennesseans up into the firing line. Breckinridge then reappeared by Johnston's side and informed the commander that he could not get the regiments in the eastern section of his brigade to charge either. Johnston replied: "Oh yes, general; I think you can."[80] Breckinridge, with tears welling in his eyes, cried: "General Johnston, I cannot get my men to make the charge." Johnston softened: "Then I will help you… We can get them to make the charge."[81]

Smith posited that the general's decision to personally lead the attack was a desperate gamble: "Johnston had to win a victory, and he was determined to do everything in his power to achieve it. But at 2:00pm on the sixth, Johnston ran out of options. He had sent in his last reserves, and they were stalled. The only choice he had left was to wade into the battle himself and hopefully inspire his men to greater efforts."[82] Smith concluded that "just as key subordinates had continually let [Johnston] down from Fort Donelson until now, he saw he had to risk his own life to personally do what needed to be done. He had to conquer or perish."[83]

When the Governor returned, Johnston turned to him and remarked: "I will go to the front, order, and lead the charge… Go to the extreme right and lead the Tennessee regiment stationed there."[84] Mounted on the imposing *Fire Eater*, Johnston accompanied Breckinridge eastwards. As he passed through the ranks of the Arkansans in Breckinridge's brigade, the general bellowed: "Soldiers, get ready! Soldiers of the 9th Arkansas Regiment – are you ready to drive the invaders of your country from our soil?" The soldiers shouted: "We are!"[85] Wearing no hat and his sword resting in its scabbard, Johnston still held the tin cup he had appropriated from the enemy camp earlier that day. He used the cup to strike the bayonets of the soldiers standing in the ranks as he rode past. "These must do the work!" Johnston yelled: "Men! They are stubborn; we must use the bayonet...a few more charges and the day [will be] ours... I will lead you!"[86] The line of soldiers roared in approval and prepared to fling themselves at the enemy once more.

One observer of the scene recalled that "those nearest to [Johnston], as if drawn to him by some overmastering magnetic force, rushed forward around him with a mighty shout. The rest of the line took it up and echoed it with a wild yell of defiance and desperate purpose and moved forward at a charge with rapid and resistless step."[87] The troops of Bowen's and Statham's brigades hurled themselves forward against Hurlbut's Federal division. Governor Harris recalled that "the charge was successful. The Federal line gave way and we advanced from a half to three-quarters of a mile [0.8-1.2 km] without opposition, when we encountered the reserve line of the enemy, strongly posted on a ridge."[88]

Johnston positioned himself in the centre and at a few feet in the rear of the advanced Confederate line. Harris galloped up to Johnston and remembered later that he "had never, in my life, seen him looking more bright, joyous, and happy than he looked at the moment that I approached him. The charge he had led was heroic. It had been successful, and his face expressed a soldier's joy and patriot's hope."[89] Although cheerful, Johnston had not survived the charge unscathed. He had been hit three times. A spent ball had struck his lateral right thigh, a shell fragment hit him above and to the rear of his right hip, and another ball cut his left boot sole. The general's clothes had also been pierced in several places. Like his rider, the valiant *Fire Eater* had been hit, suffering three or four wounds in the charge. However, none of the injuries were serious.

An aide-de-camp observed the general smile and slap his thigh in jest in reference to the bruise from the spent ball.[90] Harris remembered: "As I approached him he said: 'Governor, they came very near putting me *hors de combat* in that charge,' holding out and pointing to his foot. Looking at it, I discovered that a musket ball had struck the edge of the sole of his boot, cutting the sole clear across and ripping it off to the toe."[91] Harris was concerned and asked: "Are you wounded? Did the ball touch your foot?" Johnston replied in the negative and "was starting to say something more when a Federal battery opened fire from a position which raked our line, which we had just established. The General paused in the midst of a sentence to say: 'Order Colonel Statham to wheel his regiment to the left, charge and take that battery.' I galloped to Colonel Statham, only about 200 yards [182 m] distant [and] gave the order."[92]

Johnston then dispatched another aide to deliver an order, leaving only Captain Watkins L. Wickham in the immediate vicinity. Still thinking of the anti-clockwise movement of the army, the general informed Wickham that "we must go to the left, where the firing is heaviest."[93] The Governor returned from his mission and stated: "General, your order is delivered, and Colonel Statham is in motion," but as he was speaking, "the General reeled from me in a manner that indicated he was falling from his horse." During the time of Harris's absence, Johnston had been struck by a random bullet from the ongoing desultory fire between the two sides. Harris recalled that "I put my left arm around his neck, grasping the collar of his coat, and righted him up in the saddle, bending forward as I did so, and looking at him in the face, said: 'General, are you hurt?' In a very deliberate and emphatic tone he replied: 'Yes, and I fear, seriously.'" At that moment I requested Captain Wickham to go with all possible speed for a surgeon… The General's hold upon his rein relaxed and it dropped from his hand, I gathered his rein with my right, in which I held my own, and guided both horses to a valley."[94]

Harris remembered that "when laid upon the ground, with eager anxiety I asked many questions about his wounds, to which he gave no answer, not even a look of intelligence. Supporting his head with one hand, I untied his cravat, unbuttoned his collar and vest, and tore his shirts open with the other for the purpose of finding the wound… In a few moments he ceased to breathe."[95] Johnston passed away at approximately 2.30pm on the 6th of April. He was the highest-ranking officer to be killed in the Civil War.[96] Command of the Army of the Mississippi devolved to Beauregard at the rear of the battlefield. Johnston's decision to personally inspire the charge was the decisive factor that enabled Bowen's and Statham's brigades to break the formidable Federal position in the Peach Orchard. He succeeded in encouraging the demoralized and exhausted troops forward when political luminaries such as Breckinridge and Harris could not. This action is further evidence that Johnston was the driving force behind the Confederate offensive on that fateful Sunday.

Conclusion

Many historians have claimed that Beauregard exerted greater influence than Johnston in managing the tactical movements of the Army of the Mississippi during the battle of Shiloh due to his location at the rear of the army. However, Johnston's decision to position himself near the front lines was no abrogation of command responsibility. His presence there enabled him to respond to rapidly evolving circumstances, which was particularly important considering that many of Johnston's subordinates at the brigade and regimental level were from non-military backgrounds and largely inexperienced in command and control. John R. Lundberg postulated that Johnston's "subordinates had failed him so many times that Johnston probably supposed that he had to lead from the front, on the spot, in order to get anything done right."[98]

The Confederate high command's ignorance of the topography of the battlefield and disposition of the Union army was also a factor in Johnston's location. Allen noted that "the passage of massed linear formations through heavy cover and across undulating terrain proved ponderous and difficult to coordinate."[99] A senior commander was required on the front lines to ameliorate this situation. Johnston's presence on the front line allowed him to make real-time adjustments, ensuring that his troops maintained offensive pressure. Wiley Sword asserted that "Johnston's presence along the battle line involved maintaining tactical control of his main offensive thrust. Thus, both his bravery and commitment to win should be apparent to all. Due to the tactical nightmare of mixed commands and random unit coordination, it was imperative that someone with high command authority be present to organize a cohesive attack."[100] This is the function that Johnston served most effectively, and interestingly, when Beauregard assumed command of the army, the Louisianian could also be found at the front lines of the battlefield on the 7th of April.

Up until his death, Johnston guided the significant manoeuvres of the Army of the Mississippi. He sent Maney's and Forrest's men to Greer's Ford, extended the front ranks of the army eastwards when advancing, repeatedly formed the concentrations of brigades necessary to launch the anti-clockwise movement of the army to push the Federals into Owl and Snake creeks, and responded to the threat of the unexpected Union forces present on the right of the battlefield. Johnston received and transmitted information through his staff and via messengers, rallied broken units, and personally directed brigades and regiments during the battle. A member of his escort company declared, "always at a gallop, we traversed a great part of the field. [Johnston] seemed cool and collected all the time... Staff and various other officers were continually galloping up to him and off again."[101]

Another officer remarked that "during the battle of Shiloh, [Johnston] was everywhere, pushing the attack, encouraging the men, and seeing that the plan of battle he had so carefully explained the night before to his subordinate generals was harmoniously and accurately carried out by them."[102] Interestingly, even though Timothy B. Smith had previously written that Beauregard was more in command at Shiloh than Johnston, he also noted that "no less than seven" of Johnston's division and brigade commanders received their orders "from him personally. For the army commander to be issuing orders to even division but certainly to brigade and especially regimental commanders during a fight was absolutely breaking the chain of command... Johnston's presence all over the battlefield at first and then concentrated on the right later in the day seemed to be the defining feature of command, with the corps and division commanders largely invisible or simply acting out his larger desires."[103]

Beauregard performed well at the rear of the army, collecting reports from the front lines, reforming stragglers, and dispatching inactive units back to the front. Roman wrote that "brigades and regiments, as well as batteries, were often... at a standstill without orders; and sometimes, from the... lack of cohesion, bodies of our own troops were mistaken for the enemy and even fired into on the flank or rear and thrown into some confusion. Other commands, after casualties, remained without leadership from a ranking officer, until so reported to General Beauregard, and by him supplied through his staff."[104] Roman recounted that "straggling also began early in the day, a great many men being engaged in the plunder of the captured camps, while numbers made their way to the rear. General Beauregard used part of the cavalry, under his staff and escort, to drive them out of the camps, and when collected, they were formed into battalions, officered as well as could be done under the circumstances, and again sent forward. Thus, all loose or halting commands were attached to the readiest lines of movement, or to those needing reinforcement."[105]

Johnston's decision to leave Beauregard at the rear of the army to direct reinforcements, collect stragglers, and attend to logistical problems does not imply that he intended Beauregard to have a more important command role in the battle. The general placed Beauregard at the rear because he was sick and seemingly incapable of serving on the battlefield. Hall maintained that it is doubtful that "Johnston relegated himself to the role of a cheerleader and left control up to Beauregard... it would leave control of the battle to someone located in the rear of the army. Most likely, what Johnston had in mind was to press the attack in the front while Beauregard controlled troops in the rear, particularly the corps of Polk and Breckinridge."[106] Perhaps Roland summed up the Confederate command situation at Shiloh most eloquently: "Notwithstanding Johnston's location during the battle, Johnston actually made every major Confederate command decision between his arrival in Corinth and his death on the field of Shiloh."[107]

24.

Was Johnston foolish to personally lead a charge?

General Albert Sidney Johnston witnessed his men break Brigadier General Stephen A. Hurlbut's obstinate defensive line in the Peach Orchard and rush forward in triumph just moments before his fatal wound. In Johnston's mind, this success opened the opportunity to outflank Major General Ulysses S. Grant's entire Union Army of the Tennessee and push it into the swamps of Owl and Snake creeks. After the war, former Confederate general and brigade commander at Shiloh, Randall L. Gibson, remarked that "it was while executing this design, in the full tide of victory, that Albert Sidney Johnston received his death-wound... as a true soldier would love to die – on the edge of battle, in the moment of triumph."[1]

The Army of the Mississippi, now led by General Pierre G.T. Beauregard, pressed the attack and finally captured the Hornet's Nest, along with the remnants of Brigadier Generals Benjamin M. Prentiss's and William H.L. Wallace's divisions, in the late afternoon of the 6th of April 1862. The victorious Southern soldiers reorganized and approached Pittsburg Landing and Grant's last line of defense. Yet darkness quickly enveloped the battlefield and the Confederate troops leading the assault on this strong Federal position soon aborted their offensive. Beauregard then officially called off the attack on Pittsburg Landing, hoping to mop up the Union remnants the following day. However, during the night, Grant's battered army received over 20,000 reinforcements in the form of Major General Don Carlos Buell's Army of the Ohio and Brigadier General Lew Wallace's division from Crump's Landing. The odds were now decidedly in Grant's favor, and after more bitter fighting on the 7th of April, Beauregard was compelled to retire his pummelled army from the battlefield.

The Confederate campaign to destroy Grant's army prior to its reinforcement by Buell was a failure. Southern losses were 10,694 from about 44,700 soldiers engaged, compared to Union losses of 13,047 from about 66,800 soldiers involved in the battle. Beauregard's exhausted men streamed back to Corinth, while the Union armies under Grant and Buell licked their wounds. Major General Henry W. Halleck blamed Grant's negligence for the massive Union losses and soon arrived at Pittsburg Landing to assume personal command of the Federal forces. On the 10th of April, Beauregard informed the men of the Army of the Mississippi that "your late commander-in-chief, General A.S. Johnston, is dead. A fearless soldier, a sagacious captain, a reproachless man, has fallen; one who in his devotion to our cause shrank from no sacrifice; one who, animated by a sense of duty and sustained by a sublime courage, challenged danger and perished gallantly for his country whilst leading forward his brave columns to victory. His signal example of heroism and patriotism, if imitated, would make this army invincible. A grateful country will mourn his loss, revere his name, and cherish his manly virtues."[2]

Major General Leonidas Polk wrote that Johnston's "loss was deeply felt. It was an event which deprived the army of his clear, practical judgment and determined character... He was a true soldier, high-toned, eminently honorable, and just. Considerate of the rights and feelings of others, magnanimous, and brave. His military capacity was also of a high order, and his devotion to the cause of the South unsurpassed by that of any of her many noble sons who have offered up their lives on her altar. I knew him well from boyhood – none knew him better – and I take pleasure in laying on his tomb, as a parting offering, this testimonial of my appreciation of his character as a soldier, a patriot, and a man."[3] President Jefferson Davis grieved: "My long and close friendship with this departed chieftain and patriot forbids me to trust myself in giving vent to the feelings which this sad intelligence has evoked. Without doing injustice to the living, it may safely be asserted that our loss is irreparable."[4] On the frontlines in Virginia, Major General Thomas J. "Stonewall" Jackson lamented that "God gave us a glorious victory [at Shiloh], but the loss of the great Albert Sidney Johnston is to be mourned. I do not remember having ever felt so sad at the death of a man whom I had never seen."[5] After the Civil War, Grant declared that "the death of so great a man as Johnston was a great loss to the South and would have been to any cause in which he might have been engaged."[6]

The impact of Johnston's death on the course of the battle has been the subject of endless discussion over the decades, with some commentators claiming that it robbed the Confederates of certain victory. Others were equally adamant that Johnston could not have achieved any more than Beauregard did in the fading twilight of the first day of battle. This debate can never be resolved and will always remain in the realm of the hypothetical. Therefore, this chapter will focus on Johnston's decision to personally command the charge at the Peach Orchard on that fateful Sunday, the 6th of April 1862.

Leading from the front

Numerous authors have condemned Johnston for leading the Army of the Mississippi from the front lines during the battle of Shiloh. Historian John F.C. Fuller wrote that "in my opinion, General Johnston was a very common type of brave and stupid soldier, and his action at the battle of Shiloh in no way disproves this."[7] Larry J. Daniel argued that "the recklessness with which Johnston exposed himself (at one point being forty yards [37 m] beyond his own line) can hardly be excused."[8] Timothy B. Smith wrote that Johnston "placed himself at the point of most danger, certainly a place he had no business being as army commander were it not for the critical nature of the moment."[9] However, there are important reasons that may help explain Johnston's behavior.

Lack of staff
Firstly, the Army of the Mississippi lacked the required number of staff officers to function effectively. When Beauregard agreed to transfer from

the Confederate Army of the Potomac in Virginia to the Western Department, he requested that the Government provide him with a complement of staff officers. Alfred Roman recalled that one of Beauregard's demands was "that he should take with him his personal and general staff, and, if he required them, ten or twelve experienced officers from the Army of the Potomac – none above the rank of colonel – some of whom were to be promoted to brigadier and major generals, the others to receive staff appointments, so as to aid in organizing and disciplining the forces to be placed under him."[10] Unfortunately, this most reasonable demand was not acted upon by the Richmond bureaucrats.

Private Yves Reni Le Monnier of the Louisiana Crescent Regiment fought at Shiloh and later commented on "the great responsibility of the War Department in not furnishing to General Beauregard the twelve – only twelve, just think – officers he had urged on that department as being absolutely necessary in an army of raw recruits." Le Monnier rightly argued that "these officers would have been at this critical moment better than that many thousands of raw troops, for they would have kept the commands together, each one in its place; instead, there were colonels leading companies, brigadiers leading regiments, and the commander-in-chief himself leading a brigade, to be slain at the most critical moment of the contest. General Johnston had no business in the front line leading a brigade; his place was in the rear; he was mortified at the ignorance, if not neglect, of the War Department with respect to the condition of his army. Had that department transferred to his command the experienced officers General Beauregard had asked for and had shown to be absolutely necessary, General Johnston would not have exposed himself unnecessarily, desultory charges would have given place to well-made and sustained attacks, dislocations of command would not have occurred."[11]

The lack of administrative staff in the principal Confederate army in the western theater had a profound impact upon the battle of Shiloh, and as Le Monnier forcefully asserted, likely contributed to Johnston's death. This troubling situation slowly improved in the months following the battle. Historian Richard J. Zimmerman observed that by the end of 1862 "it is interesting to note that on both sides respective staff sizes had grown significantly, and staff officers were becoming more professional. Gone were some of the personal relatives, friends, and hangers-on seen earlier in 1862. For example, Bragg's staff had swelled to 36 men on the day of battle [at Stones River on the 31st of December]."[12] If Johnston had enjoyed the services of 36 professional staff officers on that fateful day in April, then perhaps he would have been more inclined to remain at a safe distance from the fighting.

Inexperienced officers and soldiers
One of Johnston's great strengths as a commander was his ability to inspire and motivate the volunteer soldier, and this had a powerful effect at the front lines during the battle of Shiloh. The general's son explained that his father's "own personal presence and inspiration and direction were often necessary with these enthusiastic but raw troops. He had personal conference on the field with most of his generals and led several brigades into battle."[13] There are numerous examples of the positive impact of Johnston's personal appearance on his subordinates.

As Johnston passed Colonel Gibson, he called out: "I hope you may get through safely today, but we must win a victory."[14] Gibson recounted that "he rode along the lines on his blood bay horse, accompanied by his staff and escort, before the battle… returning the frequent salutations with earnest dignity and gentleness, stopping for a moment here to greet some old comrade of other wars, or there to take the hand of some inexperienced young soldier in whom he felt a personal interest, animating all by his words of good cheer, and by a bearing free of excitement, yet inspiring the conviction everywhere of his purpose to conquer or die."[15]

Riding past Brigadier General Thomas C. Hindman, Johnston told him that he had "earned [his] spurs as a major-general. Let this day's work win them."[16] One Confederate officer noted "the majestic presence of General Johnston. He looked like a hero of the antique type, and his very appearance on the field was a tower of more than kingly strength. I saw him as our lines were forming and talked and shook hands with him for the last time."[17] Such gestures steeled Johnston's inexperienced officers to the task at hand. He appreciated that he was leading a volunteer army, composed largely of green troops, and wished to buoy their spirits for the terrible ordeal by fire. It cannot be denied that Johnston's decision to lead from the front was exceedingly effective in inspiring his troops forward. Beauregard recalled that "our commander-in-chief, General A.S.

Johnston [showed] the highest qualities of the commander, and a personal intrepidity that inspired all around him and gave resistless impulsion to his columns at critical moments."[18]

Similarly, Captain Joseph B. Allison of the 45th Tennessee declared that the "impulse given the Confederate line by General Johnston's presence was irresistible."[19] A sergeant in Bowen's brigade observed that "Johnston was a large heavy-set man, and I liked his appearance very much."[20] Based on these and other such accounts, Smith declared in his narrative on the battle of Shiloh that "amazingly, the attack worked on almost the entire front, mostly because of Johnston's personal leadership… [Johnston could achieve] almost superhuman things, much like he did at the Peach Orchard."[21] The general's personal presence on the battlefield was instrumental to the success of the Confederate army.

Fuller's assessment of Johnston as "brave and stupid" is simplistic and unreasonably harsh. In the mid-nineteenth century it was common practice for the commanding general to personally lead his troops into battle if required by circumstances. Johnston's son explained that "the criticism upon this conduct, that he exposed himself unnecessarily, is absurd to those who know how important rapid decision and instantaneous action are in the crisis of conflict."[22] Similarly, Zimmermann maintained that "to be successful, the commanding officer needed to be reasonably close to the critical areas of combat where he could intervene forcefully and direct or correct the course of the battle. In the West, however, with the largest armies seldom exceeding more than 40,000 men, a commander needed to be visible among his soldiers."[23]

Common practice at the time
There are innumerable examples of Civil War commanders behaving in a similar fashion to Johnston at Shiloh. During the battle of Wilson's Creek in August 1861, Brigadier General Ben McCulloch, "was literally everywhere; he trusted nothing to others; and exposed his person to the fire of the enemy with a reckless temerity which he would have rebuked in one of his men."[24] During the same battle, the Union commander, Brigadier General Nathaniel Lyon, was killed in action attempting to rally his disintegrating army. At the battle of Shiloh, Wiley Sword observed that "like Johnston, the other senior commanders, Grant, [Brigadier

General William T.] Sherman, and later Beauregard, personally exposed themselves along the front line to obtain information, rally troops, and direct the fighting. All had close calls and were occasionally fired at."[25] After arriving on the battlefield on the morning of the 6th of April, one of Grant's escorts reported that the general "continuously rode along the line of battle, through the hottest of their fire, for the whole distance of about five miles [8 km]."[26]

At one point, Grant was splashed in the blood and gore of his aide-de-camp, Captain Irving W. Carson, after his head was taken off by a cannon ball. A canister shot also hit Grant on his sword scabbard and bent it. An inch or two in either direction could have killed or mortally wounded him. On the second day of Shiloh, Beauregard wore a bright red shirt, grabbed a battle flag, and personally led the troops of Colonel Preston Pond's brigade into the fray. It was reported that: "Beauregard himself, on two occasions, seized the colors of slowly advancing regiments and led them forward. When an officer friend reproved him for rashness, he answered, 'The order must now be follow, not go!'"[27] Over the two-day conflict, Major General Braxton Bragg had two horses killed from under him. Polk subjected himself to risks that "might better have been left to subordinates," as he considered that the fate of the South "hung almost in the balance" during this crucial battle. Yet the bishop's "frequent exposure of himself to the hottest of the enemy's fire tended to greatly reassure" the soldiers around him.[28] Major General William J. Hardee was slightly wounded, had a horse shot out from under him, and his coat was penetrated by two bullets. Brigadier General John C. Breckinridge was struck by two spent balls.

Much later in the Civil War, the general officers from both sides were still taking significant personal risks. At the battle of Stones River, Tennessee, from the 31st of December 1862 to the 2nd of January 1863, the commander of the Union Army of the Cumberland, Major General William S. Rosecrans, "seemed to be everywhere, trying to see personally to all his dispositions." A Federal surgeon observed that "wherever the battle raged most fiercely, General Rosecrans bore his charmed life." As with Grant at Shiloh, one of Rosecrans's aides, Lieutenant Colonel Julius P. Garesché, was decapitated by a cannon ball during the battle when riding close to his commander, spattering the latter in blood. The unfortunate Garesché had previously warned Rosecrans to be more careful, but the general had responded "Never mind me. Make the sign of the cross and go in."[29]

In November 1864, Breckinridge was serving as commander of the Department of East Tennessee and West Virginia. At the battle of Bull's Gap in eastern Tennessee, one Confederate officer noted that "Breckinridge exposed himself in a manner that called forth the almost indignant remonstrance of the men, and it is a matter of wonder that he escaped unhurt."[30] During the battle of the Wilderness in 1864, the commander of the Army of Northern Virginia, General Robert E. Lee, felt that his personal intervention was necessary to close a breach in the Confederate line. One of his subordinates recalled, "calmly and grandly, [Lee] rode to a point near the center of my line and turned his horse's head to the front, evidently resolved to lead in person the desperate charge and drive [the Federals] back or perish in the effort."[31]

Any criticism of Johnston's decision to position himself on the front lines throughout the battle of Shiloh should equally be applied to Grant, Beauregard, Sherman, and other prominent commanders. Johnston suffers the obloquy of historians merely because the fickle finger of fate selected him for death that day. Sword asserted that "Johnston's limited exposure, and the random, chance nature of his fatal wound seems to have involved more ill-luck than a reckless abuse of command responsibility."[32] Indeed, Beauregard emphasized that "Johnston was not wounded while leading a charge, as has been so frequently asserted, but while several hundred yards in the rear of [Colonel Walter S.] Statham's brigade after it had made a successful advance."[33]

Smith contends that Johnston's involvement in the charge at the Peach Orchard was a gamble borne of desperation. However, the general had exhibited similar risky behavior throughout his military career. There was the infamous 1837 duel with Brigadier General Felix Huston, the participation in the battle of the Neches as Texan Secretary of War, and the rallying of the division of volunteers at the battle of Monterrey. This behaviour continued with the onset of the Civil War. At Columbus in October 1861, Johnston and Polk stood on the bluffs to observe Union gunboats in the Mississippi River. One witness observed that a "64-pounder landed near Johnston and Polk, but the departmental commander 'merely looked back over his shoulder at it and resumed his spy glass.' Such a noble gesture could not help but impress naïve country boys experiencing their first taste of enemy fire." When cautioned by a subordinate, Johnston casually responded: "We must all take our risks." Soon "the entire army... conceived the greatest admiration of and confidence in him."[34]

Johnston's actions at the Peach Orchard are unremarkable in the context of his entire career. Exposure to danger was the most effective method of commanding the respect and obedience of the unruly volunteer soldier. One commentator remarked that if Johnston "had kept the least aloof, or had exhibited the slightest trace of hesitancy or waver of purpose, his attack would have failed at the first firm resistance."[35] George St. Leger Grenfell, a visiting British observer, once noted that the Confederate soldiers "hold a man in great esteem who in action sets them as example of contempt of danger."[36] Historian Bruce Catton wrote that "above everything else, that in battle the officer had to be absolutely fearless... From army commander on down, he had to show physical courage rather ostentatiously. If he could not do this, he could not do anything."[37]

The tourniquet

A little over a decade after the Civil War, Grant speculated that Johnston "lost his life because he would not abandon his troops in order to have his wound properly dressed. If he had gone to the rear and had the wound attended to, he might have lived. If he had had no anxiety about his army, to see if it was victorious, there could be no reason why he should not go to the rear; but the battle was so pressing that he would not leave his command, and so he bled to death."[38] Some historians have followed this line of reasoning. Thomas K. Hall declared that "in a move that would later cost him his life, Johnston sent his surgeon, Dr. D[avid] W. Yandell to care for the wounds of the prisoners. Yandell protested, saying that his proper place was with Johnston. Johnston assured the doctor that he would tell him when he was ready to move. In his haste, Johnston left the doctor. In just a few more hours, Johnston's haste would be fatal... Johnston's actual cause of death was from a loss of blood. A minié ball struck him in the back of the right leg below the knee. Johnston may not have initially felt the wound because his right leg sometimes went numb from a previous wound. A tourniquet could have easily stopped the loss of blood."[39]

An irony many authors delight to attribute to Johnston's death is that he could have been saved if he, or someone else, had applied the tourniquet in his pocket to the wound. Johnston's son claimed his father's injury "was not necessarily fatal. General Johnston's own knowledge of military surgery was adequate for its control by an extemporized tourniquet had he been aware or regardful of its nature."[40] Stanley F. Horn asserted that "it was a wound which, given instant medical attention – even the first-aid treatment of an improvised tourniquet – need not have been fatal."[41] They contend that Johnston did not feel the bullet that hit his leg due to numbness caused by long term damage to the sciatic nerve from the 1837 duelling wound incurred in Texas. However, in a modern review of the general's injury, a team of neurosurgeons stated that "clinically severe injury to the sciatic nerve and posterior cutaneous nerve do not match the descriptions of Johnston after his return to the army."[42] They noted that the general rode a horse and walked without difficulty. There were no reports that he ever suffered from pressure sores on the back of his right thigh.

As a matter of fact, Johnston's son reported that various medical treatments "in time, almost entirely restored him. In later life he was troubled with a slight lameness after any severe fatigue and with numbness and occasional pain in one foot, with some shrinkage of the muscles."[43] If there was a lack of sensation in his right leg, it was not persistent nor complete. Thus, there is minimal evidence to support the idea that the medical sequelae of Johnston's 1837 duelling injury directly or indirectly contributed to his death. After Johnston's passing, Yandell inspected the body and observed that the popliteal artery in the right leg had been severed just above the point where it branched into the anterior and posterior tibial arteries. In their review of the case, the neurosurgeons pointed out that such an injury would have been intensely painful: "It should also be noted that after a bullet injury, deep nocioceptors and mechanoreceptors are usually activated, in addition to the more superficial cutaneous receptors. Because deep pain is usually one of the first sensations to return after a bullet wound, this would add further support to bleeding and not superficial nerve injury as the underlying problem leading to Johnston's death."[44]

Many authors contend that the bleeding could have been staunched by the tourniquet in Johnston's pocket. Yandell asserted that if he had been present at the time of the incident, he could have easily treated the wound and saved the general's life. However, the doctor's opinion was far too optimistic. Modern neurosurgeons attest that "based on the description of the completely severed popliteal artery... General Johnston, sitting in the saddle of his horse with his leg extended, would quickly lose consciousness and bleed to death within a few minutes of the injury described by his surgeon."[45] In addition, Yandell only assessed the impact of the severed popliteal artery. "He fails to mention the vein... it is likely that the vein was injured just by virtue of the proximity to the artery and size of the standard minié ball (0.577-caliber). This artery-vein combination, if true, would further hasten his death... In actual battlefield medical practice, by the time they navigated Johnston on his horse with his leg extended (and bleeding) to a safe place, the blood loss may have already led to his death, even if the wound was immediately identified."[46]

Finally, and most importantly, the people on the scene who were assisting Johnston would not have been able to apply the tourniquet. This is because the location of the fatal wound was not immediately identified. Governor Isham G. Harris "described his attempts to find a wound upon the general's torso, because he was confident that 'he had a more serious wound than the one which I knew was bleeding profusely in the right leg.'"[47] The neurosurgeons note that "this is the only mention by anyone at the scene, or at the battle, that a leg injury was even noticed."[48] Harris's account was written long after the tragic event of the 6th of April 1862 and it appears that he only mentioned the profuse bleeding from Johnston's right leg because of his later knowledge of Yandell's post-mortem examination. One of the general's closest associates and brother-in-law, Colonel William Preston, observed that Johnston "had neither escort nor surgeon with him. His horse was wounded and bleeding... I searched but found no wound upon his body."[49]

The failure to detect Johnston's leg wound by the people present and rapid blood loss sealed the general's fate. When Harris returned from his errand, Johnston was aware that he was severely wounded, responding to the Governor's inquiry with the words: "Yes, and I fear, seriously" but it is "unclear whether he was aware of the locations of his multiple wounds because of his rapid deterioration and likely shock from blood loss. The general quickly lost consciousness from blood loss and died within minutes of his injury."[50] Thus, despite the entertaining story, the tourniquet in Johnston's pocket could not have saved him from death on the battlefield at Shiloh.

Conclusion

The reproach from various historians regarding Johnston's decision to lead a crucial charge in the Peach Orchard has validity but seems unfair when viewed in the context of the situation and the time. The general lacked an adequate staff to undertake the actions necessary to the efficient operation of command headquarters and had to fulfil many of these functions by himself. A significant proportion of the soldiers and officers of the Army of the Mississippi were inexperienced and frightened, and Johnston needed to personally inspire and steel these men to endure the brutal fighting conditions ahead. The commanding general's behavior on the 6th of April was relatively commonplace during that period of the Civil War, and Grant, Beauregard, and Buell also recklessly exposed themselves to enemy fire during the battle of Shiloh. In addition, Johnston had previously exhibited such bravery at the battle of the Neches, the battle of Monterrey, and at Columbus, so the incident at Shiloh was unremarkable in the context of his entire military career. In the culture of the day, courage under fire was often the only way for an officer to win the respect and obedience of the volunteer soldier. Finally, the assertion that Johnston's life could have been saved by the tourniquet in his pocket is unrealistic considering the extent of the injury, the rapidity of blood loss, and the failure to identify the wound.

Epilogue

It is evident that the relentless criticism of General Albert Sidney Johnston's Civil War generalship, particularly those by authors Thomas L. Connelly, T. Harry Williams, Larry J. Daniel, and Timothy B. Smith is frequently misguided or overstated. Connelly was the worst offender. He omitted information that can easily be located in the *Official Records* to disparage Johnston, such as the movement of Brigadier General Felix K. Zollicoffer's forces into eastern Kentucky, the purpose of the Russellville detachment, Johnston's instructions to Zollicoffer regarding the crossing of the Cumberland River, the threat against Fort Donelson versus Columbus after the fall of Fort Henry, Johnston's awareness of the lack of fortifications at Nashville, and the true catalyst for the concentration of Confederate forces at Corinth – the fall of Fort Henry. Connelly was even guilty of distorting the actual chronology of events on occasion to denigrate Johnston's generalship, such as the sequence of telegrams relating to the concentration at Corinth.

Smith's theory of Johnston as a "chess player who preferred to methodically plot his every move" who was "essentially out of place in a fast-moving poker-style game of war" is an unusual metaphor that oversimplifies his thought processes and decision-making.[1] The theory does not align with Johnston's bold decisions to expand the invasion of Kentucky, threaten the Union high command with illusions of strength to buy time, divide his Central Kentucky Army between Bowling Green and Russellville in the face of Major General Don Carlos Buell's significantly larger Army of the Ohio, organize a counterstrike after the disasters of Fort Henry, Fort

Donelson, and the fall of Nashville, and launch an aggressive surprise attack at Shiloh. These are not the actions of a purely "chess-like" general. They suggest a commander willing to gamble and seize opportunities – more in line with the "poker-playing" style Smith says Johnston lacked. Historian Albert Castel declared that "Johnston possessed many of the same attributes that made [Robert E.] Lee a great commander: aggressiveness, willingness to take risks, resolution and persistence in overcoming obstacles, composure and decisiveness when faced with a crisis, and an intellect and personal character that inspired trust, even devotion, in others."[2]

Smith's criticism that Johnston was slow and vacillating is also unwarranted. At a command level, Johnston responded decisively and quickly to enemy movements. He was simply outnumbered, had a vast border to defend, and was hamstrung by the inability of Confederate infrastructure to rapidly move large bodies of troops in response to Union offensives. He lacked a navy to defend the Tennessee and Cumberland rivers, and his obstructions and mines were rendered harmless by the abnormally large increase in the water levels in January and February 1862. The accusation that Johnston was too lenient with his subordinates can be countered by the fact that he over-ruled the protests of both Leonidas Polk and Gideon J. Pillow regarding the transfer of troops from Columbus; ignored the doubts of William J. Hardee, Jeremy F. Gilmer, and William W. Mackall regarding the move to Corinth rather than Chattanooga; and most decisively, over-ruled the objections of both Pierre G.T. Beauregard and Braxton Bragg regarding the surprise attack at Shiloh Church.

All too frequently, post-war authors have been guilty of attributing the failure of the Confederate cause in the Western theatre to Johnston's generalship alone rather than to the multitude of geographic, meteorologic, military, political, logistic, and personnel factors beyond his control. Connelly, Williams, and other authors have not recognised the impossibility of Johnston's assignment and refused to acknowledge his successes. This makes for more simplistic and entertaining storytelling, but it is a false representation of history. In Jefferson Davis's own words, these authors "have no correct measure for military operations, and... are very reckless in their statements."[3]

Dr. David W. Yandell recalled that Johnston "had written at

Tuscumbia, Alabama, his report of the operations of the army from Bowling Green, [and] read it to [Colonel William] Preston and myself. I was struck with the expression, 'Success is the test of merit,' and objected to its use. He said, 'Well, critically perhaps it is not correct, but, as the world goes, it is true, and I am going to let it stand.'"[4] Connelly, Williams, and other critics have accepted Johnston's self-deprecating statement and denounced his generalship based on the lack of Confederate military success in the Western Department from September 1861 to April 1862. Yet, as Johnston noted, the statement is not critically correct. It is hoped that the evidence presented in each chapter of this book has demonstrated that Johnston was a competent, resourceful, and responsive commander, simply thwarted by the intractable complexities of the military environment he found himself in.

The objective of this book was to provide some of the missing context and analysis that is required to make a more accurate representation of Johnston's ability as a Civil War general. Success is most definitely not the test of merit, and its achievement is often due to many other factors, including plain dumb luck. World War II general, and later President of the United States, Dwight D. Eisenhower, perhaps echoing a statement anecdotally attributed to the French Emperor Napoleon I, remarked: "I'd rather have a lucky general than a smart general. They win battles."[5] Unfortunately for Johnston, he was not a lucky general and was plagued by miserable weather at the most critical of times. Flooded rivers facilitated the range of Union ironclads, submerged his forts, washed away his naval mines, destroyed bridges and roads, and delayed his army's marches.

It is apparent that no general could have succeeded in command of the Western Department. Each of Johnston's successors in command of the Army of the Mississippi, and later renamed Army of Tennessee, failed to defend the territorial integrity of the Western Department. Highly educated and experienced military veterans such as Braxton Bragg, Joseph E. Johnston, and John B. Hood all experienced failure when in command of the western army. Pierre G.T. Beauregard was removed a couple of months after Shiloh due to ongoing illness and a dysfunctional relationship with President Jefferson Davis. The Confederate generals responsible for the defense of the Mississippi Valley after Johnston's death, Earl Van Dorn, John C. Pemberton, and Joseph E. Johnston, all failed too. The complexities of the military environment were too difficult to overcome. Just over eighteen months after his death on the battlefield at Shiloh, Southern diarist, Mary Chesnut, lamented: "Oh, for a day of Albert Sidney Johnston out West!"[6]

Bibliography

Albert Sidney and William Preston Johnston Papers, Mason Barret Collection, Manuscripts Division, Howard-Tilton Memorial Library, Tulane University, New Orleans, Louisiana.

Allen, Stacy D. (2018). Shiloh. *Blue & Gray Magazine*. Blue & Gray Enterprises Incorporated: Columbus, Ohio.

Ambler, Charles H. (Editor) (1918). Correspondence of R.M.T. Hunter. *Annual Report of the American Historical Association for the Year 1916*. American Historical Association: Washington D.C., Volume II.

Anderson, Jonathan, Peace, David, and Okun, Michael S. (2008). Albert Sidney Johnston's Sciatic Dueling Injury Did Not Contribute to His Death at the Battle of Shiloh. *Neurosurgery*, Volume LXIII, Number 6.

Anderson, Robert (1888). Reminiscences of the Black Hawk War. Report and Collections of the State Historical Society of Wisconsin, Volume X.

Ash, Stephen V. (2010). *The Black Experience in the Civil War South*. Praeger: Santa Barbara, California.

Badeau, Adam (1881). *Military History of Ulysses S. Grant*. Applewood Books: Bedford, Massachusetts, Volume I.

Basler, Roy P. (Editor) (1953). *The Collected Works of Abraham Lincoln*. Rutgers University Press: Springfield, Illinois.

Bassham, Ben L. (Editor) (1999). *Conrad Wise Chapman's Civil War Memoir: Ten Months in the "Orphan Brigade."* Kent State University Press: Kent, Ohio.

Baxter, William (1957). *Pea Ridge and Prairie Grove*. The University of Wisconsin: Madison.

Baylor, George W. (1897). With Gen. A.S. Johnston at Shiloh. *Confederate Veteran*, Volume V.

Beauregard, Pierre G.T. (1872). Notes on E.A. Pollard's 'Lost Cause.' *The Southern Magazine*, Volume X.

Beauregard, Pierre G.T. (1876). *Remarks of General Beauregard relative to the criticism of the Count de Paris on the Battle of Shiloh*, discussed in Mr. W. [L.] Marnis's letters of 1896, Western Reserve Historical Society. Cleveland, Ohio.

Beauregard, Pierre G.T. (1886). The Shiloh Campaign. Part I. *The North American Review*, Volume 142, Number 350.

Beauregard, Pierre G.T. (1886). The Shiloh Campaign. Part II. *The North American Review*, Volume 142, Number 351.

Beauregard, Pierre G.T. (1887). The Campaign of Shiloh. In Johnson, Robert U. and Buel, Clarence C. (Editors). *Battles and Leaders of the Civil War*. Century Company: New York, Volume I.

Bedford, Hugh L. (1885). Fight between the Batteries and Gunboats at Fort Donelson. In United States War Department (1912). *Donelson Campaign Sources: Supplementing Volume VII of the Official Records of the Union and Confederate Armies in the War of the Rebellion*. Army Service Schools Press: Fort Leavenworth, Kansas.

Berlin, Ira, Fields, Barbara J., Glymph, Thavolia, Reidy, Joseph P., and Rowland, Leslie S. (Editors) (1967). The Destruction of Slavery. In *Freedom: A Documentary History of Emancipation, 1861-1867*. Series I, Volume I, Chapter IX.

Bierce, Ambrose (1909, 1994). What I Saw of Shiloh. In *Civil War Stories*. Dover: New York.

Blackburn, J.K.P. (1918). Reminiscences of the Terry Texas Rangers. *Southwestern Historical Quarterly*, Volume XXII.

Broome, John P. (1908). How Gen. A.S. Johnson Died. *Confederate Veteran*, Volume XVI, Number 12.

Brown, Campbell H. (1967). Book Reviews. *Tennessee Historical Quarterly*, Volume XXVI, Number 4.

Buell, Don Carlos (1887). Shiloh Reviewed. In Johnson, Robert U. and Buel, Clarence C. (Editors). *Battles and Leaders of the Civil War*. Century Company: New York, Volume I.

The Burlington Free Press, Burlington, Vermont.

Burress, L.R. (1913). Who Lost Shiloh to the Confederacy? *Confederate Veteran*, Volume XXI, Number 8.

The Camden Confederate, Camden, South Carolina.

Carter, Arthur B. (1999). *The Tarnished Cavalier: Major General Earl Van Dorn, C.S.A.* University of Tennessee Press: Knoxville.

Castel, Albert (1968). Book Reviews. *The Kent State University Press*. Volume XIV, Number 1.

Castel, Albert (1997). Dead on Arrival: The Life and Sudden Death of General Albert Sidney Johnston. *Civil War Times Illustrated*, Volume XXXVI, Number 1.

Castel, Albert (1997). Savior of the South? Was Albert Sidney Johnston the 'Robert E. Lee of the West' – The Missing Ingredient for Southern Victory? *Civil War Times Illustrated*, Volume XXXVI, Number 1.

Cathey M. Todd and Robnett, Ricky W. (2021). *The River Batteries at Fort Donelson: Construction, Armament, and Battles, 1861-1862*. McFarland and Company: Jefferson, North Carolina.

Catton, Bruce (1958, 2012). *America Goes to War: The Civil War and its Meaning in American Culture*. Wesleyan University Press: Middletown, Connecticut.

The Charleston Daily Courier, Charleston, South Carolina.

Chesnut, Mary B. (1905). *A Diary from Dixie*. D. Appleton and Company, New York.

Chick, Sean Michael (2022). *Dreams of Victory: General P.G.T. Beauregard in the Civil War*. Savas Beatie: El Dorado Hills, California.

Chumney, James R. (1964). *Don Carlos Buell: Gentleman General*. Dissertation, Rice University.

Chumney, James R. (1968). Book Reviews. *The Mississippi Quarterly*, Volume XXII, Number 1.

Cimprich, John (1985). *Slavery's End in Tennessee, 1861-1865*. University of Alabama Press: Tuscaloosa.

Cincinnati Commercial, Cincinnati, Ohio.

Clark, Victor (2012). *A.W. Bradley: A Confederate in Company E of the 30th Tennessee Infantry*. Retrieved from http://awbradley.com/.

Cochran, J.A. (1898). Vivid Story of A. S. Johnston. *Confederate Veteran*, Volume VI, Number 2.

Coffin, Charles C. (1866). *Four Years of Fighting: A Volume of Personal Observation with the Army and Navy, from the First Battle of Bull Run to the Fall of Richmond*. Tickner and Fields: Boston, Massachusetts.

Connelly, Thomas L. (1967). *The Army of the Heartland: 1861-1862*. Louisiana State University Press: Baton Rouge.

Connelly, Thomas L. and Jones, Archer (1973). *The Politics of Command: Factions and Ideas in Confederate Strategy*. Louisiana State University Press: Baton Rouge.

Cooling, Benjamin F. (1987). *Forts Henry and Donelson: The Key to the Confederate Heartland*. The University of Tennessee Press: Knoxville.

Cooling, Benjamin F. (1997). *Fort Donelson's Legacy: War and Society in Kentucky and Tennessee, 1862-1863*. The University of Tennessee Press, Knoxville.

Cooney, Charles F. (Editor) (1985). The Fall of a Confederate Commander. *Civil War Times Illustrated*, Volume XXIV, Number 1.

Cooper, William J., Jr. (2000). *Jefferson Davis, American*. Vintage Books: New York.

Cope, Alexis (1916). *The Fifteenth Ohio Volunteers and its Campaigns: War of 1861-5*. Miller Company: Columbus, Ohio.

The Courier-Journal, Louisville, Kentucky.

Crisp, John T. (1894). General John R. Baylor of Texas. *Confederate Veteran*, Volume II.

Crist, Lynda L. and Dix, Mary S. (Editors) (1971), *The Papers of Jefferson Davis*. Louisiana State University Press: Baton Rouge.

Cummings, Charles M. (1968). *Forgotten Man at Fort Donelson: Bushrod Rust Johnson*. Tennessee Historical Quarterly, Volume XXVII, Number 4.

Cunningham, O. Edward (1966; 2009). *Shiloh and the Western Campaign of 1862*. Savas Beatie: New York.

Cunningham, Sumner A. (1895). To whom honor is due. *Confederate Veteran*, Volume III.

Daniel, Larry J. (1997). *Shiloh: The Battle that Changed the Civil War*. Simon and Schuster: New York.

Daniel, Larry J. (2019). *Conquered: Why the Army of Tennessee Failed*. The University of North Carolina Press: Chapel Hill.

Davidson, Eddy W. and Foxx, Daniel (2007). *Nathan Bedford Forrest: In Search of the Enigma*. Pelican Publishing Company: Gretna, Mississippi.

Davis, Jefferson (1881). *Rise and Fall of the Confederate Government*. Appleton and Company: New York.

Davis, Reuben O. (1891). *Recollections of Mississippi and Mississippians*. Houghton, Mifflin, and Company: Boston and New York.

Davis, William C. (1974, 2010). *Breckinridge: Statesman, Soldier, Symbol*. University Press of Kentucky: Lexington.

Davis, William C. (Editor) (2005). *Secret History of Confederate Diplomacy Abroad* by Edwin De Leon. University Press of Kansas, Lawrence.

Dawes, E.C. (1896). My First Day Under Fire at Shiloh. In Chamberlin, W.H. (Editor), *Sketches of War History 1861-1865: Papers Prepared for the Ohio Commandery of the Military Order of the Loyal Legion of the United States*. The Robert Clarke Company: Cincinnati, Volume IV.

Deseret News, Salt Lake City, Utah Territory.

Dillard, H. M. (1897). Beauregard-Johnston-Shiloh. *Confederate Veteran*, Volume V, number 3.

Dillon, John F. (1973). The Role of Riverine Warfare in the Civil War. *Naval War College Review*, Volume XXV, Number 4.

Dixon, Thomas W. (1914). *The Victim: A Romance of the Real Jefferson Davis*. Copp Clark: Toronto.

Drake, E.L. (Editor), (1878). The Annuals of the Army of Tennessee and Early Western History: Including a Chronological Summary of Battles and Engagements in the Western Armies of the Confederacy. A.D. Haynes: Nashville, Vol. I.

Duke, Basil W. (1867). *History of Morgan's Cavalry*. Miami Printing and Publishing Company: Cincinnati, Ohio.

Duke, Basil W. (1883). The Battle of Shiloh. *The Southern Bivouac*, Volume II, Number 4.

Duke, Basil W. (1911). *The Civil War Reminiscences of General Basil W. Duke, C.S.A.* Doubleday: Garden City, New York.

Eggleston, George C. (1910). *The History of the Confederate War: Its Causes and its Conduct*. Sturgis & Walton Company: New York, Vol. I.

Eisterhold, John A. (1974). Fort Heiman: Forgotten Fortress. *The West Tennessee Historical Society Papers*, Volume 38.

Elliott, Sam D. (2010). *Isham G. Harris of Tennessee*. Louisiana State University Press: Baton Rouge.

Engle, Stephen D. (1999). *Don Carlos Buell: Most Promising of All*. The University of North Carolina Press: Chapel Hill.

Fayetteville Observer, Fayetteville, Tennessee.

Fitch, John (2003). *Annals of the Army of the Cumberland*. Stackpole Books: Mechanicsburg, Pennsylvania.

Fletcher, Henry C. (1865). *History of the American War*. Richard Bentley: London, United Kingdom.

Foote, Shelby (1958, 1994). *The Civil War, A Narrative: Fort Sumter to Perryville*. Pimlico: London, United Kingdom.

Force, Manning F. (1883). *Fort Henry to Corinth*. Charles Scribner's Sons: New York.

Friend, Llerena (1965). Book Reviews. *The Southwestern Historical Quarterly*, Volume 68, Number 4.

Freehling, William W. (2002). *The South vs. the South: How Anti-Confederate Southerners Shaped the Course of the Civil War*. Oxford University Press: New York.

Freehling, William W. (2002). Why Civil War Military History Must Be Less than 85 Percent Military. *North & South*, Curtis Circulation Company: New Milford, New Jersey, Vol. V, No. 2.

Fremantle, Arthur J.L. (1864). *Three Months in the Southern States: April-June 1863*.

University of Nebraska Press: Lincoln.

The Fremont Weekly Herald, Nebraska.

Fry, James B. (1884). *Operations of the Army under Buell*. D. Van Nostrand: New York.

Fuller, John F.C. (1929). *The Generalship of Ulysses S. Grant*. Dodd, Mead, and Company: New York.

Gabel, Christopher R. (2002). *Rails to Oblivion: The Decline of Confederate Railroads in the Civil War*. U.S. Army Command and General Staff College Press: Fort Leavenworth, Kansas.

Gallagher, Gary W. (Editor) (1989). *Fighting for the Confederacy: The Personal Recollections of General Edward Porter Alexander*. University of North Carolina Press: Chapel Hill.

The Galveston Daily News, 10th April 1887 edition, Galveston, Texas.

Gentsch, James (1994). *A Geographic Analysis of the Battle of Shiloh*. Master's thesis, Memphis State University.

Gibson, Randall L. (1887). *Shiloh. Equestrian Monument, erected by the Veterans of the Army of Tennessee: Unveiled 6th April 1887*. Metairie Cemetery, New Orleans. Picayune Job Print: New Orleans.

Girardi, Robert I. (2011). Leonidas Polk and the Fate of Kentucky in 1861. In Hewitt, Lawrence L. and Bergeron, Arthur W. Jnr. (Editors), *Confederate Generals in the Western Theater, Volume 3, Essays on America's Civil War*. The University of Tennessee Press: Knoxville.

Goggin, Leigh S. (2011). Morbidity and mortality of the Confederate generals during the American Civil War, Letter to the editor. *American Surgeon*, Vol. 77, Number 11.

Gordon, John B. (1903). *Reminiscences of the Civil War*. Scribner's Sons: New York.

Gott, Kendall D. (2003). *Where the South Lost the War: An Analysis of the Fort Henry-Fort Donelson Campaign, February 1862*. Stackpole: Mechanicsburg, Pennsylvania.

Gott, Kendall D. (2014). *Confederate Command During the Fort Henry-Fort Donelson Campaign, February 1862*. Golden Springs: Electronic publication.

Grant, Ulysses S. (1885). *Personal Memoirs of U.S. Grant*. Webster and Company: New York.

Griffling, William (Editor), (accessed 2024). *Billy Yank & Johnny Reb Letters*. https://billyyankjohnnyreb.wordpress.com

Grose, William (1891). *The Story of Marches, Battles and Incidents of the Thirty Sixth Regiment Indiana Infantry*. The Courier Company Press: New Castle, Indiana.

Gudmens, Jeffrey J. (2005). *Staff Ride Handbook for the Battle of Shiloh, 6-7 April 1862*. Combat Studies Institute Press: Fort Leavenworth, Kansas.

Hall, Thomas K. (1995). *The Confederate High Command at Shiloh*. U.S. Army Command and General Staff College: Fort Leavenworth, Kansas.

Hamilton, James (1968). *The Battle of Fort Donelson*. Modern Literary Editions Publishing Company: New York.

Hannaford, Ebenezer (1868). *The Story of a Regiment: A History of the Campaigns, and Associations in the Field, of the Sixth Regiment Ohio Volunteer Infantry*. Self-published: Cincinnati, Ohio.

Hardin, Bayless (1943). Book Reviews. *Register of Kentucky State Historical Society*, Volume XLI, Number 136.

Harrison, Lowell H. (1972). A Confederate View of Southern Kentucky 1861. *Register of Kentucky Historical Society*.

Hodge, George B. (1874). *Sketch of the First Kentucky Brigade*. Major & Johnston, Frankfort, Kentucky.

Horn, Huston (2019). *Leonidas Polk: Warrior Bishop of the Confederacy*. University Press of Kansas: Lawrence.

Horn, Stanley F. (1941). *The Army of Tennessee*. University of Oklahoma Press: Norman.

Horn, Stanley F. (1945). Nashville During the Civil War. *Tennessee Historical Quarterly*, Vol. IV, No. 1, p. 9.

Horsley, A.S. (1894). Reminiscences of Shiloh. *Confederate Veteran*, Volume II.

Hughes, Nathaniel C., Jr. (1985). *Liddell's Record, St. John Richardson Liddell, Brigadier General, CSA, Staff Officer and Brigade Commander, Army of Tennessee*. Louisiana State University Press: Baton Rouge and London.

Hughes, Nathaniel C., Jr. (1991). The Battle of Belmont: Grant Strikes South. The University of North Carolina Press: Chapel Hill.

Hughes, Nathaniel C., Jr. (1992). *General William J. Hardee: Old Reliable*. Louisiana State University Press: Baton Rouge.

Hughes, Nathaniel C., Jr. and Stonesifer, Roy P. Jr. (2011). *The Life and Wars of Gideon J. Pillow*. The University of Tennessee Press: Knoxville.

Hutchinson, R.R. (1898). Albert Sidney Johnston at Shiloh. *Confederate Veteran*, Volume VI, Number 7.

Hyde, Anne B. (1923). The Battle of Shiloh, Confederate Veteran, Vol. XXXI.

The Indianapolis Star, Indianapolis, Indiana.

Inge, F.A. (1909). Corinth, Miss., in Early War Days. *Confederate Veteran*, Volume XVII, Number 8.

Inge, F.A. (1909). Corinth, Miss., in War Times. *Confederate Veteran*, Volume XXIII, Number 9.

Jackson, Mary A. (1895). *Memoirs of Stonewall Jackson.* Prentice Press, Courier-Journal Job Printing Company: Lexington, Kentucky.

Johnson, Richard W. (1886). A Soldier's Reminiscences in Peace and War. Lippincott Company: Philadelphia.

Johnston, William P. (1878). *The Life of General Albert Sidney Johnston: Embracing his Services in the Armies of the United States, the Republic of Texas, and the Confederate States.* Appleton and Company: New York.

Johnston, William P. (1887). Albert Sidney Johnston at Shiloh. In Johnson, Robert U. and Buel, Clarence C. (Editors), *Battles and Leaders of the Civil War.* Century Company: New York, Volume I.

Johnston, William P. (1895). General Albert Sidney Johnston. *Confederate Veteran,* Volume III.

Jones, John B. (1866). *A Rebel War Clerk's Diary at the Confederate States Capital.* J.B. Lippincott & Company: Philadelphia, Vol. I.

Jones, Katherine M. (1995). *Heroines of Dixie.* Smithmark: New York.

Jordan, Thomas (1880). Recollections of General Beauregard's Service in West Tennessee in the Spring of 1862. *Southern Historical Society Papers,* Volume VIII.

Jordan, Thomas. (1888). The Battle of Shiloh. *Southern Historical Society Papers,* Volume XVI.

Jordan, Thomas (1904). The Campaign and Battle of Shiloh. *The United Service,* Volume VI, Numbers 4 and 5.

Kincaid, Gerald, A. (2014). *The Confederate Army, A Regiment: An Analysis of the Forty-Eighth Tennessee Volunteer Infantry Regiment, 1861-1865.* Golden Springs Publishing.

The Knoxville Whig, Knoxville, Tennessee.

The Lantern, New Orleans, Louisiana.

Le Monnier, Yves Reni (1913). *General Beauregard at Shiloh.* The Graham Press: New Orleans.

Le Monnier, Yves Reni (1913). Who Lost Shiloh to the Confederacy? *Confederate Veteran,* Volume XXI, Number 11.

Leon, T.C. De. (1892). *Four Years in Rebel Capitals.* The Gossip Printing Company, Mobile, Alabama.

Leonidas Polk Memorial Society (2014). *Introductory Hermeneutics of Sword Over the Gown.* Retrieved from http://www.leonidaspolk.org/sword_over_the_gown.html

Lexington Herald Leader, Lexington, Kentucky.

Liedtke, Gregory P. (2023). Operation Ziethen: The Evacuation of the Demyansk Salient, February 1943. In Heck, Timothy G. and Mills, Walker D. (Editors),

Armies in Retreat: Chaos, Cohesion, and Consequence. Army University Press: Fort Leavenworth, Kansas.

The Louisville Daily Courier, Louisville, Kentucky.

The Louisville Journal, Louisville, Kentucky.

Lockett, Samuel H. (1887). Surprise and Withdrawal at Shiloh. In Robert U. Johnson and Clarence C. Buel, (Editors), *Battles and Leaders of the Civil War,* Volume I, Century: New York.

Louisville Daily Courier, Louisville, Kentucky.

The Louisville Journal, Louisville, Kentucky.

Lundberg, John R. (2009). I must save this army: Albert Sidney Johnston and the Shiloh Campaign. In Woodworth, Steven E. (Editor). *The Shiloh Campaign.* Southern Illinois University Press: Carbondale.

The Macon Telegraph, Macon, Georgia.

Martin, Samuel J. (2011). *General Braxton Bragg, C.S.A.* McFarland and Company: Jefferson, North Carolina.

McClendon, Charles B. (2011). A Terrain and Meteorological Analysis of the Battlefield at Shiloh, Tennessee. *Theses and Dissertations*. Mississippi State University.

McCord, Franklyn (1964). J.E. Bailey: A Gentleman of Clarksville. *Tennessee Historical Quarterly*, Volume 23, Number 3.

McDonough, James L. (1977). *Shiloh: In Hell before Night.* University of Tennessee Press: Knoxville.

McDonough, James L. (1980). *Stones River: Bloody Winter in Tennessee.* University of Tennessee Press: Knoxville.

McDonough, James L. (1998). Tennessee in the Civil War. In Van West, Carroll (Editor), *Tennessee History: The Land, the People, and the Culture*, University of Tennessee Press: Knoxville.

McGavock, Randal W. (1959). *Pen and Sword: The Life and Journals of Randal W. McGavock.* Tennessee Historical Commission.

McMurry, Richard M. (2002). *The Fourth Battle of Winchester: Toward a New Civil War Paradigm.* The Kent State University Press: Kent, Ohio.

The Memphis Daily Appeal, Memphis, Tennessee.

Mendoza, Alexander (2009). A Terrible Baptism by Fire: David Stuart's Defense of the Union Left. In Woodworth, Steven E. (Editor). *The Shiloh Campaign.* Southern Illinois University Press: Carbondale.

Merrill, Catharine (1866). *The Soldier of Indiana in the War for the Union.* Merrill and Company: Indianapolis, Vol. I.

Moore, Avery C. and Segerstrom, Donald I. (1954). *Destiny's Soldier*. Fearon Publishers: San Francisco, California.

Moore, Frank (Editor) (1862). The Rebellion Record: A Diary of American Events, With Documents, Narratives, Illustrative Incidents, Poetry, etc. G.P. Putnam: New York, Vol. IV.

Morrison, James L. (Editor) (1974). *The Memoirs of Henry Heth*. Greenwood Press: Westport, Connecticut.

The Murfreesboro Post, Murfreesboro, Tennessee.

The National Tribune, Washington D.C.

The New Orleans Crescent, Louisiana.

The New York Times, New York.

Parks, Joseph H. (1992). *General Edmund Kirby Smith, C.S.A.* Louisiana State University Press: Baton Rouge.

Parks, Joseph H. (1962, 1990). *General Leonidas Polk, C.S.A.: The Fighting Bishop*. Louisiana State University Press: Baton Rouge.

Pickett, William D. (1910). *Sketch of the Military Career of William J. Hardee*. Hughes: Lexington, Kentucky.

Pinnegar, Charles (2002). *Brand of Infamy: A Biography of John Buchanan Floyd*. Greenwood Press: Westport, Connecticut.

Polk, William M. (1880). Facts Connected with the Concentration of Army of the Mississippi Before Shiloh, April 1862. *Southern Historical Society Papers*, Volume VIII.

Polk William M. (1881). The Concentration Before Shiloh–Reply to General Ruggles. *Southern Historical Society Papers*, Volume IX.

Polk, William M. (1893, 1915). *Leonidas Polk: Bishop and General*. Longmans, Green, and Company: New York.

Pollard, Edward A. (1866). *The Lost Cause: A New Southern History of the War of the Confederates*. E.B. Treat: New York.

The Port Allen Observer, Port Allen, Louisiana.

Porter, George C. (1910). Gen. Braxton Bragg at Shiloh. *Confederate Veteran*, Volume XVIII, Number 2.

Powell, David A. (2023). *Decisions at Shiloh: The Twenty-Two Critical Decisions that Defined the Battle*. The University of Tennessee Press, Knoxville.

Prokopowicz, Gerald J. (2001). *All for the Regiment: The Army of the Ohio, 1861-1862*. The University of North Carolina Press, Chapel Hill and London.

The Providence Journal, Providence, Rhode Island.

Raab, James W. (2006). *Confederate General Lloyd Tilghman: A Biography.* McFarland and Company: Jefferson, North Carolina.

Republican Banner, Nashville, Tennessee.

Rich, Joseph W. (Editor) (1918). Isham G. Harris: The Death of General Albert Sidney Johnston on the Battlefield of Shiloh. *Iowa Journal of History*, Volume XVI.

The Richmond Enquirer, Richmond, Virginia.

The Richmond Times-Dispatch, Richmond, Virginia.

Roland, Charles P. (1957). Albert Sidney Johnston and the Loss of Forts Henry and Donelson. *The Journal of Southern History*, Volume XXIII, Number 1.

Roland, Charles P. (1964, 2001). *Albert Sidney Johnston: Soldier of Three Republics.* The University Press of Kentucky: Lexington.

Roland, Charles P. (2000). *Jefferson Davis's Greatest General: Albert Sidney Johnston.* McWhiney Foundation Press: Abilene, Texas.

Roland, Charles P. (2000). The Confederate Defense of Kentucky. In Brown, Kent M. (Editor). *The Civil War in Kentucky: Battle for the Bluegrass State.* Savas Publishing Company: Mason City, Iowa.

Roland, Charles P. (2004). P.G.T. Beauregard. In Gallagher, Gary W. and Glatthaar, Joseph T. (Editors). *Leaders of the Lost Cause: New Perspectives on the Confederate High Command.* Stackpole Books: Mechanicsburg, Pennsylvania.

Roland, Charles P. (2010). *History Teaches Us to Hope: Reflections on the Civil War and Southern History.* The University Press of Kentucky: Lexington.

Roman, Alfred (1884). *Military Operations of General Beauregard.* Harper and Brothers: New York, Volume I.

Rose, Joseph A. (2015). *Grant Under Fire: An Exposé of Generalship and Character in the American Civil War.* Alderhanna: New York.

Rose, Victor M. (1888). *The Life and Services of Ben McCulloch.* Pictorial Bureau of the Press: Philadelphia.

Rowland, Dunbar (Editor) (1923). *Jefferson Davis, Constitutionalist: His Letters, Papers, and Speeches.* Mississippi Department of Archives and History: Jackson, Mississippi.

Ruggles, Daniel. (1881). The Concentration Before Shiloh–Reply to Captain Polk. *Southern Historical Society Papers*, Volume IX.

Savas, Theodore P. (2024). George Washington Rains, the Augusta Powder Works, and Forts Henry and Donelson: How Union Riverine Warfare Almost Ended the Civil War in 1862. In Mackowski, Chris and Bierle, Sarah K. (Editors), *The War in the Western Theater: Favorite Stories and Fresh Perspectives from the Historians at Emerging Civil War*, Savas Beatie: El Dorado Hills, California.

Scott, Winfield (1864). *Memoirs of Lieut.-General Scott*. Sheldon and Company: New York.

Selma Morning Times, Selma, Alabama.

Shaw, John T. (1924). The Fatal Half-Mile Gap at Shiloh. *The National Tribune*, September 4, 1924.

Shaw, Arthur M. (Editor) (1942). *Albert Sidney Johnston in Texas: Letters to Relatives in Kentucky, 1847-1860*. Register of Kentucky State Historical Society, Volume XL, Number 132.

Shea, William L. and Hess, Earl J. (1992). *Pea Ridge: Civil War Campaign in the West*. The University of North Carolina Press: Chapel Hill.

Sherman, William T. (1875). *Memoirs of General William T. Sherman*. Appleton and Company: New York.

Shoup, Francis A. (1884). The Art of War in '62 – Shiloh. *The United Service: A Monthly Review of Military and Naval Affairs*, Volume XI.

Shoup, Francis A. (1894). How We Went to Shiloh. *Confederate Veteran*, Volume II, Number 5.

Simpson, Brooks D. (Editor) (1999). *Sherman's Civil War: Selected Correspondence of William T. Sherman, 1860-1865*. University of North Carolina Press: Chapel Hill.

Smith, Timothy B. (2006). *The Untold Story of Shiloh: The Battle and the Battlefield*. University of Tennessee Press: Knoxville.

Smith, Timothy B. (2009). Anatomy of an Icon: Shiloh's Hornets' Nest in Civil War Memory. In Woodworth, Steven E. (Editor). *The Shiloh Campaign*. Southern Illinois University Press: Carbondale.

Smith, Timothy B. (2011). To Conquer or Perish: The Last Hours of Albert Sidney Johnston. In Hewitt, Lawrence L. and Bergeron, Arthur W. Jnr. (Editors), *Confederate Generals in the Western Theater, Volume 3, Essays on America's Civil War*. The University of Tennessee Press: Knoxville.

Smith, Timothy B. (2013). *Rethinking Shiloh: Myth and Memory*. University of Tennessee Press: Knoxville.

Smith, Timothy B. (2014). *Shiloh: Conquer or Perish*. University Press of Kansas: Lawrence.

Smith, Timothy B. (2016). *Grant Invades Tennessee: The 1862 Battles for Forts Henry and Donelson*. University Press of Kansas: Lawrence.

Smith, Timothy B. (2021). Lasting Void: The Western Confederate Army Never Recovered from Albert Sidney Johnston's April 1862 Death at Shiloh. *America's Civil War*, Volume XXXIV, Number 2.

Smith, Timothy B. (2022). "Persistently Misunderstood": The What Ifs of Shiloh. In Mackowski, C. and Jordan, B.M. (Editors). *The Great What Ifs of the American*

Civil War: Historians Tackle the Conflict's Most Intriguing Possibilities. Savas Beatie: El Dorado Hills, California.

Smith, Timothy B. (2023). *The Iron Dice of Battle: Albert Sidney Johnston and the Civil War in the West.* Louisiana State University Press: Baton Rouge.

Speed, Thomas (1907). *The Union Cause in Kentucky*, 1860–1865. New York.

The Spirit of the Age, Raleigh, North Carolina.

Steele, Matthew F. (1909). *American Campaigns.* Byron S. Adams, Washington, Vol. I.

Stevenson, William G. (1862). *Thirteen Months in the Rebel Army.* A.S. Barnes & Burr: New York.

Stickles, Arndt M. (1940). *Simon Bolivar Buckner: Borderland Knight.* The University of North Carolina Press: Chapel Hill.

The Sunday Delta, New Orleans, Louisiana.

Sword, Wiley (2001). *Shiloh: Bloody April.* Morrow and Company: New York.

Sword, Wiley (2011). General G.T. Beauregard's Role at the Battle of Shiloh: Hero or Villain? In Hewitt, Lawrence L. and Bergeron, Arthur W. Jnr. (Editors), *Confederate Generals in the Western Theater, Volume 3, Essays on America's Civil War.* The University of Tennessee Press: Knoxville.

Symonds, Craig L. (1992). *Joseph E. Johnston: A Civil War Biography.* Norton and Company: New York.

Tagg, Larry (2017). *The Generals of Shiloh: Character in Leadership, April 6-7, 1862.* Savas Beatie: El Dorado Hills, California.

Taylor, Richard (1879). *Destruction and Reconstruction: Personal Experiences of the Late War.* Appleton and Company: New York.

T.E.C. (1864). *Battlefields of the South: From Bull Run to Fredericksburg; With Sketches of Confederate Commanders, and Gossip of the Camps.* New York.

The Times-Democrat, New Orleans, Louisiana.

The Times-Picayune, New Orleans, Louisiana.

Thompson, Edwin P. (2011). *History of the First Kentucky Brigade.* Nabu Press: New York.

Thompson, Porter (Editor) (1942). Letters of George W. Johnson: Provisional Governor of Kentucky Under the Confederacy. *Register of Kentucky State Historical Society*, Volume XL, Number 133.

Throne, Mildred (Editor) (1953). *The Civil War Diary of Cyrus F. Boyd, Fifteenth Iowa Infantry.* State Historical Society of Iowa: Iowa City.

Tunnard, William H. (1866). *Southern Record: The History of the Third Regiment Louisiana Infantry.* Self-published: Baton Rouge, Louisiana.

Ulmer, J.B. (1907). A Glimpse of Albert Sidney Johnston through the Smoke of Shiloh. *The Quarterly of the Texas State Historical Association*, Volume X, Number 4.

United States War Department (1880-1901). *The War of the Rebellion: A Compilation of the Official Records of the Union and Confederate Armies*. Government Printing Office: Washington D.C.

The United States War Department (1921). *Official Records of the Union and Confederate Navies*. Government Printing Office: Washington D.C.

Vandiver, Frank E. (Editor) (1947). *The Civil War Diary of General Josiah Gorgas*. University of Alabama Press: Tuscaloosa.

Vermont Watchman and State Journal, 28th January 1885 edition, Montpelier, Vermont.

Von Clausewitz, Carl (1873). *On War*. Trübner: London, England.

Wagenhoffer, Andrew J. (2024). Civil War Books and Authors. Reviews. https://cwba.blogspot.com/2024/01/review-iron-dice-of-battle-albert.html

Walker, Peter F. (1957). Building a Tennessee Army: Autumn, 1861. *Tennessee Historical Quarterly*, Volume XVI, Number 2.

Walker, Peter F. (1957). Command Failure: The Fall of Forts Henry and Donelson. *Tennessee Historical Quarterly*, Volume XVI, Number 4.

Warren, Amanda L. (2024). *Southern Cross: A New View of Leonidas Polk and His Clashes with Braxton Bragg*. McFarland & Company: Jefferson, North Carolina.

Watkins, Samuel R. (1882, 2011). *Company Aytch or a Side Show of the Big Show*. Turner Publishing Company: New York.

The Weekly Mississippian, Jackson, Mississippi.

Weekly Pioneer, St. Paul, Minnesota.

Weekly Raleigh Register, Raleigh North Carolina.

Wiart, Peter and Oppenheimer, Clive (2000). *Largest known historical eruption in Africa: Dubbi volcano, Eritrea, 1861*. Geology, vol. 28, no. 4.

Williams, T. Harry (1954). *P.G.T. Beauregard: Napoleon in Gray*. Louisiana State University Press: Baton Rouge.

Winter, William C. (Editor) (2011). *Captain Joseph Boyce and the 1st Missouri Infantry, C.S.A*. Missouri Historical Society: St. Louis.

Woodworth, Steven E. (1990). *Jefferson Davis and his Generals: The Failure of Confederate Command in the West*. University Press of Kansas: Lawrence.

Woodworth, Steven E. (1999). *Civil War Generals in Defeat*. University Press of Kansas: Lawrence.

Woodworth, Steven E. (2013). *Shiloh: Confederate High Tide in the Heartland*. ABC-CLIO: Santa Barbara, California.

Wyllie, Arthur (2016). *The Battles and Men of the Republic of Texas*. Lulu Press: Morrisville, North Carolina.

Yandell, Maria (1926). Surgeons of the Confederacy: David W. Yandell M.D., L.L.D. *Confederate Veteran*, Volume **XXXIV**, Number 7.

Young, John R. (1879). *Around the World with General Grant: A Narrative of the Visit of General U.S. Grant, Ex-President of the United States, to Various Countries in Europe, Asia, and Africa, in 1877, 1878, 1879*. The American News Company, New York, Vol. II.

Zimmermann Richard J. (2023). *More Than Just Grit: Civil War Leadership, Logistics and Teamwork in the West, 1862*. McFarland and Company: Jefferson, North Carolina, p. 6.

Notes

Notes to Preface

[1] Rowland, Dunbar (Editor) (1923). *Jefferson Davis, Constitutionalist: His Letters, Papers, and Speeches*. Mississippi Department of Archives and History: Jackson, Mississippi, Vol. VIII, p. 232, hereafter referred to as *Jefferson Davis*.

[2] Crist, Lynda L. and Dix, Mary S. (Editors) (1971). *The Papers of Jefferson Davis*. Louisiana State University Press: Baton Rouge, Louisiana, Vol. I, p. 61, 67, 73, 75.

[3] Woodworth, Steven E. (1990). *Jefferson Davis and his Generals: The Failure of Confederate Command in the West*. University Press of Kansas: Lawrence, Kansas, p. 8, hereafter referred to as *Davis and his Generals*; Roland, Charles P. (1964, 2001). *Albert Sidney Johnston: Soldier of Three Republics*. The University Press of Kentucky: Lexington, Kentucky, p. 138, hereafter referred to as *Soldier of Three Republics*.

[4] Johnston, William P. (1878). *The Life of General Albert Sidney Johnston: Embracing his Services in the Armies of the United States, the Republic of Texas, and the Confederate States*. Appleton and Company: New York, p. 143-144, hereafter referred to as *Life of Johnston*; Roland, *Soldier of Three Republics*, p. 138.

[5] Johnston, *Life of Johnston*, p. 144.

[6] Rowland, *Jefferson Davis*, Vol. VIII, p. 232.

[7] Johnston, *Life of Johnston*, p. 291.

[8] Crisp, John T. (1894). General John R. Baylor of Texas. *The Confederate Veteran Magazine*. Nashville, Tennessee, Vol. II, p. 116, hereafter referred to as the *Confederate Veteran*.

[9] Pollard, Edward A. (1866). *The Lost Cause: A New Southern History of the War of the Confederates*. E.B. Treat: New York, p. 378.

[10] Grant, Ulysses S. (1885). *Personal Memoirs of U.S. Grant*. Webster & Company: New York, hereafter known as *Memoirs of U.S. Grant*, p. 213-214.

[11] United States War Department (1880-1901). *The War of the Rebellion: A Compilation of the Official Records of the Union and Confederate Armies*. Government Printing Office: Washington D.C., Series I, Volume X, Part II, Chapter XXII, p. 314, hereafter referred to as the O.R.

[12] Johnston, *Life of Johnston*, p. 733.

[13] O.R., Vol. VII, Ch. XVII, p. 257-258.

[14] Dixon, Thomas W. (1914). *The Victim: A Romance of the Real Jefferson Davis*. Copp Clark: Toronto, p. 313-314.

[15] Davis, Jefferson (1881). *Rise and Fall of the Confederate Government*. Appleton and Company: New York, Volume II, p. 67, hereafter referred to as *Rise and Fall*.

[16] Johnston, William P. (1887). Albert Sidney Johnston at Shiloh. In Johnson, Robert U. and Buel, Clarence C. (Editors). *Battles and Leaders of the Civil War*. Century Company: New York, Volume I, p. 568, hereafter referred to as *Johnston at Shiloh*.

[17] McMurry, Richard M. (2002). *The Fourth Battle of Winchester: Toward a New Civil War Paradigm*, Kent State University: Ohio, p. xvi.

[18] Johnston, *Life of Johnston*, p. v-viii.

[19] Hardin, Bayless (1943). Book Reviews. *Register of Kentucky State Historical Society*, Volume XLI, Number 136, p. 266.

[20] Williams, T. Harry (1954). *P.G.T. Beauregard: Napoleon in Gray*. Louisiana State University Press: Baton Rouge, p. 309, hereafter referred to as the *Napoleon in Gray*.

[21] Williams, *Napoleon in Gray*, p. 310.

[22] Horn, Stanley F. (1941). *The Army of Tennessee*. University of Oklahoma Press: Norman, p. ix.

[23] Horn, *The Army of Tennessee*, p. 52.

[24] Roland, *Soldier of Three Republics*, p. xiii.

[25] *Lexington Herald Leader*, 9th April 2018 edition, Lexington, Kentucky.

[26] Roland, *Soldier of Three Republics*, p. xiii.

[27] Friend, Llerena (1965). Book Reviews. *The Southwestern Historical Quarterly*, Volume 68, Number 4, p. 521

[28] Roland, Charles P. (2000). *Jefferson Davis's Greatest General: Albert Sidney Johnston*. McWhiney Foundation Press: Abilene, Texas.

[29] Connelly, Thomas L. (1967). *The Army of the Heartland: 1861-1862*. Louisiana State University Press: Baton Rouge, p. xiii, hereafter referred to as *Army of the Heartland*.

[30] Connelly, *Army of the Heartland*, p. xiv.

[31] Connelly, *Army of the Heartland*, cover page.

[32] Castel, Albert (1968). Book Reviews. *The Kent State University Press*, Volume XIV, Number 1, p. 80.

[33] Chumney, James R. (1968). Book Reviews. *The Mississippi Quarterly*, Volume XXII, Number 1, p. 88.

[34] Brown, Campbell H. (1967). Book Reviews. *Tennessee Historical Quarterly*, Volume XXVI, Number 4, p. 404.

[35] Castel, *Book Reviews*, p. 80.

[36] Daniel, Larry J. (1997). *Shiloh: The Battle that Changed the Civil War*. Simon and Schuster: New York, hereafter referred to as *Shiloh*; Daniel, Larry J. (2019). *Conquered: Why the Army of Tennessee Failed*. The University of North Carolina Press: Chapel Hill, hereafter referred to as *Conquered*.

[37] Wagenhoffer, Andrew J. (2024). Civil War Books and Authors. Reviews. https://cwba.blogspot.com/2024/01/review-iron-dice-of-battle-albert.html

[38] Smith, Timothy B. (2023). *The Iron Dice of Battle: Albert Sidney Johnston and the Civil War in the West*. Louisiana State University Press: Baton Rouge, loc. 780 of 977, hereafter referred to as *Iron Dice of Battle*.

[39] Woodworth, Steven E. (1999). *Civil War Generals in Defeat*. University Press of Kansas: Lawrence, p. 2, hereafter referred to as *Civil War Generals in Defeat*.

[40] Woodworth, *Civil War Generals in Defeat*, p. 2-3.

[41] Woodworth, *Civil War Generals in Defeat*, p. 3.

Notes to Chapter 1

[1] Johnston, *Life of Johnston*, p. 12.

[2] Johnston, *Life of Johnston*, p. 13.

[3] Parks, Joseph H. (1962, 1990). *General Leonidas Polk, C.S.A.: The Fighting Bishop*. Louisiana State University Press: Baton Rouge, p. 24, hereafter referred to as *The Fighting Bishop*.

[4] Johnston, *Life of Johnston*, p. 11.

[5] Johnston, *Life of Johnston*, p. 2.

[6] Roland, *Soldier of Three Republics*, p. 21.

[7] Johnston's Black Hawk War Diary, 29th May 1832. *Albert Sidney and William Preston Johnston Papers*, Mason Barret Collection, Manuscripts Division, Howard-Tilton Memorial Library, Tulane University, New Orleans, Louisiana, hereafter referred to as *Johnston papers*.

[8] Roland, *Soldier of Three Republics*, p. 46.

[9] Henry Atkinson to Mr. Carson, 25th June 1836. *Johnston Papers*.

[10] Anderson, Robert (1888). Reminiscences of the Black Hawk War. *Report and Collections of the State Historical Society of Wisconsin*, Volume X, p.170.

[11] Smith, *Iron Dice of Battle*, loc. 129, 135, 137-138 of 977.
[12] Roland, *Soldier of Three Republics*, p. 55.
[13] Johnston, *Life of Johnston*, p. 70.
[14] Johnston, *Life of Johnston*, p. 80.
[15] Johnston, *Life of Johnston*, p. 80.
[16] Roland, *Soldier of Three Republics*, p. 61.
[17] Johnston, *Life of Johnston*, p. 81.
[18] Johnston, *Life of Johnston*, p. 84.
[19] Thomas C. Reynolds to William P. Johnston, 13th November 1875, *Johnston Papers*.
[20] Roland, *Soldier of Three Republics*, p. 63, 69.
[21] Johnston, *Life of Johnston*, p. 113.
[22] Wyllie, Arthur (2016). *The Battles and Men of the Republic of Texas*. Lulu Press: Morrisville, North Carolina, p. 44.
[23] Roland, *Soldier of Three Republics*, p. 98.
[24] Johnston, *Life of Johnston*, p. 114.
[25] Smith, *Iron Dice of Battle*, loc. 162 of 977.
[26] Johnston, *Life of Johnston*, p. 120, 129.
[27] Smith, *Iron Dice of Battle*, loc. 169 of 977.
[28] Johnston to George Hancock, 10th July 1846, *Johnston Papers*.
[29] Johnston to George Hancock, 1st November 1847, *Johnston Papers*.
[30] Johnston, *Life of Johnston*, p. 9.
[31] Johnston, *Life of Johnston*, p. 135.
[32] Johnston, *Life of Johnston*, p. 217.
[33] Joseph Hooker to William P. Johnston, 3rd June 1875, *Johnston Papers*.
[34] Johnston, *Life of Johnston*, p. 139-140.
[35] Taylor, Richard (1879). *Destruction and Reconstruction: Personal Experiences of the Late War*. Appleton and Company: New York, hereafter referred to as *Destruction and Reconstruction*, p. 232.
[36] Johnston, *Life of Johnston*, p. 154.
[37] Johnston, *Life of Johnston*, p. 153.
[38] Shaw, Arthur M. (Editor) (1942). *Albert Sidney Johnston in Texas: Letters to Relatives in Kentucky, 1847-1860*. Register of Kentucky State Historical Society, Vol. XL, No. 132, p. 314, hereafter referred to as *Letters to Relatives*, p. 302.
[40] Shaw, *Letters to Relatives*, p. 314.
[41] Johnston to Henrietta Johnston, 27th February 1856, *Johnston Papers*.

⁴² Johnston to William P. Johnston, 21ˢᵗ August 1856, *Johnston Papers*.

⁴³ Johnston, *Life of Johnston*, p. 191-192.

⁴⁴ Johnston, *Life of Johnston*, p. 215.

⁴⁵ *Deseret News*, 13ᵗʰ of October 1858 edition, Salt Lake City, Utah Territory.

⁴⁵ Roland, Charles P. (2010). *History Teaches Us to Hope: Reflections on the Civil War and Southern History*. The University Press of Kentucky: Lexington, p. 164, hereafter referred to as *History Teaches Us to Hope*.

⁴⁶ Moore, Avery C. and Segerstrom, Donald I. (1954). *Destiny's Soldier*. Fearon Publishers: San Francisco, California, p. 176, hereafter referred to as *Destiny's Soldier*.

⁴⁷ Johnston, *Life of Johnston*, p. 271-272.

⁴⁸ Johnston, *Life of Johnston*, p. 289.

⁴⁹ *Selma Morning Times*, 22ⁿᵈ November 1871, Selma, Alabama.

⁵⁰ Johnston, William P. (1895). General Albert Sidney Johnston. *Confederate Veteran*, Vol. III, p. 83.

Notes to Chapter 2

¹ O.R., Vol. IV, Ch. XII, p. 405.

² Berlin, Ira, Fields, Barbara J., Glymph, Thavolia, Reidy, Joseph P., and Rowland, Leslie S. (Editors) (1985). The Destruction of Slavery. In *Freedom: A Documentary History of Emancipation, 1861-1867*. Series I, Vol. I, Ch. IX, p. 664; Ash, Stephen V. (2010). *The Black Experience in the Civil War South*. Praeger: Santa Barbara, California, p. 43-44.

³ Woodworth, *Davis and his Generals*, p. 18-19; Davis, William C. (Editor) (2005). *Secret History of Confederate Diplomacy Abroad* by Edwin De Leon. University Press of Kansas, Lawrence, Kansas, p. xi.

⁴ O.R., Vol. III, Ch. X, p. 717-718; Connelly, *Army of the Heartland*, p. 8-9.

⁵ Connelly, *Army of the Heartland*, p. 6.

⁶ Connelly, *Army of the Heartland*, p. 9-10; Woodworth, *Davis and his Generals*, p. 18-19.

⁷ Woodworth, *Davis and his Generals*, p. 21-22.

⁸ Gott, Kendall D. (2003). *Where the South Lost the War: An Analysis of the Fort Henry-Fort Donelson Campaign, February 1862*. Stackpole: Mechanicsburg, Pennsylvania, p. 21, hereafter referred to as *Where the South Lost*.

⁹ Dillon, John F. (1973). The Role of Riverine Warfare in the Civil War. *Naval War College Review*, Vol. XXV, No. 4, p. 60.

¹⁰ Connelly, Thomas L. and Jones, Archer (1973). *The Politics of Command: Factions*

and Ideas in Confederate Strategy. Louisiana State University Press: Baton Rouge, p. 88-92, hereafter referred to as *Politics of Command*; Woodworth, *Davis and his Generals*, p. 33, 123-124.

[11] Von Clausewitz, Carl (1873). *On War*. Trübner: London, England, Vol. VI, Ch. XXII, hereafter known as *On War*.

[12] Von Clausewitz, *On War*, Vol. VI, Ch. XXII.

[13] O.R., Vol., IV, Ch. XII, p. 562-563.

[14] Rowland, *Jefferson Davis*, Vol. V, p. 184.

[15] O.R., Vol. IV, Ch. XII, p. 423.

[16] O.R., Vol. III, Ch. X, p. 226.

[17] O.R., Vol. IV, Ch. XII, p. 499.

[18] *The Burlington Free Press*, 20th October 1862, Burlington, Vermont.

[19] O.R., Vol. LII, Pt. II, Ch. LXIV, p. 183.

[20] Connelly, *Army of the Heartland*, p. 70.

[21] Harrison, Lowell H. (1972). A Confederate View of Southern Kentucky 1861. *Register of Kentucky Historical Society*, p. 170.

[22] Daniel, *Conquered*, p. 2.

[23] O.R., Vol. IV, Ch. XII, p. 445.

[24] Klein, Lloyd W. (2022). The Critical Role of Railroads in Influencing Military Strategy in the Civil War. *Emerging Civil War*. Accessed from https://emergingcivilwar.com/2022/02/15/the-critical-role-of-railroads-in-influencing-military-strategy-in-the-civil-war/

[25] Connelly, *Army of the Heartland*, p. xi.

[26] Gabel, Christopher R. (2002). *Rails to Oblivion: The Decline of Confederate Railroads in the Civil War*. U.S. Army Command and General Staff College Press: Fort Leavenworth, Kansas, p. 2-16.

[27] Gott, *Where the South Lost*, p. 21.

[28] Johnston, *Life of Johnston*, p. 485.

[29] Johnston, *Life of Johnston*, p. 338.

[30] Munford, Edward W. (no date). Albert Sidney Johnston. *Johnston papers*.

[31] *The Knoxville Whig*, 26th January 1861, Knoxville, Tennessee.

[32] O.R., Vol. IV, Ch. XII, p. 509; Parks, Joseph H. (1992). *General Edmund Kirby Smith, C.S.A*. Louisiana State University Press: Baton Rouge, Louisiana, p. 158; McDonough, James L. (1998). Tennessee in the Civil War. In Van West, Carroll (Editor), *Tennessee History: The Land, the People, and the Culture*, University of Tennessee Press: Knoxville, p 155.

[33] Gibson, Randall L. (1887). *Shiloh. Equestrian Monument, erected by the Veterans of the Army of Tennessee: Unveiled 6th April 1887*. Metairie Cemetery, New Orleans.

Picayune Job Print: New Orleans, hereafter referred to as *Equestrian Monument*.

[34] Polk, William M. (1893, 1915). *Leonidas Polk: Bishop and General*. Longmans, Green, and Company: New York, Vol. II, p. 34, hereafter referred to as *Bishop and General*.

[35] Woodworth, *Civil War Generals in Defeat*, p. 4.

[36] Smith, Timothy B. (2016). *Grant Invades Tennessee: The 1862 Battles for Forts Henry and Donelson*. University Press of Kansas: Lawrence, Kansas, p. 16, hereafter referred to as *Grant Invades Tennessee*.

Notes to Chapter 3

[1] Speed, Thomas (1907). *The Union Cause in Kentucky, 1860–1865*. New York, p. 109.

[2] *The Louisville Journal*, 28th April 1861, Louisville, Kentucky.

[3] *The Louisville Journal*, 28th April 1861, Louisville, Kentucky.

[4] *The Louisville Journal*, 10th August 1861, Louisville, Kentucky.

[5] O.R., Vol. IV, Ch. XII, p. 252.

[6] Basler, Roy P. (Editor) (1953). *The Collected Works of Abraham Lincoln*. Rutgers University Press: Springfield, Illinois, Vol. IV, p. 497.

[7] *Louisville Daily Journal*, 6th September 1861, Louisville, Kentucky.

[8] *Louisville Daily Courier*, 26th August 1861, Louisville, Kentucky.

[9] O.R., Vol. III, Ch. X, p. 142.

[10] Robert H. Wood to his father-in-law, 16th September 1861, in Griffling, William (Editor), *Billy Yank & Johnny Reb Letters*. Accessed 28th September 2024 at https://billyyankjohnnyreb.wordpress.com, hereafter referred to as *Billy Yank & Johnny Reb Letters*.

[11] Girardi, Robert I. (2011). Leonidas Polk and the Fate of Kentucky in 1861. In Hewitt, Lawrence L. and Bergeron, Arthur W. Jnr. (Editors), *Confederate Generals in the Western Theater, Volume 3, Essays on America's Civil War*. The University of Tennessee Press: Knoxville, p. 13.

[12] Connelly, *Army of the Heartland*, p. 20.

[13] Hughes, Nathaniel C., Jr. and Stonesifer, Roy P., Jr. (2011). *The Life and Wars of Gideon J. Pillow*. The University of Tennessee Press: Knoxville, p. 172, hereafter referred to as *Pillow*.

[14] Cooling, Benjamin F. (1987). *Forts Henry and Donelson: The Key to the Confederate Heartland*. The University of Tennessee Press: Knoxville, p. 13-14, hereafter referred to as *Forts Henry and Donelson*.

[15] Hughes and Stonesifer, *Pillow*, p. 172.

[16] O.R., Vol. LII, Ch. LXIV, Pt. II, p. 116.

[17] Elliott, Sam D. (2010). *Isham G. Harris of Tennessee.* Louisiana State University Press: Baton Rouge, p. 85, hereafter referred to as *Harris*.

[18] O.R., Vol. IV, Ch. XII, p. 384.

[19] O.R., Vol. VI, Ch. XVI, p. 788.

[20] O.R., Vol. IV, Ch. XII, p. 189.

[21] O.R., Vol. IV, Ch. XII, p. 193-194.

[22] O.R., Vol. IV, Ch. XII, p. 420-21.

[23] Johnston to Samuel Cooper, 17th October 1861, *Johnston papers*.

[24] O.R., Vol. IV, Ch. XII, p. 469.

[25] O.R., Vol. IV, Ch. XII, p. 222-223.

[26] Johnston, *Life of Johnston*, p. 518.

[27] Freehling, William W. (2002). *The South vs. the South: How Anti-Confederate Southerners Shaped the Course of the Civil War.* Oxford University Press: New York, p. 68-69, 72-73; Daniel, *Conquered*, p. 14.

[28] Freehling, William W. (2002). Why Civil War Military History Must Be Less than 85 Percent Military. *North & South*, Curtis Circulation Company: New Milford, New Jersey, Vol. V, No. 2, p. 19.

[29] Connelly, *Army of the Heartland*, p. 62-63.

[30] Connelly, *Army of the Heartland*, p. 63.

[31] Roland, *Soldier of Three Republics*, p. 271.

[32] Johnston, *Life of Johnston*, p. 307-308.

[33] Johnston, *Life of Johnston*, p. 518.

[34] Johnston, *Life of Johnston*, p. 362.

[35] *The Times-Picayune*, 21st March 1862, New Orleans, Louisiana.

[36] O.R., Vol. IV, Ch. XII, p. 467.

[37] O.R., Vol. IV, Ch. XII, p. 531.

[38] Smith, *Iron Dice of Battle*, loc. 332-333 of 977.

[39] O.R., Vol. III, Ch. X, p. 226.

[40] Bassham, Ben L. (Editor) (1999). *Conrad Wise Chapman's Civil War Memoir: Ten Months in the "Orphan Brigade."* Kent State University Press: Kent, Ohio, p. 43, 52, 59.

[41] O.R., Vol. III, Ch. X, p. 515.

[42] O.R., Vol. III, Ch. X, p. 199.

[43] O.R., Vol. IV, Ch. XII, p. 339.

[44] Roland, *Soldier of Three Republics*, p. 271-272.
[45] Sherman, William T. (1875). *Memoirs of General William T. Sherman*. Appleton and Company: New York, Vol. I, p. 199, hereafter referred to as *Memoirs*.
[46] O.R., Vol. IV, Ch. XII, p. 297.
[47] Simpson, Brooks D. (Editor) (1999). *Sherman's Civil War: Selected Correspondence of William T. Sherman, 1860-1865*. University of North Carolina Press: Chapel Hill, p. 154-155.
[48] O.R., Vol. IV, Ch. XII, p. 353.
[49] *The Indianapolis Star*, 16th October 1911, Indianapolis, Indiana.
[50] Sherman, *Memoirs*, Vol. I, p. 200.
[51] Pollard, *Lost Cause*, p. 210.
[52] Roland, *Soldier of Three Republics*, p. 271, 272.
[53] Johnston, *Johnston at Shiloh*, p. 545.
[54] Woodworth, *Davis and his Generals*, p. 55.
[55] Cooling, *Forts Henry and Donelson*, p. 42.
[56] Roland, *History Teaches Us to Hope*, p. 165.
[57] O.R., Vol. IV, Ch. XII, p. 433.
[58] Johnston, *Life of Johnston*, p. 413.
[59] *The Times-Picayune*, 21st March 1862, New Orleans, Louisiana.
[60] O.R., Vol. IV, Ch. XII, p. 419-20.
[61] Connelly, *Army of the Heartland*, p. 62-63.
[62] O.R., Vol. IV, Ch. XII, p. 423.
[63] Gudmens, Jeffrey J. (2005). *Staff Ride Handbook for the Battle of Shiloh, 6-7 April 1862*. Combat Studies Institute Press: Fort Leavenworth, Kansas, p. 35-36, hereafter referred to as *Staff Ride Handbook*.
[64] O.R., Vol. IV, Ch. XII, p. 539.
[65] O.R., Vol. IV, Ch. XII, p. 527-528.
[66] O.R., Vol. VII, Ch. XVII, p. 928.
[67] O.R., Vol. IV, Ch. XII, p. 454.
[68] O.R., Vol. IV, Ch. XII, p. 454.
[69] Connelly, *Army of the Heartland*, p. 63.
[70] Johnston to John J. Pettus, 24th December 1861, *Johnston papers*.

Notes to Chapter 4

1. O.R., Vol. IV, Ch. XII, p. 418.
2. *The Port Allen Observer*, 19th October 1861, Port Allen, Louisiana.
3. Horn, Stanley F. (1941). *The Army of Tennessee*. University of Oklahoma Press: Norman, p. 56.
4. Walker, Peter F. (1957). Building a Tennessee Army: Autumn, 1861. *Tennessee Historical Quarterly*, Vol. XVI, No. 2, p. 111.
5. Connelly, *Army of the Heartland*, p. 93.
6. O.R., Vol. IV, Ch. XII, p. 194.
7. O.R., Vol. IV, Ch. XII, p. 436.
8. O.R., Vol. IV, Ch. XII, p. 452-453.
9. O.R., Vol. IV, Ch. XII, p. 452-453.
10. O.R., Vol. IV, Ch. XII, p. 474.
11. O.R., Vol. VII, Ch. XVII, p. 807.
12. O.R., Vol. VII, Ch. XVII, p. 827-828.
13. O.R., Vol. IV, Ch. XII, p. 412.
14. O.R., Vol. IV, Ch. XII, p. 454.
15. O.R., Vol. VII, Ch. XVII, p. 779.
16. O.R., Vol. VII, Ch. XVII, p. 779.
17. O.R., Vol. VII, Ch. XVII, p. 792-794.
18. O.R., Vol. VII, Ch. XVII, p. 820.
19. O.R., Vol. IV, Ch. XII, p. 194.
20. O.R., Vol. IV, Ch. XII, p. 412-413.
21. O.R., Vol. IV, Ch. XII, p. 416.
22. O.R., Vol. IV, Ch. XII, p. 417.
23. O.R., Vol. IV, Ch. XII, p. 510.
24. O.R., Vol. IV, Ch. XII, p. 436.
25. O.R., Vol. IV, Ch. XII, p. 436.
26. Hughes, Nathaniel C., Jr. (1985). *Liddell's Record, St. John Richardson Liddell, Brigadier General, CSA, Staff Officer and Brigade Commander, Army of Tennessee*. Louisiana State University Press: Baton Rouge and London, p. 39, 41, hereafter referred to as *Liddell's Record*.
27. Hughes, *Liddell's Record*, p. 42.
28. Hughes, *Liddell's Record*, p. 46.
29. O.R., Vol. IV, Ch. XII, p. 194.

30 O.R., Vol. IV, Ch. XII, p. 453.
31 O.R., Vol. IV, Ch. XII, p. 426.
32 O.R., Vol. IV, Ch. XII, p. 426.
33 O.R., Vol. IV, Ch. XII, p. 429.
34 O.R., Vol. IV, Ch. XII, p. 452.
35 O.R., Vol. IV, Ch. XII, p. 459.
36 O.R., Vol. IV, Ch. XII, p. 469-470.
37 Cooling, Benjamin F. (1997). *Fort Donelson's Legacy: War and Society in Kentucky and Tennessee, 1862-1863*. The University of Tennessee Press, Knoxville, p. 11, hereafter referred to as *Fort Donelson's Legacy*.
38 O.R., Vol. IV, Ch. XII, p. 478.
39 Hughes, *Liddell's Record*, p. 42-44.
40 Jones, John B. (1866). *A Rebel War Clerk's Diary at the Confederate States Capital*. J.B. Lippincott & Company: Philadelphia, Vol. I, p. 86, hereafter referred to as *Rebel War Clerk*.
41 Jones, *Rebel War Clerk*, p. 106.
42 Pollard, *Lost Cause*, Vol. I, p. 210, 239.
43 Davis, Reuben O. (1891). *Recollections of Mississippi and Mississippians*. Houghton, Mifflin, and Company: Boston and New York, p. 435.
44 Roland, *Soldier of Three Republics*, p. 272-273.
45 Smith, *Iron Dice of Battle*, loc. 335 of 977.
46 Roland, *Soldier of Three Republics*, p. 272-273.
47 *The Times-Picayune*, 21st March 1862 edition, Louisiana, New Orleans.
48 Roman, Alfred (1884). *Military Operations of General Beauregard*. Harper and Brothers: New York, Vol. I, p. 238, hereafter referred to as *Beauregard*.
49 Cunningham, Sumner A. (1895). To whom honor is due. *Confederate Veteran*, Vol. III, p. 208.
50 Davis, *Rise and Fall*, Vol. II, p. 69.
51 Johnston, *Life of Johnston*, p. 732.

Notes to Chapter 5

1 O.R., Vol. IV, Ch. XII, p. 436.
2 Johnston, *Life of Johnston*, p. 318.
3 Leonidas Polk Memorial Society (2014). *Introductory Hermeneutics of Sword Over the Gown*. Retrieved from http://www.leonidaspolk.org/sword_over_the_gown.html

on 16th September 2021.

4 Johnston, *Life of Johnston*, p. 321-322.

5 Parks, *The Fighting Bishop*, p. 113.

6 Fremantle, Arthur J.L. (1864). *Three Months in the Southern States: April-June 1863*. University of Nebraska Press: Lincoln, Nebraska, p. 139.

7 Polk, *Bishop and General*, Vol. II, p. 389.

8 Hughes, Nathaniel C., Jr. (1991). *The Battle of Belmont: Grant Strikes South*. The University of North Carolina Press: Chapel Hill, p. 36-37, hereafter referred to as Belmont.

9 Horn, Huston (2019). *Leonidas Polk: Warrior Bishop of the Confederacy*. University Press of Kansas: Lawrence, p. 171, 210, hereafter referred to as *Warrior Bishop*.

10 Parks, *The Fighting Bishop*, p. 199.

11 Johnston, *Life of Johnston*, p. 326.

12 Connelly, *Army of the Heartland*, p. 54-55.

13 Connelly, *Army of the Heartland*, p. 54-55.

14 O.R., Vol. IV, Ch. XII, p. 432.

15 O.R., Vol. IV, Ch. XII, p. 440.

16 Connelly, *Army of the Heartland*, p. 80.

17 O.R., Vol. IV, Ch. XII, p. 440.

18 O.R., Vol. VII, Ch. XVII, p. 710.

19 O.R., Vol. IV, Ch. XII, p. 513.

20 O.R., Vol. IV, Ch. XII, p. 513.

21 O.R., Vol. III, Ch. X, p. 149.

22 O.R., Vol. III, Ch. X, p. 169.

23 O.R., Vol. IV, Ch. XII, p. 517.

24 O.R., Vol. IV, Ch. XII, p. 517.

25 O.R., Vol III, Ch. X, p. 310.

26 Grant, *Memoirs*, p. 185.

27 O.R., Vol. IV, Ch. XII, p. 529.

28 O.R., Vol. IV, Ch. XII, p. 529.

29 O.R., Vol. IV, Ch. XII, p. 532.

30 Winfield Scott (1864). *Memoirs of Lieut.-General Scott*. Sheldon and Company: New York, Volume II, p. 583.

31 T.E.C. (1864). *Battlefields of the South: From Bull Run to Fredericksburg; With Sketches of Confederate Commanders, and Gossip of the Camps*. New York, p. 121.

32 O.R., Vol. IV, Ch. XII, p. 550.

33 O.R., Vol. IV, Ch. XII, p. 550.
34 O.R., Vol. IV, Ch. XII, p. 553.
35 O.R., Vol. IV, Ch. XII, p. 553.
36 Connelly, *Army of the Heartland*, p. 104-105.
37 Connelly, *Army of the Heartland*, p. 47-48.
38 Woodworth, *Jefferson Davis and his Generals*, p. 58-60.
39 O.R., Vol. III, Ch. X, p. 730.
40 Connelly, *Army of the Heartland*, p. 34-35.
41 Connelly, *Army of the Heartland*, p. 32-35.
42 Hughes, *Belmont*, p. 38.
43 O.R., Vol. IV, Ch. XII, p. 553.
44 O.R., Vol. IV, Ch. XII, p. 553-554.
45 O.R., Vol. IV, Ch. XII, p. 553-554.
46 O.R., Vol. IV, Ch. XII, p. 564.
47 O.R., Vol. LII, Pt. II, Ch. LXIV, p. 222.
48 O.R., Vol. LII, Ch. LXIV, Pt. II, p. 222.
49 O.R., Vol. VII, Ch. XVII, p. 692.
50 O.R., Vol. VII, Ch. XVII, p. 731.
51 Connelly, *Army of the Heartland*, p. 105.
52 O.R., Vol. IV, Ch. XII, p. 557.
53 O.R., Vol. LII, Ch. LXIV, p. 224.
54 *The New York Times*, 18th December 1861, New York.
55 O.R., Vol. VII, Ch. XVII, p. 773.
56 O.R., Vol. VII, Ch. XVII, p. 773-774.
57 O.R., Vol. VII, Ch. XVII, p. 774.
58 Connelly, *Army of the Heartland*, p. 47.
59 Woodworth, Steven E. (2013). *Shiloh: Confederate High Tide in the Heartland*. ABC-CLIO: Santa Barbara, California, p. 7, hereafter referred to as *High Tide*.
60 Connelly, *Army of the Heartland*, p. 47.
61 Smith, *Iron Dice of Battle*, loc. 386 of 977.
62 Smith, *Iron Dice of Battle*, loc. 373 of 977.
63 O.R., Vol. VII, Ch. XVII, p. 797.
64 O.R., Vol. VII, Ch. XVII, p. 790.
65 O.R., Vol. VII, Ch. XVII, p. 808.
66 O.R., Vol. VII, Ch. XVII, p. 808.

[67] Johnston, *Life of Johnston*, p. 318.
[68] Johnston, *Life of Johnston*, p. 323.

Notes to Chapter 6

[1] Roland, Charles P. (2000). The Confederate Defense of Kentucky. In Brown, Kent M. (Editor). *The Civil War in Kentucky: Battle for the Bluegrass State*. Savas Publishing Company: Mason City, Iowa, p. 27-28.

[2] Cunningham, O. Edward (1966; 2009). *Shiloh and the Western Campaign of 1862*. Savas Beatie: New York, p. 6, hereafter referred to as *Shiloh*.

[3] O.R., Vol. IV, Ch. XII, p. 527-528.

[4] *The Times-Picayune*, 21st March 1862, New Orleans, Louisiana.

[5] O.R., Vol. IV, Ch. XII, p. 444.

[6] O.R., Vol. IV, Ch. XII, p. 454.

[7] O.R., Vol. IV, Ch. XII, p. 484.

[8] Hughes, Nathaniel C., Jr. (1992). *General William J. Hardee: Old Reliable*. Louisiana State University Press: Baton Rouge, p. 56, hereafter referred to as *Hardee*.

[9] Fremantle, *Three Months in the Southern States*, p. 138.

[10] Johnston, *Life of Johnston*, p. 353-354.

[11] *Republican Banner*, 28th and 31st October 1857 and 23rd February 1858, Nashville Tennessee; Stickles, *Buckner*, p. 43; Hughes and Stonesifer, *Pillow*, p. 151.

[12] O.R., Vol. IV, Ch. XII, p. 194.

[13] Coffin, Charles C. (1866). *Four Years of Fighting: A Volume of Personal Observation with the Army and Navy, from the First Battle of Bull Run to the Fall of Richmond*. Tickner and Fields: Boston, Massachusetts, p. 83.

[14] Williams, *Napoleon in Gray*, p. 117.

[15] Cooling, *Forts Henry and Donelson*, p. 44.

[16] Smith, *Iron Dice of Battle*, loc. 387 of 977.

[17] O.R., Vol. VII, Ch. XVII, p. 734.

[18] *The Times-Picayune*, 11th December 1861, New Orleans, Louisiana.

[19] *The Charleston Daily Courier*, 18th December 1861, Charleston, South Carolina.

[20] Horn, *Warrior Bishop*, p. 168.

[21] Cooling, *Forts Henry and Donelson*, p. 42.

[22] Hughes, *Hardee*, p. 87.

[23] *The New York Times*, 18th December 1861, New York.

[24] O.R., Vol. LII, Ch. LXIV, Pt. II, p. 407.

25 Hughes, *Liddell's Record*, p. 170.
26 O.R., Vol. XXXI, Ch. XLIII, Pt. III, p. 764-765.
27 Hughes, *Hardee*, p. 185.
28 Chesnut, Mary B. (1905). *A Diary from Dixie*. D. Appleton and Company, New York, p. 320.
29 Smith, *Iron Dice of Battle*, loc. 208 of 977.
30 Hughes, *Hardee*, p. 184.
31 Hughes, *Hardee*, p. 88.
32 Polk, *Bishop and General*, Vol. II, p. 204.
33 Fremantle, *Three Months in the Southern States*, p. 137-138.
34 Jones, Katherine M. (1995). *Heroines of Dixie*. Smithmark: New York, p. 84, hereafter referred to as *Heroines*.
35 Jones, *Heroines*, p. 85-86.
36 Fitch, John (1864). *Annals of the Army of the Cumberland*. Lippincott and Company: New York, p. 544.
37 Hughes, *Liddell's Record*, p. 37.
38 Stickles, Arndt M. (1940). *Simon Bolivar Buckner: Borderland Knight*. The University of North Carolina Press: Chapel Hill, p. 122, hereafter referred to as *Buckner*.
39 Stickles, *Buckner*, p. 122-123; Gott, *Where the South Lost*, p. 131.
40 Stickles, *Buckner*, p. 121.
41 Stickles, Buckner, p. 121.
42 *The Courier-Journal*, 27th September 1861, Louisville, Kentucky.
43 Johnston, *Life of Johnston*, p. 365.
44 Jones, *Rebel War Clerk*, p. 197.
45 Bassham, *Chapman's Memoir*, p. 43, 52.
46 Connelly, *Army of the Heartland*, p. 62, 65.
47 O.R., Vol. VII, Ch. XVII, p. 773.

Notes to Chapter 7

1 Connelly, *Army of the Heartland*, p. 65.
2 Connelly, *Army of the Heartland*, p. 63.
3 Connelly, *Army of the Heartland*, p. 62-63, 65.
4 Cooling, *Forts Henry and Donelson*, p. 43-44.
5 Smith, *Iron Dice of Battle*, loc. 369 of 977.

⁶ Cooling, *Forts Henry and Donelson*, p. 33.

⁷ O.R., Vol. VII, Ch. XVII, p. 707.

⁸ O.R., Vol. IV, Ch. XII, p. 527-528.

⁹ O.R., Vol. VII, Ch. XVII, p. 746.

¹⁰ O.R., Vol. VII, Ch. XVII, p. 788.

¹¹ O.R. Vol. VII, Ch. XVII, p. 792-793.

¹² Johnston to Benjamin, 8th January 1862, *Johnston papers*.

¹³ Savas, Theodore P. (2024). George Washington Rains, the Augusta Powder Works, and Forts Henry and Donelson: How Union Riverine Warfare Almost Ended the Civil War in 1862. In Mackowski, Chris and Bierle, Sarah K. (Editors), *The War in the Western Theater: Favorite Stories and Fresh Perspectives from the Historians at Emerging Civil War*, Savas Beatie: El Dorado Hills, California, loc.185-186 of 1320.

¹⁴ O.R., Vol. IV, Ch. XII, p. 342.

¹⁵ Engle, Stephen D. (1999). *Don Carlos Buell: Most Promising of All*. The University of North Carolina Press: Chapel Hill, p. 102, 104, 107, hereafter referred to as Buell.

¹⁶ Engle, *Buell*, p. 104.

¹⁷ *The New York Times*, 15th November 1861, New York.

¹⁸ O.R., Vol. VII, Ch. XVII, p. 585.

¹⁹ O.R., Vol. IV, Ch. XII, p. 403.

²⁰ O.R., Vol. IV, Ch. XII, p. 192.

²¹ O.R., Vol. LII, Ch. LXIV, Pt. II, p. 237-238.

²² Thomas S. English to his brother, 1st December 1861, *Billy Yank & Johnny Reb Letters*.

²³ Dabney S. Wier to his mother, 3rd December 1861, *Billy Yank & Johnny Reb Letters*.

²⁴ *The Macon Telegraph*, 27th December 1861, Macon, Georgia.

²⁵ *The Memphis Daily Appeal*, 26th January 1862, Memphis, Tennessee.

²⁶ *The New Orleans Crescent*, 11th February 1862, New Orleans, Louisiana.

²⁷ *The New Orleans Crescent*, 11th February 1862, New Orleans, Louisiana.

²⁸ O.R., Vol. IV, Ch. XII, p. 470.

²⁹ Smith, *Iron Dice of Battle*, loc. 385 of 977.

³⁰ Smith, *Iron Dice of Battle*, loc. 300, 385 of 977.

Notes to Chapter 8

[1] Cooling, *Forts Henry and Donelson*, p. 46-48; Smith, *Grant Invades Tennessee*, p. 13-14.
[2] Cooling, *Forts Henry and Donelson*, p. 46-48; Gott, *Where the South Lost*, p. 16-18.
[3] O.R., Vol. VII, Ch. XVII, p. 390.
[4] Hughes and Stonesifer, Pillow, p. 172.
[5] Johnston, *Life of Johnston*, p. 419.
[6] O.R., Vol. IV, Ch. XII, p. 448.
[7] Gott, *Where the South Lost*, p. 48-49.
[8] Smith, *Grant Invades Tennessee*, p. 21.
[9] Connelly, *Army of the Heartland*, p. 62, 65.
[10] Daniel, *Conquered*, p. 15.
[11] Roland, *Soldier of Three Republics*, p. 284-285.
[12] O.R., Vol. IV, Ch. XII, p. 454.
[13] O.R., Vol. IV, Ch. XII, p. 456.
[14] O.R., Vol. IV, Ch. XII, p. 463.
[15] O.R., Vol. IV, Ch. XII, p. 459.
[16] O.R., Vol. IV, Ch. XII, p. 461-62.
[17] O.R., Vol. IV, Ch. XII, p. 461-62.
[18] O.R., Vol. IV, Ch. XII, p. 481.
[19] O.R., Vol. IV, Ch. XII, p. 491.
[20] O.R., Vol. IV, Ch. XII, p. 491-492.
[21] Polk, *Bishop and General*, Vol. II, p. 36.
[22] O.R., Vol. IV, Ch. XII, p. 496-497.
[23] O.R., Vol. IV, Ch. XII, p. 506.
[24] O.R., Vol. IV, Ch. XII, p. 501.
[25] O.R., Vol. IV, Ch. XII, p. 527-528.
[26] O.R., Vol. IV, Ch. XII, p. 526.
[27] O.R., Vol. IV, Ch. XII, p. 560.
[28] O.R., Vol. IV, Ch. XII, p. 560.
[29] O.R., Vol. III, Ch. X, p. 306.
[30] Eisterhold, John A. (1974). Fort Heiman: Forgotten Fortress. *The West Tennessee Historical Society Papers*, Vol. XXXVIII, p. 45.
[31] O.R., Vol. VII, Ch. XVII, p. 132.

32 Cathey M. Todd and Robnett, Ricky W. (2021). *The River Batteries at Fort Donelson: Construction, Armament, and Battles, 1861-1862*. McFarland and Company: Jefferson, North Carolina, hereafter referred to as *The River Batteries*, p. 46.

33 Bedford, Hugh L. (1885). Fight between the Batteries and Gunboats at Fort Donelson. In United States War Department (1912). *Donelson Campaign Sources: Supplementing Volume VII of the Official Records of the Union and Confederate Armies in the War of the Rebellion*. Army Service Schools Press: Fort Leavenworth, Kansas, p. 134, hereafter referred to as *Fight between the Batteries*.

34 O.R., Vol. VII, Ch. XVII, p. 719.

35 O.R., Vol. VII, Ch. XVII, p. 723.

36 Johnston, *Life of Johnston*, p. 416.

37 O.R., Vol. VII, Ch. XVII, p. 731-32.

38 Cathey and Robnett, *The River Batteries*, p. 49.

39 O.R., Vol. VII, Ch. XVII, p. 132.

40 Johnston, *Life of Johnston*, p. 424.

41 Johnston, *Life of Johnston*, p. 424.

42 Pickett, William D. (1910). *Sketch of the Military Career of William J. Hardee*. Hughes: Lexington, Kentucky, p. 6.

43 Johnston, *Life of Johnston*, p. 424.

44 O.R., Vol. VII, Ch. XVII, p. 132.

45 O.R., Vol. VII, Ch. XVII, p. 845.

46 O.R., Vol. VII, Ch. XVII, p. 845.

47 Hughes, *Hardee*, p. 89.

48 Johnston, *Life of Johnston*, p. 411-412, 423.

49 Horn, *Army of Tennessee*, p. 78.

50 Eggleston, George C. (1910). *The History of the Confederate War: Its Causes and its Conduct*. Sturgis & Walton Company: New York, Vol. I, p. 308, hereafter referred to as *The Confederate War*.

51 O.R., Vol. VII, Ch. XVII, p. 685.

52 O.R., Vol. VII, Ch. XVII, p. 693.

53 O.R., Vol. IV, Ch. XII, p. 485-486.

54 Johnston, *Life of Johnston*, p. 416.

55 Cimprich, John (1985). *Slavery's End in Tennessee, 1861-1865*. University of Alabama Press: Tuscaloosa, p. 14.

56 O.R., Vol. VII, Ch. XVII, p. 698.

57 Cooling, *Forts Henry and Donelson*, p. 60.

58 O.R., Vol. VII, Ch. XVII, p. 685.

[59] Johnston, *Life of Johnston*, p. 411-412, 423.

[60] Roman, *Beauregard*. p. 216.

[61] Daniel, *Conquered*, p. 12.

[62] Johnston, *Life of Johnston*, p. 411-412, 423.

[63] O.R., Vol. IV, Ch. XII, p. 452.

[64] O.R., Vol. VII, Ch. XVII, p. 711.

[65] O.R., Vol. VII, Ch. XVII, p. 923-924.

[66] McClendon, Charles B. (2011). A Terrain and Meteorological Analysis of the Battlefield at Shiloh, Tennessee. *Theses and Dissertations*. Mississippi State University.

[67] Wiart, Peter and Oppenheimer, Clive (2000). Largest known historical eruption in Africa: Dubbi volcano, Eritrea, 1861. *Geology*, vol. 28, no. 4, p. 291-294.

[68] Woodworth, *Davis and his Generals*, p. 57.

[69] O.R., Vol. VII, Ch. XVII, p. 144.

[70] Clark, Victor (2012). *A. W. Bradley: A Confederate in Company E of the 30th Tennessee Infantry*. Retrieved from http://awbradley.com/, hereafter referred to as *Bradley*.

[71] McCord, Franklyn (1964). J.E. Bailey: A Gentleman of Clarksville. *Tennessee Historical Quarterly*, Vol. XXIII, No. 3, p. 253.

[72] Clark, *Bradley*.

[73] Raab, James W. (2006). *Confederate General Lloyd Tilghman: A Biography*. McFarland and Company: Jefferson, North Carolina, p. 55, hereafter referred to as *Tilghman*.

[74] Roland, *Forts Henry and Donelson*, p. 59.

[75] Roland, *Soldier of Three Republics*, p. 285, 287-288.

[76] Polk, *Bishop and General*, Vol. II, p. 63.

[77] O.R., Vol. VII, Ch. XVII, p. 711.

[78] Daniel, *Shiloh*, p. 20.

Notes to Chapter 9

[1] Dabney S. Wier to his sister, 16th September 1861, *Billy Yank & Johnny Reb Letters*.

[2] Johnston, *Life of Johnston*, p. 394-395.

[3] Connelly, *Army of the Heartland*, p. 14.

[4] Connelly, *Army of the Heartland*, p. 15.

[5] Connelly, *Army of the Heartland*, p. 95.
[6] Connelly, *Army of the Heartland*, p. 95.
[7] Horn, *Army of Tennessee*, p. 67.
[8] Johnston, *Life of Johnston*, p. 395, 400, 406.
[9] O.R., Vol. XXXVII, Part II, Ch. XLIX, p. 433.
[10] O.R., Vol. IV, Ch. XII, p. 429.
[11] Johnston, *Life of Johnston*, p. 390.
[12] O.R., Vol. IV, Ch. XII, p. 495.
[13] O.R., Vol. IV, Ch. XII, p. 527.
[14] Fletcher, Henry C. (1865). *History of the American War*. Richard Bentley: London, United Kingdom, p. 200.
[15] *Cincinnati Commercial*, 18th November 1861, Cincinnati, Ohio.
[16] O.R., Vol. IV, Ch. XII, p. 515.
[17] O.R., Vol. IV, Ch. XII, p. 515.
[18] O.R., Vol. IV, Ch. XII, p. 509.
[19] O.R., Vol. IV, Ch. XII, p. 509.
[20] O.R., Vol. IV, Ch. XII, p. 231.
[21] Connelly, *Army of the Heartland*, p. 43.
[22] O.R., Vol. IV, Ch. XII, p. 554.
[23] O.R., Vol. IV, Ch. XII, p. 244.
[24] O.R., Vol. VII, Ch. XVII, p. 687.
[25] O.R., Vol. VII, Ch. XVII, p. 734.
[26] O.R., Vol. VII, Ch. XVII, p. 706.
[27] O.R., Vol. VII, Ch. XVII, p. 725.
[28] Connelly, *Army of the Heartland*, p. 96.
[29] Johnston, *Life of Johnston*, p. 396.
[30] Johnston, *Life of Johnston*, p. 395, 400, 406.
[31] Horn, *Army of Tennessee*, p. 67-68.
[32] O.R., Vol. VII, Ch. XVII, p. 753.
[33] O.R., Vol. VII, Ch. XVII, p 46.
[34] O.R., Vol. VII, Ch. XVII, p. 48-49.
[35] O.R., Vol. IV, Ch. XII, p. 554.
[36] O.R., Vol. VII, Ch. XVII, p. 754-755.
[37] O.R., Vol. LII, Ch. LXIV, Pt. II, p. 239.
[38] O.R., Vol. VII, Ch. XVII, p. 103.

39 O.R., Vol. VII, Ch. XVII, p. 106.
40 *Weekly Pioneer*, 31 January 1862 edition, St. Paul, Minnesota.
41 O.R., Vol. VII, Ch. XVII, p. 104.
42 O.R., Vol. VII, Ch. XVII, p. 109.
43 Johnston, *Life of Johnston*, p. 406.
44 Connelly, *Army of the Heartland*, p. 95-96.
45 O.R., Vol. VII, Ch. XVII, p. 844.
46 O.R., Vol. VII, Ch. XVII, p. 844.
47 O.R., Vol. VII, Ch. XVII, p. 849.
48 Smith, *Iron Dice of Battle*, loc. 416-417 of 977.

Notes to Chapter 10

1 Rose, Victor M. (1888). *The Life and Services of Ben McCulloch*. Pictorial Bureau of the Press: Philadelphia, p. 201.
2 Smith, *Iron Dice of Battle*, loc. 395-396 of 977.
3 O.R., Vol. VII, Ch. XVII, p. 758.
4 The United States War Department (1921). *Official Records of the Union and Confederate Navies*. Government Printing Office: Washington D.C., Series I, Vol. XXII, p. 814, hereafter referred to as O.R.N.
5 O.R., Vol. VII, Ch. XVII, p. 817.
6 O.R.N., Series I, Vol. XXII, p. 815.
7 O.R., Vol. VII, Ch. XVII, p. 561.
8 O.R., Vol. VII, Ch. XVII, p. 74-75.
9 O.R., Vol. VII, Ch. XVII, p. 840.
10 O.R., Vol. VII, Ch. XVII, p. 847.
11 O.R.N., Series I, Vol. XXII, p. 816.
12 O.R., Vol. VII, Ch. XVII, p. 841.
13 Connelly, *Army of the Heartland*, p. 109-110.
14 O.R., Vol. VII, Ch. XVII, p. 844.
15 Johnston, *Life of Johnston*, p. 379.
16 O.R., Vol. VII, Ch. XVII, p. 571.
17 O.R., Vol. VII, Ch. XVII, p. 572.
18 Johnston, *Life of Johnston*, p. 411-412, 423.
19 O.R., Vol. VII, Ch. XVII, p. 149.

20 O.R., Vol. VII, Ch. XVII, p. 858.
21 O.R., Vol. VII, Ch. XVII, p. 149.
22 Gott, *Where the South Lost*, p. 86; Smith, *Grant Invades Tennessee*, p. 87.
23 Kincaid, Gerald, A. (2014). *The Confederate Army, A Regiment: An Analysis of the Forty-Eighth Tennessee Volunteer Infantry Regiment, 1861-1865*. Golden Springs Publishing, p. 12.
24 Johnston, *Life of Johnston*, p. 428.
25 Johnston, *Life of Johnston*, p. 429.
26 Gott, *Where the South Lost*, p. 91.
27 Connelly, *Army of the Heartland*, p. 108.
28 Connelly, *Army of the Heartland*, p. 108.
29 Smith, *Iron Dice of Battle*, loc. 429 of 977.
30 Force, Manning F. (1883). *Fort Henry to Corinth*. Charles Scribner's Sons: New York, p. 19.
31 Johnston, *Life of Johnston*, p. 129-130.
32 Hughes, *Belmont*, p. 33.
33 Johnston, *Life of Johnston*, p. 424.
34 O.R., Vol. VII, Ch. XVII, p. 137.
35 O.R., Vol. VII, Ch. XVII, p. 138.
36 Johnston, *Life of Johnston*, p. 429.
37 O.R., Vol. VII, Ch. XVII, p. 858.
38 O.R., Vol. VII, Ch. XVII, p. 859.
39 Johnston, *Life of Johnston*, p. 429.
40 Smith, *Grant Invades Tennessee*, p. 82.
41 O.R., Vol. VII, Ch. XVII, p. 139.
42 O.R., Vol. VII, Ch. XVII, p. 134.
43 O.R., Vol. VII, Ch. XVII, p. 134.
44 O.R., Vol. VII, Ch. XVII, p. 134.
45 O.R., Vol. VII, Ch. XVII, p. 141.
46 O.R., Vol. VII, Ch. XVII, p. 139, 143.
47 O.R., Vol. VII, Ch. XVII, p. 145-147.
48 Hughes, *Liddell's Record*, p. 49.
49 Rowland, *Jefferson Davis*, Vol. V, p. 216.

Notes to Chapter 11

[1] Fremantle, *Three Months in the Southern States*, p. 193.
[2] Chick, Sean Michael (2022). *Dreams of Victory: General P.G.T. Beauregard in the Civil War*. Savas Beatie: El Dorado Hills, California, p. 54, hereafter referred to as *Dreams of Victory*.
[3] Williams, *Napoleon in Gray*, p. 97-98, 102-108, 113-115.
[4] Roman, *Beauregard*, Vol. I, p. 213.
[5] Roman, *Beauregard*, Vol. I, p. 214.
[6] Roman, *Beauregard*, Vol. I, p. 213-214.
[7] Chick, *Dreams of Victory*, p. 8.
[8] Roman, *Beauregard*, Vol. I, p. 215.
[9] O.R., Vol. VII, Ch. XVII, p. 861-862.
[10] O.R., Vol. VII, Ch. XVII, p. 130-131.
[11] O.R., Vol. VII, Ch. XVII, p. 130-131.
[12] O.R., Vol. VII, Ch. XVII, p. 130-131.
[13] O.R., Vol. VII, Ch. XVII, p. 861-862.
[14] O.R., Vol. VII, Ch. XVII, p. 861-862.
[15] O.R., Vol. VII, Ch. XVII, p. 861.
[16] Connelly, *Army of the Heartland*, p. 109.
[17] O.R., Vol. VII, Ch. XVII, p. 844.
[18] O.R., Vol. VII, Ch. XVII, p. 130.
[19] Hamilton, James (1968). *The Battle of Fort Donelson*. Modern Literary Editions Publishing Company: New York, p. 44, hereafter referred to as *Fort Donelson*.
[20] O.R., Vol. VII, Ch. XVII, p. 869.
[21] R.L. Brodie to Johnston, 8th of February 1862, *Johnston papers*.
[22] O.R., Vol. VII, Ch. XVII, p. 880.
[23] Roman, *Beauregard*, Vol. I, p. 217.
[24] Horn, *Army of Tennessee*, p. 85-86.
[25] Horn, *Army of Tennessee*, p. 85-86.
[26] Horn, *Army of Tennessee*, p. 86.
[27] Horn, *Army of Tennessee*, p. 86.
[28] Williams, *Napoleon in Gray*, p. 118-119.
[29] Parks, *The Fighting Bishop*, p. 209-210.
[30] Roman, *Beauregard*, Vol. I, p. 217-218.

[31] Roman, *Beauregard*, Vol. I, p. 217-218.

[32] Roman, *Beauregard*, Vol. I, p. 219-220.

[33] O.R., Vol. VII, Ch. XVII, p. 258-259.

[34] Smith, *Iron Dice of Battle*, loc. 501 of 977.

[35] Roland, Charles P. (1957). Albert Sidney Johnston and the Loss of Forts Henry and Donelson. *The Journal of Southern History*, Vol. XXIII, No. 1., p. 58, hereafter referred to as *Forts Henry and Donelson*.

[36] Johnston, *Johnston at Shiloh*, p. 548.

[37] O.R., Vol. VII, Ch. XVII, p. 259-260.

[38] Roland, *Forts Henry and Donelson*, p. 58, 60, 65-66, 68.

[39] *The Times-Picayune*, 21st March 1862 edition, New Orleans, Louisiana.

[40] Cooling, *Forts Henry and Donelson*, p. 35.

[41] Roland, *Forts Henry and Donelson*, p. 58, 60, 65-66, 68; Roland, *Soldier of Three Republics*, p. 289.

[42] Roland, *Forts Henry and Donelson*, p. 66-67.

[43] Roland, *Forts Henry and Donelson*, p. 66-67.

[44] Johnston, *Johnston at Shiloh*, p. 548.

[45] O.R., Vol. VII, Ch. XVII, p. 595.

[46] Walker, Peter F. (1957). Command Failure: The Fall of Forts Henry and Donelson. *Tennessee Historical Quarterly*, Vol. XVI, No. 4, p. 343.

Notes to Chapter 12

[1] Raab, *Tilghman*, p. 94.

[2] Ambler, Charles H. (Editor) (1918). Correspondence of R.M.T. Hunter. *Annual Report of the American Historical Association for the Year 1916*. American Historical Association: Washington D.C., Vol. II, p. 244.

[3] Grant, *Memoirs*, p. 114.

[4] Pinnegar, Charles (2002). *Brand of Infamy: A Biography of John Buchanan Floyd*. Greenwood Press: Westport, Connecticut, p. 124-125, hereafter referred to as *Brand of Infamy*.

[5] Morrison, James L. (Editor) (1974). *The Memoirs of Henry Heth*. Greenwood Press: Westport, Connecticut, p. 152.

[6] Daniel, *Shiloh*, p. 29-30.

[7] Symonds, Craig L. (1992). *Joseph E. Johnston: A Civil War Biography*. Norton and Company: New York, p. 91.

8 Connelly, *Army of the Heartland*, p. 113.
9 Gott, *Where the South Lost*, p. 249.
10 Bedford, *Fight between the Batteries*, p. 135.
11 *The Richmond Enquirer*, 6th September 1861, Richmond, Virginia.
12 *The Sunday Delta*, 15th September 1861, New Orleans, Louisiana.
13 *The Spirit of the Age*, 25th September 1861, Raleigh, North Carolina.
14 *Weekly Raleigh Register*, 25th September 1861, Raleigh, North Carolina.
15 O.R., Vol. V, Ch. XIV, p. 148.
16 Jones, *Rebel War* Clerk, p. 116.
17 O.R., Vol. VII, Ch. XVII, p. 259-260.
18 O.R., Vol. VII, Ch. XVII, p. 860.
19 Cooling, *Forts Henry and Donelson*, p. 128.
20 O.R., Vol. XXXI, Ch. LXIV, Pt. III, p. 268.
21 O.R., Vol. VII, Ch. XVII, p. 865.
22 Hamilton, James (1968). *The Battle of Fort Donelson*. Modern Literary Editions Publishing Company: New York, p. 44, hereafter referred to as *Fort Donelson*.
23 Connelly, *Army of the Heartland*, p. 112.
24 O.R., Vol. VII, Ch. XVII, p. 865.
25 O.R., Vol. VII, Ch. XVII, p. 865.
26 Johnston, *Life of Johnston*, p. 434-435, 439.
27 Roland, *Soldier of Three Republics*, p. 281.
28 Roman, *Beauregard*, Vol. I, p. 231.
29 Horn, *Army of Tennessee*, p. 87.
30 Horn, *Army of Tennessee*, p. 87.
31 Smith, *Iron Dice of Battle*, loc. 504 of 977.
32 O.R., Vol. VII, Ch. XVII, p. 864.
33 Liedtke, Gregory P. (2023). Operation Ziethen: The Evacuation of the Demyansk Salient, February 1943. In Heck, Timothy G. and Mills, Walker D. (Editors), *Armies in Retreat: Chaos, Cohesion, and Consequence*. Army University Press: Fort Leavenworth, Kansas, p. 177, hereafter referred to as *Operation Ziethen*.
34 Hughes, *Hardee*, p. 95.
35 Hughes, *Hardee*, p. 95.
36 Moore and Segerstrom, *Destiny's Soldier*, p. 67.
37 Merrill, Catharine (1866). *The Soldier of Indiana in the War for the Union*. Merrill and Company: Indianapolis, Vol. I, p. 355.
38 William W. Mackall to Captain Lindsay, 9th of February 1862, *Johnston papers*.

Notes to Chapter 13

[1] O.R., Vol. VII, Ch. XVII, p. 867-868.
[2] McGavock, Randal W. (1959). *Pen and Sword: The Life and Journals of Randal W. McGavock*. Tennessee Historical Commission, p. 589, hereafter referred to as *Pen and Sword*.
[3] O.R., Vol. VII, Ch. XVII, p. 869.
[4] O.R., Vol. VII, Ch. XVII, p. 870.
[5] O.R., Vol. LII, Ch. LXIV, Pt. II, p. 269.
[6] O.R., Vol. LII, Ch. LXIV, Pt. II, p. 269.
[7] O.R., Vol. VII, Ch. XVII, p. 272.
[8] McGavock, *Pen and Sword*, p. 589.
[9] O.R., Vol. VII, Ch. XVII, p. 328.
[10] Johnston, *Life of Johnston*, p. 438.
[11] Johnston, *Life of Johnston*, p. 438.
[12] O.R., Vol. LII, Ch. LXIV, Pt. II, p. 271.
[13] O.R., Vol. VII, Ch. XVII, p. 329.
[14] O.R., Vol. LII, Ch. LXIV, Pt. II, p. 271.
[15] O.R., Vol. LII, Ch. LXIV, Pt. II, p. 272.
[16] Steele, Matthew F. (1909). *American Campaigns*. Byron S. Adams, Washington, Vol. I, p. 165, hereafter referred to as *American Campaigns*.
[17] Connelly, *Army of the Heartland*, p. 111-112.
[18] Connelly, *Army of the Heartland*, p. 111-112.
[19] Woodworth, *Davis and his Generals*, p. 80.
[20] Smith, *Iron Dice of Battle*, loc. 469 of 977.
[21] Williams, *Napoleon in Gray*, p. 119.
[22] Williams, *Napoleon in Gray*, p. 119.
[23] Roland, *Soldier of Three Republics*, p. 290-291.
[24] Smith, *Iron Dice of Battle*, loc. 377, 502, 506 of 977.
[25] O.R., Vol. VII, Ch. XVII, p. 864.
[26] O.R., Vol. VII, Ch. XVII, p. 869.
[27] O.R., Vol. LII, Ch. LXIV, Pt. II, p. 269.
[28] O.R., Vol. LII, Ch. LXIV, Pt. II, p. 269.
[29] Smith, *Grant Invades Tennessee*, p. 156.
[30] O.R., Vol. VI, Ch. XVI, p. 825.
[31] O.R., Vol. VII, Ch. XVII, p. 259-260.

[32] O.R., Vol. VII, Ch. XVII, p. 880.
[33] O.R., Vol. VII, Ch. XVII, p. 267.
[34] Smith, *Iron Dice of Battle,* loc. 472 of 977.
[35] O.R., Vol. VII, Ch. XVII, p. 426.

Notes to Chapter 14

[1] O.R., Vol. VII, Ch. XVII, p. 267.
[2] Smith, *Grant Invades Tennessee*, p. 207.
[3] Roland, *Soldier of Three Republics*, p. 292, 296-297.
[4] Bedford, *Fight between the Batteries*, p. 134.
[5] Gott, *Where the South Lost*, p. 277.
[6] Smith, *Grant Invades Tennessee*, p. 123.
[7] O.R., Vol. VII, Ch. XVII, p. 162.
[8] Steele, *American Campaigns*, p. 164.
[9] Stickles, *Buckner*, p. 145.
[10] Cooling, *Forts Henry and Donelson*, p. xii.
[11] Smith, *Grant Invades Tennessee*, p. 173.
[12] Badeau, Adam (1881). *Military History of Ulysses S. Grant*. Applewood Books: Bedford, Massachusetts, Vol. I, p. 39.
[13] Steele, *American Campaigns*, p. 164.
[14] Gott, *Where the South Lost*, p. 127.
[15] Steele, *American Campaigns*, p. 165.
[16] O.R., Vol. VII, Ch. XVII, p. 690.
[17] O.R., Vol. LII, Ch. LXIV, Pt. II, p. 272-273.
[18] Cooling, *Forts Henry and Donelson*, p. 151.
[19] Gott, *Where the South Lost*, p. 171.
[20] Johnston, *Life of Johnston*, p. 453.
[21] Hamilton, *Fort Donelson*, p. 127.
[22] O.R., Vol. VII, Ch. XVII, p. 880.
[23] Steele, *American Campaigns*, p. 164.
[24] Stickles, *Buckner*, p. 145-146.
[25] O.R., Vol. VII, Ch. XVII, p. 861-862.
[26] O.R., Vol. VII, Ch. XVII, p. 260.

27 Pinnegar, Brand of Infamy, p. 124-125.
28 O.R., Vol. VII, Ch. XVII, p. 265-266.
29 O.R., Vol. VII, Ch. XVII, p. 282.
30 O.R., Vol. VII, Ch. XVII, p. 263, 266.
31 O.R., Vol. VII, Ch. XVII, p. 265-266.
32 Cummings, Charles M. (1968). Forgotten Man at Fort Donelson: Bushrod Rust Johnson. Tennessee Historical Quarterly, Vol. XXVII, No. 4, p. 388.
33 Gott, Kendall D. (2014). Confederate Command During the Fort Henry-Fort Donelson Campaign, February 1862. Golden Springs: Electronic publication, loc. 830 of 1333, hereafter referred to as Confederate Command.
34 Cummings, p. 388.
35 O.R., Vol. VII, Ch. XVII, p. 331.
36 Gott, Confederate Command, loc. 841 of 1333.
37 Gott, Confederate Command, loc. 988-998 of 1333.
38 Gott, Where the South Lost, p. 220.
39 O.R., Vol. VII, Ch. XVII, p. 267, 269.
40 Pinnegar, Brand of Infamy, p. 140, 143.
41 Hughes and Stonesifer, Pillow, p. 230.
42 O.R., Vol. VII, Ch. XVII, p. 269.
43 Smith, Iron Dice of Battle, loc. 502-503 of 977.
44 Roman, Beauregard, Vol. I, p. 231.
45 Roland, Soldier of Three Republics, p. 292, 296-297.
46 Young, John R. (1879). Around the World with General Grant: A Narrative of the Visit of General U.S. Grant, Ex-President of the United States, to Various Countries in Europe, Asia, and Africa, in 1877, 1878, 1879. The American News Company, New York, Vol. II, p. 471, hereafter referred to as Around the World.
47 O.R., Vol. VII, Ch. XVII, p. 386.
48 O.R., Vol. VII, Ch. XVII, p. 255.
49 Johnston, Life of Johnston, p. 495.
50 O.R., Vol. VII, Ch. XVII, p. 283.
51 O.R., Vol. VII, Ch. XVII, p. 386.
52 O.R., Vol. VII, Ch. XVII, p. 283.
53 O.R., Vol. VII, Ch. XVII, p. 302.
54 O.R., Vol. VII, Ch. XVII, p. 283.
55 O.R., Vol. VII, Ch. XVII, p. 334.
56 O.R., Vol. VII, Ch. XVII, p. 334.

57 O.R., Vol. VII, Ch. XVII, p. 409.
58 Roland, *Soldier of Three Republics*, p. 292, 296-297.
59 Smith, *Iron Dice of Battle*, loc. 502 of 977.
60 Steele, *American Campaigns*, p. 164.
61 O.R., Vol. VII, Ch. XVII, p. 260.
62 Johnston, *Johnston at Shiloh*, p. 548.
63 Johnston, *Life of Johnston*, p. 434-435, 439.
64 Johnston, *Life of Johnston*, p. 550.
65 Vandiver, Frank E. (Editor) (1947). *The Civil War Diary of General Josiah Gorgas*. University of Alabama Press: Tuscaloosa, p. 3.

Notes to Chapter 15

1 Roland, *Soldier of Three Republics*, p. 292, 296-297.
2 Gott, *Where the South Lost*, p. 155.
3 O.R., Vol. LII, Ch. LXIV, p. 265.
4 Bassham, *Chapman's Memoir*, p. 59-60.
5 *The Times-Picayune*, 21st March 1862 edition, New Orleans.
6 *The Times-Picayune*, 21st March 1862 edition, New Orleans.
7 O.R., Vol. VII, Ch. XVII, p. 610.
8 Moore, Frank (Editor) (1862). *The Rebellion Record: A Diary of American Events, With Documents, Narratives, Illustrative Incidents, Poetry, etc.* G.P. Putnam: New York, Vol. IV, p. 30, hereafter referred to as *The Rebellion Record*.
9 O.R., Vol. VII, Ch. XVII, p. 881.
10 O.R., Vol. VII, Ch. XVII, p. 881.
11 O.R., Vol. VII, Ch. XVII, p. 882.
12 Eggleston, *The Confederate War*, p. 308.
13 Roman, *Beauregard*, Vol I, p. 224.
14 O.R., Vol. VII, Ch. XVII, p. 597.
15 O.R., Vol. VII, Ch. XVII, p. 606.
16 Cope, Alexis (1916). *The Fifteenth Ohio Volunteers and its Campaigns: War of 1861-5*. Miller Company: Columbus, Ohio, p. 73.
17 O.R., Vol. VII, Ch. XVII, p. 607.
18 Stickles, *Buckner*, p. 132.
19 Prokopowicz, Gerald J. (2001). *All for the Regiment: The Army of the Ohio, 1861-*

1862. The University of North Carolina Press, Chapel Hill and London, p. 89.

[20] *The Providence Journal*, 16th February 1862 edition, Providence, Rhode Island.

[21] *New York Times*, 3rd March 1862 edition, New York.

[22] O.R., Vol. VII, Ch. XVII, p. 881.

[23] *The Times-Picayune*, 21st March 1862 edition, New Orleans.

[24] Hodge, George B. (1874). *Sketch of the First Kentucky Brigade*. Major & Johnston, Frankfort, Kentucky, p. 11, hereafter referred to as *First Kentucky*.

[25] Johnston, *Life of Johnston*, p. 495.

[26] Hodge, *First Kentucky*, p. 12.

27 *New York Times*, 3rd March 1862 edition, New York.

[28] *New York Times*, 3rd March 1862 edition, New York.

[29] Eggleston, *The Confederate War*, p. 309.

[30] Hodge, *First Kentucky*, p. 10.

[31] Johnston, *Life of Johnston*, p. 493.

[32] Moore, *The Rebellion Record*, p. 87.

[33] Hodge, *First Kentucky*, p. 13.

[34] Jones, *Rebel War Clerk*, p. 111.

[35] Hodge, *First Kentucky*, p. 12.

Notes to Chapter 16

[1] Johnston, *Life of Johnston*, p. 495.

[2] Johnston, *Life of Johnston*, p. 495.

[3] O.R., Vol. VII, Ch. XVII, p. 263.

[4] O.R., Vol. VII, Ch. XVII, p. 426.

[5] O.R., Vol. VII, Ch. XVII, p. 426.

[6] Connelly, *Army of the Heartland*, p. 74.

[7] Connelly, *Army of the Heartland*, p. 74.

[8] Tagg, Larry (2017). *The Generals of Shiloh: Character in Leadership, April 6-7, 1862*. Savas Beatie: El Dorado Hills, California, p. 133, hereafter referred to as *Generals of Shiloh*.

[9] O.R., Vol. VII, Ch. XVII, p. 792.

[10] O.R., Vol. IV, Ch. XII, p. 476.

[11] O.R., Vol. IV, Ch. XII, p. 479.

[12] O.R., Vol. VII, Ch. XVII, p. 757.

[13] O.R., Vol. LII, Ch. LXIV, Pt. II, p. 233.
[14] O.R., Vol. LII, Ch. LXIV, Pt. II, p. 233.
[15] O.R., Vol. VII, Ch. XVII, p. 811.
[16] Munford, Edward W. (no date). Albert Sidney Johnston. *Johnston papers*.
[17] Cooling, *Forts Henry and Donelson*, p. 33.
[18] Johnston, *Life of Johnston*, p. 491.
[19] Johnston, *Life of Johnston*, p. 417.
[20] Johnston, *Life of Johnston*, p. 496.

Notes to Chapter 17

[1] Johnston, *Life of Johnston*, p. 495.
[2] Johnston, *Life of Johnston*, p. 495.
[3] Duke, Basil W. (1867). *History of Morgan's Cavalry*. Miami Printing and Publishing Company: Cincinnati, Ohio, p. 114, hereafter referred to as *Morgan's Cavalry*.
[4] Johnston, *Life of Johnston*, p. 496.
[5] Horn, Stanley F. (1945). Nashville During the Civil War. *Tennessee Historical Quarterly*, Vol. IV, No. 1, p. 9.
[6] Connelly, *Army of the Heartland*, p. 136.
[7] Johnston, *Life of Johnston*, p. 518.
[8] Johnston, *Life of Johnston*, p. 520
[9] Johnston, *Life of Johnston*, p. 497.
[10] O.R., Vol. VII, Ch. XVII, p. 428.
[11] *The National Tribune*, 24th September 1903 edition, Washington D.C.
[12] Johnston, *Life of Johnston*, p. 498.
[13] Johnston, *Life of Johnston*, p. 498.
[14] O.R., Vol. VII, Ch. XVII, p. 431-432.
[15] Connelly, *Army of the Heartland*, p. 135.
[16] Roman, *Beauregard*, Vol. I, p. 218.
[17] Jones, *Rebel War Clerk*, p. 111.
[18] Daniel, *Shiloh*, p. 43.
[19] *The Richmond Times-Dispatch*, 5th March 1862, Richmond, Virginia.
[20] *The Weekly Mississippian*, 5th March 1862, Jackson, Mississippi.
[21] Davidson, Eddy W. and Foxx, Daniel (2007). *Nathan Bedford Forrest: In Search of*

the Enigma. Pelican Publishing Company: Gretna, Mississippi, p. 59-60.

22 *The Camden Confederate*, 7th March 1862, Camden, South Carolina; *Fayetteville Observer*, 13th March 1862, Fayetteville, Tennessee.

23 *The Camden Confederate*, 7th March 1862, Camden, South Carolina; *Fayetteville Observer*, 13th March 1862, Fayetteville, Tennessee.

24 O.R., Vol. VII, Ch. XVII, p. 430-431.

25 *The Murfreesboro Post*, 23rd February 2014, Murfreesboro, Tennessee.

26 *The Courier-Journal*, 3rd April 1862, Louisville, Kentucky.

27 O.R., Vol. VII, Ch. XVII, p. 428.

28 O.R., Vol. VII, Ch. XVII, p. 429.

29 O.R., Vol. VII, Ch. XVII, p. 428.

30 Connelly, *Army of the Heartland*, p. 136; Daniel, Shiloh, p. 42-43.

31 *The National Tribune*, 24th September 1903 edition, Washington D.C.

32 O.R., Vol. VII, Ch. XVII, p. 427.

33 O.R., Vol. VII, Ch. XVII, p. 427.

34 Cooling, *Fort Donelson's Legacy*, p. 14.

Notes to Chapter 18

1 O.R., Vol. VII, Ch. XVII, p. 257.

2 O.R., Vol. VII, Ch. XVII, p. 260-261.

3 Roman, *Beauregard*, Vol. I, p. 226.

4 Connelly, *Army of the Heartland*, p. 4.

5 Roman, *Beauregard*, Vol. I, p. 243.

6 Connelly, *Army of the Heartland*, p. 138.

7 Rowland, *Jefferson Davis*, Vol. IX, p. 570.

8 Hughes, *Liddell's Record*, p. 42.

9 Johnston to Lovell, 10th February 1862, *Johnston papers*.

10 O.R., Vol. X, Ch. XXII, Pt. I, p. 566.

11 Roman, *Beauregard*, Vol. I, p. 506.

12 Roman, *Beauregard*, Vol. I, p. 506.

13 Smith, *Iron Dice of Battle*, loc. 531 of 977.

14 O.R., Vol. VII, Ch. XVII, p. 905.

[15] Horn, *Army of Tennessee*, p. 107-108.
[16] Horn, *Army of Tennessee*, p. 107-108.
[17] O.R., Vol. VII, Ch. XVII, p. 427.
[18] O.R., Vol. VII, Ch. XVII, p. 427.
[19] O.R., Vol. VII, Ch. XVII, p. 259-261.
[20] Johnston, *Life of Johnston*, p. 548.
[21] O.R., Vol. VII, Ch. XVII, p. 427.
[22] O.R., Vol. VII, Ch. XVII, p. 427.
[23] Johnston, *Life of Johnston*, p. 507.
[24] O.R., Vol. VII, Ch. XVII, p. 666.
[25] Connelly, *Army of the Heartland*, p. 139.
[26] Connelly, *Army of the Heartland*, p. 126, 131.
[27] Roman, *Beauregard*, Vol. I, p. 215.
[28] O.R., Vol. VII, Ch. XVII, p. 880.
[29] Roman, *Beauregard*, Vol. I, p. 232.
[30] Roman, *Beauregard*, Vol. I, p. 233.
[31] Johnston, *Life of Johnston*, p. 541.
[32] Smith, *Iron Dice of Battle*, loc. 530 of 977.
[33] O.R., Vol. VII, Ch. XVII, p. 890.
[34] Johnston, *Life of Johnston*, p. 526.
[35] O.R., Vol. VII, Ch. XVII, p. 896.
[36] O.R., Vol. VII, Ch. XVII, p. 912.
[37] Parks, *The Fighting Bishop*, p. 214-215.
[38] Johnston, *Life of Johnston*, p. 542.
[39] Martin, Samuel J. (2011). *General Braxton Bragg, C.S.A.* McFarland and Company: Jefferson, North Carolina, p. 113, hereafter referred to as *Bragg*.
[40] Connelly, *Army of the Heartland*, p. 140.
[41] O.R., Vol. VI, Ch. XVI, p. 823, 828.
[42] O.R., Vol. VI, Ch. XVI, p. 823, 828.
[43] O.R., Vol. VII, Ch. XVII, p. 862-863.
[44] Williams, *Napoleon in Gray*, p. 123.
[45] Smith, *Iron Dice of Battle*, loc. 439-440 of 977.

Notes to Chapter 19

1. Roland, *Soldier of Three Republics*, p. 303.
2. Smith, *Iron Dice of Battle*, loc. 534 of 977.
3. Roman, *Beauregard*, Vol I, p. 262.
4. Steele, *American Campaigns*, p. 183.
5. Connelly, *Army of the Heartland*, p. 148.
6. Daniel, *Shiloh*, p. 90.
7. Steele, *American Campaigns*, p. 183.
8. Steele, *American Campaigns*, p. 183.
9. Johnston, *Life of Johnston*, p. 508.
10. Roland, *Davis's Greatest General*, p. 48.
11. Thompson, Edwin P. (2011). *History of the First Kentucky Brigade*. Nabu Press: New York, p. 79, hereafter referred to as *Kentucky Brigade*.
12. Hodge, *First Kentucky*, p.17.
13. Thompson, *Kentucky Brigade*, p. 83.
14. O.R., Vol. X, Ch. XXII, Pt. II, p. 326.
15. O.R., Vol. X, Ch. XXII, Pt. II, p. 327.
16. Roland, *Soldier of Three Republics*, p. 303.
17. Johnston, *Life of Johnston*, p. 516-517.
18. O.R., Vol. X, Pt. II, Ch. XXII, p. 310.
19. Hall, Thomas K. (1995). *The Confederate High Command at Shiloh*. U.S. Army Command and General Staff College: Fort Leavenworth, Kansas, p. 17, hereafter referred to as *Confederate High Command*.
20. Thompson, *Kentucky Brigade*, p. 83.
21. Johnston, *Life of Johnston*, p. 516-517.
22. Cunningham, *Shiloh*, p. 97.
23. Moore, *The Rebellion Record*, p. 55.
24. Johnston, *Life of Johnston*, p. 507.
25. O.R., Vol. X, Pt. II, Ch. XXII, p. 340.
26. Daniel, *Shiloh*, p. 89.
27. O.R., Vol. X, Pt. II, Ch. XXII, p. 310.
28. Smith, *Iron Dice of Battle*, loc. 537 of 977.
29. Johnston, *Life of Johnston*, p. 508.
30. O.R., Vol. X, Pt. I, Ch. XXII, p. 31-32.
31. O.R., Vol. VII, Ch. XVII, p. 666.

[32] O.R., Vol. VII, Ch. XVII, p. 671.

[33] O.R., Vol. X, Pt. II, Ch. XXII, p. 11.

[34] O.R., Vol. VII, Ch. XVII, p. 261.

[35] Moore and Segerstrom, *Destiny's Soldier*, p. 67.

[36] Johnston, *Life of Johnston*, p. 505.

[37] Hodge, *First Kentucky*, p. 13.

[38] Lundberg, John R. (2009). I must save this army: Albert Sidney Johnston and the Shiloh Campaign. In Woodworth, Steven E. (Editor). *The Shiloh Campaign*. Southern Illinois University Press: Carbondale, p. 9, hereafter referred to as *I Must Save this Army*.

Notes to Chapter 20

[1] O.R., Vol. VI, Ch. XVI, p. 797-798.

[2] Carter, Arthur B. (1999). *The Tarnished Cavalier: Major General Earl Van Dorn, C.S.A.* University of Tennessee Press: Knoxville, p. 4, hereafter referred to as *Tarnished Cavalier*.

[3] Carter, *Tarnished Cavalier*, p. 185.

[4] O.R., Vol. VII, Ch. XVII, p. 826.

[5] Carter, *Tarnished Cavalier*, p. 42.

[6] O.R., Vol. VIII, Ch. XVIII, p. 751.

[7] O.R.N., Series I, Vol. XXII, p. 828.

[8] O.R.N., Series I, Vol. XXII, p. 828.

[9] O.R., Vol. VIII, Chapter XVIII, p. 755.

[10] O.R., Vol. X, Pt. II, Ch. XXII, p. 27.

[11] O.R., Vol. VIII, Ch. XVIII, p. 789-90.

[12] O.R., Vol. VIII, Ch. XVIII, p. 791.

[13] O.R., Vol. X, Pt. II, Ch. XXII, p. 354.

[14] Roland, *Soldier of Three Republics*, p. 309.

[15] Roland, *Soldier of Three Republics*, p. 311.

[16] Baxter, *Pea Ridge*, p. 98-101.

[17] Shea, William L. and Hess, Earl J. (1992). *Pea Ridge: Civil War Campaign in the West*. The University of North Carolina Press: Chapel Hill, p. 267.

[18] Tunnard, William H. (1866). *Southern Record: The History of the Third Regiment Louisiana Infantry*. Self-published: Baton Rouge, Louisiana, p. 139, 146-147.

Notes to Chapter 21

[1] Johnston, *Life of Johnston*, p. 541.
[2] *The Fremont Weekly Herald*, 7th April 1887 edition, Nebraska.
[3] O.R., Vol. X, Ch. XXII, Pt. II, p. 310.
[4] Daniel, *Shiloh*, p. 72.
[5] Cunningham, *Shiloh*, p. 85.
[6] Engle, *Buell*, p. 212-214.
[7] Martin, *Bragg*, p. 116.
[8] Force, *Fort Henry to Corinth*, p. 110.
[9] Roland, *Soldier of Three Republics*, p. 309.
[10] Young, *Around the World*, p. 471.
[11] Hannaford, Ebenezer (1868). *The Story of a Regiment: A History of the Campaigns, and Associations in the Field, of the Sixth Regiment Ohio Volunteer Infantry*. Self-published: Cincinnati, Ohio, p. 231.
[12] Johnston, *Life of Johnston*, p. 549.
[13] Davis, William C. (1974, 2010). *Breckinridge: Statesman, Soldier, Symbol*. University Press of Kentucky: Lexington, p. 297, hereafter referred to as *Breckinridge*.
[14] Johnston, *Life of Johnston*, p. 549.
[15] Lundberg, *I Must Save this Army*, p. 16.
[16] O.R., Vol. X, Pt. II, Ch. XXII, p. 381.
[17] Beauregard, Pierre G.T. (1887). The Campaign of Shiloh. In Johnson, Robert U. and Buel, Clarence C. (Editors). *Battles and Leaders of the Civil War*. Century Company: New York, Volume I, p. 579, hereafter referred to as *Campaign of Shiloh*.
[18] O.R., Vol. X, Pt. II, Ch. XXII, p. 387.
[19] Sword, Wiley (2001). *Shiloh: Bloody April*. Morrow and Company: New York, p. 99, hereafter referred to as *Bloody April*; Daniel, *Shiloh*, p. 118-119; Smith, Timothy B. (2014). *Shiloh: Conquer or Perish*. University Press of Kansas: Lawrence, p. 60, hereafter referred to as *Conquer or Perish*.
[20] Horn, *Army of Tennessee*, p. 124; Allen, Stacy D. (2018). Shiloh. *Blue & Gray Magazine*. Blue and Gray Enterprises Incorporated: Columbus, Ohio, p. 11, 15, hereafter referred to as *Shiloh*.
[21] Bragg to William P. Johnston, 16th December 1874, *Johnston papers*.
[22] *The Lantern*, 30th April 1887 edition, New Orleans.
[23] Johnston, *Johnston at Shiloh*, p. 552.
[24] Roland, *Soldier of Three Republics*, p. 321.
[25] Parks, *The Fighting Bishop*, p. 231.

[26] Woodworth, *Davis and his Generals*, p. 98.

[27] Smith, *Iron Dice of Battle*, loc. 611-612 of 977.

[28] *The Times-Picayune*, 5th June 1887 edition, New Orleans.

[29] Beauregard, Pierre G.T. (1876). *Remarks of General Beauregard relative to the criticism of the Count de Paris on the Battle of Shiloh*, discussed in Mr. W. [L.] Marnis's letters of 1896, Western Reserve Historical Society. Cleveland, Ohio, p. 2-3.

[30] Roman, *Beauregard*, Vol. I, p. 269-270.

[31] Gallagher, Gary W. (Editor) (1989). *Fighting for the Confederacy: The Personal Recollections of General Edward Porter Alexander*. University of North Carolina Press: Chapel Hill, p. 307.

[32] Smith, Timothy B. (2006). *The Untold Story of Shiloh: The Battle and the Battlefield*. University of Tennessee Press: Knoxville, p. 17, hereafter referred to as *Untold Story*.

[33] Hughes, *Hardee*, p. 101.

[34] Roman, *Beauregard*, Vol. I, p. 328.

[35] Johnston, *Johnston at Shiloh*, p. 553.

[36] Johnston, *Life of Johnston*, p. 552.

[37] Roman, *Beauregard*, Vol. I, p. 271-272.

[38] Hughes, *Liddell's Record*, p. 59.

[39] Johnston, *Life of Johnston*, p. 553.

[40] Horn, *Army of Tennessee*, p. 124.

[41] Hall, *Confederate High Command*, p. 26.

[42] Johnston, *Life of Johnston*, p. 553.

[43] Hall, *Confederate High Command*, p. 2.

[44] Buell, Don Carlos (1887). Shiloh Reviewed. In Johnson, Robert U. and Buel, Clarence C. (Editors). *Battles and Leaders of the Civil War*. Century Company: New York, Vol. I, p. 505, hereafter referred to as *Shiloh Reviewed*.

[45] Roman, *Beauregard*, Vol. I, p. 329.

[46] Powell, David A. (2023). *Decisions at Shiloh: The Twenty-Two Critical Decisions that Defined the Battle*. The University of Tennessee Press, Knoxville, p. 46-47.

Notes to Chapter 22

[1] O.R., Vol. X, Ch. XXII, Pt. II, p. 297.

[2] Hall, *Confederate High Command*, p. 21-22.

[3] Roman, *Beauregard*, Vol. I, p. 233.

[4] Johnston, *Life of Johnston*, p. 549.

[5] Munford, Albert Sidney Johnston. *Johnston papers*.
[6] Johnston, *Life of Johnston*, p. 549.
[7] Roman, *Beauregard*, Vol. I, p. 266.
[8] Williams, *Beauregard*, p. 125.
[9] Cunningham, *Shiloh*, p. 98.
[10] Hall, *Confederate High Command*, p. 22-23.
[11] Hughes, *Liddell's Record*, p. 58.
[12] Drake, E.L. (Editor) (1878). *The Annals of the Army of Tennessee and Early Western History: Including a Chronological Summary of Battles and Engagements in the Western Armies of the Confederacy*. A.D. Haynes: Nashville, Vol. I, p. 239, hereafter referred to as *The Annals*.
[13] Hughes, *Liddell's Record*, p. 49.
[14] Johnston, *Life of Johnston*, p. 550.
[15] Johnston, *Life of Johnston*, p. 550.
[16] Hyde, Anne B. (1923). The Battle of Shiloh, *Confederate Veteran*, Vol. XXXI, p. 130.
[17] Roman, *Beauregard*, Vol. I, p. 266.
[18] Chick, *Dreams of Victory*, p. 57.
[19] Roman, *Beauregard*, Vol. I, p. 267.
[20] Johnston, *Life of Johnston*, p. 549.
[21] Roman, *Beauregard*, Vol. I, p. 276.
[22] Baylor, George W. (1897). With Gen. A.S. Johnston at Shiloh. *Confederate Veteran*, Vol. V, p. 609.
[23] Ulmer, J.B. (1907). A Glimpse of Albert Sidney Johnston through the Smoke of Shiloh. *The Quarterly of the Texas State Historical Association*, Volume X, Number 4, p. 288, hereafter referred to as Smoke of Shiloh.
[24] Munford, *Johnston papers*.
[25] Sword, *Bloody April*, p. 105; Lundberg, I Must Save this Army, p. 19.
[26] Roland, *Soldier of Three Republics*, p. 320.
[27] Roman, *Beauregard*, Vol. I, p. 276.
[28] Cunningham, *Shiloh*, p. 132.
[29] Johnston, *Life of Johnston*, p. 566.
[30] Beauregard, *Campaign of Shiloh*, p. 583.
[31] O.R., Vol. X, Ch. XXII, Pt. I, p. 407.
[32] O.R., Vol. X, Ch. XXII, Pt. I, p. 407.
[33] *The Times-Picayune*, 5th June 1887 edition, New Orleans.
[34] Davis, *Breckinridge*, p. 303.

35 Roman, *Beauregard*, Vol. I, p. 278.
36 Johnston, *Life of Johnston*, p. 568
37 Davis, *Breckinridge*, p. 303; Johnston, *Johnston at Shiloh*, p. 555.
38 Johnston, *Johnston at Shiloh*, p. 555.
38 Johnston, *Life of Johnston*, p. 571.
40 Yandell to William P. Johnston, 11th November 1877, *Johnston papers*.
41 Johnston, *Life of Johnston*, p. 570.
42 Yandell to William P. Johnston, 11th November 1877, *Johnston papers*.
43 Sword, Bloody *Shiloh*, p. 108.
44 O.R., Vol. X, Ch. XXII, Pt II, p. 93-94.
45 O.R., Vol. X, Ch. XXII, Pt I, p. 89.
46 O.R., Vol. X, Ch. XXII, Pt I, p. 330-331.
47 Grose, William (1891). *The Story of Marches, Battles and Incidents of the Thirty Sixth Regiment Indiana Infantry*. The Courier Company Press: New Castle, Indiana, p. 101.
48 Ulmer, *Smoke of Shiloh*, p. 289.
49 Smith, Timothy B. (2011). To Conquer or Perish: The Last Hours of Albert Sidney Johnston. In Hewitt, Lawrence L. and Bergeron, Arthur W. Jnr. (Editors), *Confederate Generals in the Western Theater, Volume 3, Essays on America's Civil War*. The University of Tennessee Press: Knoxville, p. 25, hereafter referred to as *Last Hours*.
50 Throne, Mildred (Editor) (1953). *The Civil War Diary of Cyrus F. Boyd, Fifteenth Iowa Infantry*. State Historical Society of Iowa: Iowa City, p. 33.
51 Daniel, *Shiloh*, p. 228.
52 Johnston, *Life of Johnston*, p. 562.
53 Johnston, *Johnston at Shiloh*, p. 558.

Notes to Chapter 23

1 Williams, *Napoleon in Gray*, p. 135.
2 Beauregard, *Campaign of Shiloh*, p. 586.
3 Williams, *Napoleon in Gray*, p. 139.
4 Connelly, *Army of the Heartland*, p. 158.
5 Daniel, *Shiloh*, p. 195.
6 Smith, *Iron Dice of Battle*, loc. 718 of 977.
7 Smith, *Untold Story*, p. 17.

8 Allen, *Shiloh*, p. 26.
9 O.R., Vol. X, Ch. XXII, Pt. I, p. 392.
10 Woodworth, *High Tide*, p. 55.
11 O.R., Vol. X, Ch. XXII, Pt. II, p. 50.
12 Roman, *Beauregard*, Vol. I, p. 270.
13 O.R., Vol. X, Ch. XXII, Pt. I, p. 392-393.
14 Cunningham, *Shiloh*, p. 140; Allen, *Shiloh*, p. 12-13.
15 Johnston, *Life of Johnston*, p. 560.
16 Sword, *Bloody April*, p. 92.
17 Roman, *Beauregard*, Vol. I, p. 330.
18 Cunningham, *Shiloh*, p. 155; Roland, *Soldier of Three Republics*, p. 329, 331; Daniel, *Shiloh*, p. 149.
19 Daniel, *Shiloh*, p. 149; Gudmens, *Staff Ride Handbook*, p. 61.
20 Smith, *Conquer or Perish*, p. 90.
21 Horsley, A.S. (1894). Reminiscences of Shiloh. *Confederate Veteran*, Vol. II, p. 234, hereafter referred to as *Reminiscences*.
22 O.R., Vol. X. Ch. XXII, Pt. I, p. 89.
23 O.R., Vol. X, Ch. XXII, Pt I, p. 454.
24 Johnston, *Life of Johnston*, p. 593.
25 Dawes, E.C. (1896). My First Day Under Fire at Shiloh. In Chamberlin, W.H. (Editor), *Sketches of War History 1861-1865: Papers Prepared for the Ohio Commandery of the Military Order of the Loyal Legion of the United States*. The Robert Clarke Company: Cincinnati, Vol. IV, p. 8.
26 Ulmer, *Smoke of Shiloh*, p. 290.
27 Johnston, *Life of Johnston*, p. 584.
28 Johnston, *Life of Johnston*, p. 589.
29 Johnston, *Life of Johnston*, p. 584; Smith, *Last Hours*, p. 25.
30 Horn, *Army of Tennessee*, p. 130.
31 Daniel, *Shiloh*, p. 153-154; Gudmens, *Staff Ride Handbook*, p. 87.
32 Roman, *Beauregard*, Vol. I, p. 285.
33 Smith, *Last Hours*, p. 26.
34 Daniel, *Shiloh*, p. 155-156; Gudmens, *Staff Ride Handbook*, p. 88.
35 Cunningham, *Shiloh*, p. 174-175.
36 Daniel, *Shiloh*, p. 196; Davis, *Breckinridge*, p. 304.
37 Johnston, *Life of Johnston*, p. 594.
38 Johnston, *Life of Johnston*, p. 598.

39 Johnston, *Life of Johnston*, p. 598.

40 Roman, *Beauregard*, Vol. I, p. 286; Davis, *Breckinridge*, p. 304.

41 Smith, *Last Hours*, p. 29.

42 Smith, *Conquer or Perish*, p. 123.

43 O.R., Vol. X, Pt. I, Ch. XXII, p. 427; Smith, *Last Hours*, p. 28.

44 Powell, *Decisions at Shiloh*, p. 64.

45 Roman, *Beauregard*, Vol. I, p. 286.

46 Roman, *Beauregard*, Vol. I, p. 286-287.

47 Allen, *Shiloh*, p. 17.

48 Johnston, *Life of Johnston*, p. 612.

49 Yandell to William P. Johnston, 11th November 1877, *Johnston papers*.

50 O.R., Vol. X, Pt. II, Ch. XXII, p. 95.

51 Allen, *Shiloh*, p. 26.

52 Allen, *Shiloh*, p. 26.

53 O.R., Vol. X, Pt. I, Ch. XXII, p. 574.

54 Allen, *Shiloh*, p. 26.

55 Johnston, *Life of Johnston*, p. 597.

56 Smith, *Conquer or Perish*, p. 130.

57 Daniel, *Shiloh*, p. 196.

58 Mendoza, Alexander (2009). A Terrible Baptism by Fire: David Stuart's Defense of the Union Left. In Woodworth, Steven E. (Editor). *The Shiloh Campaign*. Southern Illinois University Press: Carbondale, p. 33, hereafter referred to as *Baptism by Fire*.

59 Ulmer, *Smoke of Shiloh*, p. 291.

60 Lockett, Samuel H. (1887). Surprise and Withdrawal at Shiloh. In Robert U. Johnson and Clarence C. Buel, (Editors), *Battles and Leaders of the Civil War*, Century Company: New York, Volume I, p. 604-605, hereafter referred to as *Surprise and Withdrawal*.

61 Johnston, *Johnston at Shiloh*, p. 562.

62 Lockett, *Surprise and Withdrawal*, p. 604-605.

63 Lockett, *Surprise and Withdrawal*, p. 604-605.

64 Davis, *Breckinridge*, p. 305.

65 Gudmens, *Staff Ride Handbook*, p. 103-105; Smith, *Conquer or Perish*, p. 197-200.

66 Johnston, *Johnston at Shiloh*, p. 562.

67 Sword, *Bloody April*, p. 257-259; Gudmens, *Staff Ride Handbook*, p. 75-76; Allen, *Shiloh*, p. 26.

68 Smith, *Conquer or Perish*, p. 168.

69 Smith, *Conquer or Perish*, p. 140.
70 Johnston, *Life of Johnston*, p. 608.
71 Mendoza, *Baptism by Fire*, p. 43.
72 Allen, *Shiloh*, p. 28-29.
73 Gudmens, *Staff Ride Handbook*, p. 80-81; Smith, *Conquer or Perish*, p. 169-170.
74 Daniel, *Shiloh*, p. 216.
75 Cunningham, *Shiloh*, p. 264.
76 Johnston, *Johnston at Shiloh*, p. 564.
77 Allen, *Shiloh*, p. 28-29.
78 Hall, *Confederate High Command*, p. 2.
79 Daniel, *Shiloh*, p. 217.
80 Daniel, *Shiloh*, p. 217.
81 Daniel, *Shiloh*, p. 217; Davis, *Breckinridge*, p. 306-307.
82 Smith, *Iron Dice of Battle*, loc. 720-721 of 977.
83 Smith, *Conquer or Perish*, p. 186-187.
84 Smith, Timothy B. (2013). *Rethinking Shiloh: Myth and Memory*. University of Tennessee Press: Knoxville, p. 39.
85 Sword, *Bloody April*, p. 297.
86 Johnston, *Johnston at Shiloh*, p. 564.
87 Johnston, *Life of Johnston*, p. 612.
88 Moore and Segerstrom, *Destiny's Soldier*, p. 68-69.
89 *The Times-Democrat*, 6th April 1887 edition, Louisiana.
90 Sword, *Bloody April*, p. 304.
91 *The Times-Democrat*, 6th April 1887 edition, New Orleans, Louisiana.
92 *The Times-Democrat*, 6th April 1887 edition, New Orleans, Louisiana.
93 *Vermont Watchman and State Journal*, 28th January 1885 edition, Montpelier, Vermont.
94 *The Times-Democrat*, 6th April 1887 edition, Louisiana; Smith, Last Hours, p. 34.
95 *The Times-Democrat*, 6th April 1887 edition, Louisiana.
96 Goggin, Leigh S. (2011). Morbidity and mortality of the Confederate generals during the American Civil War, Letter to the editor. *American Surgeon*, Vol. 77, Number 11, p. 1563.
97 Johnston, *Johnston at Shiloh*, p. 559; Sword, *Bloody April*, p. 447.
98 Lundberg, *I Must Save this Army*, p. 22.
99 Allen, *Shiloh*, p. 16.
100 Sword, *Bloody April*, p. 447.

[101] Ulmer, *Smoke of Shiloh*, p. 291.

[102] Hutchinson, R.R. (1898). Albert Sidney Johnston at Shiloh. *Confederate Veteran*, Vol. VI, p. 313.

[103] Smith, *Iron Dice of Battle*, loc. 687-688 of 977.

[104] Roman, *Beauregard*, Vol. I, p. 294.

[105] Roman, *Beauregard*, Vol. I, p. 294.

[106] Hall, *Confederate High Command*, p. 37.

[107] Roland, *Soldier of Three Republics*, p. 345.

Notes to Chapter 24

[1] *The Galveston Daily News*, 10th April 1887 edition, Galveston, Texas.

[2] O.R., Vol. X, Ch. XXII, Pt. II, p. 408-409.

[3] O.R., Vol. X, Ch. XXII, Pt. I, p. 409.

[4] O.R., Vol. LII, Ch. LXIV, Pt. II, p. 298-299.

[5] Jackson, Mary A. (1895). *Memoirs of Stonewall Jackson*. Prentice Press, Courier-Journal Job Printing Company: Lexington, Kentucky, p. 248.

[6] Young, *Around the World*, p. 472.

[7] Fuller, John F.C. (1929). *The Generalship of Ulysses S. Grant*. Dodd, Mead, and Company: New York, p. 82.

[8] Daniel, *Conquered*, p. 22.

[9] Smith, *Iron Dice of Battle*, loc. 707 of 977.

[10] Roman, *Beauregard*, p. 212.

[11] Le Monnier, Yves Reni (1913). *General Beauregard at Shiloh*. The Graham Press: New Orleans, p. 28-29.

[12] Zimmermann Richard J. (2023). *More Than Just Grit: Civil War Leadership, Logistics and Teamwork in the West, 1862*. McFarland and Company: Jefferson, North Carolina, p. 322, hereafter referred to as *More Than Just Grit*.

[13] Johnston, *Johnston at Shiloh*, p. 559.

[14] Johnston, *Life of Johnston*, p. 584.

[15] *The Galveston Daily News*, 10th April 1887 edition, Galveston, Texas.

[16] Johnston, *Johnston at Shiloh*, p. 557.

[17] Johnston, *Life of Johnston*, p. 568.

[18] O.R., Vol. X, Ch. XXII, Pt. I, p. 387.

[19] Johnston, *Life of Johnston*, p. 618.

[20] Franklin A. O'Neil to his wife, 18th April 1862, *Billy Yank & Johnny Reb Letters*.

[21] Smith, *Conquer or Perish*, p. 190.

22 Johnston, *Johnston at Shiloh*, p. 559.

23 Zimmermann, *More Than Just Grit*, p. 6.

24 Rose, *McCulloch*, p. 140.

25 Sword, *Bloody April*, p. 447.

26 Tagg, *Generals of Shiloh*, p. 9.

27 Williams, *Napoleon in Gray*, p. 145.

28 Horn, *Warrior Bishop*, p. 233.

29 McDonough, James L. (1980). *Stones River: Bloody Winter in Tennessee*. University of Tennessee Press: Knoxville, p. 114-115.

30 Duke, Basil W. (1911). *The Civil War Reminiscences of General Basil W. Duke, C.S.A.* Doubleday: Garden City, New York, p. 186-187.

31 Gordon, John B. (1903). *Reminiscences of the Civil War*. Scribner's Sons: New York, p. 278.

32 Sword, *Bloody April*, p. 447.

33 Beauregard, *Campaign of Shiloh*, p. 589.

34 Thomas C. Reynolds to William P. Johnston, 13th November 1875, *Johnston papers*.

35 Drake, *The Annals*, p. 288.

36 Fremantle, *Three Months in the Southern States*, p. 160.

37 Catton, Bruce (1958, 2012). *America Goes to War: The Civil War and its Meaning in American Culture*. Wesleyan University Press: Middletown, Connecticut, p. 53.

38 Young, *Around the World*, p. 472.

39 Hall, *Confederate High Command*, p. 39, 62.

40 Johnston, *Johnston at Shiloh*, p. 565.

41 Horn, *Army of Tennessee*, p. 134.

42 Anderson, Jonathan, Peace, David, and Okun, Michael S. (2008). Albert Sidney Johnston's Sciatic Dueling Injury Did Not Contribute to His Death at the Battle of Shiloh. *Neurosurgery*, Vol. LXIII, Number 6, p. 1194, 1196, hereafter referred to as *Dueling Injury*.

43 Anderson et al., *Dueling Injury*, p. 1193.

44 Anderson et al., *Dueling Injury*, p. 1196.

45 Anderson et al., *Dueling Injury*, p. 1195-1196.

46 Anderson et al., *Dueling Injury*, p. 1195-1196.

47 Anderson et al., *Dueling Injury*, p. 1195-1196.

48 Anderson et al., *Dueling Injury*, p. 1195-1196.

49 O.R., Vol. X, Pt. I, Ch. XXII, p. 404.

50 Anderson et al., *Dueling Injury*, p. 1195-1196.

Notes to Epilogue

[1] Smith, *Iron Dice of Battle*, loc. 509-510 of 977.

[2] Castel, Albert (1997). Savior of the South? Was Albert Sidney Johnston the 'Robert E. Lee of the West' – The Missing Ingredient for Southern Victory? *Civil War Times Illustrated*, Vol. XXXVI, No. 1, p. 40.

[3] O.R., Vol. VII, Ch. XVII, p. 257-258.

[4] Johnston, *Life of Johnston*, p. 725.

[5] Macintyre, Ben (2016). *SAS: Rogue Heroes*. Penguin: London, loc. 96 of 384.

[6] Chesnut, *A Diary from Dixie*, p. 265.

Index

Page numbers in bold refer to illustrations or their captions

Adams, John Quincy, 16
Adams, William W., 287
Alabama, 75, 78, 137-139, 142-143, 180, 285, 295, 336
Alabama 19th Infantry Regiment, 343
Alabama 27th Infantry Regiment, 138
Alcorn, James, L., 67, 134
Alexander, Edward P., 80
Allen, Stacy D., 324, 338-339, 349
Allison, Joseph B., 357
Ampudia, Pedro de, 2, 27
Anderson, Adna, 129-130
Anderson, Patton, 334
Anderson, Robert, 51, 56, 64-65
Arkansas, 22, 31, 35, 38, 41-42, 51, 58, 67, 69, 74-75, 102, 111, 114, 167, 289-290, 292-294, 298, 332, 345
Arkansas 3rd Infantry Regiment, 332
Arkansas 9th Infantry Regiment, 346
Arkansas 15th Infantry Regiment, 138
Army of Northeastern Virginia, Union, 185

Army of Northern Virginia, Confederate, 39, 42, 69, 80, 359
Army of Southwest Virginia, Confederate, 154
Army of Tennessee, Confederate, 7-9, 112, 366
Army of the Cumberland, Union, 358
Army of the Kanawha, Confederate, 201
Army of the Mississippi, Confederate, 7, 13, 298-299, 301, 310-312, 315-318, 321-323, 325, 329, 333, 348-349, 352-354, 363, 366
Army of the Ohio, Union, 61, 101, 106, 120-124, 127, 156, 172, 184, 194-195, 206-207, 209, 220, 225, 240, 243, 246, 269, 274, 287, 296, 330, 353, 364
Army of the Potomac, Confederate, 355
Army of the Potomac, Union, 27, 116
Army of the Southwest, Union, 102, 290
Army of the Tennessee, Union, 274, 296, 318-319, 325, 345, 352

Atkinson, Henry, 16-17
Atlanta, Georgia, 258, 266, 269-270, 273

Bacon Creek, 187, 243
Bad Axe, battle of, 17
Baldwin, William E., 108, 175
Ball's Bluff, battle of, 47
Barbary War, Second, 15
Barbourville, Kentucky, 152
Barren River, 119, 121, 193, 244, 246
Baylor, George W., 316
Bear Creek Landing, Tennessee, 225
Beauregard, Pierre G.T., 6, 9, 12-13, 67, 84, 117, 143, 172, 184, **185**, 186-195, 198, 201-204, 206, 209-211, 215, 217, 234, 243, 249, 259, 269, 270-278, 280-282, 284-288, 291, 293, 295, 297-305, 308-309, 311-324, 328-329, 333-336, 338, 340, 343-345, 348-356, 358-359, 363, 365-366
Bedford, Hugh L., 138, 202, 223
Beech Grove, Kentucky, 159, 163-164
Bell's Tavern, Kentucky, 243
Belmont, battle of, 91-92, 95-96, 98, 101, 196
Belmont, Missouri, 51, 55, 91-92, 95-96, 98, 101, 196
Benjamin, Judah P., 58, 75-77, 79-81, 83, 120, 125, 188, 193, 251, 270, 278, 289-290
Bethel Station, Tennessee, 297, 300
Bird's Point, Missouri, 100
Black Hawk, Chief, 16-17
Black Hawk War, 16-17, 25, 153
Black River, 51
Bolívar, Simón, 15

Bowen, John S., 67, 103, 245, 337, 340, 342, 344-348, 357
Bowling Green, Kentucky, 12, 44-45, 59-71, 81, 83, 89-91, 97, 101-128, 133-135, 138-143, 147-148, 150, 154-157, 165-177, 182-210, 213-215, 218, 220, 226-227, 235-237, 240-251, 254, 259-260, 268-269, 273-274, 281, 290, 313, 364, 366
Bradley, A.W., 146
Bragg, Braxton, 24, 33, 68, 111-112, 117, 219-221, 239, 273, 276-280, 285, 289, **290**, 297-305, 308, 311, 314-319, 322-323, 329, 333-336, 339, 344, 356, 358, 365-366
Breckinridge, John C., 240-241, 245, 247, **299**, 300-302, 319, 323, 329, 333, 335-336, 338, 340-348, 351, 358-359
Brown, John C., 108
Brown, Neill S., 125, 131
Buchanan, James, 30, 199, 257
Buckner, Simon B., 12, 59, 67, 69, 85, 106, 108, **109**, 110-117, 123, 126, 144, 157, 171, 176, 184, 190, 199, 202-210, 212-214, 217, 220-223, 226, 229-240, 249
Buell, Don Carlos, 65, 79, 101-102, 106, 114, 118-127, 133, 141, 148-149, 155-156, 161, 165-167, 171-172, 184, 186, 191-195, 198, 206-210, 220, 225, 239-246, 250, 255, 260-261, 265, 269, 274, 286-287, 296-302, 305, 309, 316, 320, 322, 330-331, 338, 353, 363-364
Bull Run, battle of, 47, 67, 167, 184-185, 313
Bull's Gap, battle of 359
Burnet, David G., 22
Burnside, Ambrose E., 116

Burnsville, Mississippi, 300
Butler, William O., 27, 28

Cairo, Illinois, 54-55, 70, 90, 97-104, 145, 148, 169, 172-173, 187, 291
California, 31-34, 48, 86
Camargo, Mexico, 25-27, 101
Camp Alcorn, Kentucky, 67
Camp Beauregard, Kentucky, 67-68, 96, 103, 168
Camp Dick Robinson, Kentucky, 54, 65, 153
Camp Fogg, Tennessee, 165, 184
Camp Goggin, Kentucky, 158
Cape Girardeau, Missouri, 55, 63, 293
Carnifex Ferry, battle of, 201, 203, 229
Carondelet, USS, warship, 173, 214, 227
Carroll, William H., 156, 299
Carson, Irving W., 358
Carthage, Tennessee, 165
Castel, Albert, 7-9, 365
Catton, Bruce, 360
Central Kentucky Army, Confederate, 7, 12, 105-117, 121, 126-127, 150, 155, 165, 170, 177, 182, 188, 191, 194-195, 198, 206-210, 215, 221, 227, 235, 240-242, 245-246, 249-250, 254, 256-263, 266, 305, 364
Chalmers, James R., 335-345
Charleston, South Carolina, 33, 42, 77, 79, 185, 201
Charlotte, Tennessee, 226
Chattanooga, Tennessee, 37, 46, 156, 258, 262, 266, 269-274, 286-287, 365

Cheatham, Richard B., 256, 261-262, 265
Cherokee, warriors, 21-23, 292
Chesnut, Mary, 112, 367
Chief Bowles (Di'wali), 21-22
China Grove, Texas, 24, 28-29
Cincinnati, Ohio, 4, 65
Cincinnati, USS, warship, 173
City of Alton, steamboat, 53
Clanton, James H., 336
Clark, Charles, 171, 176, 184, 190, 199, 204, 212
Clarksville, Tennessee, 37, 67-68, 89-96, 100, 104, 132-133, 136, 142, 144, 171, 176-177, 184, 188, 190, 192, 195, 199, 204-206, 212, 214-215, 252, 259
Clausewitz, Carl von, 41
Clay, Henry, 16
Cleburne, Patrick R., 107, 331-335, 338, 340, 342
Coleto River, 18
Columbia, Kentucky, 157, 286
Columbia, Tennessee, 296, 300
Columbus, Kentucky, 50-56, 59-60, 63-64, 67, 70, 74, 80, 85-106, 111, 124, 133-136, 140-141, 144-148, 167-175, 183, 186, 189-193, 198, 204, 215, 225, 229, 272-280, 287, 291, 297, 298, 311-312, 322, 359, 363-365
Comanche, warriors, 23, 29-30, 290
Commerce, Missouri, 271
Conestoga, USS, warship, 132, 169, 173, 227
Confederate Government, see *Richmond*
Connelly, Thomas L., 8-13, 56, 61, 69, 71, 74, 82-84, 88, 94-97, 100-103,

116, 118, 133, 151-158, 165-166, 171, 175, 190, 198, 202, 210, 215-216, 220, 250-251, 254, 257, 259-260, 264, 266, 270-282, 286, 314, 323, 364-366

Cooling, Benjamin F., 11-12, 66, 109, 111, 118-119, 196, 224, 253, 266

Cooper, Samuel, 76, 79, 80-82, 124, 190

Cordon defense, 41-51, 66-74, 82, 85, 105, 118, 126, 167, 186, 275

Corinth, Mississippi, 270-289, 293-313, 316-320, 324, 328, 330, 351, 353, 364-365

Courtland, Alabama, 283

Covington House, Kentucky, 183, 187-194, 198, 204, 211, 215, 221, 229, 240, 274

Crittenden, George B., **162**, 163-166, 176, 184, 205, 242, 258, 265-266, 281, 283, 288, 298-299

Cross Hollow, Arkansas, 292

Crump's Landing, Tennessee, 296-300, 338, 353

Culbertson, Jacob, 139

Cumberland City, Tennessee, 212-214, 217

Cumberland Gap, Kentucky, 59-62, 105, 122-123, 150-152, 157

Cumberland River, 7, 11-12, 37-39, 50, 56, 62, 67-68, 88, 97, 118-121, 124, 129-151, 155, 157-159, 162-163, 166-171, 176-177, 182-183, 187-229, 236-245, 250, 252, 255, 258, 260, 264-265, 272, 275, 287, 291, 364-365

Cumming, Alfred, 30

Cunningham, O. Edward, 284, 313

Curtis, Samuel R., 102, 290-292, 298

Daniel, Larry J., 9-10, 12, 133, 201, 210, 260, 264, 266, 282, 324, 354, 364

Danville, Tennessee, 174-175, 177

Davidson, T.J., 204

Davis, Jack, 237

Davis, Jefferson, 1-3, **4**, 5-9, 29, 34, 37, 41-43, 48-49, 57, 59, 66, 69, 71, 74, 78-86, 89, 107, 109, 112, 126, 131, 148, 153, 162, 165, 182, 185-186, 194-195, 203, 205, 210, 219, 229, 238, 257, 267-268, 270-273, 284, 288, 300-303, 310, 314, 353, 365-366

Davis, Reuben O., 83

Davis, William C., 341

Decatur, Alabama, 266, 270-274, 281-288

Deception strategy, 61-67, 71-72, 115-116, 122, 241, 253-254, 305, 364

Delaware, 42

Department Number Two, see *Western Department*

Dill Branch, 328

Dillon, John F., 39

Disease and illnesses in the army, 25-26, 44, 67, 95-96, 106, 120-121, 142, 155, 164, 196, 229, 236, 241-242, 246-247, 264, 284

Dixon, Joseph K., 88-89, 103, 132-139

Dixon, Thomas W., 5

Donelson, Daniel S., 129-130

Douglass, Kelsey H., 22

Dover, Tennessee, 134, 169, 172, 213, 223, 226-227

Dripping Springs, Kentucky, 70

Dubbi stratovolcano, 145

Duck River, 296, 298
Duke, Basil W., 256, 257, 259

East Tennessee, District of, Confederate, 59, 123-124, 150-153, 157, 161-166, 176, 184, 242, 258, 266, 281, 364
East Tennessee, rebellion, 47-48, 54, 57-58, 65, 122, 124, 155-157, 166
Eastport, CSS, warship, 137, 149, 180, 182
Eastport, Mississippi, 295, 300
Edgefield, Tennessee, 196, 220, 242, 245, 254, 260, 265
Eggleston, George C., 141, 242, 246
Eisenhower, Dwight D., 366
El Paso, Texas, 33
Elizabethtown, Kentucky, 106, 114
Engineers, 16, 21, 54, 67, 68, 80-81, 88-89, 126, 129-136, 139-140, 143-147, 184, 186, 202, 205, 223, 244, 251-254, 272, 275, 282, 286, 296, 298, 304, 339, 341
Essex, USS, warship, 173, 179

Fayetteville, Arkansas, 294
Fayetteville, Tennessee, 281-282, 287-288, 296
Federal Government, see *Washington*
Feliciana, Kentucky, 103
Fire Eater, horse, 73, 317, 321, 329, 337, 346-347
Fishing Creek, battle of, 163-166, 176, 183-186, 189, 281, 313, 316
Florence, Alabama, 287
Florida, 68, 149, 184, 278, 289-290
Floyd, John B., 77, 128, 168, 171, 176, 184, 188, 190, 199, **200**, 201-207, 210-230, 233-242, 247, 249, 256-259, 262-265, 272, 275, 280, 287
Foote, Andrew H., 172-173, 178, 180, 206, 215-216, 222, 227, 229
Forrest, Nathan B., 33, 206, 231, 235-237, 258-265, 287, 300, 330-331, 349
Fort Bridger, Utah, 31
Fort Defiance, Tennessee, 144, 183
Fort Donelson, Tennessee, 7, 9-12, 50, 68, 80, 88-89, 92, 96, 119, 127-149, 153, 167, 170-178, 183, 186-227, **228**, 229, 231, 234-251, 254-262, 265-271, 275, 281, 283, 299, 313, 316, 320, 346, 364
Fort Heiman, Kentucky, 137-139, 147, 170, 174, 177
Fort Henry, Tennessee, 11-12, 50, 67-68, 80, 88-92, 96, 103, 119-120, 127-149, 167-180, **181**, 182-192, 196-199, 202-204, 207, 209, 211, 213, 218-225, 238, 243, 272, 275-283, 295, 313, 316, 364
Fort Holt, Kentucky, 100, 197
Fort Leavenworth, Kansas, 112
Fort Pillow, Tennessee, 51, 96, 189
Fort Sumter, South Carolina, 33, 53, 184-185, 313
Foster, Robert C., 50, 125
Foster, William E., 129-130
France, 20, 37
Freehling, William W., 61
Fremantle, Arthur, J.L., 86, 107, 113, 185
Frémont, John C., 51, 55-58, 63-65, 90, 102
Fuller, John F.C., 354, 357

Galveston, Texas, 25

Gantt, George, 177
Garesché, Julius A., 358-359
Garfield, James A., 161
Georgia, 30, 75, 78, 107, 258
German soldiers, 26, 337
Gibson, Randall L., 5, 48, 339, 344, 352, 356
Gilmer, Jeremy F., 68, 112, 126, 132-139, 143, 146-147, 173-174, 177-179, 190, 211, 218, 230, 249-254, 269, 273, 281-285, 288, 365
Girardi, Robert I., 56
Gladden, Adley H., 333-334
Gorgas, Josiah, 139, 176
Gott, Kendall G., 175, 202, 223-226, 232-233, 238, 240
Grant, Ulysses S., 4-5, 12, 24, 34, 55, 64-65, 79, 90-92, 101-102, 133, 141, 148, 152, 169-173, 178-183, 187, 190-200, 206-207, 210-226, 229, 232-238, 243, 247, 250, 255, 269, 272-274, 287, 292, 295-302, 305, 316-322, 325, 330, 337-342, 352-360, 363
Gray, Asa B., 89
Great Britain, 37
Green River, 64, 77, 79, 101, 106, 111, 120, 125, 136, 171, 243
Greer's Ford, Tennessee, 330, 331, 349
Grenfell, George St. Leger, 360
Guthrie, James, 123

Hall, Thomas K., 284, 308-315, 345, 351, 360
Halleck, Henry W., 102, 124, 127, 141, 148, 172, 183-184, 197, 243, 269, 271, 274, 287, 292-296, 320, 330, 353

Hamburg, Tennessee, 330-331,
Hamer, Thomas L., 27-28
Hanson, Roger W., 108
Hardee, William J., 12, 51, 64, 67, 106-107, **108**, 110-117, 126, 140, 155, 171, 187-190, 193, 198-216, 242, 244, 270-273, 287, 298-302, 308, 317-323, 329, 331, 333, 339, 340, 342, 344, 358, 365
Harris, Isham G., 56, **58**, 59, 66, 73-74, 93, 96-97, 100, 129-130, 137, 156, 208, 214, 251-256, 259, 271, 276, 288, 345-348, 362
Harrison, H.H., 134-136
Hayden, Dudley M., 318
Haynes, Landon C., 165
Haynes, Milton A., 136
Head, John W., 43, 138, 146
Hébert, Louis, 292, 294
Heiman, Adolphus, 134, 169, 173-175, 188
Helm, Benjamin H., 287
Helm, John L., 125
Henry, Gustavus A., 130, 133, 135-136
Hess, Earl J., 294
Heth, Henry, 200, 289
Hickman, Kentucky, 55, 67
Hindman, Thomas C., 107, 165, 240-241, 244, 246, 271, 281, 283, 331-334, 337, 339, 343, 356
Ho-Chunk (Winnebago), warriors, 16-17
Hodge, George B., 247
Hollins, George N., 98, 189
Holly Springs, Mississippi, 270
Holmes, Theophilus H., 24
Hood, John B., 366

433

Hooker, Joseph, 27
Hopkinsville, Kentucky, 67-68, 70, 96, 134, 142, 171, 176, 184, 188, 199, 204, 212
Horn, Stanley F., 6-12, 141, 152, 158, 191-194, 206-207, 210, 257, 272, 301, 332, 361
Hornet's Nest, 342-345, 352
Houston, Sam, 19-20
Hughes, Nathaniel C., Jnr, 96
Humboldt, Tennessee, 189, 190, 286, 295
Huntsville, Alabama, 266, 271, 281
Hurlbut, Stephen A., 328, 333, 340-347, 352
Huston, Felix, 19-22, 359
Hyde, Anne B. 315

Illinois, 16, 94, 98, 101, 121, 290
Illinois 8th Regiment, 53
Indian Territory (Oklahoma), 3, 22, 35, 289-290
Ingram's Shoals, Tennessee, 134, 136
Intelligence gathering, 37, 70, 94, 97, 102, 153, 168-169, 172, 194, 207-210, 217-218, 220, 300, 328
Ironclad warships, 39, 46, 49, 98, 100, 145, 147, 149, 169, 173, 179-183, 187-188, 205, 214-218, 220, 222, 226-227, 236, 238, 242, 272, 366
Island Number Ten, Tennessee, 89, 96, 143, 183, 189, 271, 278, 291, 297
Iuka, Mississippi, 270

Jacksborough, Kentucky, 157
Jackson, John K., 335, 339-345
Jackson, Tennessee, 271, 276-277, 295, 311

Jackson, Thomas J. "Stonewall", 206, 310, 354
Jamestown, Kentucky, 154-156
Jefferson Barracks, Missouri, 16
Johnson, Bushrod R., 130, 230-231, 234-237
Johnson, George W., 239
Johnston, Eliza G. (second wife), 24-25, 28
Johnston, Henrietta P. (first wife), 17
Johnston, Joseph E., 111, 143, 185, 201-202, 267, 366
Johnston, William P. (eldest son), 6, 10, 13, 18, 23-24, 28, 46-47, 62, 66, 86, 104, 107, 140-144, 150, 152, 154, 158, 172, 176, 194, 197, 205, 227, 238-239, 273, 283, 308-309, 314, 328, 339, 342, 357, 361
Jones, John B., 82-83, 116, 203, 247, 260
Jordan, Thomas, 300-303, 308, 310, 318, 325

Kansas, 35, 290
Kennett, John, 265
Kentucky, 3-5, 13-21, 24, 35, 38, 41-42, 46, 48, 51, 53-71, 74, 76, 81-83, 87-90, 93-94, 103-113, 115-133, 140, 145, 150-159, **160**, 161-172, 184, 187, 192, 194, 198, 205, 208, 217, 239-240, 243, 247-248, 254, 264, 275, 278, 291, 299, 312-313, 364
Kentucky 1st Cavalry Regiment, 153, 287
Kentucky 3rd Infantry Regiment, 63, 116
Kentucky Army, Confederate, 273-274, 280-288, 297-298, 311-315

Kentucky Home Guard, 53, 152
Kentucky Legislature, 53-55, 58-60, 115
Kentucky State Guard, 53, 59, 109, 115
Kessler's Cross Lanes, battle of, 200, 202
Kirby Smith, Edmund, 8, 273
Knoxville, Tennessee, 37, 46, 50, 59, 85, 122, 124, 144, 150-151, 155-156, 162, 269, 273, 290

Lady Polk, cannon, 86, 91-92
Lamar, Mirabeau B., 21, 23
Le Monnier, Yves R., 355
Lebanon, Kentucky, 163, 243
Lee, Robert E., 34, 77, 116, 201, 297, 359, 365
Lexington, battle of, 47, 51
Lexington, Kentucky, 1, 65
Lexington, Missouri, 51
Lexington, USS, warship, 169, 173, 295
Lick Creek, 305, 324-325, 328, 333, 336-340
Liddell, St. John R., 79-82, 111-113, 180, 270, 308, 313-314
Liedtke, Gregory P., 207
Lincoln, Abraham, 33, 53-57, 65, 70, 122, 124-125, 152, 156
Lockett, Samuel H., 339-342
Locust Grove Branch, 343
Logan's Crossroads, battle of, see *Fishing Creek*
Logan's Crossroads, Kentucky, 163-164, 286
London, Kentucky, 154
Los Angeles, California, 33

Louisiana, 15, 48, 75, 85, 184, 278, 280, 287, 291
Louisiana 18th Regiment, 6
Louisiana Crescent Infantry Regiment, 355
Louisville, Kentucky, 56, 64-65, 111, 114, 119-125, 155, 161, 165, 207, 263
Louisville, USS, warship, 227
Lovell, Mansfield, 270, 277
Lundberg, John R., 288, 299, 349
Lyon, Nathaniel, 357

Mackall, William W., 88-91, 94, 134, 137, 139, 153-154, 157, 161, 170, 273, 288, 365
Madison Barracks, New York, 16
Magoffin, Beriah, 108
Manassas, battle of, see *Bull Run*
Maney, George E., 330, 331, 349
Marmaduke, John S., 332
Marshall, Humphrey, 152-153, **154**, 159, 161-162, 166
Maryland, 42, 135
Maury City, Tennessee, 7
Mayfield, Tennessee, 56, 67, 169
Maysville, Arkansas, 51
McArthur, John A., 344-345
McClellan, George B., 33, 79, 122, 124, 172, 287
McClernand, John A., 173, 226, 231-232, 235, 328, 333, 338-339, 342-345
McCook, Alexander M., 65, 114, 243
McCulloch, Ben, 51, 167, 292, 294, 357
McDowell, Irvin, 185
McDowell, John A., 335

McGavock, Randal W., 134, 211, 213
McIntosh, James M., 292, 294
McMurry, Richard M., 5
McWhiney, Grady, 8
Memphis, Tennessee, 37-38, 44, 46, 50, 57, 91, 93, 144, 156, 167, 189, 256, 269-273, 278, 293
Mendoza, Alexander, 340, 343
Mexican-American War, 2, 25-29, 34, 44, 93-94, 101, 107-108, 153, 162, 184, 290
Mexico, Republic of, 18-25, 28-29
Middle Creek, battle of, 161
Milburn, Tennessee, 67
Mill Springs, battle of, see *Fishing Creek*
Mill Springs, Kentucky, 151, 157-159, 162-163
Miller, Madison, 332-337
Minerals and resources, 38, 40, 60
Mississippi, 9, 35, 41-42, 56, 69, 72-75, 83, 103, 270, 287, 289, 291
Mississippi 4th Infantry Regiment, 134
Mississippi 6th Infantry Regiment, 334
Mississippi 14th Infantry Regiment, 125, 150, 175
Mississippi 22nd Infantry Regiment, 44
Mississippi River, 3, 16, 37, 39, 50-59, 67, 87-88, 91, 97, 102, 105, 122, 124, 131-135, 142-145, 148, 168, 183, 192, 269-273, 276, 289-294, 359
Mississippi River bloc, 56-57, 86, 91, 144
Mississippi Valley, 11, 19, 85-89, 97, 100, 126, 132, 135, 142, 187, 193, 225, 269-278, 280, 366

Missouri, 35, 38, 41-43, 51, 58, 63, 69, 72, 74, 87, 90, 94, 98, 102, 140, 144, 148-149, 183, 187, 193, 269-271, 289, 290, 291, 292
Missouri 1st Infantry Regiment, 257
Missouri State Guard, 51
Mitchel, Ormsby M., 243-244, 265, 296, 300
Mobile, Alabama, 42, 68, 79, 149, 184, 239, 277-278, 290, 297, 312
Monterey, Tennessee, 300-301, 316
Monterrey, battle of, 2, 26-28, 290, 359, 363
Monticello, Kentucky, 157
Morgan, John H., 287, 296
Mormon War, 30-32, 199, 202, 332
Mosquito Fleet, 98, 100
Mountain Meadows, Utah, 31
Munford, Edward W., 245, 249, 253-256, 308-309, 312, 315, 319
Munfordville, Kentucky, 114, 243
Murfreesboro, Tennessee, 113, 250, 257-258, 262, 265-266, 270-273, 281-288, 296, 298, 311
Murray, John P., 156
Murray, Tennessee, 169-170
Myers, Abraham C., 81

Napoleon I, Emperor, 4, 301, 366
Nashville, Tennessee, 12, 37-38, 46, 50, 57-59, 62, 65, 68, 70-74, 77-81, 85, 105-110, 114-127, 133-134, 137-139, 142, 144, 148, 151, 157, 163, 165, 171, 175-177, 180, 188-198, 206, 209, 213-216, 219-221, 226-229, 233, 236-275, 281-283, 287-288, 297, 313, 364-365

Native Americans, 16-17, 21-23, 29-31, 44, 51, 292
Naval mines, 87, 134, 146, 149, 169, 173, 178, 182, 366
Neches, battle of, 22, 28, 359, 363
Nelson, William, 153, 265, 298, 320-321, 330, 338
New Madrid, Missouri, 96, 183, 271, 276, 291, 293
New Orleans, Louisiana, 8, 42, 68, 74, 79, 149, 184, 185, 269-270, 277-280, 302, 312
Nolin, Kentucky, 65
North Carolina, 85, 289
Northrop, Lucius B., 81, 267

Oglesby, Richard J., 53-55
Ohio, 121
Ohio River, 55, 56, 61, 67, 71, 140, 159, 189, 192-195, 270
Owl Creek, 305, 322-325, 333-336, 339, 343, 345, 349, 352

Pacific, Department of the, 32
Paducah, Kentucky, 55-56, 64, 70, 102-103, 135, 169-170, 173, 180, 187, 291
Panther Island, Tennessee, 169, 173, 178, 182
Paris, Tennessee, 92, 169, 172, 190
Parks, Joseph H., 193-194, 302
Pea Ridge, battle of, 292-294
Peabody, Everett, 329, 331-334, 337
Peach Orchard, 345, 348, 352, 354, 357, 359-360, 363
Pearce, Nathan B., 51
Pearl Harbor, Hawaii, 5
Pemberton, John C., 366

Pensacola, Florida, 68, 78-79, 149, 239, 277-289, 297, 312
Pike, Albert, 292
Pillow, Gideon J., 11, 57, 66, 85-92, **93**, 94-104, 108-109, 141, 143, 168, 176-177, 184, 190, 200, 203-207, 211-227, 230-240, 249, 256-257, 299, 365
Pinnegar, Charles, 200, 230, 233
Pittsburg, USS, warship, 227
Pittsburg Landing, Tennessee, 286, 295-305, 309-310, 316, 320-321, 324-325, 328, 330, 337-338, 343-344, 352, 353
Plummer, Joseph B., 63
Pocahontas, Arkansas, 291, 293
Point Isabel, Texas, 25
Polk, James K., 93
Polk, Leonidas, 8, 11, 15, 24, 48, 50, 55-60, 66, 75, 85, **86**, 87-105, 111-112, 118, 124-125, 131-149, 168-170, 174-178, 182-183, 187-190, 193, 215, 225, 229, 276-277, 280, 286, 297-302, 308, 311-312, 316-319, 323, 329-330, 333-336, 339, 344, 351, 353, 358-359, 365
Pond, Preston, 334, 342, 358
Pontoons, 193, 194, 287, 296
Pope, John, 102, 141, 187, 269, 271
Potawatomi, warriors, 17
Pound Gap, Virginia, 157
Powell, David A., 310, 336
Prentiss, Benjamin M., 102, 298, 325, 329, 331-343, 345, 352
Preston, William, 362, 366
Prestonburg, Kentucky, 154
Price, Sterling, 51, 144, 149, 291, 292

Railroads, 35, 36, 38, 41, 42, 45-46, 53, 58, 61, 67, 70, 80-81, 97, 105-106, 114-115, 119, 122-124, 127, 133, 135-136, 148, 155-156, 165-166, 169, 172, 187, 190, 195-196, 213, 241, 244, 250, 262-266, 269-274, 285-288, 295-296, 300, 328

Rains, George W., 121, 122

Ready, Alice, 113

Red Bird, Chief, 16

Reynolds, Arthur E., 103

Richmond, Confederate Government, 11, 35, 37, 41-44, 47-48, 53, 57-59, 66, 69-70, 73-85, 94, 96, 106, 121, 131-132, 135-136, 140-141, 146-149, 155-156, 161, 165-166, 171, 180-182, 184, 186, 203, 220, 235, 239, 250, 252, 258-266, 270-273, 276-277, 280, 289-290, 295, 304, 355

Richmond, Virginia, 4, 39, 42, 51, 79, 81-82, 86, 116, 156, 243, 247, 260

Ridley, Alonzo, 33

Rio Grande River, 25

Rodgers, John, 55

Roland, Charles P., 7-12, 18, 62, 66, 83, 133, 148, 194-197, 206, 216-217, 223-234, 238, 240, 284, 293-294, 297, 302, 317, 351

Roman, Alfred, 6, 186, 191, 193-194, 270, 275, 304-305, 309, 333-336, 350, 355

Rosecrans, William S., 201, 358, 359

Ruggles, Daniel, 270, 312, 317, 328

Rusk, Thomas J., 18-19

Russell, Robert M., 334

Russellville, Kentucky, 68, 136, 170-171, 176, 182, 184, 199, 204, 207, 212, 364

Salt Lake City, Utah, 31, 32, 199

Sauk, warriors, 16

Saunders, James E., 139

Savannah, Georgia, 42, 78-79

Savannah, Tennessee, 274, 295-296, 300, 320, 321, 337, 338

Schoepf, Albin F., 153, 155, 159, 163

Schofield, John M., 102

Scott, John, 287

Scott, Winfield, 16, 24, 32, 56, 93, 108, 201

Seminole War, 44, 107, 150, 290

Shaaf, John T., 81

Shaver, Robert G., 107

Shea, William L., 294

Shelbyville, Kentucky, 24

Shelbyville, Tennessee, 267, 284-288

Sheridan, Philip H., 33

Sherman, William T., 64-65, 71, 115, 118, 122, 155, 296, 299-300, 320-321, 325, 328, 331-339, 342-345, 358-359

Shiloh, battle of, 5-9, 12-13, 234, 266, 284, 294, 302-305, **306-307**, 309-315, 321-325, **326-327**, 328-363, 365-367

Shiloh Branch, 331-334, 338

Shiloh Church, 297, 316, 318, 321, 324-325, 336, 365

Slack, William Y., 292, 294

Slavery, 33, 36-37, 42, 47, 51, 53-54, 57, 67, 93, 137-138, 142-143, 146, 176, 198, 252, 254, 260

Smith, Charles F., 64, 102-103, 169-170, 173, 177, 190, 201, 234-235, 295-296

Smith, Gustavus W., 80
Smith, Persifor, 29
Smith, Timothy B., v, 9-13, 18, 24, 49, 83, 101, 109, 119, 126, 133, 166, 168, 175, 194, 207, 216, 217, 220, 224, 234, 238, 271, 276, 280, 286, 303, 305, 324, 336, 339, 343, 346, 350, 354, 357, 359, 364, 365
Smith, William R., 170, 176
Smithland, Kentucky, 56
Snake Creek, 325, 328, 345, 349, 352
Snowden, J. Hudson, 89
Somerset, Kentucky, 157, 159, 163
South Carolina, 287
South Carrollton, Kentucky, 132, 171
Spanish American Wars of Independence, 15
Springfield, Missouri, 51
St. Louis, Missouri, 16, 55, 290, 291, 293
St. Louis, USS, warship, 173, 227
Stacker, George W., 146
Stanton, Sydney S., 44, 156, 158
Statham, Walter S., 337, 340-348, 359
Steele, Matthew F., 215, 224-225, 229, 238, 282
Stephen, William H., 339, 344-345
Stevenson, Alabama, 188
Stevenson, Vernon K., 209, 262, 263
Stewart, Alexander P., 80, 134, 147-148, 202, 336, 337, 339
Stewart's Hill, Kentucky, 137
Stickles, Arndt M., 224, 229, 243
Stones River, battle of, 358
Stuart, David R., 328, 333, 339-344
Submarine batteries, see *naval mines*

Sugar Creek, 292
Sugg, Cyrus A., 146
Sword, Wiley, 310, 349, 357, 359

Tagg, Larry, 251
Tate, Samuel, 97, 98
Taylor, Jesse, 132
Taylor, Richard, 4
Taylor, Zachary, 25, 27, 28, 32
Telegraph communications, 38, 45, 48, 69-70, 90, 115, 138, 152, 156, 172, 175, 177, 212, 214, 241, 264, 276, 300
Tennessee, 4-9, 13, 35, 38, 41-43, 46-51, 54-62, 65-70, 74-75, 79, 81, 88, 90, 93, 96-97, 100, 103, 105, 118-119, 121-125, 130-131, 134, 136, 140-142, 145, 150-151, 154-157, 162, 165-166, 173, 176, 187, 193, 200, 202, 208, 213, 217, 221, 240, 243, 250, 254-255, 258, 269-278, 280, 284-285, 287, 291-292, 295-296, 298, 312, 322, 346, 359
Tennessee, Provisional Army of, Confederate, 50, 55, 57, 93, 125, 136
Tennessee 1st Infantry Regiment, 330
Tennessee 3rd Infantry Regiment, 125
Tennessee 9th Cavalry Battalion, 177
Tennessee 10th Infantry Regiment, 211
Tennessee 22nd Infantry Regiment, 56
Tennessee 25th Infantry Regiment, 44
Tennessee 30th Infantry Regiment, 138, 146
Tennessee 43rd Infantry Regiment, 95
Tennessee 45th Infantry Regiment, 357
Tennessee 48th Infantry Regiment, 174
Tennessee 50th Infantry Regiment, 146
Tennessee 51st Infantry Regiment, 174

Tennessee River, 11-12, 37-39, 50, 55-58, 62, 67, 88, 90, 104, 118-120, 124, 129-137, 140-149, 167-184, 187-189, 193, 195, 197, 204, 207, 217-219, 223-235, 250, 270, 272-275, 280, 287, 291-300, 310, 319, 321, 324-325, 328, 330, 333, 365

Terry, Benjamin F., 76

Texas, 4, 25, 29-30, 33-34, 76, 112, 290, 303, 343, 361

Texas, Department of, 29-30

Texas, Republic of, 2, 18-24

Texas 1st Infantry Regiment, 25

Texas Army, 18-23

Texas Rangers, 76, 107, 244

Texas Volunteer Infantry Regiment, 237

Thomas, George H., 33, 64-65, 153, 155, 163-165, 184, 243, 250, 286

Thompson, Jacob, 320

Thompson, Meriwether J., 43, 51, 63, 72

Tilghman, Lloyd, 43, 55, 80, 128, 135, **136**, 137-148, 169-170, 173-182, 188, 204, 213

Torpedoes, see *naval mines*

Trabue, Robert P., 337, 344-345

Trans-Mississippi, 58, 102, 269, 290-293

Transylvania University, Kentucky, 1, 15

Tredegar Iron Works, 42

Trenton, Tennessee, 51, 78

Tulane University, Louisiana, 8

Turchin, John B., 244, 246

Tuscumbia, Alabama, 170, 176, 295, 366

Tyler, USS, warship, 173, 227, 295

Tyler's Landing, Tennessee, 296

Ulmer, J.B., 316

Union City, Tennessee, 50-51, 55, 64, 96, 103

United States 2nd Cavalry Regiment, 29, 30, 107, 112, 290

United States 6th Infantry Regiment, 16

United States Military Academy, 1, 4, 14-16, 44, 48, 51, 80, 85-86, 101, 107-108, 135, 153, 162, 184, 185, 202, 210, 223, 229, 231, 235, 289

United States Navy, 15, 29, 39, 42-43, 46, 55, 68, 70, 85, 98, 102, 130, 132, 134, 136, 158, 167, 173, 178, 180, 182, 185, 187, 215, 216, 252, 255, 272

University of the South, Tennessee, 8

Utah Expedition, see *Mormon War*

Utah Territory, 30-34

Van Buren, Arkansas, 293-294

Van Dorn, Earl, 289-290, **291**, 292-294, 366

Virginia, 39, 41-42, 46, 69-70, 76-84, 90, 116, 121-122, 142, 154, 159, 161, 168, 185, 187, 199-202, 204, 213, 237, 267, 269, 278, 287, 289, 315, 330, 354-355, 359

Virginia, Provisional Army of, Confederate, 200

Waagner, Gustav, 55

Walker, Leroy P., 82, 156

Walker, Peter F., 73, 198

Walker's Gap, Kentucky, 122
Wallace, Lew, 222-226, 232, 234, 296-298, 300, 338, 353
Wallace, William H.L., 328, 333, 341, 343, 345, 352
War of 1812, 15-16, 43
Washington, D.C., 16
Washington, Federal Government, 25, 28, 30, 32, 39, 53, 55, 60, 64, 77, 114, 162, 172, 184
Weather, 24, 25, 31, 34, 43-44, 87, 145, 155, 164, 196, 222, 226, 241, 246-247, 264-266, 282-284, 286, 288, 293-296, 316-317, 366
Webster, Daniel, 16
West Point, New York, see *United States Military Academy*
Western Department, 3-4, 6, 10-13, 34-35, **36**, 37-38, **40**, 41-42, 45-51, **52**, 57-58, 65-79, 82-86, 89, 95, 97, **99**, 102, 104, 106, 109, 115, 117, 119, 124, 126-127, 129, 131, 141, 144, 147, 149-150, 151, 157, 165-167, 172, 177, 180, 182-183, 186-187, 190, 198, 201-206, 208-210, 215, 221, 238, 262, 266, 268-269, 274, 276, 280, 286, 289, 304, 314, 316, 355, 366
Wickham, Watkins L., 348
Wildcat Mountain, battle of, 153
Wilderness, battle of the, 359
Williams, John S., 153, 154, 159
Williams, T. Harry, 12-13, 109-110, 192-195, 216, 312-313, 323, 364-366
Wilmington, North Carolina, 42
Wilson's Creek, battle of, 47, 167, 357
Wisconsin River, 16
Wise, Henry A., 201

Wood, Sterling A.M., 114, 331-334, 337, 339
Wood, Thomas J., 243
Woodsonville, Kentucky, 111
Woodworth, Steven E., 10-13, 49, 66, 94, 101, 103, 146, 216, 303, 325
Woolley, Robert W., 68, 83, 106, 195, 241, 244, 246
Worth, William J., 14, 15
Wright, Moses, 259

Yandell, David W., 247, 319-321, 360-362, 365
Yellow Creek, Tennessee, 296
Young, Brigham, 30-32

Zimmerman, Richard J., 355, 357
Zollicoffer, Felix K., 50, 59, 65-70, 85, 123-124, 128, 144, 150, **151**, 152-166, 186, 205, 275, 280, 364

www.ingramcontent.com/pod-product-compliance
Lightning Source LLC
Chambersburg PA
CBHW021758220426
43662CB00006B/98